PITT LATIN AMERICAN SERIES

The Overthrow of Allende
and
the Politics of Chile,
1964–1976

The Overthrow of Allende
and
the Politics of Chile,
1964-1976

†

PAUL E. SIGMUND

University of Pittsburgh Press

Published by the University of Pittsburgh Press, Pittsburgh, Pa. 15260
Feffer and Simons, Inc., London
Manufactured in the United States of America

Library of Congress Cataloging in Publication Data

Sigmund, Paul E
  The overthrow of Allende and the politics of Chile,
1964-1976.

  (Pitt Latin American series)
  Includes bibliographical references and index.
  1. Chile—Politics and government—1970–
2. Chile—Politics and government—1920–   I. Title.
F3100.S5   320.9'83'064   77-7181
ISBN 0-8229-3355-1
ISBN 0-8229-5287-4 (pbk.)

Contents

Illustrations

Preface

I became a Chile-watcher in the early 1960s, when my interest in ideologies of development and in the prospects for constitutional democracy naturally led me to a country where both seemed to flourish. A teaching stint at the two major universities in Santiago in 1967 under the auspices of the Rockefeller Foundation gave me a deeper understanding of a complex society at a crucial point in its development. Direct observation of the 1970 presidential election and visits to Chile and articles on Chilean politics over a decade induced me to begin to write this book during the last part of the Allende regime.

Since the book was begun before the 1973 coup, it was not written with a preestablished thesis in mind, although I was interested initially in comparing the effectiveness of the Frei reforms, which were based on a blend of Christian Democratic, populist, and technocratic prescriptions, with the Marxist-inspired changes being introduced by the Allende regime. The tragic overthrow of Chilean democracy in September 1973 led me to shift the focus to a more direct analysis of the proximate and remote causes of the coup as well as its consequences in the drastic changes which followed. Finally the post-coup revelations of the extent of U.S. intervention in Chile since the early 1960s required a consideration of the relative influence of external and domestic factors on the course of Chilean politics.

While I did not and still do not possess a single explanation around which to organize the narrative that follows, I have operated with certain assumptions which probably should be stated at the outset. As befits a scholar whose original training and writing was in political philosophy, I have assumed that ideas are not mere epiphenomena, but, particularly in a literate and free society, exert a direct influence on conduct and political decision-making. When, as in Chile, they are organized into ideologies which form part of the raison d'être of a multiparty system, they mobilize to political action, influence policy, and complicate the task of developing democratic consensus. I also believe that in a political system with the strong constitutional and legalist tradition of Chile, institutions and legitimated patterns of political action make a difference in political outcomes. That the Frei government could adopt the strongest agrarian reform law ever adopted under democratic auspices, that a committed Marxist could come to the presidency of what was basically a very "bourgeois" society, and that he would only be overthrown after the breakdown of the economy and the widespread belief that his government was systematically violating the constitution, are all explicable in terms of the strength of Chilean political institutions which until September 1973 endured strains that no other democratic system in the world could have supported for such a period of time.

In keeping with this, I also believe that Chilean politics is influenced principally by internal factors, and that, contrary to the dependency school now dominant in Latin American social science, external influences have not been central determinants of the course of political life there. This emphasis therefore distinguishes this study from those which attempt to explain recent Chilean politics primarily in terms of either U.S., Soviet, or Cuban intervention. I take account of the role of the CIA and U.S. policy, but I do not believe it made a decisive difference. I am now convinced—with the benefit of hindsight—that even if the CIA had not been giving substantial financial support to the opposition, Allende would not have lasted a full six-year term unless he had drastically altered his policies, so long as the armed forces retained the autonomy and independence which they were guaranteed from the outset of his administration. There were also external pressures inspired or influenced by U.S. policy, but Allende's self-defeating domestic economic policies and polarizing politics were adopted from the outset of his administration and seemed to ignore or disregard what his predecessor had recognized—that, particularly with as fragile and inflation-prone an economy as Chile's, there are serious economic constraints on the possibilities of more than incremental changes in a democratic system, although over time those changes may in fact result in a "revolutionary" shift in political and economic power.

Recognizing the political, economic, and institutional limits on policy-making, I also have assumed that there was no inevitability about the course of recent Chilean history, and that there were always alternatives available —some of which might have avoided the tragic dénouement of 1973. In particular, at the beginning of both the Frei and Allende administrations, alternative ways of dealing with those outside the government party or parties could have made a difference in Chile's subsequent political evolution. Similarly, in the middle of their periods in office, both presidents had opportunities to alter their political and economic policies in ways which could have avoided the downward spiral which occurred in both cases— with far greater intensity and adverse effects, of course, in Allende's case than in Frei's. To identify these and other crucial turning points in the stormy recent history of Chile, I refer the reader to the following chapters.

As I hope this book will demonstrate, neither Frei nor Allende fits into the neat categories that the mythmakers of left and right have assigned to them. Frei was neither the willing tool of foreign and domestic reaction nor the initiator of a social revolution in Chile, but a dedicated democrat who tried to use constitutional channels to promote a greater degree of social justice for low-income groups. Allende was neither an innocent social democrat overthrown by fascist thugs and the CIA, nor a Marxist revolutionary who manipulated Chile's democratic institutions in order to set the stage for a violent Communist seizure of power. Rather, he was a skilled parliamentary politician committed to aiding the poor and under-privileged, who could never abandon his romantic admiration for those, like Castro and Guevara, who had waged a successful armed revolution. When at last the contradiction between parliamentarism and revolution led to his overthrow, he chose to die holding a submachine gun which was a gift from Fidel Castro.

There is not space to identify and thank all those who have helped me, especially the hundreds of Chileans with whom I have discussed politics since my first visit in 1963. Besides the Rockefeller Foundation, which supported my teaching there, I should also express my gratitude to the Committee on Regional and International Studies and the Committee on Research in the Social Sciences and the Humanities of Princeton University, which made possible repeated visits to Chile over more than a decade, and to the Princeton Center of International Studies for its support for two summers of research and writing. The Twentieth Century Fund's sponsorship of my current work on nationalization in Latin America was also helpful in the sections on Chilean policy toward the copper industry. Finally I wish to thank my wife for her continued advice, assistance, and example as to what a dedicated democratic (and Democratic) politician can accomplish. This book is dedicated to the Chilean people in the hope that they may soon reestablish the free society concerned with social justice that all those who have worked with them have known and loved.

The Overthrow of Allende
and
the Politics of Chile,
1964–1976

CHAPTER ONE

The Coup and Its Causes

At 8:30 A.M. on September 11, 1973, Radio Agricultura in Santiago interrupted its regular programming to play the Chilean national anthem, following it with the announcement, "This is the network of the armed forces and carabineros." Citing "the grave social and moral crisis in the country, the government's inability to control the chaos, and the constant increase in paramilitary groups trained by the Popular Unity parties which will lead Chile to an inevitable civil war," the pronunciamiento demanded that President Salvador Allende turn over his office to the military and the national police, and declared that "the armed forces and carabineros are united in carrying out their historic mission and responsibility to fight for the liberation of the fatherland [*patria*], to prevent the country from falling under the Marxist yoke, and to seek the restoration of order and institutionality." The military declaration promised that the workers would not be deprived of their "economic and social conquests," advised Santiago residents to remain in their homes, and ordered the progovernment press, radio, and television to cease to function "beginning at this instant" or be subject to attack by the Chilean army and air force.[1]

Informed earlier that the Chilean navy had seized Valparaíso, President Allende had left his residence in Santiago's fashionable Barrio Alto for the presidential palace, La Moneda, shortly after 7:00 A.M. He was joined there by his ministers of foreign affairs, economy, and interior, as well as his close friend, José Tohá, former minister of interior and defense. In addition, several doctors, his two daughters, his personal secretary (and, as the pro-junta press noted after the coup, "intimate friend") Miria Contreras, along with a well-known journalist, Augusto Olivares, and the undersecretary of the interior, Daniel Vergara, came to the palace. The armed personal bodyguard of the president (usually referred to as the GAP, an acronym for Allende's description of them as a group of personal friends, "Grupo de Amigos Personales"), twenty detectives from the Investigation Squad (Investigaciones), and the three hundred carabineros of the Special Services section of the national police were also on hand to defend the

3

palace. (After the carabineros were informed that the national police had joined the coup, they left the palace, dismantling the machine-gun emplacements which had been set up in front of the building.)

Allende replied over the radio to the military ultimatum, expressing his determination to resist "by whatever means, even at the cost of my life." The military countered with a communiqué which accused his government of violating fundamental rights, "artificially fomenting class struggle, violating the constitution, destroying the economy, and endangering the security of the country," concluding that the Allende government was "illegitimate, immoral, and unrepresentative of the overwhelming sentiment of the nation."

By 9:30 A.M. only one progovernment radio station continued to broadcast, and on it Allende delivered his last message to the Chilean people:

> This is surely the last time that I will be able to speak to you. . . . My words are not spoken in bitterness, but in disappointment. In the face of these events, I can only say to the workers, "I am not going to resign." At this historic juncture, I will pay with my life for the loyalty of the people.

Allende thanked the workers for their support and insisted that he had kept his promise to respect the constitution and the law. Blaming "foreign capital and imperialism allied to reaction" for creating the climate which persuaded the armed forces to break their tradition of nonintervention, he said he was speaking to

> the worker, the peasant, and the intellectual, to those who will be persecuted because fascism is already present in our country, blowing up bridges, cutting railroad lines, destroying pipelines in the face of the silence of those who should have taken action. History will judge them. . . . My voice will no longer come to you, but it does not matter. You will keep hearing it; it will always be with you. At the least you will remember me as an honorable man who was loyal to the revolution.

During the speech, Allende said that the people should "defend themselves but not sacrifice themselves," which seemed to indicate that he did not wish the workers to carry out armed resistance if it was evident that the armed forces possessed overwhelming military superiority.

The military leaders in charge of the siege of the presidential palace were situated in the Ministry of Defense just across Santiago's main boulevard, and Allende was in telephone contact with them throughout the morning. They gave him until 11:00 A.M. to surrender, repeating several times an offer of safe conduct out of the country for him and his family. At about 10:00 A.M. the president permitted his military aides to leave, as well as those of the twenty-man detachment of detectives from Investigaciones who wished to do so. Over their objections, Allende finally persuaded his two daughters to leave the palace an hour later. He donned a helmet, gas mask, and bulletproof vest, and carried a submachine gun which had been a gift to him from Fidel Castro, inscribed "To my friend and comrade in arms, Salvador." Along with progovernment snipers located in the upper floors of government buildings around Constitution Square behind the palace, the only armed defenders of the palace besides Allende himself were the thirty members of the personal bodyguard and some detectives from Investigaciones.

When the telephone negotiations were concluded with the announcement by the military that Hawker Hunter fighter bombers were already on their way to bomb the palace, those within took refuge in its side subcellars on the theory that the pilots would hit only the central portion to avoid damaging surrounding buildings. At 11:55 A.M. the rocket bombing runs began. A total of eighteen rockets hit the building, and when the seven bombing runs were completed at 12:15 P.M., a thick cloud of black smoke billowed out of the north central facade and flames leapt out of the main entrance. After 140 years of almost uninterrupted constitutional rule, the Chilean armed forces, long known for their adherence to constitutionalism and civilian rule, had set fire to the building that for most of that period had been the symbol of civilian constitutional government in Chile.

After the bombing, a four-man delegation from Allende crossed over in an armored car from the palace to the Ministry of Defense to conduct surrender negotiations, but sniper fire prevented them from returning. Tanks and army troops began to advance on the palace amid sporadic firing from surrounding buildings. Shortly after 1:30 P.M. the besieging troops gave the defenders a four-minute deadline to capitulate. Allende, who was defending the palace from the second floor, is quoted as saying, "Surrender. This is a massacre. La Payita [Miria Contreras] should leave first. I will go at the end." A white handkerchief was tied to a broom, and the group began to file through the side door of the palace; but Allende did not follow them. Sniper fire forced those who had left the building to lie on the sidewalk, and the fighting continued within the palace between the members of the GAP and the soldiers led by General Javier Palacios, who had entered through the main gate. When they reached the Independence Salon on the second floor of the east side of the building, the soldiers found one of the president's doctors with the body of Allende. The doctor, Patricio Guijón, said that he had seen the president shoot himself through the chin with his submachine gun. At 6:15 P.M., after examination by medical and ballistics experts, Allende's body was taken out of the building wrapped in a poncho

The Chilean presidential palace, symbol of civilian rule, after rocket bombing by the Chilean air force, September 11, 1973. (United Press International)

Daniel Vergara leads the delegation leaving the presidential palace after the bombing in order to negotiate its surrender at the Ministry of Defense. (Hernan Morales)

and flown the next day to Viña del Mar, a resort city near Valparaíso, where it was buried in the family plot. Allende's widow has said that she was not permitted to see the body and could only make a brief lamentation at the grave, telling the gravediggers, "Salvador Allende cannot be buried in such an anonymous way. I want you at least to know the name of the person whom you are burying."

A nationwide twenty-four-hour curfew was imposed as of 3:00 P.M., and military patrols were sent out to arrest wanted leaders of the deposed regime. Some turned themselves in as ordered in radio announcements, and many more sought asylum in various embassies. The head of the Socialist Party, Senator Carlos Altamirano, escaped the country, as did some of the leaders of the Movement of the Revolutionary Left (MIR). Allende's close friend, Augusto Olivares, committed suicide before the bombing of La Moneda, and Eduardo Paredes, one-time head of Investigaciones, was reported by the military to have died in a clash with an army patrol (it seems more likely that he and other captured members of the GAP and Investigaciones were shot in the Tacna regimental headquarters the day after the coup), but the coup itself had been relatively bloodless.

Much more blood was shed later, as the new military rulers initiated the brutal process of destroying the power of the Marxist left. In succeeding weeks the military junta headed by General Augusto Pinochet closed the Chilean Congress, outlawed the pro-Allende political parties and declared the other parties in recess, appointed military men to head all Chile's universities including those under private auspices, dissolved the Chilean trade union confederation, established censorship of the media, and conducted continuous roundups of real or suspected enemies of the regime, many of whom were held in Santiago's two large soccer stadiums. The courts continued to function, but they refused jurisdiction over the political arrests, citing the "state of siege in time of war" which had been unilaterally declared by the military. The junta legislated by a series of decree-laws, one of which later stated that if any of the military decrees was in violation of the constitution it was to be considered as a constitutional amendment. Continuing reports came out of Chile from journalists, churchmen, and international investigating agencies of torture, repression, and prisoners "shot while trying to escape." One of the world's oldest constitutional democracies had become a harsh military dictatorship.

Why did it happen? Was it inevitable that Allende's *vía chilena*, which he had described as "a second model" of a peaceful transition to socialism, would end with the presidential palace in flames, blood in the streets of Santiago, and corpses in the Río Mapocho? How does one explain and understand the sequence of events that culminated on September 11—and the regime that followed? Initially, foreign observers blamed the U.S. Central Intelligence Agency and ITT, since their earlier anti-Allende activities had been widely publicized. The left attributed the coup to imperialism and its domestic allies, citing the so-called invisible blockade organized by the United States and the continuing sabotage, black-market activity, and violence organized by the extreme right within Chile. The Moderates such as the Left Radicals (PIR), the Chilean equivalent of Europe's Social Democrats, and the Christian Democrats, Chile's largest party, cited the runaway inflation produced by Allende's economic policies (an annual rate of 323 percent shortly before the coup) and his failure to maintain democratic legitimacy as the principal causes of the coup. The right pointed to the proliferation of armed leftist groups and claimed that a left-wing coup had been planned for September 1973 which would have involved the assassination of the military commanders and the leaders of the civilian opposition. Social scientists in other countries saw the coup as a confirmation of their theories about rapid social mobilization, the exhaustion of populism in Latin America, or the pernicious effects of an electoral and party system geared to proportional representation and frequent elections.[2]

Who was right? In the complex patterns of this hyperpoliticized country one could find confirmation of almost any theory, and left and right could produce completely consistent—and totally contradictory—interpretations of recent Chilean history. Inevitably the many Chileans who were forced into exile by the coup have produced selective accounts of the Allende period which are highly sympathetic to the Popular Unity government, while the Chilean government has attempted to reply with government publications and documents aimed at demonstrating that Allende had been solely concerned with self-aggrandizement and, aided by thousands of Cubans and other Latin American leftists, the establishment of a Marxist dictatorship.[3] The lessons to be derived from a careful examination of the Chilean experience are in danger of being lost in the partisan propaganda which has followed the coup.

To understand what happened on September 11 and to evaluate the conflicting interpretations of its meaning, it is necessary to go back before Allende's accession to power in 1970. Some might say that one should begin with the early 1950s, when a considerable expansion of electoral participation took place in Chile and political leaders began to promise more to the electorate than the Chilean political and economic system could deliver. The 1958 presidential election, in which the figures that were to dominate Chilean politics for fifteen years—Jorge Alessandri on the right, Eduardo Frei for the Christian Democrats, and Salvador Allende on the left—first ran against one another, is another possible point of departure. However, 1964 seems more appropriate as the year with which to begin, both for reasons of space and because of the close relationship between what happened during Eduardo Frei's six-year term—dubbed by him "the revolution in liberty"—and the policies carried out between 1970 and 1973 by his successor, Salvador Allende.

A comparison of the policies of Frei and Allende is also useful as an illustration of the alternative possibilities available to, and the limits upon, the democratic reformer. Both promised "revolutionary" changes in Chilean society within the framework of that country's democratic institutions. Both were faced with policy choices which often, although not always, involved trade-offs between conflicting goals. The problem for both was how to achieve development, reform, and social justice, while maintaining a productive economy, popular support, and political democracy. The methods they chose, however, and the choices they made, were very different.

There are fairly precise indicators to measure the effects of government policy on stability, economic growth, democracy, and social justice. A government is stable when antigovernment violence is nonexistent or at a low level. Economic growth is usually measured by the annual rate of increase in per capita income. Political democracy is indicated by competitive elections, civil liberties, and the percentage of adults of voting age who vote. Social justice is more difficult to measure, but recent writers have emphasized income distribution and, in agricultural countries, land-tenure arrangements.

Along with a generally shared objective of national autonomy and a reduction of *dependencia*,[4] these goals and measures have become central elements of Chilean political debate in recent years. Part of the fascination of the Chilean drama is the extent to which a highly ideologized multiparty system in a centralized but democratic state offered the Chilean voter alternative policy choices which ranged from the conservative's preference for order and stability to the socialist's belief in equality and equity—and successive governments of right, center, and left tried to implement their political philosophies.

Dissatisfied with the conservatism of the Alessandri "businessman's government" which had ruled Chile since 1958, Eduardo Frei, the victorious Christian Democratic candidate in 1964, called for a "revolution in liberty," altering property relationships in the countryside, asserting national control over the copper industry, and mobilizing the "marginal" sectors of the population. This was to be carried out within the framework of constitutional democracy through an appeal for broad popular support to overcome the opposition which would inevitably arise on both left and right. There is no doubt that Chile was a more prosperous, just, and democratic (if less stable) society at the end of Frei's term of office than it had been at the beginning. Yet he did not succeed in solving Chile's chronic problems of inflation and economic stagnation, and in 1970 he turned over power to the very forces to which he had offered himself as an alternative six years before. This study will attempt to determine whether his policy was a failure, as its critics on the left and right (for different reasons) contend, and whether the problems he encountered were an inevitable consequence of the inherent contradictions of populist reformism, or were related to particular characteristics of the Chilean political system, or, alternatively, were the result of policy errors and wrong choices at crucial points by his administration.

As a Marxist, Salvador Allende pursued a policy which was actuated by very different value priorities from those of his predecessor. For both ideological and political reasons, the rapid expansion of state control of industry and agriculture and an immediate increase in the living standards and political participation of low-income groups were given first priority, and the political instability and economic dislocations which were likely to result were accepted as "the costs of revolution." In the course of Allende's three years in power, class polarization, violence, and, after mid-1972, runaway inflation convulsed Chilean society and made it increasingly unlikely that the transition to socialism could be carried out peacefully. Allende's domestic problems were exacerbated by external pressures, chiefly from the United States, and by the intransigence both of the left wing of his own coalition, whose predictions of the inevitability of a violent confrontation eventually became a self-fulfilling prophecy, and of the extreme right wing of the opposition, which did not hesitate to use subversive methods and armed violence to overthrow him. Again the question will be asked whether the violent end of the Allende regime was the result of factors that were systemic (the contradiction between democracy and Marxism), national (the fragile Chilean economy and archaic political system), or personal (Allende's policy errors)—or more accurately, how one is to weigh the importance of each, since they all played a role in the Chilean tragedy.

I conclude with a brief examination of the policies pursued by the military junta which overthrew Allende's Popular Unity government. All sides agree that September 11, 1973, marked the end of an era in Chile. The military government is committed to a very different policy—postponing for many years a return to democratic rule, giving first priority to economic recovery and the elimination of Marxist influence, and relying ideologically on a combination of Catholic integralism and free-enterprise economics. Why that government has felt it necessary to engage in repressive measures is also related to what went before, and this study will attempt to determine why one of the freest democracies in the contemporary world has been replaced with a government which, legally and psychologically, is in a permanent "state of siege." Once again the systemic explanation ("fascism" as the only alternative to socialism) is offered, but historical factors (the particular situation of Chile in 1973 in an economic and political "blind alley" from which only an authoritarian government could extricate it) and personal factors (the Chilean military's political socialization, or lack thereof) provide alternative or additional explanations.

The political experience of Chile since the early 1960s suggests a broader range of questions of fundamental importance for modern politics. First, it provides a series of case studies of the policy prescriptions of the ideologies of the left, right, and center, and compels the observer to define his own attitude toward them, as they apply not only to Chile but more generally. Is it true, as the left suggests, that capitalism and imperialism are the major obstacles to the achievement of social justice in the contemporary world, and that only a socialist system can provide a minimum level of human dignity to mankind? Or is the problem, as the center maintains, that formal democracy has not yet been translated into genuine effective participation by the poor and less privileged so that they can make use of the mechanisms of the modern state to moderate the excesses of private enterprise, and provide the populace with access to the advantages of modern life, while maintaining political freedom and pluralism? Or is the solution basically economic, as the right maintains, lying in economic development which can only be achieved by restraining political demagoguery and social unrest—by authoritarian means, if necessary? All three of these positions are represented and can be evaluated in the policies of the various Chilean parties and governments that are examined in this book.

The period under study raises related questions about democracy and development. In the decade before 1973, increasing sectors of Chilean society (although by no means a majority) began to question Chile's tradition of constitutional democracy. The democratic center believed that social reform and economic development could be carried out through incremental change within a framework of freedom, legality, and compromise. But the center found itself increasingly under attack both from the left, which insisted that any "fundamental" change must inevitably involve a violent confrontation with the forces of reaction, and from the right, which looked to military intervention to give Chile the stability required for economic growth and social peace. For the left and the right, Cuba and Brazil respectively offered examples of the successful implementation of alternative models of political change to the democratic system which in theory had previously had a quasi monopoly on legitimacy in the Western Hemisphere. Chileans and "Chile-watchers" were compelled to ask themselves, Is democracy compatible with basic socioeconomic reform, and if not, what are the alternatives?

The conduct of various social groups and classes within Chile also suggests broader questions about their role in the modernization process. Are the workers (or the workers and peasants, or the workers, peasants, and slum dwellers) a revolutionary force which once catalyzed by class-conscious intellectuals can transform society? Or are they basically conservative, especially once they receive better wages, a small plot of land, or a house of their own? Does Marxism unite or divide exploited groups in their effort to achieve a more human existence? Is the middle class revolutionary, reformist, or reactionary, or all three at the same or different times? Can the upper classes be persuaded, cajoled, or frightened into sharing their wealth and power with other groups, or is violence the only way to achieve social justice, with repression by those in control of the instruments of political power the likely response? More generally, is man actuated primarily if not exclusively by motives of self-interest and competition which neither persuasion nor appeals to social consciousness and cooperation, nor even a fundamental alteration in social institutions, can modify?

The role of the United States in relation to Chile during the period has also been cited as an illustration of more general conclusions. At the beginning of the period, the Alliance for Progress appeared to symbolize a U.S. commitment to land reform, tax reform, and educational reform under democratic auspices, and the government of Eduardo Frei seemed to be one of the showcases for U.S. policy. Later, as Frei ran into increasing difficulties, it was said that U.S. policy was turning away from democratic regimes and toward those under military auspices, notably in Brazil. With the election of Salvador Allende, U.S. policy became increasingly hostile to Chile, and after his overthrow it was revealed that a deliberate policy of "destabilization" of his government had been pursued. It was therefore concluded by some that Chile demonstrated that U.S. policy always and everywhere is opposed to regimes—even democratically elected regimes—that are committed to social changes which may threaten U.S. power or economic interests. U.S. assistance to the military junta which followed the September 1973 coup was taken as additional confirmation. This book will give considerable attention to U.S. policy toward Chile and will attempt to determine the extent to which these assertions are true.

The most disturbing generalization which may be drawn from the Chilean case is not restricted to the developing nations or to recent U.S. foreign policy, but involves the relationship of politics, economics, and the modern state. It is the question whether in recent Chilean experience we have "seen the future" and perceived that it does *not* work. The trends that have been evident in accelerated fashion in Chile in recent years are worldwide trends. Not merely in Latin America or the Third World but everywhere in the world we see persistent inflation and unemployment, increasingly scarce resources, the extension of state regulation, heightened demands on government, and diminished capability of *any* economic system to satisfy those demands. Is the Chilean experience of increasing politicization, inflation, and polarization, followed by the imposition of authoritarian rule, likely to be repeated in many other parts of the world, including major democracies in the so-called developed world? Is it true, as Lord Acton asserted when he observed similar trends in nineteenth-century Europe, that "the passion for equality makes vain the hope of freedom"? A closer look at Chile since the early 1960s may give us some insight into these perennial questions.

CHAPTER TWO

The Context of Chilean Politics

Chile in the early 1960s was ready for reform. Coming to Chile from other Latin American countries, one was struck by the comparative weakness of conservative forces and the ferment and dynamism of those calling for change. Yet that change was to be carried out within the constitutional "rules of the game"—and, at least at the beginning of the decade, the proponents of violence on both the right and the left had little influence or support. Salvador Allende and Eduardo Frei were both elected to office on programs that promised "revolutionary" transformation in the distribution of power in Chile. Yet both also affirmed their commitment to the constitutional framework. This adherence to constitutionalism on the part of Chileans, while not unique in Latin America (Costa Rica, Colombia, and more recently Venezuela also have developed constitutionalist traditions), was more deeply rooted than anywhere else in the continent. Between 1833 and 1973 Chile had only two constitutions, and throughout most of its history it has been a constitutional democracy in law, if not in fact. With the exception of a comic-opera barracks revolt for higher pay in October 1969, prior to the 1973 coup the military had not attempted to interfere with the operation of Chilean constitutional processes since the 1930s.[1]

The Institutional Context

It was the military that made it possible to write the constitution of 1925, under which Chile operated until 1973. The 1833 constitution had established a strong presidency, but this had been reinterpreted after the brief 1891 civil war to permit the establishment of a parliamentary regime in which the legislature dominated the executive. When the Congress resisted President Arturo Alessandri's attempt to adopt a welfare program and to strengthen the presidency, the military stepped in to resolve the deadlock. President Alessandri left the country but was recalled five months later by a group of reformist military men. With the assistance of a civilian group of experts, he wrote the 1925 constitution returning Chile to the system of presidential dominance which had characterized its politics in the nineteenth century.

According to the 1925 constitution, the Chilean president was elected for a six-year term and was not eligible to succeed himself (although he could run again if there was an intervening presidency). In the event that he did not receive an absolute majority of the votes cast (as was usual), the Congress was to decide in joint session fifty days after the election between the two candidates with the largest numbers of votes. The president could appoint and remove members of his cabinet, and the 1925 constitution took away from Congress the power to remove ministers by withdrawal of confidence (although it could achieve the same result by accusing the minister of violating the law or the constitution). The president had the exclusive right to propose the budget, create new administrative posts, and increase government salaries. In addition, he could expedite his legislative proposals by attaching various degrees of urgency to his bills and by calling extraordinary sessions of Congress. He had an item veto over legislation, which also enabled him to add amendments to bills passed by Congress. Additions and vetoes could be overridden only by a two-thirds majority of Congress. The 1925 constitution also granted the president the power (broadened in 1970) to call a plebiscite in the event of conflict with the Congress over a proposal for a constitutional amendment.

While the Chilean Congress was weakened by the 1925 constitution, it remained the oldest and strongest in Latin America. It consisted of two houses, a Senate and a Chamber of Deputies. The Senate had 45 members until 1969, when it was enlarged to 50, elected for eight-year terms, half of them every four years. Five senators were elected by proportional representation for each of ten groups of provinces. The 147 (later 150) members of the Chamber of Deputies were elected every four years, again under a system of proportional representation by province, or, in the case of Santiago, by district. Congressional elections never coincided with those for the presidency.

The Congress met in ordinary session from May 21 to September 18, and was always called into extraordinary session by the president for other parts of the year. Except for the reservation to the president of the right of exclusive initiative on certain types of laws already mentioned and the time limits on budgetary and urgency laws, the Congress's legislative powers during ordinary sessions were very broad. The legislative stages for the adoption of a law were lengthy and complex. Most bills were first considered by a specialized committee, then discussed and voted on as a whole in order to determine whether the chamber wished to legislate on the subject. Then, after another committee consideration, the bill was discussed and voted on in detail. If the bill was approved by one house, it went to the other. If the second house modified or rejected the bill, the initiating chamber could insist on its bill by a two-thirds majority, in which case the second house was obliged to insist on its version by two-thirds. A joint committee then attempted to work out differences between the two versions. If both houses approved, the item veto of the president could still delay the bill's adoption. Legislation thus went through many stages (*trámites*) before adoption, and opponents of legislation had many opportunities to prevent its passage. Constitutional amendments went through similar stages but had to be adopted by an absolute majority and confirmed in a joint legislative session sixty days later. In addition, there were provisions for a popular referendum in the event of certain disagreements between the president and Congress.

Local municipalities elected municipal councils, although the mayors of municipalities with over ten thousand inhabitants were appointed by the president (as were the governors of the eighty-seven departments and the *intendentes* of Chile's twenty-five provinces). Municipal elections were highly politicized and were regarded as referenda on the conduct of the national government.

The combination of presidential elections every six years, congressional elections every four years in which the lower house and half of the upper house were elected, and politicized municipal elections in the intervening years meant that Chile was in a perpetual state of electoral fever, and elections became a favorite preoccupation of Chileans at every social and economic level. The constitutional tradition became closely tied to Chilean nationalism; Chileans were proud that unlike their neighbors, Argentina, Bolivia, and Peru, they had been able to govern themselves freely throughout most of their history. Critics could observe that until the last two decades, electoral participation was low, partly due to a literacy requirement (removed in 1970), partly due to apathy, and mostly due to the delay until 1949 in extending the suffrage to women. By the 1960s, however, 85 percent of the registered voters were participating in presidential elections, and 75 percent of those eligible to vote were registered.[2]

The proportional representation system encouraged the proliferation of parties and gave each some representation in the legislature. A president who represented a new tendency often found that he was faced with a hostile "lame-duck" legislature—although since the death of Juan Antonio Rios in 1946, every second president had been able to benefit from having a legislative election six months after he was elected (Eduardo Frei benefited from this in 1964–65, but Salvador Allende did not in 1970). Yet the combination of proportional representation and staggered elections (even when the legislative elections followed shortly after the election of the president, only half the Senate was elected), plus the lack of immediate reeligibility of the president, built into the constitution a bias against more than incremental change. Thus, a new president would come to power with high hopes and strong support but would soon run into serious legislative opposition and find it necessary to compromise major portions of his program or be obliged to wait either five or seven years for the election of a Senate favorable to him. By that time his term was either nearing its end or had been concluded.

The judiciary was somewhat less politically significant in the Chilean system than in the United States, since the Chilean Supreme Court did not have a general power of judicial review. However, it could declare a statute or executive act unconstitutional in specific cases. Furthermore, after 1970 a special Constitutional Tribunal was established with the right to rule on the constitutionality of laws and to decide disputes between the executive and the legislature. The judiciary was independent, in the sense that judges could not be removed except for gross malfeasance and were appointed by the president on the basis of lists of candidates prepared by the judiciary itself. Enjoying the same guarantees of tenure as the members of the Supreme Court was the Controller General's Office (Contraloría General), which audited government accounts and pronounced on the legality of executive decrees (although the president could insist on his decree if he had the countersignatures of his entire cabinet).

The Chilean political parties were not mentioned in the constitution of 1925, but they formed a very important part of the institutional system. While there was a bewildering variety of splits and alliances among the parties, they were divided into six, and after the mid-1960s five, principal parties and three main orientations. On the right, the oldest parties (dating back to the early days of the Republic), the Liberals and Conservatives, joined together after 1966 to form the National Party. In the center, the Radical Party, dating to 1861, combined diverse orientations from moderate to socialist linked by a shared anticlericalism and, after 1967, deeply divided by their attitudes toward cooperation with the Marxist left. The other centrist group, the Christian Democratic Party (PDC), was relatively new. It drew on Catholic reformist thought to advance the cause of a "communitarian" society characterized by considerable state influence in the economy, as well as the democratization of participation in politics and economics through neighborhood associations, agricultural cooperatives, and worker shares in ownership, management, and profits in industry. After 1970 the Christian Democrats described their program as "communitarian socialism," and in 1969 and 1971 they too suffered internal divisions over the issue of cooperation with the Popular Unity coalition of Salvador Allende.

On the left were two Marxist parties, the Communists and the Socialists. Most observers placed the Communists to the right of the Socialists because they appeared to be more flexible about cooperation with the center parties and more strongly committed to electoral participation (the *vía pacífica*) as the means to attain power. Perhaps it would be more accurate to say that a part of the Socialist Party, including its secretary general between 1971 and 1973, Carlos Altamirano, was critical of "bourgeois" parliamentarism. Salvador Allende, as one would expect of someone who was a presidential candidate four times, president of the Chilean Senate in the 1960s, a minister in the Popular Front government in 1940, and a member of Congress for over thirty years, was deeply committed to parliamentary government.

The Communist Party was founded in 1921, but its history goes back before World War I to the foundation of the Socialist Workers Party in 1912. The Socialist Party was founded in 1931 (Allende was involved in its foundation) and had adopted a variety of ideologies and political positions. The Communist Party was outlawed from 1948 until 1958. Thereafter the Communists worked in close alliance with the Socialists through the Popular Action Front (Frente de Acción Popular, FRAP) and, after 1970, in the Popular Unity coalition dominated by the two Marxist parties.[3]

In addition to the Chilean political parties, one might also consider Chilean organized interest groups as part of the institutional structure. Big business has been represented by the Sociedad de Fomento Fabril (SFF), small business by the Confederación de la Producción y Comercio, agriculture by the Sociedad Nacional de Agricultura (SNA), students at the University of Chile by the Chilean Student Federation (FECH), and labor by the Central Workers Confederation (CUT); professionals, civil servants, and many other occupational groups had their representative organizations (*gremios*); and in recent years women, peasants, and neighborhood committees have been organized with official approval and support.

The Economic Context

The political system gave the Chilean voter a much broader choice of alternative ideologies and approaches than is available in most other countries in the contemporary world. That choice was more meaningful both because of the openness of the Chilean political system and because the severity of Chile's economic and social crisis induced the parties to offer sharply divergent solutions to the country's problems.

The seeming permanence of an inflation which dated back nearly a century provided a continuing reminder to every Chilean consumer of his country's economic difficulties. Since the 1930s there had been wage readjustments each year to compensate, wholly or in part, for the inflation, but purchasing power rarely managed to keep up with price increases. This in turn led the Chilean voter to look to the government for a solution to his economic squeeze, to raise his hopes that each new government would end the inflationary spiral, and, when it did not succeed, to turn to another political formula. At least part of the reason for the fickleness of the Chilean voter which brought successively a moderate business regime, reformist Catholicism, and Marxism to the presidency lies in Chile's endemic inflation.

For years Chile was second only to South Vietnam in the seriousness of its inflation, and in 1972, 1973, and 1974, it held the world record. To make matters worse, the inflation rate fluctuated wildly from one year to the next, making economic planning or even business forecasts and cost estimates very difficult. Thus, in 1955, when the inflation rate had reached 83 percent, a group of U.S. business consultants, the Klein-Saks Mission, persuaded the Chilean government that restriction of credit and a modified freeze on wage readjustments for the cost of living was necessary. The program brought the inflation rate down to 17 percent in 1957, but it also resulted in widespread unemployment, strikes, demonstrations, and a sharp reduction in per capita income. By 1958, the presidential election year, the rate had risen to 33 percent. When Jorge Alessandri, the right-wing candidate who narrowly won the election, reorganized the currency, adopted a more realistic exchange rate, and pushed through further economic stabilization measures, the inflation rate came down to almost zero in early 1960, although this was accompanied by a massive balance-of-payments deficit. Then in May 1960 earthquakes forced an increase in government spending, resulting in an upturn in the inflation rate with predictable effects on political support for the Alessandri government.[4]

Relatively high inflation rates have been justified by some Latin American economists in cases where the alternative is economic stagnation like that which followed the Klein-Saks measures, but in Chile inflation does not seem to have been accompanied by anything more than moderate economic growth. Chilean industry had expanded in the 1930s and 1940s as a result of import substitution, but by the mid-1950s the potential for expansion to meet the relatively limited market of (at the time) 7 million people (only about a third of whom were really in the market economy) had been seriously diminished. Between 1953 and 1959 per capita industrial production had only increased at 0.9 percent per year, and this record was improved only slightly in the early 1960s. (It is important to note the words *per capita*, since the growth rate of the Chilean population of around 2 percent reduces what appear to be more respectable figures on the overall increase in industrial production.)

To finance industrialization, all developing countries need foreign exchange. Copper is the principal source of Chile's earnings in hard currency, accounting for about 75 percent of export earnings. The copper industry until the 1960s was principally U.S.-owned, with the Anaconda and Kennecott companies controlling the largest mines. Since 1955, under the so-called Nuevo Trato (New Deal), the companies had paid profit taxes which declined as production expanded, an attempt to induce them to increase output. The fact that such a major factor in the Chilean balance of payments was subject to production decisions made by foreigners meant that this would be a central issue of Chilean politics in the period we are examining.

Since World War II and through the Korean War, copper exports had been sold to the United States at an agreed-upon fixed price, but increasingly since then copper sales had been carried out on the London International Metals Exchange market and were subject to the fluctuations of supply and demand. A sharp drop in the international price of copper in 1957, for instance, had much to do with the difficulties of the Klein-Saks stabilization program.

The area in which Chile's state of underdevelopment seemed most pronounced in the early 1960s was agriculture. Blessed by a fertile Central Valley with nearly ideal agricultural conditions, Chilean agricultural production was notoriously inefficient, its landowning pattern antiquated, and wages in the countryside far below the official minimum wage. According to a widely quoted study, 7 percent of Chilean landowners owned 65 percent of the land (78 percent of the irrigated land); while at the other end of the landholding spectrum, 37 percent owned 1 percent of the land.[5] The concentration of agricultural production into large estates or *fundos* might have been justified if they had been able to produce the food necessary to feed the Chilean population, but by the 1960s the importation of over $100 million worth of food each year constituted a major drain on foreign exchange earnings. The emphasis on agrarian reform in the Charter of Punta del Este which established the Alliance for Progress in 1961 helped to draw further attention to an already desperate situation in Chilean agriculture. That situation comprised two problems, one of efficiency and the other of social justice. Between 1962 and 1973 three administrations attempted to resolve those problems, making agrarian reform a central issue of Chilean politics throughout the period.

In the early 1960s Chile was by no means totally underdeveloped. Besides copper and nitrate mining, it had a basic industrial infrastructure— including communications, steel, cement, chemical, and paper industries, as well as domestic petroleum resources. With per capita income around $500 a year, Chile had moved further in the direction of economic development than most countries in the Third World. Ironically, it was just this state of partial development which accounted for the frustration of educated Chileans as they looked at their economy and society. Broadly educated and literate, politically competitive, urbanized, and living in a society in which economic data had become part of the regular substance of political debate, they were more conscious of the shortcomings of the existing system than citizens of many other countries of the Third World. Books such as Ricardo

Lagos's *La concentración del poder económico en Chile* showed how tight was the control of the financial and economic elite. Jorge Ahumada's *En vez de la miseria* appealed to the educated middle class on Christian and humanist grounds for an end to exploitation of peasants and slum dwellers. As in the United States in the same period, the mass of politically conscious Chileans began in the 1960s to be aware of the injustice of many aspects of their society; but unlike their North American counterparts, they did not live in a society whose economy was sufficiently productive and well organized to handle the strains involved in attempting to remedy those injustices. Despite criticism by the extremes of left and right, there was until the early 1970s a broad spectrum of acceptance of the Chilean political system of constitutional democracy. But the Chilean economic system, because of the problems outlined above, commanded much less general support, and much of the political debate of the sixties was concerned with the search for alternatives to, or at least serious modifications of, existing economic arrangements.

The Social Context

The conventional picture of the Latin American class structure divides Latin America into two social groups, a small group of the very wealthy and a large group of the poor. This is not an accurate description of the situation in Chile. By 1960 about 30 to 35 percent of the Chilean population belonged to the middle or upper strata, with a higher proportion in Santiago and Valparaíso, where almost half of the population lives. Many more identified with the middle class even when their incomes did not justify it. The large and increasing middle group was literate, educated, upwardly mobile, and striving to advance itself. It was also chronically dissatisfied, and this dissatisfaction expressed itself at the polls.

The urban population of Chile had expanded at a rapid rate—between 1952 and 1960 at 5.9 percent per annum, so that by 1960 about 70 percent of the population lived in urban centers. This population was 90 percent literate, and the national literacy figure for Chile, including rural areas, was 84 percent.[6]

Yet despite the existence of a relatively large middle class, the disparity between rich and poor in Chile was still very great. One estimate put the annual per capita income of the upper 5 percent of the population at $2,300, while that of the lower 50 percent was estimated at $140.[7]

Racial differences have not been a serious factor in Chilean society. Except in parts of the south with a large Indian population, the Chileans have solved their problems with Indians by killing them in continual wars, or by intermarrying with them. There is a noticeable darkening of skin color as one descends the socioeconomic scale, while the "best families" of

Santiago have distinctly Spanish or even northern European features. Since the mid-nineteenth century there has been a considerable German colony in Chile, especially in the south. English cultural and genetic influence is evident among the upper classes, and the full names of recent presidential candidates, such as Jorge Alessandri Rodriguez, Eduardo Frei Montalva, Radomiro Tomic Romero, and Salvador Allende Gossens, indicate the diversity of national backgrounds.

The old families are still influential in economic and social life but distinctly less so in politics, the civil service, and the military. The family names of former presidents, literary figures, and leaders of the last century continue to recur in business, the society pages, the meetings of the National Agricultural Society, and diplomatic life.

Widespread access to education, at least in the urban areas, has meant a broadening of opportunity for advancement and an openness to talent in Chilean life that contrasts with the narrowness of many other Latin American countries. Yet attendance at a private secondary school (where tuition is low by U.S. standards but prohibitive for anyone below the upper middle classes in Chile) and the Catholic University in Santiago has long been a passport to a successful career. The graduates of the public schools and the University of Chile are more likely to go into public service, government, education, and certain professions such as medicine. As elsewhere, certain marks of background including pronunciation, accent, foreign travel, and cosmopolitan culture mark the upper and upper-middle classes, but they are less ostentatious about it in Santiago (even in the style of their homes) than in most other Latin American capitals.

Besides educational opportunity, there is also a wide range of social welfare institutions. Chile was one of the first Latin American countries to develop a social security system and a national health service. While both systems are inefficient (and until recently the social security system, comprising several separate funds, was blatantly unfair in its coverage), they provide a minimum level of security for many Chileans, principally, again, those in the urban areas.

What emerges from this description is that Chile in the early 1960s was neither an egalitarian, meritocratic, pluralistic, open society nor a hierarchical, ascriptive, two-class closed society, but somewhere in between—and moving from one to the other. That movement has been considerably accelerated in recent years; and in a politicized, centralized, but economically fragile society like Chile's this has placed great strains on the system. Yet uniting and integrating the whole society was a strong sense of nationalism which until 1973 prevented social, economic, or political differences from destroying the basic consensus that enabled the society to function. Why and how that consensus broke down, succeeding chapters will attempt to describe.

CHAPTER THREE

The "Revolution in Liberty"

The story of the breakdown of Chilean institutions does not begin with the 1970 elections. To understand the events of the early seventies it is important to examine the politics of the preceding administration which framed the issues, focused upon the alternative solutions, and conditioned the responses of the political actors to later events. It is also useful to analyze the experience of the Christian Democratic government of Eduardo Frei (1964–70) in order to understand and evaluate the alternative approach to political and economic change he offered, and to assess the respective charges of the right (that the Frei administration, in raising hopes that only the left could satisfy and in forging legal instruments for the expansion of control over Chile by a minority president, was responsible for the advent of Marxism to power) and of the left (that Frei was "the new face of reaction" delivering Chile to neocapitalism, the multinationals, and the U.S. government, thus provoking "contradictions" which led the Chilean people to opt for more radical solutions).

Frei promised an alternative to the solutions of right and left—a "revolution in liberty," a fundamental transformation of Chilean political and economic structures to be carried out within the framework of constitutional democracy. To a considerable degree he delivered on that promise, but after he had successfully secured the adoption of a number of important reforms, the constraints which the Chilean political and economic system placed upon the implementation of those policies, and some serious tactical errors on his part and that of his party, led to the debacle of 1970. To understand those constraints and to identify those errors, we must begin with the preceding presidential election of September 1958, which marked the onset of mass politics in Chile and set the stage for the debate between clearly defined alternatives of left, center, and right which continued until the 1973 coup. Eduardo Frei and Salvador Allende were the candidates of the Christian Democrats and the FRAP, respectively. The Radicals also presented a candidate, Luis Bossay, while the right supported Jorge Alessandri, the son of former president Arturo Alessandri and a self-styled "independent" who had been elected to the Senate with Liberal Party backing in 1957. The fifth candidate, Antonio Zamorano, a leftist ex-priest, was given no chance of winning.

Alessandri, Frei, and Allende were to dominate Chilean politics for the next fifteen years. On the right, Alessandri bore the name of a famous Chilean politician and president, but he made no secret of his aversion to traditional Chilean party politics. An engineer by training and a business-man by profession, he offered managerial ability, honesty, and fiscal conservatism at his program. State involvement in the economy would be retained, but only as an aid to the basic productive forces of private enter-prise. Attacking the corruption and mismanagement of the outgoing regime of the aging military ex-caudillo, Pedro Ibáñez, the abstemious bachelor candidate promised to restore rationality, austerity, and efficiency to Chilean government.

In contrast, Eduardo Frei, a member of the Chilean Senate since 1949, was a professional politician with a mission. Austere and deeply influenced by Catholic social thought, he was a brilliant orator who could make both neo-Thomist philosophy and the arguments of the Santiago-based Economic Commission for Latin America comprehensible to the average Chilean. He promised to combine democracy with planning, popular participation with technical expertise in government, and growth through a mixed economy with equity and structural reform. In the 1958 election, it became evident for the first time that the newly reorganized Christian Democratic Party, with its combination of mysticism and professionalism, was out to make a strong bid to capture the center of the Chilean political spectrum from its long domination by the Radical Party.

On the left, in his second bid for the presidency, this time at the head of a Marxist-dominated alliance of the Socialists and the Communists, was Salvador Allende. From his days as a medical student during the depression, when he helped to organize the Socialist Party, he had been deeply involved in Chilean politics. He had been in the Chilean Congress for twenty years and had participated in the Popular Front cabinet as minister of health in 1940. Thus, the fact that he was a committed Marxist did not carry the same challenge to Chilean political democracy as might have been the case in other countries. Moreover, his "bourgeois" tastes in dress, drink, and the enjoyment of the good life made him less threatening to the middle and upper classes than a more proletarian candidate—although there was never any doubt of his commitment to the poor and the oppressed. His program called for radical reform of Chilean economic structures, in particular, the nationalization of the U.S.-owned copper mines, the banks, and some basic industry, as well as far-reaching agrarian reform involving the distribution of land among the peasantry along with technical assistance to increase productivity. The political changes these economic reforms would necessitate were not spelled out beyond a call for popular democracy and a movement toward socialism rather than an immediate socialist revolution.

Frei, Bossay, and Allende had all agreed that an unwritten constitutional tradition prescribed that in the congressional run-off between the top two candidates the Congress should confirm whichever candidate received a plurality—even if it was by a single vote. Alessandri, whose Liberal and Conservative backers formed a large bloc in Congress, hesitated to do so. As it turned out, Alessandri won the election by 33,500 votes (of 1,235,552) over his nearest rival, Salvador Allende.

Allende came very close to victory in 1958, and the breakdown of the election figures reveals that two factors accounted for his defeat. Antonio Zamorano, the ex-priest from Catapilco ("el cura de Catapilco"), received 42,000 votes, so that if all those who voted for him had cast their ballots for the FRAP candidate, Allende would have won. In addition, Allende ran much more strongly among male than among female voters (32.4 and 22.3 percent, respectively); the women divided their votes between Alessandri and Frei.[1]

The strongholds of the left were in the mining districts of the north, the coal-mining and industrial areas around Concepción in south-central Chile, and in two provinces in the far south—a pattern that was to be repeated in all subsequent elections. Alessandri did well in Santiago, where among women in the Third District, for instance, he received 42 percent of the vote, and in southern agricultural areas such as Cautín and Osorno. Frei came in third with 20.7 percent of the vote but ran well in many parts of the country, especially in Valparaíso, where he received 26 percent of the vote. The Radical candidate received 15.6 percent, and it was not clear whether the difference between that figure and the 21 percent which the Radicals received in the legislative elections meant that a number of Radicals had deserted the party for Allende or for Alessandri. More likely the Radical vote, like the party itself, was split between left and right, since more conservative Radical provinces like Osorno voted heavily for Alessandri, while Coquimbo, where the Radicals were also strong, gave Allende a large vote. If the votes of the two centrist candidates, the Radical Bossay and the Christian Democrat Frei, are combined, a three-way division emerges with about a third of the voters supporting the center, right, and left respectively—another pattern which was to persist until 1973, with a crucial effect on the 1970 presidential election.

The Alessandri Administration, 1958–64

The Chilean constitutional tradition gave the presidency to Alessandri, but to adopt legislation he needed the support, if not the participation, of one of the center parties in Congress. Despite its formal commitment to socialism in 1931 and its earlier alliance with the Socialists and Communists in the 1938 Popular Front, the Radical Party had been moving right ever since the mid-forties. In a contrary evolution, the Christian Democrats, despite their origins in the Conservative Party, had within them a group led by Radomiro Tomic, the most influential party leader after Frei, which saw in an alliance with the Communists a way to carry out necessary social and economic changes and abolish capitalism, the source of the country's ills.[2] Alessandri, therefore, selected a cabinet made up of Liberals, Conservatives, and independents (principally businessmen), but he also counted on the votes of the Radicals for the adoption of legislation.

That legislation was concerned principally with economic stabilization. At the outset, Alessandri was strikingly successful in this area. For about two years, from mid-1959 to mid-1961, a program which combined price controls, restriction of credit, limits on wage increases, and austerity in government spending resulted in near stability of prices and a virtual end to Chile's seventy-year-old inflation. The program was also relatively successful politically as measured by the 1960 municipal elections, which gave the two right-wing parties about 30 percent of the vote.

In the classic Chilean pattern, however, by the third year of the Alessandri administration, things began to come apart. In 1960 a serious earthquake wreaked massive destruction in the south, and the government was called upon to engage in large-scale reconstruction and aid. Lacking budgetary resources for this purpose, the government engaged in deficit financing, upsetting the delicate economic balance established in the stabilization program. In the congressional elections of March 1961 both the Liberals and Conservatives lost seats, while the FRAP obtained 31 percent of the votes and 27.5 percent of the seats in the Chamber of Deputies. The Christian Democrats also increased their vote to 16 percent, and the Radicals held their usual share of the vote, about 22 percent.[3]

It was thus necessary for Alessandri to cooperate more closely with the Radicals if he wished to govern, and the vote on the organization of the two houses of Congress indicated that a coalition of the right with the Radicals was in the making. The Christian Democrats were determined to make another try on their own at the presidency in 1964, but the Radicals, who also had presidential ambitions, computed electoral figures and decided that on the basis of the 1961 congressional elections a coalition with the Liberals and Conservatives would pay off in 1964. Radical ministers therefore began to participate in the Alessandri cabinet in August 1961, but for a price—a further increase in government spending, and support for an agrarian reform bill which the Radicals needed to preserve their image as a reformist party.

The increase in government spending, which was prompted by the earthquake and by Radical pressures, set off inflation again. By 1963 the inflation rate was up to 44 percent, and the government coalition was in serious trouble. Since October 1962 a formal coalition of the Liberals, Conservatives, and Radicals—the Democratic Front—had been established, and it was already clear that its candidate would be a Radical, probably Julio Durán, a leader of the right wing of the party. The Radicals, however, wishing to demonstrate that they were not averse to change and reform, took the lead in securing the adoption of the first agrarian reform law in Chile's history.

In retrospect, it is surprising that agrarian reform became a major political issue in Chile only in the 1960s. Despite clear evidence published by such bodies as the United Nations Economic Commission for Latin America (ECLA) that the latifundia were economically inefficient and socially unjust, agrarian reform had not figured earlier as a major issue in political campaigns. However, increased political competition in the countryside, plus the Cuban Revolution in 1959 and the not unconnected establishment of the Alliance for Progress in 1961, focused attention on the issue of land distribution.

Chile from the outset was a principal recipient of Alliance funds; in terms of per capita aid it received more during the first years of the Alliance than any other country. The figure was inflated by the inclusion of $100 million in earthquake assistance appropriated by the U.S. Congress in 1961, but an additional $120 million in assistance was authorized in early 1962. The Alliance was looking for a "showcase" of reform, and Chile was willing to play that role, especially since its chronic need for foreign exchange had become desperate in the early 1960s.

The Alessandri agrarian reform as finally signed into law in November 1962 was principally concerned with the use of idle lands, although it also gave the government broad powers of expropriation. Arable land which was badly cultivated or unused could be taken over by the government upon payment of 10 percent of its value in cash and the remainder in bonds redeemable over a period of fifteen years. This required a constitutional amendment, since the 1925 constitution stated that expropriated property was to be paid for in cash, and the issue of deferred payments nearly broke up the coalition of Conservatives, Liberals, and Radicals. However, concessions by the Radicals (the reduction of the payment period from thirty to fifteen years, and the limitation of bond payments to abandoned and inefficient properties) and the desire of the Frente Democrático to come into the 1964 elections with a reformist record led to the acceptance of the measure and to the adoption of the corresponding constitutional amendment in 1963.[4] This set an important precedent for subsequent reform efforts, since the right had accepted the principle of payment in bonds. In addition, two important agrarian reform agencies were established: the Corporation for Agrarian Reform (CORA) and the Institute for Agricultural Development (INDAP). Expropriation (with payment in cash) was also permitted in cases other than those of idle or inefficient lands. The Alessandri administration never remotely approached its announced goal of creating 5,000 new proprietors a year (between November 1962 and November 1964 when it left office, the Alessandri government distributed land to 1,066 families),[5] but a beginning had been made.

Progress was made under Alessandri in two other areas as well. The percentage of children in primary and secondary schools had increased rapidly in the last decade, but university expansion had been slower. In the last half of the Alessandri administration the expansion at the lower levels began to have an effect on the university, where enrollments increased strikingly. More directly related to government policy was a government program to expand available housing. The Housing Corporation (Corporación de la Vivienda), created in 1953, greatly expanded its activities after the launching of the Alliance for Progress in 1961. Middle-class housing was promoted by the creation of savings and loan associations in which private savings for housing were protected by annual readjustments for inflation, and by the establishment of important tax advantages for those who built new houses within certain specified limits as to size and materials. Alessandri also began a program to deal with the burgeoning shantytowns (*callampas*, or mushrooms) which were springing up on every available piece of land around Santiago. A government program provided a foundation, water, and electricity to *callampa* dwellers who were willing to build their own houses with whatever materials they could obtain. In 1961 Alessandri's ten-year development plan called for the construction of 200,000 new housing units in the next five years, and in 1962 more than 42,000 new dwellings were completed.[6]

The government was chronically short of money for these programs, however. Once the choice was made to abandon the austerity and financial retrenchment of the early Alessandri years in favor of government-financed reform efforts (half-hearted as they appeared to the Christian Democratic and Marxist critics of the government), a price had to be paid in serious inflation, balance-of-payments difficulties, increasing government deficits, and foreign borrowing. A major devaluation in October 1962 demonstrated that the currency reform several years earlier (when the escudo had replaced the devalued peso at a rate of a thousand to one) had not produced a stable currency. The next electoral referendum on the government policy, the municipal elections of April 1963, showed that the country's increasing economic problems were producing rising demands for change. The FRAP continued to receive about 30 percent of the vote. The principal change was a large increase in the center-left Christian Democratic vote, which moved from 16 percent to 22 percent. This gain was mainly at the expense of the Liberals and Conservatives, since the Radicals lost less than half a percentage point, dropping from 22 percent to 21.6 percent, so that they were narrowly displaced by the Christian Democrats as the largest party in Chile. The election confirmed the earlier Christian Democratic decision to "go it alone" with Frei's candidacy in the 1964 presidential elections, but it did not diminish the resolve of the Democratic Front to present a Radical candidate, since the 1963 figures seemed to indicate that the combined strength of the Liberals, Conservatives, and Radicals (47 percent) could easily elect their candidate.

The 1963 municipal elections also demonstrated that Chile was undergoing a process of political mobilization. In the 1958 presidential elections, a record number of Chileans—1,250,350—had voted. Yet in the less important municipal elections of 1963 the number of voters reached 2,070,188. A good part of the increase resulted from increased political participation by women, who composed 27 percent of the voters in the 1963 elections.[7] A large number of new voters without established loyalties had entered the political arena, rendering the kind of prognostications based on past elections that Chilean politicians had previously used much less reliable indicators of the future.

The Curicó By-Election

The political calculations of the right were definitively upset in March 1964 in a by-election to replace a deceased deputy in Curicó. In what had hitherto been regarded as a conservative rural bastion, the Frente Democrático dropped from 49 percent to 32 percent of the vote, while the FRAP jumped 10 percent, winning the seat with 39 percent. The Christian Democrats also increased their vote from 21.5 percent to nearly 28 percent. The right-wing parties, recalling the narrowness of Alessandri's victory over Allende in 1958, were thrown into a panic at the prospect of an Allende triumph in the September presidential elections. The Democratic Front collapsed, and the Liberal and Conservative parties endorsed Frei's candidacy despite the Christian Democrats' insistence that they would make no concessions in return for their support. The Radicals decided to run Durán as a token candidate ("as a salute to the [party] banner," to use the Chilean description), if only to provide an alternative for those Radicals who could not bring themselves to vote for someone whom they viewed as a clerical candidate.[8]

Despite the loss of support for the right which had been demonstrated in recent elections, President Alessandri continued to maintain his personal popularity. He attributed his government's difficulties to pressures from the politicians, and through his personal habits (he is a teetotaling bachelor who walked from his apartment to the presidential office every day) and public image gave an impression of abstemiousness and independence from politics to which many Chileans responded.

Alessandri could not succed himself, however (he opposed proposals from his supporters to amend the constitution to make this possible), and it seemed clear from the election figures and from the inflation levels that neither the right-wing parties nor the Radicals who had been allied with them could win the presidency in 1964. The contest was between two candidates who both were committed to fundamental change in the Chilean system. The Chilean voter was harried by inflation and economic dislocation and was aware, because of the propaganda of the left and now of many centrists as well, that there were fundamental injustices in the present system. He seemed to be ready for more radical alternatives. Yet underneath this receptivity to radical proposals was a basic conservatism which abhorred violence, and a belief that social reform was possible without any sacrifice in living standards except by the very rich. What the Chileans wanted was a "revolution" without revolution.[9]

Not only the right and the Radicals were discredited. Classical economics and conventional treatments of balance-of-payments problems were considered to have failed, since the Klein-Saks recommendations and the Alessandri austerity program had brought unemployment and a reduction of economic growth. By the end of the Alessandri administration, the Chilean state was deeply in debt to foreign and international creditors and suffered persistent balance-of-payments problems. Chile had entered into a stabilization agreement with the International Monetary Fund to remedy the latter problem, and the Alliance for Progress had begun to make program loans for general budget support, which were also contingent on economic "performance." The question of Chile's dependence on foreign governments and international agencies was raised by the left and by the Christian Democrats, and in different degrees each group was critical of what they saw as the abdication of Chilean independence.

The Frei and Allende Programs

The center and the left, as represented by the two leading candidates in the 1964 elections, both called for an extension of state activity—but with important differences. The FRAP, dominated by the two Marxist parties, blamed Chile's economic and social problems on the bankers, capitalists, large landowners, and foreign interests—in particular the U.S.-owned copper companies. Allende's economic brain trust, the Oficina Central de Planificación (OCEPLAN), proposed that the copper, nitrate, and iron mines, as well as utilities, insurance companies, and private banks, be taken over by the state and integrated into a national system. In addition, a more progressive tax system was to use the excess purchasing power of the rich for state-promoted investment, while the purchasing power of the people was to be expanded through price controls and increased production of consumer goods. In agriculture, about one-third of the arable land would be expropriated with payment in thirty-year bonds at 4 percent (readjustable for inflation) and redistributed into state, collective, and private holdings. Peasants would be unionized and small plots combined into larger units.[10]

The Allende program also called for expansion of unionization, abolition of the literacy requirement for voting and lowering the voting age to eighteen, as well as a foreign policy "of dignity" which included an end to military pacts with the United States. The question of how his program could be implemented in the face of opposition from the military or from Congress was skirted when the Allende program referred to the need to democratize the army and perhaps to write a new constitution.

He insisted, however, that many of the changes that he called for could be achieved through existing institutions. His program was thus revolutionary in the sense of calling for a considerable alteration in property relations in Chile, but it did not demand an immediate transformation of the political system. Despite its Marxist inspiration, it was not couched in terms of the class struggle or of an inevitable opposition between capital and labor; in fact, it made a special effort to reassure the small businessman that his interests would be protected. It was only "exploitative" capital, not all capital, that was opposed.

Observers pointed out at the time that the Christian Democratic program was not very different from that of the FRAP. Yet there *were* important differences, both of degree and of kind. The differences in kind related to the ideological inspiration of Christian Democracy. While it was a relatively new party in Chile, dating in its present form only from 1957, its philosophy had very ancient roots. The Christian Democratic view of society was influenced by the papal social encyclicals, *Rerum Novarum* of Leo XIII (1891) and *Quadragesimo Anno* of Pius XI (1931), which had been critical of the excesses of "liberal" capitalism and of "collectivist" socialism, calling for the establishment of a new form of society which responded to both the individual and the social aspects of man's nature. The encyclicals recognized the right of workers to organize into unions, and *Quadragesimo Anno* recommended that intermediate groups between the individual and the state be encouraged and that workers be given a share in ownership and management of industry. The latter proposal became a common element in the programs of all the Christian Democratic parties in Europe and Latin America.

The underlying assumption of this view of society was that these "natural" communities were not irreconcilably opposed to one another, but could work together for "the common good." Implicit in the Christian Democratic view, therefore, was a rejection of the class struggle of the Marxists and a belief that government could operate by conciliation and consensus.

Catholic social doctrine could be given an authoritarian and corporatist character as in Portugal, Austria of the 1930s, and Franco's Spain, but the Christian Democratic movement, as its name implies, was also strongly committed to representative democracy. Influenced particularly by the writings of French Catholic philosopher Jacques Maritain (Frei had heard him lecture during a trip to Europe in 1935 and Jaime Castillo, the party ideologist, had written often on his work), the Chilean Christian Democrats like their European counterparts saw democracy as the form of government most in keeping with the Gospel message. They saw the religiously neutral state as a positive contribution of the modern age rather than as a reluctant concession to contemporary religious divisions, as it had appeared in the writings of the popes up to that time. The party therefore was Catholic in terms of the sources of its ideology and of the educational background of most (but not all) of its leaders, but it was not a confessional party.[11]

Chilean Christian Democrats had also been influenced by the economic theorists associated with the UN Economic Commission for Latin America. Frei's writings and speeches were studded with references and concepts drawn from ECLA (CEPAL) publications, and the 1964 program was influenced by young, well-trained economists who saw in the technical tools of economics the way to get Chile out of its stagnation. That these young *técnicos* were attracted to the Christian Democrats rather than to the Radicals was explicable in terms partly of age (a young party versus one long in or near power), partly of social background (the upper-middle class could afford to send their children to private, usually Catholic, schools and universities), and partly of Christian Democratic organizational strength and propaganda in the Chilean universities in the early 1960s.

The differences which emerged later among those Christian Democrats who gave a greater emphasis to the party's proposals for the "replacement of capitalist exploitation by a new social organization," those who saw the expansion of political participation as the cure for Chile's ills, and those who gave the highest priority to economic development were not yet evident. In formulating its program, the party was not forced to make hard choices among economic development, political democracy, and social justice, but could promise all things to all men.

Thus, without going into detail on where the money for these reforms would come from, the Christian Democratic "revolution in liberty" promised 360,000 new houses in the next presidential term, an expansion of education which would put every child in the first year of primary school by the beginning of the next academic year, and an agrarian reform which would give land to 100,000 families in six years. The program also promised tax reform, economic development, an end to inflation over several years (not immediately, because recent Chilean experience had shown that this was harmful to economic growth), and Latin American economic integration (a long-time ECLA proposal which tied in neatly with the internationalism of the Christian Democrats) as the basis for an economic recovery which would make this possible. Mentioned, but not emphasized, were proposals for reform of industrial enterprises to give workers a share in "profits, management, and ownership."

The copper industry was also seen as an important source of economic growth. Despite the fact that a group within the party led by Radomiro Tomic had been pressing for outright nationalization of the foreign-owned copper mines, the party came out for what became known as "Chileanization," the purchase by the Chilean state of majority ownership of the mines with the payments to be reinvested in the expansion of production and refining capacity. In addition, sales decisions were to be made by a government agency, the Corporación del Cobre, so that the Chilean national interest, rather than the maximization of profit of the U.S. companies, would be the determining factor. As Frei put it, Chileanization was a "way to give concrete expression to the association of the interests of [foreign] investors and those of the Chilean national community."[12]

The decision in favor of Chileanization rather than nationalization was an important difference between the Frei and Allende programs. It related both to the differing philosophical and ideological stands of the two candidates and to the greater importance given by Frei to economic considerations such as the maintenance of production and the continued influx of foreign investment and U.S. assistance.

A similar combination of philosophical and pragmatic considerations influenced the differing approaches of the two candidates toward agrarian reform. The Christian Democrats were committed to land reform with deferred payment (twenty-five-year bonds at 5 percent interest with 10 percent payment in cash). When the program discussed the form of redistribution, it avoided the word *collectivization* but spoke of cooperatives and the extension of individual ownership to "peasant proprietors." Like the FRAP, the Christian Democrats supported unionization of the peasantry, but from a different philosophical basis—communitarianism rather than Marxism. The need to promote agricultural production through tax and other incentives also received much more emphasis in the Christian Democratic program.

Peasant unionization was only one part of a broader Christian Democratic program of the organization of many groups in society. In the program that the Christian Democrats called Promoción Popular, shantytown inhabitants, neighborhood residents, women, youth, workers, and peasants would be organized into representative groups which could present their views and needs to the government, supplementing the often ineffective geographically based representative organs (and potentially competing with them). If this recalled European corporatism and paternalism to the program's critics, it was because those critics did not believe in the sincerity of the Christian Democratic commitment to democratic grassroots organization.[13] The question of the role of the government in "encouraging" (and supporting financially) such organizations was not faced until later, after the Christian Democrats were in power.

Besides the differences in ideological inspiration and view of society, and those on nationalization and agrarian reform, the two parties differed in the groups which formed their social base. As the 1958 election had demonstrated, Allende had strong backing in the areas where trade unions were strong, most of them either Socialist- or Communist-controlled. He also had support from many intellectuals and academics in Chilean universities and secondary schools. His problem was to extend his backing to the middle classes, the shantytown inhabitants who were becoming politically active, and the peasantry (where he had already made inroads in 1958). Frei, on the other hand, could count on many of the women's votes and had the backing of many students, young professionals, and a part of the middle class. He also had the reluctant support of the upper classes and the industrialists, if only because he was the lesser of two evils. His Catholic background helped him with women, but could have cost him support among the more anticlerical males in the middle and lower classes. Like Allende, he actively sought the vote of the newly politicized shantytown dwellers and peasants.[14]

The Campaign and Election

In retrospect, it seems that Frei's election was assured once he had added the support of the Liberals and Conservatives to his Christian Democratic base. Yet with the influx of so many new voters (half the voters in 1964 were participating in a presidential election for the first time) and with the clear indication of a swing to the left in Chilean opinion, the Christian Democrats ran a well-financed and tough campaign. Over half the cost of the campaign, a total of $2.6 million, came from the U.S. Central Intelligence Agency through various intermediaries and without Frei's knowledge as to its source.[15] Considerable CIA money also went to the Liberals and Conservatives, who could pull out all the stops in making anti-Communist appeals without compromising the Christian Democrats as a party. Thus, thousands of posters showing children with the hammer and sickle stamped on their foreheads and hundreds of radio programs dramatizing the danger of communism appealed to the Chilean fear that an Allende victory would mean the establishment of a Communist totalitarian state.[16]

Allende's known sympathy for Fidel Castro became a campaign issue as Frei's supporters emphasized Cuba's dependence on the Soviet Union and its isolation in the Western Hemisphere. In 1964 this isolation had become even more pronounced because the Organization of American States had voted that its members should break relations with Cuba after Venezuela demonstrated that the Cubans had shipped arms to the guerrilla movement there. A few weeks before the election, when Alessandri severed diplomatic relations in accordance with the OAS vote (although Chile had voted against the rupture), the FRAP did not react since demonstrations or violent actions might have alienated potential voters.[17]

The campaign concluded with mass demonstrations in Santiago in favor of the two candidates. Allende's was more restrained, but years later many Santiago residents recalled the quasi-religious fervor which gripped them as they participated in a candlelight procession down Chile's main thoroughfare and heard the impassioned tones of Frei promising a new society. Chilean law prohibits electoral propaganda within forty-eight hours of elections, but the night before the election, a recorded message was broadcast from Fidel Castro's sister, Juana, warning Chileans of the dangers of voting for Allende. Like Fidel Castro, Che Guevara, and Nikita Krushchev, she said, Allende "only follows the line established by the Communist party. If the Reds win in Chile, no type of religious activity will be possible. The new Gods will be Marx, Lenin, and the Communist party. Chilean mother, I know you will not allow your children to be taken from you and sent to the Communist bloc, as is the case in Cuba."[18] Allende asked for and received the right to reply, but this seems to have been a clear case of propaganda overkill.

That Eduardo Frei was the victor on September 4, 1964, did not come as a surprise, but the magnitude of his triumph was unexpected. In an election in which 88 percent of those registered voted (voting is compulsory in Chile, but no one has been prosecuted for failing to vote), he received 56.1 percent of the vote to Allende's 38.9 percent, while Durán received only 5 percent. Frei carried all the provinces except three northern mining provinces, the coal and industrial area around Concepción, and the province of Magallanes in the extreme south. His biggest majorities were in Valparaíso and Santiago, which together compose nearly 50 percent of the electorate, where he received over 60 percent of the vote, and in the southern conservative rural province of Cautín, where he secured 63 percent.[19]

Male and female votes are reported separately in Chile, and it was evident that Frei had done extraordinarily well among women, who had turned out in numbers nearly equal to those of the men. While Frei received slightly over half of the male votes, he secured nearly two-thirds of those of the women and carried the female vote in every province except one. This has been attributed by many observers to Frei's Catholicism, but the index of religious practice among women in Chile, while higher than among males, does not approach 63 percent. More probable influences were the female aversion to Marxism and the appeal of Frei's personality;

in the campaign he appeared upright, passionate, and (despite his thirty years in Chilean politics), in a certain sense, above ordinary politics.

In the glow of Frei's triumph, it was easy for the Christian Democrats to ignore the real advances made by the left. Besides retaining the left fiefdoms in the copper-mining areas of the north and the coal mines of the south, Allende had gained substantial support among male voters in the agricultural Central Valley (winning male majorities in the provinces of O'Higgins, Talca, and Linares) and in the lower-class areas of Santiago (but, interestingly, not of Valparaíso, the area he represented in the Senate). He received 52 percent of the valid male vote in the Santiago working-class commune of San Miguel, and it was only the women's votes that kept him from carrying several other lower-class communes in Santiago.[20] His overall percentage (39 percent) was well above anything that the left had been able to achieve in the past. As the 1970 election was to demonstrate, in a race among candidates representing all three major political tendencies in Chile, this figure would have carried him to victory.

Initial Christian Democratic Successes

The political force of the right had been obscured by the two-way contest in 1964, but it could still make itself felt in the Congress, which had been elected in 1961 and earlier. When Frei sent his proposals for legislation to the Congress after his inauguration, they were blocked by the combined opposition of both left and right. Included in those proposals were a bill to acquire partial control of the U.S.-owned copper mines, a wealth tax (*impuesto patrimonial*) of 1.5 to 3 percent to finance housing, agrarian reform, education, and health care, a constitutional reform granting the president power to call a plebiscite on legislation, and a program for improvement and organization of the urban shantytowns. Frei also promised to submit bills subsequently on agrarian reform and a new labor code.[21]

Frei thus chose to begin his administration with an appeal for legislative support which he knew he would not receive. His strategy was to dramatize his need for a Christian Democratic victory in the forthcoming legislative elections, scheduled for March 1965. He knew that the right would not cooperate with his tax proposals and that neither right nor left would support his slum improvement program, since in their minds this was designed to ensure the "thirty years of Christian Democratic dominance" of which Radomiro Tomic had spoken shortly after the 1964 election.

Frei received mixed reactions from the U.S.-owned copper companies slated for action in his program of Chileanization. Within a month of taking office he was able to reach agreement in principle with the Kennecott and Cerro Corporations, although the details of the new relationship had to be worked out in legislation which required two years of intensive effort in the Chilean Congress. Anaconda flatly refused to Chileanize its large mines at El Salvador and Chuquicamata but agreed to a 25 percent arrangement for its new Exótica mine, and Cerro agreed to a 30 percent arrangement for its new Rio Blanco mine. Kennecott agreed at once to a 51 percent arrangement with the purchase price to be invested in the expansion of the capacity of the Chilean copper industry. Kennecott was attracted to the proposal because it involved a reduction in the effective tax rate, an upward revaluation of the company's assets for tax purposes, and continued management by Kennecott of the joint operation for twenty (later reduced to ten) years.[22]

Frei was also able to work out an agreement for the phased purchase of 90 percent of the shares of the Chilean Electrical Company owned by the American and Foreign Power Company, and he initiated negotiations with ITT which led to an agreement in 1967 for the purchase of 49 percent of the Chilean Telephone Company's shares, with the purchase price to be reinvested in expansion of the telephone system. The agreement also provided for Chilean majority control at a later point.

In other areas of his program, Frei was also able to take action without congressional authorization. He had not received additional funds for housing, but he ordered the housing authorities to recognize the legality of fifteen thousand housing titles, and he reduced the payments on government housing loans. In education, he promised that schools would be built and teachers trained so that every seven-year-old could begin his primary education in March 1965. In his wage readjustment bill, Frei requested a full adjustment for 100 percent of the increase in the cost of living in the preceding year and an increase in the rural minimum wage to equal that of the urban worker. In foreign policy, he reestablished relations with the Soviet Union and Eastern Europe (but not with Cuba) and took steps to develop trade with Africa and Asia.

These actions both fulfilled campaign promises and increased the electoral appeal of his party in the coming elections. In effect, Frei asked the voters to confirm his stunning victory in September by giving him a legislature with which he could work in March. While only half of the Senate was to be chosen, the entire Chamber of Deputies was to be elected, and Chilean legislative procedure makes it possible for a president with one-third of the Senate and a majority in the lower house to override senatorial amendments to presidential bills initiated in the Chamber of Deputies. The question the 1965 elections posed was whether Frei's large vote was transferable to his party, or whether a considerable proportion of it was made up of conservative anti-Marxist voters who would revert to support of the right-wing parties in the legislative elections.

The results of the March 1965 congressional election indicated that the

Christian Democratic sweep was continuing. Although the party did not get an absolute majority, as Frei had, the Christian Democrats secured 42 percent of the vote, far more than any party in recent history had received. The Chilean electoral system translated that figure into a comfortable working majority in the Chamber of Deputies (82 of 147, or 55 percent of the seats). In the Senate they won 12 of the 21 seats up for election, a gain of 11 seats for a total of 13, 2 seats short of the one-third which in combination with a majority in the Chamber can adopt legislation. (Ironically, the party could have elected an additional senator from the Fourth District of Santiago if it had presented a candidate.) The right-wing parties lost heavily. The Conservatives received 5 percent of the vote, winning only 3 seats in the Chamber, and the Liberals secured 10 percent and 6 seats. Neither party won any seats in the Senate. (In the 1961 elections, the two parties had received 14.7 percent and 16.5 percent respectively.) The Radicals also suffered serious losses, dropping from 22 percent to 12.8 percent of the vote. It seemed that the country had definitively rejected the right and had chosen the Christian Democrats over the Radicals as the center-left party which, together with a dynamic president with a large popular mandate, could carry out long-overdue reforms.

There was an usually high turnout for the election—over 80 percent—and the Christian Democrats won pluralities in all the provinces of Chile except the hard core of the left: Tarapacá in the extreme north, Magallanes and Chiloé in the extreme south, and the depressed coal-mining province of Arauco near Concepción. Despite the fact that there were twelve parties on the ballot, the Christian Democrats won absolute majorities in Valparaíso and in the First and Second Districts of Santiago. In lower-class areas of Valparaíso, they received as much as 57 percent of the vote.[23]

The new Chamber of Deputies included many who were elected for the first time. Among the Christian Democrats, sixty-six of the party's eighty-two deputies were new. Their enthusiasm and commitment to the party program made it appear that Frei would have a relatively easy time securing his legislation. Yet there was still the opposition-dominated Senate, half of which had not been up for election; and high on the list of Frei's legislative priorities were two difficult pieces of legislation—the Chileanization of copper and the agrarian reform bill.

In a way, the Christian Democratic victories were *too* sweeping. It made them resistant to any idea of compromise, and their ideological fervor gave them an arrogance (*prepotencia*) which made it difficult to arrange the kinds of compromises traditional in Chilean politics—and almost necessitated by the system of staggered elections. But no amount of compromise would have satisfied the left that Frei was not simply "the new face of capitalist reaction," and the ease with which he had arrived at agreement with the copper companies seemed to confirm their suspicions. The leader of the

Socialist Party, Aniceto Rodriguez, early announced the intention of the FRAP to "deny salt and water" to the Christian Democrats. The rightist parties were bracing themselves to resist the forthcoming agrarian reform bill, the adoption of which was made more difficult by the fact that a constitutional amendment would be necessary if payment was to be made in bonds for other than unused or abandoned land. This left the Radicals as possible allies, with ten Senators who could bring Frei one vote short of a majority in the Senate. Yet the Radicals appeared to be in decline, losing their middle-class clientele to the more dynamic Christian Democrats. Furthermore, they seemed clearly identified with the right wing in Chilean politics, so that an arrangement with them would have been viewed as an ideological sellout by party militants.[24]

Under these circumstances, it is understandable that Frei calculated that his government could go it alone without forming a coalition with any other party. He thought, correctly as it turned out, that he could secure the adoption of his agrarian reform law with the votes of all or part of the left-wing parties, and that of his copper Chileanization proposal with the support of the right. But this was to be a lengthy and complicated process of negotiation, and it would be difficult to maintain the momentum of the "revolution in liberty" through the lengthy bickering and compromises involved in congressional approval. Frei, however, placed his considerable prestige and energy behind these two key legislative proposals as central to his efforts to restructure the Chilean economy, leaving other aspects of his program until later—in many cases, until too late.

The agrarian reform bill was still being drafted within the government (it was not presented to the legislature until November 1965), but the lame-duck Congress continued to debate the copper agreements. In April, the position of the Radicals seemed to harden against the Christian Democrats, as they began to vote in the Chamber against the copper bill when earlier they had abstained. In the Senate a tentative agreement had been reached between a Christian Democratic and a Radical senator that the two parties should each preside over the Senate for a period of two years, but the Radical Party's National Executive Council (CEN) voted that the party should maintain an independent line and make no agreements with other parties.[25] On both sides, therefore, there was a lack of enthusiasm for a Christian Democratic–Radical coalition, which appears in retrospect to have been the only way in which democratic reform could have been successfully achieved in Chile.

Relations with the United States

Frei's election in September had been greeted with a favorable statement from the White House. Following his inauguration, President Lyndon

Johnson appointed as ambassador Ralph Dungan, a White House aide who remained from the Kennedy administration and a Catholic with a strong interest in Latin America. From the beginning of his two-and-a-half-year career as ambassador to Chile, Dungan exhibited a style which was very different from that of his predecessors. He made statements and gave interviews which made no attempt to conceal his support for the Christian Democrats. Thus, he added to the usual left-wing opposition to the U.S. embassy a strong right-wing feeling against the ambassador, particularly when he made favorable comments on the impending agrarian reform bill. On the other hand, Dungan developed a close personal relationship with the Christian Democrats, who valued him as a Kennedyite attuned to their aspirations and sympathetic to their programs.

Only a few months after his arrival in Chile, however, Dungan was faced with two serious threats to the good relations he had developed with the new government: the U.S. intervention in the Dominican Republic in late April 1965, and the exposure of a research program, Project Camelot, which had attempted to involve many Chilean social scientists without revealing that it was sponsored and financed by the U.S. Department of the Army.

Ralph A. Dungan, U.S. ambassador to Chile, 1964–67. (U.S. Department of State)

When President Johnson landed fourteen thousand marines in Santo Domingo at the end of April, this appeared to the Chileans and to most Latin Americans as a return to the "gunboat diplomacy" the United States had practiced in the early part of the century. The Chilean foreign minister, Gabriel Valdés, issued a statement denouncing the unilateral intervention as contrary to the OAS charter, and the Chilean ambassador to the OAS, Alejandro Magnet, introduced a resolution calling for an immediate end to the U.S. intervention and suggesting the establishment of an inter-American peace force under OAS command. On May 4, student demonstrators in Santiago attacked the U.S. consulate and threw paint on its walls (it remained there for several years), and two days later Averell Harriman arrived as a special presidential emissary to explain to Frei the U.S. position. By this time, what had originally been a Chilean suggestion for the replacement of U.S. troops by an OAS peace force had become instead a means of legitimating the U.S. presence by sending a few Brazilian soldiers and some Costa Rican policemen, placing all the troops under a Brazilian commander, and nominally incorporating the U.S. troops in an inter-American peace force. The proposal was viewed as a subterfuge by the Chileans, who along with Mexico, Ecuador, Peru, and Uruguay voted against it, but it carried 14 to 5.

The Chilean attitude was consistent with a long-held belief in nonintervention in inter-American affairs, but in this case, it was reinforced by the Chilean view that the U.S. intervention had prevented the return to power of Juan Bosch, the democratically elected president who had been overthrown by a military coup in September 1963. Along with the unseemly haste of the White House in endorsing the overthrow of João Goulart in Brazil in April 1964, it appeared to substantiate the belief of many Chileans that U.S. policy had now given up the support for constitutional democracy which the Alliance for Progress had symbolized at its inception under John Kennedy.

The widely reported uproar over Project Camelot was related psychologically and chronologically to the Dominican intervention. In July 1964, the chief of research and development for the U.S. Department of the Army had requested the Special Operations Research Office of American University in Washington, D.C., to develop "a social systems model" which would have among its purposes "measurement of internal war potential: a means for identifying, measuring, and forecasting the potential for internal war." As the project developed, a number of social scientists were invited to participate, including Johan Galtung, a Norwegian professor who in early 1965 was teaching at the UNESCO-sponsored Latin American Faculty of Social Science in Santiago. Galtung declined to participate, principally on the grounds of the army sponsorship, which had not been any secret in the discussions about the project in the United States. The army role was concealed, however, when efforts were made to involve Chilean academics in the project. When Galtung denounced the deception, the case became a *cause célèbre* in the Chilean press and Congress, and there was an immediate adverse reaction to what appeared to be another case of intervention, more subtle than, but just as dangerous as, the Dominican example.

Ambassador Dungan denied any knowledge of Camelot and sent cables to Washington demanding to know the nature and sponsorship of the project; the House Foreign Affairs Committee held a special closed hearing on the matter; and in early July Dungan was able to announce that the project had been canceled.[26]

The tension between Chile and the United States could have had serious repercussions for the developing relationship between the new Christian Democratic government and the Johnson administration. However, the personal relations between the U.S. ambassador and leading figures in the government (reinforced by the impression that he represented the Kennedy inter-American policy which would not have engaged in such adventures), along with the combination of Frei's need for external economic assistance and an evident U.S. readiness to respond, meant that the Dominican and Camelot affairs did not seriously impede cooperation in other areas. However, they may have reinforced Frei's determination to work harder to involve Europe in Latin American development in the European tour he planned for July.

Economic Development and Social Justice

On May 21, the new Chilean Congress, elected in March, formally opened its sessions, and Frei delivered the first of his annual state-of-the-nation addresses reviewing his government's accomplishments and outlining its program for the future. It was an important statement both for the details it gave and for the general political philosophy underlying it. At the outset Frei defined the problem of Chile and indeed of all Latin America as the necessity to develop a "political regime which can overcome the obstacles to economic development and social justice without sacrificing freedom."[27]

Running through the speech was a continuing emphasis on the importance of economic growth as a prerequisite to social justice. At the beginning of the message, Frei observed that Chile's per capita income between 1940 and 1964 had grown at only 1.5 percent per year, and he promised that by 1970 he would increase that growth rate to 3.2 percent and raise average incomes by 50 percent.[28] He proposed to do this through a combination of government and private investment, foreign assistance, and self-restraint on the part of trade unions and consumers. Noting that no country had developed without restricting its consumption to secure investment capital, Frei indicated that sacrifices in their standard of living would have to be made by the 35 percent of the population who received more than twice the minimum wage. He became more specific when he said that "the highest groups" would have to reduce their consumption by 4 percent if the economy was to grow.

As the workers' contribution to economic growth Frei called for no reduction in the hours of work, a limit on holidays, and a reduction in strikes and slowdowns. To counterbalance this, he indicated that his government would support full annual wage readjustments for purchasing power lost through inflation and promised to reduce inflation to relative price stability by 1968. He added that he already had cut the inflation rate in half from the rate during the last year of the Alessandri regime.

An emphasis on economic factors also characterized Frei's discussion of his proposed agrarian reform. He announced as the program's first goal a rapid increase in production, and he described its other objectives as "the creation of thousands of new property owners, the strengthening of the small and medium proprietors already in existence, and the stimulation of the agricultural producers who are cultivating their land efficiently today." It was evident from his description of the family-sized medium landholders ("with 20 percent of the land and labor, they produce 40 percent of the farm production") that his agrarian reform would be directed at expanding this sector, although not without opposition from those who favored other methods of production.

Yet it would be an error to describe Frei's approach as exclusively devoted to economic expansion. True to the ideology of Christian Democracy, he was concerned with the promotion of social justice, and he saw the further extension of democratic organization as the way to achieve that goal. To represent the interests of the lower social and economic groups, Frei described his Popular Promotion program—a network of neighborhood committees, mothers' centers, youth organizations, cooperatives, and other representative organizations which would be given legal recognition and would be represented on a national council. Their special purpose would be to give effective participation in politics to the "marginal" sectors of the population. A similar belief in the virtues of organization led Frei to propose the official recognition of the Central Unica de Trabajadores (CUT) and the adoption of a law to encourage the organization of peasant unions.

The government, however, was not to wait for demands from these organizations. Frei repeated his promise to construct 360,000 housing units during his six-year term and cited figures to demonstrate that he had already initiated a vast expansion of primary education (186,000 new registrations for the current school year versus an average of 40,000 per year in the past; 5,000 new primary-school teachers; and 3,500 new schools). He also described his recent decree equalizing the rural minimum wage and family allowances with those of urban workers as a significant contribution to raising the standard of living in rural areas. In so doing, he implicitly recognized that agrarian reform was not the sole or even the principal way to achieve social justice in the countryside since, as he noted, there were 280,000 peasant families with little or no property. Thus, even the unattainable goal of redistributing land to 100,000 families cited during the 1964 presidential campaign (Frei did not repeat the figure in his 1965 speech) would not have aided a majority of the peasant population.

The last section of the speech was devoted to foreign policy, an area in which Frei took a special interest. He described the opening of diplomatic relations with the Soviet Union and Eastern Europe, as well as his efforts to increase relations with Africa and Asia. In the latter case, Frei singled out the United Nations Conference on Trade and Development (UNCTAD), which had had its first meeting in Geneva in 1964, as worthy of special support. Then, as if to dispel any impression that his government was moving toward the neutralism which was becoming increasingly fashionable in the less-developed areas, he asserted, "We belong irrevocably to the West because of ineradicable spiritual and cultural ties." This then led to an affirmation of the necessity of giving the European spiritual heritage a new form and content in Latin America through the promotion of Latin American integration.

One of Frei's first acts as president had been to write an open letter to four leading Latin American economists soliciting their ideas on progress beyond the limited integration achieved in the 1960 Treaty of Montevideo which had established the Latin American Free Trade Area. Speaking a few weeks after the Dominican intervention, Frei also referred to the need for restructuring the Organization of American States so that it would promote democracy and social and economic development rather than concern itself exclusively with the threat of subversion.[29] Almost immediately, Chilean representatives in the OAS began to work on constitutional changes which were adopted several years later.

Frei's message concluded with a brief allusion to his forthcoming European trip. This was the next major event in his presidency, and it was directly related to ideas put forth in his presidential message and his earlier writings. Through further contacts with Western Europe, he hoped to interest the Europeans in extending aid to Latin America. His Christian Democratic party affiliation made him particularly interested in France, Italy, and Germany, where the party was or had been strong, and a visit to England was to complete the trip.

The European trip took place in July and was a great success politically, although much less fruitful economically. The world press had taken a great interest in the Chilean election in 1964, and it covered Frei's trip extensively.

Considerable significance was attributed to a joint communiqué issued by Frei and De Gaulle which was critical of the U.S. action in the Dominican Republic. Political commentators read into it an attempt by De Gaulle to play a more important role in Latin America, which seemed to be confirmed by his announcement that he planned to return Frei's visit.[30]

When Frei returned to Chile on July 24, he was met by large crowds at the airport. His popular support was great, and his new government seemed to be acting with initiative and creativity in a wide range of areas. One observer returning from Chile in 1965 compared it to the early days of the New Deal. Tomic's prediction that the Christian Democrats would be in power for thirty years was widely repeated and believed.

Yet for all the optimism and confidence of Frei and his party, he had to deliver on the ambitious program he had outlined during and after the campaign. And characteristically for a president who had spent sixteen years in the Chilean Senate, he tried to bring about change through legislation. He had sent a torrent of bills to the lame-duck Congress in the period between his inauguration and the March 1965 congressional elections. Now with a majority in the lower house and just a few votes short of one-third of the Senate, it was time for Frei to push through his reform program.

The Congress, Copper, and Agrarian Reform

Top priority was given to the Chileanization of copper and to agrarian reform. The preliminary agreements with the copper companies made it possible to go ahead with legislation, and debate had begun on the bill establishing the Copper Corporation to join with them in owning and operating the mines. The agrarian reform was more complicated, and before the law could be adopted the constitution had to be amended to allow for compensation in bonds for property that was neither abandoned nor poorly utilized. Opponents of the agrarian reform circulated rumors that the government would also use the constitutional amendment to carry out a massive reform of urban property to relieve Chile's desperate housing shortage. Right-wing Catholic groups responded by forming "Fiducia," the Society for the Defense of Tradition, Family, and Property. Open letters were printed in Santiago's leading newspaper, El Mercurio, citing Pope Leo XIII's defense of property rights in Rerum Novarum, while omitting his references to "the social function of property," a term specifically used in the proposed constitutional amendment to justify compensation in bonds.

The objection to compensation in bonds was related to Chile's chronic inflation. At then current inflation rates, unless provision was made for readjustment for inflation such bonds would be worthless in a few years, and the so-called compensation would be confiscatory. Even after their electoral victory in March, the Christian Democrats only had thirteen senators of a total of forty-five. They assumed that the twelve Communist and Socialist senators would vote for the agrarian reform, but that they were certain to oppose the Chileanization of copper as a sellout to the foreign investors whose holdings, in their view, should be nationalized outright with little or no compensation. The seven Liberal and Conservative senators (with the exception of one Liberal who also supported nationalization) were likely to favor the Chileanization proposals, although they might withhold their support to extract concessions on the property amendment or the agrarian reform. But even with support by the right-wing parties, Frei needed the Radical Party to secure adoption of his proposal.

At their biennial convention in June, the Radicals reaffirmed their line of opposition to the Frei government. Julio Durán, the leader of the right wing of the party and its former presidential candidate, declared to the press that the Christian Democratic Party was "a movement of quasi-fascist character [which] is trying to convert Chile into an experimentation ground for a system which hides beneath a demagogic exterior the dogmatic sectarianism of its foreign inspirers and directors." The left wing of the party added to the anticlericalism of the right its commitment to democratic socialism, which was supported in particular by the party youth organization. The draft resolution presented by the leader of the left group called for "the most firm and intransigent opposition to the dogmatist government of Christian Democracy . . . in social and political affairs, in parliamentary behavior, and in professional and trade union activities." The policy vote as finally adopted read: "The National Convention of the Radical Party reaffirms its opposition to the Christian Democratic government, and declares that its political action can only consider the establishment of agreements with forces which are democratic, socialist, and secular." In a press conference after his election, the new Radical president, Humberto Enriquez, interpreted the requirement that other groups be "democratic" to exclude agreements with the Marxist parties. The party thus was to pursue an independent opposition course.[31]

The first effect of the convention was the resignation of Radical senators from senatorial committees to which they had been elected with the support of the Christian Democrats and the right-wing parties. When the National Executive Committee elected by the convention met in July, it also voted to oppose the copper agreements in the Senate. The principal objection mentioned by the Radicals was the delegation of legislative decisions to the president in making agreements with the copper companies. They later also cited the excessively generous tax reductions given to the U.S.-owned companies in return for their agreement to expand their investments in Chile.

Frei was aware that without agreement by the Radicals his project would fail, and he spent the month of August in intense negotiation with them on various modifications which would answer their objections. At its meeting on August 31, the Radical National Executive Committee (CEN) modified its opposition slightly. It voted to continue to oppose the presidential bill even with the changes Frei had made, but it announced that rather than reject the bill it would attempt to amend it with a view to "safeguarding the national interest." Negotiations continued until the Senate vote on September 8. At 3 A.M. the CEN authorized its senators to support the measure if its last demands were met, and later that day the Senate voted for the copper bill, 26 to 14.[32]

There remained many stages before the bill was finally adopted in early 1966. Each of its provisions had to be voted on individually by both houses, but once the Senate had given its general approval, the lower house could override the Senate on specific clauses unless the Senate could mobilize a two-thirds vote to override the Chamber's version. In fact, the Chamber even removed some of the concessions made earlier to the Radicals in the Senate—a move which strengthened the Radical currents opposed to co-operation with the Christian Democrats.

Considering the copper agreements the master plank (*viga maestra*) of his program, Frei had concentrated all his efforts on securing their adoption as the first major order of business. This was understandable, since his other major objective, agrarian reform, was much more complex and required a constitutional amendment. But the fact that the first major piece of legislation pushed through by the Frei government was supported by most of the right and could be accused of benefiting foreign investors had already had an adverse effect on the dynamism of the revolution in liberty. Like the Radicals, the Christian Democrats were divided into right and left sectors. The left was already dissatisfied that the transformation of property relations promised by the party had not taken place and, aside from the beginnings on agrarian reform, did not seem to be likely in the near future. Concerned as he was with governmental matters, Frei made little attempt to defend his policy to the party, and the left could strike a response among the more ideologically committed party members who tended to be elected to the party's National Assembly (Junta). The division was expressed in the vote for the officers of the party held on August 2, 1965. Senator Patricio Aylwin, the candidate of what later became known as the *oficialista* wing of the party, was elected president of the party by a vote of 220 to 188 over Alberto Jerez, a deputy who was one of the leaders of the rebel (*rebelde*) wing. Jerez left the party in 1969 and helped to form a movement which participated in Allende's Popular Unity coalition in the 1970 elections. The support he was able to attract so early in Frei's presidency indicated that Frei was in for serious trouble from the leftist elements within his own party in the future. As an ideologically motivated party, the Christian

Democrats could inspire dedication and hard work among their militants, but in putting that ideology into practice once in power, they would inevitably make choices and compromises which would alienate some of the most dedicated of the party's members.

The copper agreements were also the principal object of attack by Salvador Allende in a lengthy critical evaluation of the Frei government published a year after Frei had taken office by a new Castroite journal, *Punto Final.* For Allende there was no third, "communitarian" way to development. The alternatives were capitalism or socialism, and the Christian Democrats were "mere reformists" who had adopted a policy of "dependence on the United States" and were carrying out a policy of "dechileanization," as the copper agreements revealed.[33]

The long-promised bill for a new agrarian reform law was finally forwarded to Congress on November 22, 1965. It contained 167 articles and was probably the strongest proposal for agrarian reform ever put before a democratic legislature. Reflecting the Christian Democratic ideology, it began with a series of definitions, including those of the "family agricultural unit" which, "when personally managed and worked by the producer, permits a family group to live and to prosper through its rational use," and of "communitarian property," "which belongs in common to those who work it, or to a cooperative formed by them which constitutes a human and economic community." As these definitions imply, the bill was directed at two goals: the expansion of the family-type intermediate-sized agricultural holding that Frei had endorsed in his 1965 message to Congress, and the creation of cooperative agricultural communities which could work the land together. The latter *asentamientos*, or "settlements," the law defined as transitional, for a period of three to five years. However, if at the end of that period the agrarian reform authorities felt the land was not suitable for individual cultivation, or if the peasants themselves so voted, the *asentamientos* could continue beyond the transitional period—a provision later used by the Allende government to postpone indefinitely land distribution to individuals.[34]

The bill also established a limit on the size of the property that any single proprietor might hold. Any landowner holding more than 80 "basic irrigated" hectares (or its equivalent) was subject to expropriation, although he could keep a "reserve" of that amount after expropriation. If he worked the land directly and efficiently at a high level of productivity, and if he gave his workers a share in the profits and paid them at twice the minimum wage plus all extras (including unionization), he could retain up to 320 hectares; but the owner had to demonstrate that he had fulfilled all the requirements, and the provision was never in fact implemented.

Compensation was fixed at two different scales. Those properties which were expropriated exclusively for reasons of size would be paid for at their evaluation for tax purposes, 10 percent in cash and the balance in twenty-five-year bonds at 3 percent interest with 70 percent of the face value of the bonds readjustable for inflation. Owners of "abandoned" land would receive only 1 percent in cash, and "poorly worked" land only 5 percent, while the balance for both types of land would be paid over thirty years with the same interest and readjustment features.

The bill was immediately attacked by both left and right. The left criticized the bill's emphasis on individual development of the land as well as the cost of its compensation features. The right saw the same features as confiscatory, since they were based on tax assessment rather than commercial value and since the rampant Chilean inflation was sure to eat away at the value of the bonds to the extent that they were not readjustable. In addition, the head of the National Agricultural Society (SNA) complained that the conversion tables were inaccurate, that the special courts established by the bill did not provide for a right of appeal, and that the determination of "efficiency" contemplated by the bill was vague and subjective. The Radicals were divided: the Radical Youth favored the bill, while Pedro Enrique Alfonso, former president of the party, was the principal spokesman for the United Front of Opposition to the bill.

By late 1965 the Congress was discussing three major pieces of reform legislation: the copper bill, the constitutional reform which included a change in the property guarantee in article 10 to authorize payment in bonds for expropriations, and the agrarian reform bill. The copper bill was well along in the legislative process, but the right (which had previously supported it) could now threaten to withhold support to extract concessions on the other two reforms.

The result of the introduction of the agrarian reform bill was thus to make passage of the copper bill more difficult. Indeed, only at the beginning of April 1966 was the impasse on the investment features of the Chileanization proposals broken, and then only after negotiations between the leaders of the Liberal and Conservative parties and Frei had extracted from the president a series of concessions on the agrarian reform bill. Among them were a change in the text of the constitutional amendment which made it possible for property owners to appeal the terms of expropriations, a change in the system of land equivalences giving owners of partially irrigated land a larger right of reserve, and the grant to the landowner instead of the agrarian reform agency of the right to decide upon the location of the "reserve" to be retained by the original owner. Despite the fact that most of these concessions were not significant, the negotiations were attacked by the left as a surrender to the landowners.

Nevertheless, Frei could feel relatively secure that his "revolution" was making progress. The inflation rate was sharply reduced, and Chile's always delicate balance of payments was in an excellent situation, thanks to a record high price for copper. (In February 1966, owing to strikes and production stoppages elsewhere—rather than the Vietnam war as the left claimed—the world market price soared to 98 cents a pound; later in the year Chile began pricing its copper on the basis of the London Metals Exchange rather than the lower U.S. price used previously.) Then in early March, in a closely watched by-election in Valparaíso, the Christian Democratic candidate won a smashing victory, receiving 49.8 percent of the vote in a three-way race and raising the number of Christian Democratic deputies in the lower house to eighty-three.[35] The election results indicated massive support for the Christian Democrats from the lower-class areas of the port city and encouraged the Frei government to think that it would not experience the "erosion" (*desgaste*) which previous governments had suffered once in power.

Strains Within the Christian Democratic Party

Since January 1966, the copper mine at El Teniente had been on strike, and after the March election the left-dominated unions called a sympathy strike at mines in the north. The government declared the strike illegal and moved in troops at the El Salvador mine. When the eighty-five soldiers were opposed by a thousand miners and their families using sticks, stones, and knives, the troops, under the command of Colonel Augusto Pinochet opened fire, killing six workers and two housewives. The left called the incident a "massacre" and cited it for years to prove that Frei was opposed to the workers.[36]

The criticism of Frei by the left elicited a response among some of the Christian Democratic militants. The fact that he was willing to weaken the agrarian reform bill to save the copper bill (with which many of the left Christian Democrats were not sympathetic to begin with) seemed to them to compromise the Christian Democratic promise to create a new, communitarian social and economic system. And when the Liberal and Conservative parties joined together in early May 1966 to form the National Party, it seemed that the right was not as moribund as the Christian Democrats had believed after the 1964 and 1965 elections.

The impression fostered by the Marxist left that Frei was moving to the right was reinforced by his message at the opening of Congress on May 21, 1966. In it, Frei reviewed the accomplishments of his government. He noted the massive increases in educational enrollments, the 52,000 housing starts which came close to the goal of 60,000 houses a year, the sharp decline in the inflation rate, the increase in wage earners' purchasing power by 12 percent, and the 40 percent increase in taxes collected from the upper classes, many of whom had never paid taxes before.

The emphasis of the address, however, was on the need for an increased rate of economic growth. Frei noted that in the last two years of the Alessandri regime economic growth had not even kept up with population increase, and he promised a growth rate of 5 percent for the current year. To do this, he said, prices paid to agricultural producers had to be substantially increased in order to induce them to produce more food, thus reducing Chile's chronic dependence on agricultural imports. Frei observed that the state was now the source of 75 percent of new investment in Chile, and he called upon the private industrial sector to increase its investments and urged all groups to increase savings. Emphasizing his "resolve to support the private sector," Frei appealed to private enterprise to increase production, noting that his income redistribution policies had already provided a stimulus to industry so that many companies were working at full capacity. But he added, "It is necessary that all social groups set aside part of the real increase in their income—those with higher incomes in higher proportion and those with lesser incomes with a relatively smaller sacrifice—so that national savings may be increased."

Frei concluded his report with an appeal for a "political truce" in Congress under which the opposition would avoid politically inspired legislative maneuvers, strikes, and spending programs for two years with the understanding that workers would receive annual wage readjustments equal to the cost-of-living increases, management would trust the government, and social change could be carried out without sacrificing economic development or employment and without increasing the inflation rate. "The country is aware that I grew up in a party, the Christian Democratic Party. . . . However, my party comrades know full well that as president and as long as I hold office, I am president of all Chileans and will serve them without distinction or discrimination."[37]

The appeal for a truce had no effect on the other parties, but the appeals to the private sector confirmed the suspicions of the left sector of the Christian Democrats about the rightward turn in Frei's policy. They seemed to see this in Frei's closing words, thanking "those members of Congress who, though belonging to other political parties, have been imbued with patriotic spirit and supported the passage of certain fundamental legislation"—an unmistakable reference to the support by the right of the copper legislation in return for concessions on agrarian reform. The ferment within the party, to which Frei as "president of all Chileans" had paid little attention, became evident at its meetings in August and September. Frei's concern was to increase economic growth to finance his social program. He saw that the private sector was lagging and that potential savings for investment were being dissipated in massive wage increases beyond the increase in the cost of living, thus continuing to fuel Chile's chronic inflation. But to a young leftist ideologue, whether Marxist or Christian Democrat (or both, as was the case with some members of the

Christian Democratic Youth), his appeals for wage restraints and his reassurances to the private sector sounded like a move to the right.

It was now almost two years since Frei's landslide election had raised nearly millennial hopes among his followers. While important changes had taken place in education, income distribution, housing, taxes, and health care, and the inflation had been sharply reduced, the major pieces of Frei's legislation were still moving only very slowly through Congress. In August 1966, the Senate finally approved the constitutional amendment on the modification of the right to property, and the copper legislation only required some finishing touches and further negotiations with the companies on details of implementation. However, the agrarian reform was still far from adoption, and to the anticapitalist ideologues in the left wing of the Christian Democratic Party no change seemed to have been made in the structure of property relationships in business, industry, and banking.

When the party had been reorganized in 1957, it had committed itself to a "communitarian" form of society which was superior to individualist liberalism and collectivist totalitarianism; but, other than to mention facilitating access to property for all citizens and giving workers a share in profits and management, it had not specified the details of the new society it envisioned. In 1961, the party had denounced both capitalism and Marxism as "inadequate solutions for the concrete problems of the Chilean nation" and had committed itself to "the replacement of the established regime in Chile" and "the creation of a new order in our country in opposition to the capitalist structures in our economy and society." But what new structures would replace the existing capitalist ones? As early as 1951, two Christian Democratic leaders, Jacques Chonchol and Julio Silva Solar, had sketched out their vision of a communitarian society. After the 1964–65 electoral victories, they issued a revised version of their thinking which argued that communitarianism was a form of socialism "because socialism is a system in which productive goods of a social character belong to the community." The state would have an important role at the outset "in bringing about a new social discipline, organizing the running of the enterprises and the economy by the workers, and planning the whole process of production, distribution, and development, but the role of the state is subsidiary to self-management by the workers."[38]

Chonchol and Silva apparently were thinking of a reorganization of the Chilean economy along Yugoslav lines. However, others in the party—including Frei himself and the party's chief ideologist, Jaime Castillo—resisted the use of the term *socialism* to describe the party's ideology and preferred to retain simply the term *communitarianism*.[39] Moreover, thus far the proposals for a revolutionary change in industrial and business relations had received a much lower priority in the government's program than the agrarian reform, copper Chileanization, the ending of inflation, and the promotion of economic growth.

The ideological divisions within the party also influenced decisions on policy. At the first Christian Democratic Congress after the establishment of the party, held in May 1959, the delegates had debated alternative "political theses." The left group supported cooperation with the FRAP in opposition to the "reactionary forces" of the Alessandri government, while the majority of the congress, led by Frei, declared its "unalterable" opposition to cooperation with the Communists. By 1966, the issue was no longer cooperation with the Marxist parties, since the Socialists had fiercely opposed the Frei government, and the Communists were only slightly less opposed. The issues now centered around the general question of the relation of party and government—whether the party should push the Frei government in a more "revolutionary" direction, or simply support its present policies—and the specific question of trade union policy—whether the government would encourage the formation of rival trade unions to those controlled by the left.

These policy issues produced major splits at the Second National Congress of the Christian Democratic Party held on August 26–29, 1966. (The congress, which numbered 1,540 delegates in 1966, is the supreme policy-making body of the party and adopts the party statutes and basic principles.) The "rebel" sector, headed by Senator Rafael Gumucio, one of the party's founders, and by Julio Silva Solar, now a deputy, presented to the congress "An Analysis and Proposals for the Execution of the Revolutionary Program," which criticized the party's failure to fulfill the revolutionary promises it had made in 1964 and declared that to subordinate the party to President Frei was to accept "the Fuehrer Principle." On the other side was the *oficialista* group, led by the outgoing president of the party, Senator Patricio Aylwin, which reaffirmed in its draft "its categorical support of the program and government of President Frei, and the principle of unity of action between the government and the party." Between the two groups, there now appeared a new third-position (*tercerista*) group led by a deputy, Bosco Parra, and Senator Renán Fuentealba, a former president of the party. The *terceristas* were critical of the government but in terms much less extreme than those of the *rebeldes*. The existence of this group permitted present members of the government such as Jacques Chonchol to criticize its action without seeming to attack the person of Frei as the *rebeldes* did.[40]

The argument of the *rebeldes* was particularly directed at the proposals for "freedom of unionization" put forward by Frei's minister of labor, William Thayer. They charged (correctly) that Thayer's proposals were aimed at reducing the quasi monopoly that Marxist-controlled unions exercised in many plants; less correctly, they saw his proposals for what they called "parallelism" in union organization as an attempt to reduce the power of the unions against employers, since employers could create company unions if they could get the support of 30 percent of the workers.

The resolution as finally adopted supported Thayer's position, although it declared that the labor code should insist that the employer negotiate with the most representative union. The final vote on the proposal was 540 to 394, and when they were defeated, the *rebeldes* announced the withdrawal of Senator Gumucio's candidacy for the presidency of the party.

The *tercerista* faction also withdrew its presidential candidate after its proposed policy thesis was defeated by a much narrower margin, 330 to 276. The influence of Frei was only felt at the end of the meeting. Pleading sickness, he was not present for the most bitter debates but appeared at the end to give a lengthy speech in support of the official position. The smaller number of voters on the policy thesis reflected the absence of many of the *rebeldes,* who had walked out of the meeting after the defeat of their trade union proposals. They reappeared at the five-hundred-member National Assembly on September 10 to voice their criticisms, but they did not oppose the reelection of Aylwin as head of the party. However, in the important election of the National Council of the party they succeeded in electing eight members while the *terceristas* elected two, and the *oficialistas,* nine. Thus, Frei could potentially be outvoted by the National Council of his own party.[41]

Criticism on the Right

Frei's problems with the legislature and with his own party did not yet appear to be serious obstacles to the accomplishment of his program. The inflation rate for 1966 was down to 17 percent, only a bit over the projected 15 percent. Tax collections were up sharply, with 16 percent of the gross national product now handed over to the government. Frei claimed that he had increased the purchasing power of wage earners by 25 percent in his first two years in office. Industrial production was up, and the prospects for the passage of the three major legislative proposals were good.

On the other hand, the pessimistic attitude of business and industry was indicated by the steady decline in the stock market since Frei's accession to office. Business leaders felt that hopes and aspirations were being raised by the Christian Democrats which the fragile Chilean economy could not satisfy. A book entitled *Frei, el Kerensky chileno,* by a right-wing Brazilian named Fabio Vidigal Xavier de Silveira, argued that Frei was preparing the way for a Communist takeover, and although the book was banned in Chile, the position it represented was widely supported on the right.

The U.S. embassy was also criticized by the right for its open support of Frei, especially on the issue of agrarian reform. The rightists contrasted what they termed the "confiscatory" expropriations proposed in the agrarian reform bill with the payment of full value in dollars to the copper companies.

A *New York Times* reporter related an incident at a dinner party in Santiago in which a leading businessman shook his finger at Ambassador Ralph Dungan and declared, "This country is being led to social chaos and you are to blame."[42]

In November 1966, Frei's finance minister, Sergio Molina, reported to Congress on the state of the Chilean economy. His report was an eloquent argument for continued reduction in inflation as a precondition to economic growth in Chile. He noted that the expansion of production which had resulted from the redistribution of income undertaken by the Frei government during its first two years had not resulted in excessive inflationary pressures because of the existence of unused industrial capacity, but he warned that the single most inflationary element in the economy was the award of wage increases in excess of the increase in the cost of living. "Every extra percentage point in the wage increase beyond the averages planned [the previous year's price increases plus productivity increases] results in a 1 percent increase in inflation. . . . The only way to carry out a real redistribution of income is to maintain a high level of production in a framework of stability." Molina's report emphasized the need to restrain wage demands and hold down government expenditures, but the opposition took it as simply another example of the increasingly conservative tenor of the Frei government. Prophetically, Molina noted that every government in Chile "has sporadic successes especially at the beginning of the presidential term, but later, as it becomes incapable of overcoming the social and political forces which are opposed to its programs, it lapses into accelerated inflation."[43]

Molina announced that Chile had a substantial surplus in its balance of payments. This was due primarily to the spectacular increase in the price of copper, but it enabled Frei to announce in a speech in December that Chile would forgo further budget-support ("program") loans from the United States, as well as standby credits from the International Monetary Fund. In his December speech, Frei also attempted to answer the charges of a move to the right. He listed the redistributive effects of his wage readjustment, public health, housing, education, and family allowance policies; his government's encouragement of unionization, especially in the countryside; the increased taxation of the wealthier classes; the acceleration of agrarian reform; and the promotion of the organization of low-income groups. He was also able to cite figures on economic growth—12 percent for 1965 and 1966 and the reduction of inflation to 17 percent—as solid accomplishments of his regime. Blaming the Senate opposition for adopting inflationary budgets with increased expenditures and reduced taxes, he called for the adoption of a proposal for the authorization of a plebiscite in the event of continued disagreement between the legislature and the executive. In a passage which anticipated some of the economic problems of the Allende regime, Frei asserted that he would not permit economic constraints to compel him either to reduce investment or to promote inflation by printing more money.[44] Within a year he would be compelled to do both.

CHAPTER FOUR

The Frei "Revolution" Stalls

At the end of 1966, it looked as if the Frei government had done the impossible. It had reduced inflation, increased production, redistributed income, and expanded education; a strong agrarian reform law was on the verge of adoption; and the most recent by-election seemed to have shown continued popular support for the Christian Democrats. Yet there were certain danger signals which portended the series of calamities which would strike the government in 1967. On the economic side, the Inter-American Committee of the Alliance for Progress, at the annual meeting of its subcommittee on Chile, expressed concern at the decline in Chilean private investment. The committee noted that the government deficits for 1965 and 1966 and the substantial increases in salaries and wages were creating inflationary pressures that were beginning to be translated into rising prices.[1] In the political arena, the beginnings of a rapprochement between the Radicals and the FRAP could be discerned in the Senate vote of December 27, 1966, in which the Radicals joined the Communists and Socialists to elect Frei's 1964 opponent, Salvador Allende, as president of the Senate. During the coming year politics and economics would interact to produce a considerably darkened political prospect for the Christian Democrats, who had been so confident, if not arrogant, during the first two years of their administration.

The tension between the president and the Senate reached its culmination in a public humiliation of Frei by the combined vote of all the opposition parties in the Senate on January 17, 1967, refusing permission for him to make an official visit to Washington in response to an invitation by President Johnson. The basis of the vote was article 43, section 2, of the Chilean constitution, which required congressional approval for the president to leave the country—a nineteenth-century provision which was aimed at preventing presidents from absconding with the national treasury.

In explaining their votes, the representatives of the FRAP attacked U.S. policy in Vietnam and Santo Domingo, while the Radicals and the National Party criticized the trip as a propaganda effort for the Christian Democrats. The National Party was particularly disturbed at the reference to Frei's revolution in liberty in President Johnson's invitation and took this as an occasion to criticize Ambassador Dungan for his favorable statements on the Frei program—in particular, the agrarian reform.

Frei's reaction was one of fury with the Senate. At a mass rally outside the presidential palace he attacked the vote as an insult to him and to Chile. At the time, he was rumored to have considered simply dissolving the Congress and calling new elections immediately. Instead, he followed proper procedures and sent the Congress a constitutional amendment giving the president the power to dissolve the legislature once during his six-year term and challenged the Congress to go to the people.

The reaction of the parties was diverse, but it amounted in one way or another to the same result: the rejection of the Frei proposal. The Socialists said they would only adopt the amendment if the president would himself resign and hold new presidential elections; the Radicals called for greater guarantees of government impartiality in the electoral process; the Communists were compelled to support the proposal because they had made similar proposals earlier; and the National Party called for postponement of a decision until after the municipal elections. scheduled for April 2. Finally, on February 23, 1967, the proposal died in the Senate for want of the absolute majority required for a constitutional amendment.[2]

Electoral Defeat

This led Frei to treat the April municipal elections as a referendum on his conduct in office. During March he made a series of public appearances throughout the country, the political purpose of which was only very thinly disguised. The opposition used the election to attack the Christian Democrats for creating a huge electoral machine financed by government spending and large payments to advisers (*asesores*). The right was also critical of the large increases in taxes suffered by the middle and upper classes. The Frei government, encouraged by polls which showed that the Christian Democrats would increase their 1965 figure of 42 percent of the vote, showered the country with electoral propaganda which called for a mandate to continue the revolution in liberty.

The turnout for the elections on April 2 was nearly as high as for the congressional elections two years before, but the results were very different. Contrary to their expectations, the Christian Democrats received 160,000 fewer votes and dropped in their electoral percentage from 43.6 percent to 36.4 percent. The party could argue that this marked a substantial increase over the 22.8 percent it had received in the last municipal elections in 1963, but there was no doubt about the political impact of the drop in voting strength. Support was waning for the revolution in liberty.

A substantial portion of the Christian Democratic losses—nearly 60 percent—occurred in Santiago, which has about 40 percent of the Chilean electorate. Most of those losses went to the new National Party on the right and came from middle-class voters who were disillusioned with reform programs that increased their taxes and gave them no direct benefits. The National Party vote in the First District of Santiago jumped 50 percent over the totals of the two right-wing parties in 1965; in the upper-class commune of Las Condes, the party received the vote of 33 percent of the electorate, compared with 20 percent in 1965. Conversely, in the working-class commune of San Miguel, south of the center of the city, the Socialists and Communists increased their combined percentages of the total vote from 39 percent to 49 percent.[3] It seemed that as the Christian Democrats failed to produce the millennium in their first two and a half years in office, a process of political division along class lines was beginning which made it most unlikely that the party would attain the long-term dominance of Chilean politics it had envisioned in 1964 and 1965.

The election had an immediate effect within the Christian Democratic Party. Despite the fact that a careful analysis of the election figures would reveal that the Christian Democrats had sustained most of their losses to the right, the left wing of the party argued that the problem was that the party had not been able to move fast enough with its reforms (the agrarian reform, for instance, was in the final stages of being voted, and the investment agreements with the copper companies had only been signed in February). The Party Council on April 6 and 7 voted to attempt to arrive at "certain basic agreements" with the FRAP "which would hasten the resolution of bills which are important to the people." The National Assembly of the party, meeting a week later, appointed a "political-technical committee" headed by Jacques Chonchol to prepare a report on the policies to be followed in pursuing "a noncapitalist way of development" between 1967 and 1970. At the same time, the party was also under pressure from its youth organization to move ahead with proposals for "banking reform" which had been mentioned in the 1964 party program and was interpreted by the president of the PDC Youth as the nationalization of Chile's private banks. Besides the pressure from the youth section of the party, the *rebelde* group also became more active in this period and began to publish its own journal, *Documentación Ideológica y Política,* which was critical of the slow progress of "revolutionary" change under Frei's direction.

The Radicals also continued to move left. On April 19, the Radical Executive Committee voted 13 to 4 to support the Socialist candidate in a June 11 senatorial by-election in the provinces of O'Higgins and Colchagua.

Economic Problems

By the time of President Frei's annual message on the state of the nation of May 21, it was also clear that the economy was running into serious trouble. The inflation rate, which had been steadily reduced during his first two years in office, had begun to climb again, and at the same time, production had started to decline. A report by the Socieded de Fomento Fabril issued in May showed February production down by 5 percent over production a year earlier and attributed the decline to a government decision to reduce spending on construction to cut inflation.[4] To make matters worse, the price of copper, vital to Chilean foreign exchange, moved into a much lower range (between 42 cents and 45 cents a pound).

In his May message, Frei mentioned the decline in the price of copper but chose to discuss inflation and production only in terms of the good results obtained in 1966. He referred to the 1966 reduction in the inflation rate and estimated the per capita increase in income at 4.3 percent, noting that this was one of the highest figures in the contemporary world. He also claimed that his policies had led wage earners to increase their share of the national income from 43 percent to 50 percent in two years and noted that the Congress had at last passed his proposal to facilitate the formation of peasant unions which would lead to a further increase in the rural standard of living. (The earlier extension of the urban minimum wage and family allowance scales to the countryside had already resulted in large increases in rural income.)[5]

In mid-June, the U.S. embassy announced that Ambassador Dungan was resigning to become chancellor of higher education of New Jersey. Chilean observers, ready as always to put a political interpretation on what had been a personal decision, assumed that this meant that the Johnson administration no longer favored the Christian Democrats or Chile and was shifting its support to more reliable military regimes such as those of Brazil, Bolivia, or Argentina. Dungan's departure was a loss for the Frei government since he had been most sympathetic to its cause, but now that the Frei experiment was running into serious difficulties, it freed the U.S. government to appoint someone who could develop closer relations with other groups, which might be victorious in the 1970 elections. This was particularly true of the right, which now was experiencing a noticeable revival both because of the 1967 elections and because of the return to prominence of Jorge Alessandri as a possible presidential candidate in 1970. Alessandri remained scrupulously out of the political arena, but after the failure of a brief flurry of interest in June in the candidacy of Felipe Herrera, the president of the Interamerican Development Bank, speculation about Alessandri's candidacy became widespread.

Realignment of the Radicals

If Alessandri ran, however, it was clear that he would not have the support of the Radicals who had cooperated with him in the last part of his previous administration. At the Radical Convention held from June 20 until July 1, 1967, a major realignment of forces took place within the party. This was evident from the outset, when Professor Alberto Baltra was elected chairman of the convention, since he was identified with a policy of seeking an alliance with the Socialists and Communists. A determined minority fought the leftward movement, but they were clearly outvoted. The influence of the leftist sectors of the Radical youth organization was particularly evident in the final votes adopted.

In the policy vote, the party expressed its determination to oppose the Christian Democrats and the National Party and to work "to achieve a grouping of all the collectivities and popular forces of the left." The convention also voted in favor of nationalizing a long list of enterprises, including the large copper mines, banking, and insurance, and called for a strict state monopoly over education. In the election of officers, the representatives of the new policy swept the field, and the convention expressed its rejection of the rightists in its ranks by expelling the editor of a right-wing journal of opinion, *PEC,* from the party.[6]

The Radical strategy was clear to most observers. The party wished to recreate the Popular Front which had elected a Radical as president in 1938. It assumed that the Communists would not put forward a candidate and that Allende, as a three-time loser, was unlikely to be supported by the FRAP. This appeared to leave the way open for the presidential candidacy of a left-wing Radical like Baltra, who was moderate enough to get centrist support but, as president of the Institute of Chilean-Soviet Culture, had very good connections on the left.

The Christian Democrats Move Left

The Catholic-influenced sectors of the political center were also moving to the left. In mid-1967, the prestigious Catholic universities of Santiago and Valparaíso were shaken by student disturbances aimed at modernizing the curriculum and bringing it in touch with the contemporary problems of Chile. A student referendum at the Católica in Santiago demonstrated that the students were overwhelmingly opposed to the present university authorities, and they went on strike to demand student participation in policymaking. The movement spread to other universities and led finally to a complete restructuring and democratization of both the Catholic and the state universities. Particularly after the restructuring, the Catholic universities increasingly lost their sectarian character (in Santiago, for example, a bishop appointed as rector was replaced by an elected layman), a process which had begun almost three decades earlier when the González Videla government began to give subsidies to nonprofit Catholic schools. By 1967, 75 percent of the budget of the Catholic University in Santiago came from the government—a financial necessity, since expenses had increased rapidly while tuition was kept very low.

The leader of the revolt at the Catholic University in Santiago was closely related to the *rebelde* sector of the Christian Democrats, a group which dominated the youth section of the party and was expanding its support in other sectors as the promised Christian Democratic revolution failed to materialize. On July 15, 1967, five hundred delegates gathered for the meeting of the National Assembly of the party. As the first order of business, they heard the report of the political-technical committee headed by Jacques Chonchol which had been appointed in April. Entitled "Proposals for Political Action for a Noncapitalistic Road to Development During the Period 1967-70," it clearly indicated the influence of Chonchol and of the left sectors of the party. It specifically rejected the "developmentalist" approach for the party, saying that it was contrary to the basic principles of Christian Democracy for it to convert itself into "The Party of Chilean Development." Rather it should prepare, the report said, "for an active confrontation with the right, especially its ultrareactionary elements." The report further recommended that the party "maintain an active and constructive dialogue with . . . political forces . . . from whom we can gain support for the execution of this program" (presumably the FRAP). The report called on the party to recognize that the state was "the fundamental dynamic element in the economic development of Chile" which should "effectively control and use the instruments and mechanisms of the economic system."[7]

The report also demanded increased control of the copper industry; nationalization of the nitrate industry and of the largest coal company, the 58 percent private shares in the national steel company (CAP), and the U.S.-owned telephone company; and total government control of the Central Bank (run by a mixed public-private council). In line with its announced goal of "the democratization of the Chilean economy and the severance of the alliance between financial power and industrial ownership" it called for development of a program to give the workers real decision-making power, subject to overall control by the state, and pointed to the National Oil Company (ENAP) as a place to begin experiments in worker control.

The report's criticisms of "developmentalism" and its emphasis on the need for real changes in the structure of ownership in industry were an implied criticism of President Frei who, from the outset, had emphasized the need to achieve economic growth as a precondition of social justice and had placed a very low priority on the elements in the Christian Democratic ideology which called for worker participation in, or control of, industry. The prospect of the FRAP-dominated unions extending their power still further was enough to discourage him from experiments in worker control. Frei felt that first priority in the revolution in liberty had to go to agrarian reform and control of Chile's copper resources, areas in which he had widespread support both within and outside the party, before attempting the much more controversial and difficult task of restructuring Chilean business and industry. He had a similar attitude toward the proposals for bank nationalization advanced by the youth of the party and proposed in various bills before the Congress. A sudden alteration of the banking structure was not a wise move, in Frei's view, at a time when the economy was running into serious difficulties.

To the party militants, these practical considerations reeked of compromise of basic principle. The party had promised a revolution, and after three years the only change in the basic capitalist structure of property relationships which had been adopted was the agrarian reform bill and even that was signed only on July 17, the day after the assembly ended its meeting. No attempt was made by the *oficialistas* to criticize the Chonchol plan, and the assembly approved it in general and referred it to the party council for application. However, there was a general debate on party-government relations between Bernardo Leighton, Frei's minister of the interior, who defended the present government policy, and Senator Rafael Gumucio, the leader of the *rebelde* faction, who called on the party to press the government in a more "revolutionary" direction. The assembly concluded with a plebiscite on the two positions in the form of a vote on the party officers for the coming year. The *rebeldes* and *terceristas* decisively defeated the *oficialista* candidates with the election of three *rebeldes* and two *terceristas* and no representative of Freiismo. Gumucio was elected chairman of the party by a vote of 244 to 197, defeating Jaime Castillo, the party's ideologist and a close friend of Frei's. As Frei officiated at the public signing of the agrarian reform law at a mass rally in the Plaza de la Constitucion, a few hours after the closing of the meeting, he must have thought it ironic that his party seemed to be abandoning him at the very moment of his greatest legislative triumph.

The psychological deterioration in the position of the Frei government was accelerated by the first instances of sporadic acts of urban violence sponsored by the Movement of the Revolutionary Left (MIR), which had been organized in 1966 among students in Concepción, and was now spreading to Santiago. In mid-July, four dynamite attacks were directed at U.S.-connected installations in Santiago. In the same month, the issue of violence became a continental one. On July 26, the anniversary of the beginning of the Cuban Revolution, the Latin American Solidarity Organization (OLAS) met in Havana and resolved to establish branches all over Latin America in support of revolutionary change. The OLAS meeting focused attention on guerrilla movements in Latin America and, in particular, the revolutionary effort that Che Guevara had initiated in Bolivia. The Chilean government permitted a branch of OLAS to be established in Santiago, but it noted that any actions beyond verbal and printed propaganda could lead to its closing.[8]

The Frei government's action was criticized elsewhere, but it was in full conformity with the Chilean tradition of freedom of expression. Less in keeping with that tradition were government-initiated prosecutions against Carlos Altamirano of the Socialist Party and, a month later, against leaders of the National Party for statements they had made—in Altamirano's case, in favor of revolution, and in the case of the Nationalists, criticizing the government's conduct of relations with Argentina. The charges were subsequently dismissed by the courts.

The tension between the new PDC leadership and President Frei became evident after a meeting at the end of July in which the new leaders of the party asked Frei to make certain changes in his cabinet, notably the removal of William Thayer as minister of labor. The opposition to Thayer arose partly from his sponsorship of the creation of new unions in factories where the existing unions were controlled by the FRAP, and partly because of his clear defense of what the left saw as a "neocapitalist" interpretation of the communitarian ideology of the party. Frei refused to fire Thayer under pressure, but he was later removed in a general cabinet reorganization. In addition, to counterbalance the impression given by reports of the party meeting, Frei gave an interview to *El Mercurio* in which he underscored his determination to carry through the 1964 program for which he had been elected "president of all Chileans." He also stressed his efforts to encourage further investment by the private sector and by foreign investors, noting that even the Eastern European countries looked upon foreign investment as a way to develop their economies.[9]

As if Frei did not have enough problems, it became clear in July and August that Chile was experiencing a severe drought that would have serious effects on agricultural production. The drought, combined with the drop in the price of copper, made it likely that the balance-of-payments situation would worsen and inflationary pressures increase. By the time the documentation was prepared in September for the annual meeting of the Chilean subcommittee of the Inter-American Committee of the Alliance for Progress, it was estimated that the growth rate for 1967 would drop to 1.5 percent, compared with 9 percent the preceding year—less than the annual rate of increase of the population. Industry was not expected to grow more than 4 percent, and agriculture was to be even slower in its growth, requiring increased imports of food. Copper earnings had fallen off sharply, and the government had substantially reduced its expenditures for construction. The report also estimated that real wages were likely to increase by 12 percent in 1967, well above the established target of 5 percent, thus creating further inflationary pressures.[10]

The Chiribono Issue

In an effort to reduce the pressures from wage increases, Frei's finance minister, Sergio Molina, included in his November budget message a proposal that 50 percent of the wage readjustment for inflation be paid in development bonds into a worker-controlled "fund of national capitalization." Molina's proposal, which he viewed as essential to controlling inflation, ran into strong resistance when it was presented to the Christian Democrats, particularly from the party's new officers, who saw it as one more step in the government's move to the right. After lengthy negotiations within the party, it was agreed that only 25 percent of the readjustment would be paid in bonds. That amount would be matched by employer contributions, and the lowest-paid workers would be exempt from the measure. The proposal, which also included a provision forbidding strikes to obtain wage increases in excess of the increase in the cost of living, elicited fierce opposition from the trade unions, which declared a general strike for November 23.[11] During the strike, violence broke out between riot police and the strikers, leaving five persons (including one child) dead and sixty-four injured. The proposal had hardly been launched under favorable auspices.

The violence of the police reaction may have been related to rumors that the strike would be used to initiate urban guerrilla activity in Santiago, but it served to discredit the *chiribonos,* as the development bonds were called (a slang reference for a bad check derived from the *chirimoya* fruit, which rots quickly in transit). Frei could point to a long list of accomplishments as he began the second half of his term, but it was clear that the way was going to be much more difficult in the remaining three years.

The Congress began to debate the proposal, but once again elections diverted attention from the legislative arena. A senatorial by-election in southern Chile exhibited a three-way division between the National Party, the Christian Democrats, and Alberto Baltra, a Radical supported and actively encouraged by the Communists. (The Socialists abstained, since they were still not ready to give a "bourgeois" candidate their official support.) By a narrow margin of fifty-eight votes, Baltra was victorious over the Christian Democrat, marking the third Christian Democratic electoral defeat in 1967.[12] The election also marked a further step toward collaboration between the Radicals and the left, although the Socialist Party still seemed unreceptive to Radical overtures.

The Molina proposal for a wage readjustment in bonds and a strike moratorium intensified the divisions among the Christian Democrats. On December 27, the Party Council met at the request of the party president, Rafael Gumucio. One of the urgent items of business was the request by Edmundo Pérez Zujovic, minister of economy, for the resignation of

Pedro Felipe Ramírez as head of the government Technical Cooperation Service after Ramírez had expressed his opposition to the wage plan. Pérez Zujovic, a strong-willed and successful businessman and a close friend of President Frei's, had in recent months been held responsible by the left sectors of the party for the rightward movement of government policy. The council rejected Pérez Zujovic's request by a vote of 12 to 2 and demanded that he appear to defend his own conduct. When he refused, it cited him, on January 2, 1968, for action by the disciplinary tribunal of the party.

The action was never taken, because at an extraordinary meeting of the Party Assembly on January 6 and 7, Frei recaptured control of his party from the left. At that meeting, Gumucio defended his leadership of the party as completely in keeping both with the April council meeting which had voted to open a dialogue with the FRAP and with the general orientation of the Chonchol report adopted in July. Yet, since his election, he observed, there had been continued friction with President Frei which had been encouraged by the right, led by the newspaper *El Mercurio*. Frei replied that the unity of the government and party were essential to progress and criticized the continual attacks made upon him by the publications of the *rebeldes*. He left the meeting, "so that no one can say I came to exert pressure," but returned at 3 A.M. to make a second speech just before the policy vote. With political skill, Patricio Aylwin had secured the support of a leading *tercerista* and former president of the party, Renán Fuentealba, for a motion critical of the present party officers. It was adopted after Frei's dramatic intervention by a vote of 278 to 202—although the assembly also voted 239 to 234 to oppose the strike moratorium provisions of the wage readjustment proposals. When the election of new officers finally took place at 7 A.M., only 252 assembly members remained; they voted 108 to 47 with 108 abstentions to elect a pro-Frei list of officers headed by Jaime Castillo.[13]

Frei had reasserted control of his party, but he still faced strong congressional opposition to the wage readjustment proposal. The opposition-controlled Senate made it clear in its committee meeting that the Molina proposal had no chance of passing, and just before the full Senate was to discuss it, the Frei government withdrew the bill. After initially threatening to send an even stronger bill, Molina finally decided to resign as finance minister, and William Thayer, controversial minister of labor, took this occasion to resign as well. The subsequent reorganization of the cabinet was seen by some observers as a further move to the right, since Edmundo Pérez Zujovic was moved from the Ministry of Economy to the post of acting minister of the interior (a position which was assuming much more importance as the problem of urban violence became more serious). Molina's position in Finance was filled by Raúl Sáez, a civil engineer and political independent who had had much to do with the negotiation of the copper agreements. The reactions to the new appointments were varied.

The stock market jumped sharply upward, while Senator Gumucio lamented the rightward movement of the government. Pérez spoke about the virtues of private enterprise, while Sáez, asked about the future of the Chonchol plan, called it "an interesting and complete study . . . for the moment impossible to apply."[14]

Sáez attempted to sound out the leaders of the opposition in order to find a way of resolving the acute financial and political crisis caused by the lack of government financial resources to pay government employees the wage readjustment. When Sáez announced his draft readjustment proposal, both the right and left parties indicated they would oppose it. Faced with this opposition, Frei agreed to a compromise with the Communist Party that removed the one item in the Sáez draft that reflected Molina's original plan—a provision that wage increases beyond the previous year's increase in the cost of living would be paid in bonds. This in turn led to Sáez's resignation on the grounds that without the much modified bond provision there was no hope of reducing inflation, which had continued to increase in 1968.

The result of the failure of the two efforts to secure a reduction in inflation and some kind of balance between government income and expenditure was three months of negotiations between the government and the Senate which only produced a deficit-financed wage readjustment on the eve of the annual presidential message on May 21. The period was punctuated by a series of strikes, especially in the public sector, and by the beginnings of pressure from the military concerning their economic problems.

Violence Increases

Little had been heard from or about the military in the first half of the Frei administration, but now the combination of an upswing in the inflation rate and the not unrelated increase in strikes, public disturbances, and occasional bombings of buildings led observers to speculate on the possibilities of military intervention. This speculation was increased when President Frei announced the appointment for the first time of a military man, retired General Tulio Marambio, as minister of defense. Reports appeared in the press concerning conversations between the PDC and the Communist Party concerning "the well-known political situation, including the question of the improvement in the situation of the armed forces." A statement on the conversations between the two parties issued by Jaime Castillo, president of the Christian Democrats, only said, "We discussed the necessity of defending the democratic system against the real or possible existent threat to it."[15]

The agitated state of Chilean politics and economics was evident in Frei's annual message on May 21. The Socialist Party resolved to boycott the message as a protest against "government repression," and the Communists decided to follow their FRAP allies. Then, after a confrontation between the police and striking teachers in Santiago (many of whom were Radical militants), the Radicals decided to join the boycott. Since the teachers' strike had not yet been settled and there were threats of protest demonstrations against the president, the Christian Democrats turned out their militants to support Frei when he rode in the traditional open carriage from the presidential palace to the Congress. He spoke to a Congress which included only representatives of the Christian Democrats and the National Party, and his speech was markedly less optimistic than in the past.

Frei blamed the spiraling inflation on excessive wage increases beyond the rise in the cost of living. The long struggle over the wage readjustment bill was reflected in Frei's recommendation of new procedures to speed up action on legislation and a special procedure for wage readjustments. He noted that the wage readjustment bill had been amended two thousand times during its legislative history.

Against the left, Frei argued that his government was not "developmentalist" (*desarrollista*) in the sense of concentrating exclusively on economic growth at the expense of concerns for social justice and political participation. He observed that 70 percent of national investment came from the state and listed the industrial areas which were either state-owned (electricity, oil, air transportation) or decisively influenced by the state (such as copper, sugar, steel, housing, and health). In answer to the right, he defended his agrarian reform against the charge of collectivism, noting that the *asentamientos* were only transitional and that the ultimate aim of the reform was individual ownership. Frei also made a specific appeal to the middle class, observing that its increasingly high aspirations could not be satisfied at once and urging it to be what it had been in the past, "the imaginative and creative motor force of great historic transformations."[16]

The appeal to the middle class was a response to an evident movement by that group in the direction of the National Party. In July, the newspaper *La Segunda* published a poll of Santiago residents in which 58 percent of the respondents said the government had failed to improve the situation of the middle class and 75 percent criticized its efforts against inflation. A majority cited as accomplishments of the Frei government its efforts to expand education, to reform agriculture, and to improve the situation of the lower classes, but the most significant statistic of all was a resounding 84 percent who felt that the country was excessively politicized. This was reflected in the preferences of those interviewed as to presidential candidates in 1970. Jorge Alessandri was overwhelmingly the first choice, drawing twice as much support as any other candidate. (Salvador Allende and Radomiro Tomic were tied for second place.)[17]

One of the programs cited by Frei in his May speech to demonstrate that his government was concerned with social justice as well as economic

development was Promoción Popular, which aimed at the political and social organization of "marginal" groups. At the outset of his administration,
Frei had used the president's discretionary funds to establish the program
and to help in the organization of mothers' centers and community development and slum housing projects. To get legislative authorization for the
program, he had proposed the creation of a Popular Promotion Council and
asked the Congress to give legal recognition to neighborhood committees
which would represent local needs to the government. The Promoción
Popular program was considered by all the opposition parties as the possible
basis for a government-controlled political "machine," and it was defeated
by the Senate. It seemed to the Marxist parties, however, that neighborhood
committees in slum areas might be as useful to them as to the Christian
Democrats, with the result that after several years of debate, a law recognizing the committees was adopted by the Congress and signed by the president on July 19, 1968. In his speech at the signing of the law, Frei stated
that more than 2,700 such committees had been set up, in addition to
85,000 mothers' centers. Once again, he returned to the subject of his government's attitude toward the middle class and appealed to it for support in
enabling the "marginal" 50 percent of the population to have a share in
national life.

Frei concluded with a criticism of those who sing "poetic songs in praise
of violence" and noted that they tended to be drawn from "privileged
groups . . . intellectual dilettantes (*pijestocracia*) who have nothing to do
with the suffering of the people." The reference seemed to be to the new
prominence of the MIR, which was being given considerable publicity by
Punto Final, a bi-monthly, which stressed the differences between the MIR
and the "traditional left," that is, the Communists. The leader of the MIR,
Miguel Enriquez, was from a prominent family in Concepción. His uncle
was a senator and had been president of the Radical Party from 1965 until
1967; his father was elected rector of Concepción University in 1969. In an
interview with *Punto Final*, Enriquez described the MIR's differences from
the Communist Party: "[The Communists believe] that it is necessary to
perfect the regime in order to generate the forces which will destroy it.
The MIR, on the other hand, believes that it is necessary . . . to implant
immediately the bases for the construction of socialism. For them [the
Communists] one should not struggle directly against capitalism. For us
the fundamental thing is to use violence to propel the working class in the
city and the countryside."[18]

Enriquez predicted that the struggle would have to be both rural and urban, thus reflecting both the general rethinking of guerrilla tactics that
had taken place following the death of Che Guevara in Bolivia and the
physical difficulty of rural guerrilla warfare in the narrow strip of land between the Andes and the Pacific that is Chile.

Beginning in March 1968, a series of bomb attacks in various parts of the country indicated that an orchestrated campaign of urban terrorism had begun. In March, the Chilean–North American Cultural Institute and the U.S. consulate were bombed, and subsequently the Chilean-American Institute in Rancagua was attacked. Then a bomb was exploded in the main office of the Christian Democratic Party, and incendiary bombs were set off at the office of *El Mercurio* and the residence of Senator Francisco Bulnes of the National Party. This was followed by attacks on the railroad line to the Sewell copper mine and an explosion at a meeting of the Christian Democrats in Chillán, the first incident in which there were injuries. The explosions had a predictable effect on public opinion, with much criticism of the government for not moving effectively against the MIR, and of the courts for releasing those arrested by the police when conclusive evidence could not be produced against them.

These developments aided the growing campaign in favor of Jorge Alessandri, and Frei's appointment of Edmundo Pérez Zujovic as interior minister in July accelerated the process of political polarization, since as acting minister, Pérez had already acquired a reputation for toughness in handling strikes and disturbances. In early August, Pérez announced that a "vast plan of subversion" had been uncovered to which the recent outbreaks of student violence, the burning of a factory, and the seizure of a farm were related.[19]

On August 10–11 a group of priests and laymen, including a number of students, occupied the Cathedral of Santiago. Calling themselves the Iglesia Joven (Young Church), they claimed to have taken this action to protest the involvement of the Catholic church with the structures of power in Latin America and its lack of concern for the poor and oppressed. The action was purely symbolic and was discontinued after two days, but it received international attention since it was timed to coincide with the visit of Pope Paul VI to the Eucharistic Congress in Bogota, Colombia. The process of radicalization of a sector of the Latin American church was clearly reflected in Chile. The Jesuits connected with the magazine *Mensaje* were now involved in a deep internal split over the question of ways to achieve social change. Before and immediately after 1964, there had been a consensus within the *Mensaje* group in favor of the Christian Democratic revolution in liberty. By 1968, however, a number of influential Jesuits felt that a much more radical process must be undertaken if any real improvement in the lot of the underprivileged was to occur. In October 1968, *Mensaje* wrote an editorial on the first anniversary of the death of Che Guevara which spoke approvingly of his "great love" and "revolutionary conviction." This elicited a protest from the cardinal (who at the time of his elevation to the cardinalate had been regarded by some Catholic sectors as dangerously radical in his social and political attitudes) and anger from President Frei. The split within the *Mensaje* group finally led to an open break when its editor, Hernán Larraín, S.J., and one of its leading contributors, Gonzalo Arroyo, S.J., left the Jesuit center in downtown Santiago to live among the poor in a slum area.[20]

Eduardo Frei, president of Chile from 1964 to 1970, with Edmundo Pérez Zujovic, his interior minister in 1968–69. Pérez's assassination in June 1971 by a militant leftist group sharply accelerated the process of political polarization under the Allende regime. (Wide World Photos)

Divisions in the Center and the Left

In 1967 the Socialist Party had divided into two groups in what was essentially a personal conflict between two of its leaders. As the 1969 congressional elections later demonstrated, most of the Socialist voters remained faithful to the Socialist Party of Salvador Allende and Aniceto Rodriguez rather than following the party's former general secretary, Raúl Ampuero, into the rival Popular Socialist Union (USP). The split had an effect on the efforts of the Radical Party to join the Marxists in an electoral coalition, since the Socialists were reluctant to open themselves to charges from their rivals of compromising with a "bourgeois" party. The Communists, however, had no such problems and were willing to cooperate with other parties when it furthered their long-range goals. However, the Communist Party, long known to be a faithful servant of Moscow, suffered a setback in its campaign for respectibility when the Soviet Union invaded Czechoslovakia on August 20, 1968. The two Socialist parties, the Christian Democrats, and the National Party all condemned the invasion, but the Communists tried to justify it. (A mass meeting on August 24 chanted "Checo, comprende; los Rusos te defienden"—"Czech, understand; the Russians are defending you.") The Radical Party issued a statement which was deliberately softened in its tone in order not to prejudice its relations with the Communists. The statement annoyed many members of the party, which was forced to issue a second, stronger statement, but not before Humberto Enriquez, its former president, had resigned in protest. The efforts to achieve unity on the left or an agreement between the FRAP and the Radicals now seemed remote, and the candidacy of Alessandri appeared to have received a further boost, accentuated by the economic problems produced by the continuation of the worst drought in the history of Chile. (By September 1968 the cost of living had risen 25 percent since the beginning of the year.)

Nevertheless, by October the invasion of Czechoslovakia had been forgotten, and the council of the Christian Democratic Party, at its meeting in Cartegena on October 19, 1968, approved a resolution by Senator Fuentealba which called for efforts to achieve "popular unity" with the parties of the left, provided that this did not compromise the basic principles of the party. However, the ideological and personal differences among the Christian Democrats which had been evident for over a year could not be concealed much longer. On November 11, Jacques Chonchol presented his resignation as head of INDAP and wrote a long letter to President Frei which criticized the lack of progress in agrarian reform and referred to obstacles to his work created by other members of the government—a clear reference to the friction between himself and Edmundo Pérez Zujovic. Fifty-three of the eighty-one Christian Democratic representatives in the Chamber of Deputies issued a declaration of support for Frei and Pérez, but it was clear that the split had been deepened by Chonchol's departure. The division among the deputies on the resolution of support predicted almost exactly which members would depart from the party in its subsequent divisions in 1969 and 1971.[21]

The divisions in the party were clear at a banquet given for Chonchol on November 29, which was attended by three thousand Christian Democrats of *tercerista* or *rebelde* orientation. Radomiro Tomic, the Christian Democratic heir-apparent as candidate for the 1970 presidential elections, was also in attendance, attempting to maintain his links with the left sector of the party while not formally identifying himself with it. Early in 1968, Tomic had returned to Chile after resigning his post as ambassador to the United States in order to devote himself exclusively to politics. When he spoke at the banquet, some opposition was expressed, but he was able to maintain his credentials with the dissidents, if only because he had always represented himself as being to the left of Frei in his views. While he was not formally identified with any specific current, he had very good relations with the *terceristas*, represented most prominently at the banquet by Senator Renán Fuentealba, president of the party.

The left received a further boost at the end of 1968 with the publication of a sensationalized book of revelations about the "invasion" of Chile, *Chile invadido*, by Eduardo Labarca Goddard. Labarca, a leading Communist journalist, had put together out of the files of *El Siglo*, the Communist Party newspaper, a pastiche of accounts of CIA intervention in Chilean affairs which was based to a considerable extent on the revelations of CIA financing of student, labor, peasant, and intellectual organizations that had appeared in the U.S. press in February 1967. At the time, those revelations had not caused much stir in Chile, but when Labarca used them to attack a number of Christian Democratic–related groups, the Chilean press, radio, and TV took up the story. Often the documentation consisted of nothing more than a quote from the *New York Times* or the *Washington Post*, and the book itself showed evidence of links with Eastern European intelligence sources in reproducing an East German list of CIA agents in its appendix. However, its publication at the end of 1968 further helped to discredit the Frei government with the left Christian Democrats and accentuated the division within the party.

The March 1969 Congressional Elections

Yet the PDC did not divide. It could not do so at this point since it faced a crucial set of congressional elections in March 1969, and even the most dissident *rebelde*, if he was a candidate for public office, was interested in receiving the support of the party machinery for his reelection. Internal differences were glossed over, therefore, in the interest of electing the Christian Democratic candidates for the 150 seats in the Chamber of Deputies and the 30 places in the Senate which were to be chosen on March 4.

The issues in the election continued to be drawn on ideological lines. The electoral system compelled each party to emphasize its distinctive characteristics so that earlier efforts at closer cooperation between the parties which had been directed at preparing for the 1970 presidential elections were suspended. The Socialists reiterated their opposition to working with the Radicals, and the internal conflicts within the Radical and Christian Democratic parties were temporarily ignored, only to reemerge after the elections.

The National Party used the election to demonstrate a groundswell of support for Alessandri's presidential candidacy. It nominated two of his relatives as deputies, and its electoral propaganda made it clear that a vote for the party, and especially for the Alessandri candidacies, would encourage "Don Jorge" to run. In February, 1969, shortly before the elections, *El Mercurio* published the results of a public opinion poll showing that in a three-way race against Tomic and Allende, Alessandri would receive 61.3 percent of the vote to Tomic's 21.3 percent and Allende's 17.4 percent. The lopsided results of this poll are enough to discredit it, especially in retrospect, but it is an additional indication of the attempt to convert the congressional elections into an Alessandri plebiscite.

The March 1969 election results revealed a further drop in the voting strength of the Christian Democrats and a marked increase in support for the right. The Christian Democrats lost about 30 percent of the votes they had received in the 1965 congressional elections, dropping from 42.3 percent of the total vote in 1965 to 29.8 percent in 1969. The Christian Democratic losses were particularly evident in the middle-class area of Santiago. In the First District, which includes most of the center of the city, the Christian Democratic percentage dropped from 52 percent to 32 percent. In the upper-middle-class suburbs of Providencia and Las Condes, the drops were from 41 percent to 27 percent and from 48 percent to 27 percent, respectively, largely owing to a rightward shift by female voters.[22]

Under the complex Chilean electoral rules, the voter cast his ballot for an individual candidate for deputy or senator, whose name appeared under his party heading along with other party candidates up to the total number of seats up for election in the district (or senatorial *agrupación*). Seats were awarded to each party in proportion to the party's electoral total in the order of the votes the individual candidates of that party had received. This made it possible to measure the popularity of individual candidates despite the fact that proportional representation was being used. One of the results of the differential vote among the PDC candidates was to demonstrate that with the exception of Senator Alberto Jerez in Concepción and Julio Silva Solar in the Third District of Santiago (both areas with sizable working-class populations) neither the *rebelde* nor the *tercerista* Christian Democratic candidates did well electorally in comparison with those who adhered to the *oficialista* position.

Another result of the system was to demonstrate the considerable electoral appeal of the Alessandri name. Gustavo Alessandri, the nephew of the former president, received 80,000 votes in the Third District of Santiago, by far the largest number received by any candidate. Silvia Alessandri, his niece, came in fourth in the country, receiving more votes than such regular vote-getters as Bernardo Leighton of the Christian Democrats and Gladys Marin of the Communists.[23] The National Party increased its vote by nearly 50 percent, obtaining 20 percent of the total vote, and thus became the second largest party in Chile. It gained votes particularly in the upper-middle-class areas, receiving more than half the votes in the commune of Providencia; but even in a working-class commune like San Miguel, it increased its vote from 5 percent to about 13 percent. Like the Christian Democrats, the National Party had significantly more support among women than men.

The general pattern of losses by the Christian Democrats also applied in rural areas. There most of the PDC losses benefited the National Party, although in areas like Aconcagua, where agrarian reform had perhaps aroused the peasantry, the Communist and Socialist vote also increased somewhat. In the lower-class urban communes, many of the former Christian Democratic voters turned to the Socialists and Communists. This was particularly evident among women, who gave the FRAP 47 percent of their votes in the Santiago working-class commune of San Miguel, compared with 33 percent in 1965. In the Valparaíso working-class commune of Las Zorras, where in 1965 nearly three times as many women had voted for the PDC as for the FRAP, the Christian Democrats barely edged out the FRAP among the women and lost heavily among men.

The election thus showed a continuation of the movement from the center to both left and right which had already been evident in the 1967 elections. As the inflation rate continued to grow (it reached 10.6 percent in the first two months of 1969) and was accelerated by the prolonged drought the lower classes found it increasingly difficult to make ends meet, even with the arrival of the annual *reajuste,* since by the time it was received a renewed round of inflation had taken away much of its value. At the other end of the economic spectrum, the upper-middle and upper classes found that they were paying substantially increased taxes for what they considered to be expensive reforms of dubious merit.

Their protest votes went, not to the Radical Party, since the left wing of that party seemed to be increasingly dominant, but to the National Party. In its postelection analysis, *El Mercurio* criticized both center parties for ignoring the middle class: "The Radicals have not taken electoral advantage of the middle class citizenry which is decisive in a country with such a high degree of income distribution as ours, and the Christian Democrats thought that they could ensure themselves of permanent control of power and elections by attending to the needs of the peasant sector and the marginal poor without taking note of the many signs that showed the need to consider the powerful middle class element."[24] The analysis of the electoral results shows that if the Christian Democrats did indeed hope that losses among the upper and middle classes would be offset by gains in the lower-class and rural areas, this hope had been frustrated by inflation and by the relatively slow pace of the agrarian reform. Indeed, as the Aconcagua results showed, the mere fact of agrarian reform did not assure an increased PDC vote, and the threat of such reforms in largely unreformed areas like

Cautín in the south may have had something to do with the considerable increase in National Party support there.

The effect of the election on Frei's relations with the Congress was mixed. On the one hand, he was able to increase Christian Democratic representation in the Senate to 22, just a few votes short of a majority of the 50-member upper house. This was a result of the fact that the 29.7 percent the Christian Democrats had received was still well above the 16 percent they had won eight years earlier, and in the interim the Senate had been enlarged by 5 members. In the lower house, on the other hand, the Christian Democrats no longer had their automatic majority, since their representation had shrunk to 53 of a total membership of 150.

This was the Congress that was to serve until May 1973. No party had a clear majority, but the National Party had made sizable gains in the Chamber of Deputies (from 8 to 33 deputies), and the right was hopeful that if Alessandri were elected in September 1970, it could develop a working majority with the Christian Democrats to govern the country. However, a lengthy process of negotiation among the parties and nomination of candidates was to ensue which would alter the electoral picture in fundamental ways, setting the stage for a three-way race from which Allende would emerge victorious by a narrow margin.

CHAPTER FIVE

The Emergence of the 1970 Candidates

With one election over, Chileans began to look to the next, the all-important presidential election of September 1970. The result of that election—the accession to power of Salvador Allende—was neither inevitable nor accidental. It was directly related to shifts within and among the parties in 1969, which had a much greater influence on the outcome than did shifts in public opinion as a result of the actual campaign in 1970. During 1969 a strong bid by the right to recapture what it had lost in 1964, increasing weakness and division within the center parties, and the forging of a broadened coalition on the left meant that by January 1970 it should have been—but was not—apparent to everyone that in his fourth bid for the presidency Salvador Allende was very likely to win.

The internal divisions in the Christian Democratic Party had been increasingly evident for at least two years. They were accentuated by an incident immediately after the March 1969 congressional elections which recalled a similar sequence of events at the El Salvador mine three years earlier. This time the locale was the southern city of Puerto Montt, where a group of ninety-one families had occupied a tract of land outside the city in order to build themselves housing which they had not been able to secure. On Saturday, March 8, the chief of the local detachment of the national police force arrived with two hundred armed men and an order that the families remove themselves from the tract. The occupants sounded an alarm, and approximately a thousand people appeared from the neighborhood to resist the attempt to dislodge the squatters. In the ensuing battle, seven people were killed and forty-seven injured (including twenty carabineros).[1]

The "massacre" at Puerto Montt was immediately denounced by the opposition parties, and the minister of the interior, Edmundo Pérez Zujovic, was held responsible although there was no evidence that the decision to dislodge the squatters was made at a level higher than that of the secretary to the governor of the province. (The governor was in Santiago at the time.) The attack on Pérez was joined by the Christian-Democratic-controlled Chilean Student Federation (FECH) and, more significantly, by the youth section of the Christian Democrats, which saw the Puerto Montt events as an attempt to appeal to right-wing voters.

The Christian Democratic National Secretariat disavowed the statement by its youth organization, but predictably the leaders of the *rebelde* faction supported it. The Party Council voted to convene a special meeting of the Party Assembly in the beginning of May, and the government removed the official responsible for the Puerto Montt actions, but the split within the party continued.

Radomiro Tomic had already resolved that he could only be assured of winning in 1970 by moving to the left, and discreet contacts had been made with the Communist Party. The Communists encouraged this, since they saw that the issue of cooperation with the left would deeply divide the Christian Democrats. In fact, there had never been any likelihood that the left would support Tomic. As Luis Corvalán, secretary-general of the Communist Party, had put it in 1968, "To mass with Tomic? Never!" ("Con Tomic ni a misa.") Yet Tomic had continued to insist: "There will be no Tomic candidacy without a popular unity coalition" ("Sin unidad popular no habrá candidatura Tomic"). Now it appeared that the Puerto Montt events had destroyed any possibility of an alliance with the left (if there ever had been such a possibility). Tomic's reaction to the controversy over Puerto Montt was to withdraw his candidacy. In a letter to the party on April 9 which alluded to the Puerto Montt shootings as a contributing factor, he announced his "irrevocable" decision not to run, in view of his conviction that there was "no basis" for a popular unity coalition "to end the capitalist regime."[2]

There were those in the party who saw this as an opportunity to follow a different strategy. In the debate over constitutional reform in which the lower house was now engaged, one Christian Democratic deputy proposed an amendment to allow Frei to run again. Others considered that either Bernardo Leighton or Foreign Minister Gabriel Valdés might be sufficiently centrist in his views to attract the support of the right and some of the left. Its success in the parliamentary elections, however, had convinced the National Party that a comeback by Alessandri was inevitable, and on April 13 its General Council voted against any electoral cooperation with the Christian Democrats. In anticipation of an Alessandri victory, the National Party's representatives began to vote with the Christian Democrats in support of Frei's proposed constitutional amendments strengthening the powers of the executive.

On May 1, an important meeting of the Christian Democratic Assembly was held to decide on a policy for the forthcoming presidential elections. The controversy centered around two resolutions. The first, supported by the *terceristas* and *rebeldes,* was offered by Senator Renán Fuentealba, the president of the party. It called for "rejection of any possible understanding, whether direct or indirect, with the right, rejection of a position of isolation for Christian Democracy," and it affirmed "the objective of popular unity, understood as a close concentration of wills which integrates all sectors of the people and the progressive middle class" on the basis of "a clear agreement on program" and with the hope that "a man from its [the Christian Democratic Party's] ranks may have the honor of leading this effort." The other resolution, offered by the *oficialistas,* called for "the replacement of capitalist structures by a way to development which is neither capitalist nor collectivist." It ruled out "any possibility of agreement with the National Party" as well as "the thesis of the Revolutionary Front" (a reference to the PDC Youth's proposal for a revolutionary union of workers, peasants, and students) and proposed the nomination of a Christian Democratic candidate (*candidato propio*) for the presidency within sixty days. The choice was thus between a proposal for negotiations with the left for a common candidate, preferably but not necessarily a Christian Democrat, and the nomination of a candidate first, followed by possible negotiations for support later.

The Creation of MAPU

The division within the party was clear when the *oficialista* resolution was adopted by a vote of 233 to 215. When the vote was announced, the party officers resigned and a largely "officialist" slate headed by Jaime Castillo was elected. In the days following the meeting a rain of resignations descended on the party as the leaders of the *rebelde* group announced their withdrawal from the PDC. Senators Rafael Gumucio and Alberto Jerez, Deputy Julio Silva Solar, Jacques Chonchol, the former head of INDAP, and most of the leaders of the youth division of the party as well as members of its peasant (*campesino*) and trade union sections announced their resignations. On May 18 the dissidents organized the Movement for Unitary Popular Action (MAPU), with Chonchol as secretary general.

The presidential elections were sixteen months away, but the maneuvering on nominations continued. A leftist independent senator, Rafael Tarud, announced that he would be a presidential candidate, although the movement he organized to nominate himself, Acción Popular Independiente (API), was not taken seriously. The Radicals began to back Senator Alberto Baltra publicly as their candidate, indicating that the left faction of that party was firmly in control. The Socialists announced their opposition to an alliance with the Radicals. Thus, given the divisions in the center and on the left, Alessandri's position as the unannounced front-runner still seemed secure.

All this made it seem most unlikely that there would be a repetition of the 1964 election scenario. The centrist parties, convinced that the country as a whole was moving left, were themselves moving in that direction; while the right wing, encouraged by the results of the March congressional elections, saw victory in 1970 as in its grasp, a view that was reinforced by the failure of the left to agree on a candidate. There was no by-election to frighten the right, and Allende, a three-time loser still far from nomination by the left, did not seem the threat that he had appeared to be in 1964.

A further factor impeding any repetition of the 1964 pattern was the pressure within the Christian Democratic Party against any kind of agreement, "direct or indirect," with the right. This was partly a matter of ideology—the party continued to call for a new system to replace capitalism, which was held responsible for the ills afflicting Chile—and partly a matter of politics, since it was assumed that a majority of the many new voters since 1964 would be sympathetic to the left.

New Copper Moves

The Christian Democratic meeting in early May had demonstrated that the left groups in the party were just short of a majority, and the most committed of the *rebelde* group had subsequently left the party. But this did not mean that the pressure from the left on the Frei administration ceased. Now that pressure centered around the question of possible nationalization of the U.S. copper companies. The high price of copper on the international market (62 cents a pound) was giving the copper companies profits in which, under the Chileanization agreements, the Chilean state shared only to a limited degree. The major benefits of that program, an expansion of production and refining, were only to be felt after 1970, and one of the two major copper producers, Anaconda, had refused to Chileanize its major mines. In addition, Radomiro Tomic, who despite his withdrawal in April was still considered the leading candidate for the Christian Democratic nomination, had supported nationalization for many years.

The result of all these pressures within his party was a last-minute addition to Frei's state-of-the-nation address on May 21, 1969. After noting that the Chileanization program had already tripled Chile's refining capacity, Frei observed that the price of copper now seemed to be stabilizing at a considerably higher level than was projected earlier, and "this obliges the government of Chile to reevaluate the share of the state in the profits of that vital activity," that is, to increase its tax share of the profits resulting from the high price of copper.

"Together with this important step I consider it necessary that the copper companies that have not participated in the past in the Chileanization program now enter into it in order that this policy, which was proposed to the country and which it approved in granting me my office, may be applied across the board without exception." Frei went on to defend Chileanization against "the insistent talk of the need for nationalization of the enterprises that were not Chileanized in the past," observing that Chileanization provides "technological and human expertise and quantities of financial capital which the country does not possess at the moment."[3] He seemed to be serving notice on Anaconda that the only way in which they could avoid outright nationalization of the remaining mines would be to agree quickly on Chileanization.

In the section of his speech on foreign affairs, Frei referred favorably to the meeting of the special Latin American Coordinating Commission (CECLA) which had just been concluded in Viña del Mar. This was a meeting of Latin American foreign ministers or their representatives which had gathered outside the framework of the Organization of American States to present a common position to the new Nixon administration concerning "new bases for social and economic inter-American cooperation." The meeting had been called by Chilean Foreign Minister Gabriel Valdés in response to a growing sense that the Alliance for Progress had failed to remedy the increasing friction between the United States and Latin America in the area of economic relations. Although the meeting was reportedly looked upon favorably by the U.S. embassy in Santiago, it pointedly excluded U.S. representatives from its deliberations and attempted to form a common front against the overwhelming U.S. financial, economic, and technical superiority. Latin American policy makers and intellectuals were increasingly resentful of their *dependencia* on the United States, and the CECLA meeting was an attempt to secure U.S. assistance for Latin American development on the basis of a Latin American rather than a U.S. analysis of the problems and priorities involved.[4]

The meeting produced an agreed statement, "The Latin American Consensus of Viña del Mar," which was presented to President Nixon in June (shortly after a scheduled visit to Santiago by Nelson Rockefeller was canceled owing to the threat of demonstrations and protests). The "Consensus" ascribed the current economic problems of Latin America to the existence of "tariff and non-tariff restrictions which impede access to world markets by the developing countries' manufactured and semi-manufactured goods, the progressive worsening of the volume, terms, and forms of international financial assistance which is practically wiped out by the burden of debt servicing . . . problems deriving from the operation of the international monetary system, . . . the conditions of marine transport . . . and the difficulties involved in transferring modern technology to the countries of the region." To remedy these problems the Latin American ministers proposed "a general, non-reciprocal and non-discriminatory system of preferences to facilitate the export of manufactures and semi-manufactures from the developing countries," "a lowering of freight rates in inter-American trade," and the recognition of "the right of Latin American countries to develop national or regional merchant fleets," the elimination of various restrictions on the use of AID funds in Latin America (especially the compulsory use of U.S. shipping lines and the prohibition on use of AID funds to buy goods from other Latin American countries), a larger part for Latin America in discussions on the reform of the international monetary system, and measures to improve the transfer of science and technology to Latin America. The document was critical of private foreign investment as a means to development since it often caused an "external financial flow," made "excessive use of local financial resources," and "[distorted] competitive conditions in internal and external markets." It asserted that such investment should be "subject to national decisions and priorities, . . . create income and prevent outflow of foreign currency, promote saving and national technical research, make a real technological contribution, and act as a complementary factor in national investment preferably in association with it."[5]

The fact that the document represented a unanimous consensus among representatives of governments of many political orientations indicated the intensity of the Latin American criticism of the U.S. aid program and the effects of foreign investment, as well as the radicalization of centrist opinion in Latin America and the region's increasing assertiveness.

The feeling against foreign, particularly U.S., investors was reflected in Chile with a twenty-four-hour student strike early in June demanding the nationalization of the Anaconda mines. Frei had already initiated negotiations with the company, and while they were proceeding a number of bills for copper nationalization were introduced in Congress, including one by a member of the *tercerista* faction of the Christian Democrats. These undoubtedly improved the bargaining position of the government during the negotiations, and they made it politically expedient for Frei to speak of the agreements finally reached not as "Chileanization" but as "agreed-upon nationalization" (*nacionalización pactada*).

In reality the agreement as announced by Frei on June 26 was for immediate Chileanization and possible nationalization later. It provided for the immediate purchase of 51 percent of the three large Anaconda mines, Chuquicamata, Potrilleros, and El Savador, with payment from the projected Chilean share of profits over a period of twelve years at 6 percent interest beginning June 30, 1970. For three years Anaconda would also have a management contract for a fee of 1 percent of sales. Beginning in 1973 the Chilean state could purchase the other 49 percent at a price based on recent earnings and payment over twelve years after payment for the first 51 percent was completed. The tax rate would be computed on a sliding scale based on the international market price and ranging up to 70 percent for copper prices exceeding 50 cents a pound. (Frei also announced that this tax policy would be extended to the other copper companies by agreement or by law as of December 30, 1970.)[6]

The opposition parties attacked the arrangement, placing special emphasis on what were conceived to be excessive payments for the management contract and for the purchase of the remaining 49 percent after 1973. MAPU also criticized the lack of provision for worker participation in management, an important element in the Christian Democratic program and principles. However, the agreement was favorably received by the public and abated the furor over copper policy. Since it had been concluded while Radomiro Tomic was temporarily out of the country, and involved an area in which he had specialized for many years, he was critical of certain of its aspects after his return, particularly the purchase provisions. In the July Plenary Council of the party he succeeded in securing the adoption of a resolution calling for a law simply nationalizing the remaining assets of Anaconda in 1973 without the specific compensation agreements worked out by Frei. Here as elsewhere the ideological and personal disagreements between Frei and Tomic were being revealed and gave rise to rumors that Frei would support someone else for the presidency when the nominating assembly met in August.

On June 26, the same day that Frei announced the agreement with Anaconda, the Radical Party opened its biennial convention. It was clear from the outset that this convention would see the continuation of the process of reorientation of the party which had begun two years before. The president of the party, Senator Hugo Miranda, spoke of the "fruitful contacts" the Radicals had had with the Communists and criticized the "intransigence" of the Socialists. Miranda also denounced "the little group" who wished to "use the name of the Radical Party as a disguise . . . for the reactionary right."[7] The convention selected Alberto Baltra as its presidential candidate and called for further negotiations with the left in the hope of concluding a Unidad Popular alliance. It also expelled the leaders of the dissident right-wing movement in the party, including Senator Julio Durán, its presidential candidate in 1964, and Humberto Enriquez, its president from 1965 until 1967. The expelled leaders and the members who disagreed with the new orientation of the Radicals formed a new party, the Radical Democrats (Democracia Radical), which included three deputies among its members, as well as Senator Durán. The new party soon began to collaborate with the National Party and supported Jorge Alessandri for the presidency after he announced his candidacy later in the year.

The main body of the Radicals hoped that the expulsions would make them more acceptable to the left, but the Socialists continued to oppose such an alliance. This opposition reflected the intransigence of the Socialist secretary general, Aniceto Rodriguez, who at this point was a rival of Salvador Allende's for the Socialist nomination for the presidency. Only after the more moderate Allende was nominated by the Socialists in late August could a rapprochement effort be undertaken.

Presidential Nominations

During July, Radomiro Tomic let it be known that he was no longer holding to his April decision to withdraw his candidacy. There were still divisions between Frei and Tomic to be overcome, but by the time the Party Assembly met on August 15 he had modified his most serious criticisms of the June agreement with Anaconda and taken a less intransigent position concerning private enterprise, which he now described as "a valuable element" in the Chilean economy. On a motion by the *oficialista* president of the party, Jaime Castillo, Tomic was nominated unanimously by the assembly. After some modification of wording to satisfy Castillo, the assembly also approved a draft statement to be used as the basis for the development of the Tomic program.

The Socialists still had not nominated their candidate, but most political discussion now focused on Alessandri's candidacy. In Santiago at least, there seemed to be a clear movement to the right as a result of a series of disturbances carried out by the MIR, which was now escalating its activities. In June, agents of Investigaciones had discovered what they called a "guerrilla school" near Santiago with quantities of explosives and material for the preparation of bombs; in the subsequent investigation the son of a Socialist senator was implicated. Four MIR-organized bank robberies had been carried out in recent months, and a number of university students were arrested in connection with them. The Socialist Party included important elements who were sympathetic to the MIR and encouraged their tactic of urban guerrilla warfare in imitation of the Uruguayan Tupamaro movement. The left sectors of the Socialists, headed by Carlos Altamirano, were opposed to Socialist participation in the discredited *vía parlamentaria,* while a slightly more moderate group supported the Socialist secretary-general, Senator Aniceto Rodriguez. When the Central Committee of the Socialist Party met on August 29, the combined opposition of the two groups meant that Allende had considerable difficulty securing the presidential nomination. On the first vote he secured 13 votes, with 14 abstentions. On the second round, two of the abstainers did not participate so as to permit him to be nominated with 13 votes against 12 abstentions. The Central Committee, however, continued to oppose cooperation with "bourgeois political parties," meaning the Radicals.[8]

Three other groups nominated candidates in September. On September 7, the new Social Democratic Party named Senator Rafael Tarud, already nominated by his own creation, API, to be its candidate. On September 27, MAPU nominated its secretary general, Jacques Chonchol, and three days later the Communist Party named the famous poet, Pablo Neruda, as its candidate. As the last nomination indicates, these candidates were only put forward as representatives of the parties of the left before a proposed round table which was to agree on a program and a single candidate. The Communist Party in particular had no intention of running Neruda, since it knew that to win, the left would have to nominate someone from one of the other parties.

The next step was to persuade the Socialist Party to agree to a meeting in which the Radical Party would be a participant. This effort was undertaken by Salvador Allende, whose unsuccessful candidacies made him aware of the importance of the Radical move to the left.

Military Discontent: The Tacnazo

The process of bringing the left together lasted several months, and in the meantime a serious problem arose in the relations between the Frei government and the army. In 1969, as the inflation rate grew worse (it was to reach nearly 30 percent for the year), the military complained of the inadequacy of their salaries and the need for an interim readjustment before the annual *reajuste*. The situation came to public attention when the minister of defense took pains to deny rumors of "indiscipline" among certain army units at the annual military parade on September 18. Two days later, in an interview in *El Mercurio*, the finance minister indicated that the government was giving special attention to the question of military salaries. The day after that, the army commander in chief admitted that certain officers had deliberately delayed the arrival of their units at the September 18 national holiday ceremonies.[9]

The military pressures were supported by two parties at the opposite ends of the political spectrum—the National Party and the Socialists. The National Party had already introduced an amendment to a bill before Congress to grant the military a 25 percent raise in pay, while the Socialists issued a statement on September 25 supporting the military cause. The Socialist attitude was related to the early history of the party. It was founded in April 1933, less than a year after the demise of a short-lived "Socialist Republic" which had been established following a coup d'état led by Air Force Colonel Marmaduque Grove. Grove himself was a co-founder of the party in the following year.[10]

The Communist Party differed from the Socialists in its policy toward the military since it was aware that, however reformist or even radical the military might be, one of the first things a military government would be likely to do would be to outlaw the Communist Party. This is why it had cooperated with the Christian Democrats in their earlier problems with the military in May 1968, and was to do so in the crisis now approaching.

On October 10, the government authorized loans to members of the armed services pending the readjustment of their salaries at the year's end. The interest rate was 6 percent, payable over three years, and given the

Chilean inflation rate, this meant that the interest along with much of the principal was likely to be canceled by the depreciation of the currency. This concession was not sufficient for some of the military leaders.

On October 16, the annual list of retirements included the name of General Roberto Viaux, commander of the Army First Division at Antofogasta. Viaux had been rumored to be heading a movement which was considering a military coup d'état as a way of resolving the military's economic problems and the general difficulties of the country, and this must have had much to do with the decision to retire him. On October 17, the officers of Viaux's division asked that the retirement be withdrawn. Their open letter in support of Viaux was published by a number of right-wing newspapers, copies of which were seized by the Frei government. The government also initiated prosecution of *La Segunda* of Santiago for violating the Internal Security Law by publishing the officers' letter and what it described as "tendentious news reports which have for their purpose the alteration of the constitutional order."

Over the weekend of October 18–19, continuous government meetings were devoted to the military crisis, and on October 20, Viaux arrived in Santiago seeking, as he said, "the solution of a problem which has been pending for a long time and has now reached crisis proportions.[11] Early on Tuesday, October 21, Viaux set himself up in the headquarters of the Tacna Artillery Regiment in Santiago with units from the Enlisted Men's School and the Second Armored Regiment. At 10 A.M., the Frei government announced the existence of a military uprising headed by Viaux at the Tacna Regiment. Frei placed all radio stations under the direct control of the Presidential Information Office and issued an appeal to the people, trade unions, peasants, workers, slum dwellers, women, and political parties "to reject the attempt at a coup and reaffirm the legal democratic regime."

Frei received expressions of support from all the political parties except the Socialists, who called on "popular forces" "to fill the vacuum of power . . . nationalize copper and iron, private banks, insurance and the monopolies of production and distribution . . . [and] radicalize the agrarian reform." The Central Workers Confederation (CUT) announced a general strike against "the reactionary coup," and the radio stations continued to broadcast messages of support for the regime. Elements from six other regiments were called to Santiago and established in a park near the Tacna headquarters. One of the more comical aspects of the day's activities was a decision to call all the garbage trucks in the city to the presidential palace in anticipation of a possible attack by the Armored Regiment.

At 3 P.M., President Frei broadcast an appeal to the citizenry in which he expressed his determination to impose respect for legitimate authority. A few minutes later, General Viaux held a press conference at which he declared that he was absolutely loyal to the president and that the actions of the units he controlled were concerned with strictly professional military matters—the question of military pay. For most of the day, negotiators and members of the press entered and left the Tacna garrison building, and by late evening (when the only violence of the day occurred as Tacna soldiers fired at students who had thrown stones at the building) a settlement of the "Tacnazo," as it was later referred to, was reached. Viaux was to be retired immediately, and he and those who had supported his action were to be tried by a military tribunal for insubordination. Although it was not asserted publicly as part of the agreement, General Marambio resigned as minister of defense, and the commander in chief of the army tendered his resignation three days later. A few days later, the government sent the Congress a bill, adopted in short order, granting the president special powers to raise the salaries of the armed forces. The coup or strike or whatever it had been was over, but General Viaux had become a hero to many of the members of the armed forces—even a martyr, since while they enjoyed a wage increase secured by his actions, he was being prosecuted under the Code of Military Justice.

The handling of the incident was later criticized on the grounds that the Frei government had overreacted to what was simply a demand for higher pay. However, the subsequent activities of General Viaux in 1970 indicated that thoughts of a coup were not absent from his mind, and the military overthrow of President Fernando Belaúnde Terry in Peru a year earlier probably had much to do with Frei's fears that an incident which began over pay might conclude with his removal from office.

The fact that it was settled peaceably reflected both the divisions among the military, most of whom did not support Viaux, and the Chilean capacity for working out face-saving compromises. However, the revolt was the beginning of a politicization—or repoliticization—of the military which was to continue in the coming months and years, culminating in the September 1973 coup. The CIA was aware of the coup plotting, and in July 1969 it began a covert program to monitor coup-oriented activity.

Constitutional Reform

In the public attention to the Tacna events, no notice was given to the fact that the Congress had finally adopted many of the constitutional reform proposals for which Frei had been working since the beginning of his term of office. The Congress had not been willing to give him the power to dissolve it once during his term, but on October 30, the Chamber approved the Senate version of a constitutional reform which strengthened an already existing provision allowing the president to call a plebiscite in the event of disagreement with the Congress on a constitutional amendment; created a Constitutional Tribunal composed of five members, three chosen by the president, and two by the Supreme Court; gave the president exclusive powers to propose the modification of the budget, tax, social security, and pension systems, as well as the minimum wage; and granted the right to vote to illiterates and those between eighteen and twenty-one years of age.[12] The Congress still had to meet once more to confirm the amendments within sixty days, but this was now simply a formality.

In most of the votes on the constitutional reforms, Frei's proposals had been supported by the National Party, which, combined with the Christian Democrats, made up a majority in the lower house and, together with Senator Durán's vote, twenty-six of the fifty votes in the Senate. As noted earlier, the National Party was now convinced that Alessandri would win the 1970 elections, and since the reforms were not to go into effect until the next presidential term of office (thus eliminating the possibly leftist vote of those under twenty-one as a factor in the September 1970 elections), the right was delighted to support them.

As an attempt to ward off further military insubordination or a possible Viaux presidential candidacy, and in anticipation of the annual demonstration on the anniversary of his departure from office on November 4, Jorge Alessandri finally announced his candidacy. In the course of his radio address, he referred to the "creation of illusory hopes that our economic capabilities do not permit us to satisfy in spite of the fact that luck has granted to certain governments vast and absolutely extraordinary resources,"[13] a clear allusion to the ambitious Christian Democratic program of reform and to the high copper prices which Frei had enjoyed during much of his tenure of office. He also alluded to his own "physical and spiritual vigor" in an attempt to answer critics who said that at seventy-three he was too old to become president again.

The Formation of Popular Unity

If the nomination of Tomic in August had not already done so, Alessandri's announcement guaranteed that the 1964 combination of forces against the left would not be repeated in 1970. However, the threat from the left which had been clear in 1964 still had not materialized, since the program and candidate of Popular Unity had not yet been decided upon.

In September, a common front for the nationalization of the copper industry had been established in which, for the first time since the breakup of the Popular Front in 1941, the Radicals and the Socialists sat together. On October 7, the Communist and Socialist parties issued a joint call for the "organization of a vast and profound movement of national liberation" which would aim at "the development of a common program, the determination of an identical understanding of popular government, and the study of the mechanisms which would make it possible to nominate one candidate as president."[14] All the left groups which had nominated presidential candidates were invited to participate on an equal basis. This arrangement gave Rafael Tarud double representation, since he had been nominated by two minuscule groups, his own Acción Popular Independiente and the new Social Democratic Party. The Popular Socialist Union, under Raúl Ampuero, which had split off from the Socialists in 1967, did not nominate a candidate and was excluded from the meeting at the request of the Socialists.

Two representatives each from the Socialists, the Communists, the Radicals, MAPU, API, and the Social Democrats met on October 9, 1969, and established a Coordinating Committee of Popular Unity. They decided that the formulation of a common program would precede the decision on a candidate and appointed an eighteen-man committee (three from each group) to draft a program during the next two months. On October 11, the program committee began two months of meetings devoted to drafting the basic program of Popular Unity. Despite the ideological differences among the participants, arrival at an agreement on a program seems to have been less difficult than the subsequent task of finding a single candidate for the presidency. The Radical Party, represented by Orlando Cantuarias, a future minister of mines in the Allende government, was especially concerned with nationalizing copper and dividing the economy into an "area of social property," that is, nationalized or state enterprises; a mixed area; and the area of private ownership, which would include smaller and intermediate-sized enterprises. The Socialist Party was responsible for the sections opposing imperialism, calling for diplomatic relations with all countries (including East Germany, North Korea, North Vietnam, mainland China, and Cuba), and supporting the Cuban Revolution. However, the program was most influenced in content and phraseology by the platform adopted by the Communist Party at its fourteenth National Congress held in the last week of November. As Alessandri supporters were to demonstrate during the campaign, whole sentences of the Popular Unity program were taken word for word from the statements of the Communist Party Congress. This was particularly true of the section on political institutions which proposed the establishment of a unicameral legislature and the subordination of the judiciary to this "Assembly of the People."[15] MAPU, headed by Jacques Chonchol, was most influential in the sections dealing with the "deepening and broadening of the Agrarian Reform," although the Communist influence was felt in the mention of "state-run agricultural enterprises" which had also figured prominently in the Communist platform adopted in November.

Aside from its proposals for constitutional changes, the most striking part of the Popular Unity Program was the list of the enterprises which would compose "the area of social property" to be expropriated. The list

included the "(1) large copper, nitrate, iodine, iron, and coal mines, (2) the
financial system of the country, particularly the private banks and insurance
companies, (3) foreign trade, (4) the large distribution enterprises and
monopolies, (5) strategic industrial monopolies, (6) in general, those activities which decisively influence [*condicionan*] the economic and social
development of the country, such as the production and distribution of
electricity; rail, air, and maritime transport; communications; the production, refining and distribution of petroleum and its derivatives including
kerosene; steel, cement, petrochemicals and heavy chemistry, cellulose,
and paper."[16]

The lengthy list was to be a principal campaign issue and a first priority
of the Allende government after it came to power. The inclusion of cellulose
and paper as an industry to be nationalized was particularly sensitive both
because of its effects on the control of newsprint, and because the principal
paper company in private hands was headed by Jorge Alessandri.

Once the program was adopted on December 17, 1969, informal consultations on a possible candidate began. Before any formal meeting devoted
to the selection of a common candidate, the Communist representatives
insisted that the coordinating commission agree on a series of documents
defining the way in which the Popular Unity electoral campaign and
elected government would be conducted. On December 26, the leaders of
the six groups signed a "Popular Unity Pact" which was to have a significant effect on the conduct of the Allende administration after it came to
power. It promised that "The Government of the People" would be multiparty in character, and provided for continual consultation by the president with a political committee representing all the parties and movements
of Popular Unity and backed up by a balanced representation of those
groups in the various governmental ministries and agencies. A second
document, "The Agreement on the Conduct and Style of the Campaign,"
established a political command for the campaign which would represent
all the sponsoring groups, and called for the establishment of local Popular
Unity committees which would be the "germinal expressions of popular
power." Finally, the commission agreed on a document regulating the
distribution of ministries which provided that after the president's election,
the ministries would be divided among the sponsoring groups so that the
Communists, Socialists, and Radicals would each have three ministries,
MAPU would have two, and API and the Social Democrats would be
considered as one party and receive three ministries. It was also agreed
that the assistant minister (*subsecretario*) in each ministry would represent
a different party from that of the minister.

On December 30, the first formal vote on a common candidate was taken.
Each party or movement submitted two nominations, and the results were
indecisive. The Radicals, API, and the Social Democrats all voted for

Baltra and Tarud, thus giving each of those candidates three votes; the MAPU voted for Chonchol and Allende; while the Communists and Socialists voted for their two nominees, Neruda and Allende. This meant that three candidates had three votes each, one (Allende) had two, and Chonchol had one. That night, representatives of the Communist Party pressured the Radicals and the Tarud parties to withdraw their candidates, arguing that Allende was acceptable to them, while their candidates were unacceptable to the Socialists. On December 31, MAPU withdrew the Chonchol candidacy, and the Radicals, API, and the Social Democrats broke off the negotiations with the parties to their left. It seemed that the efforts to reach agreement had ended in a draw. MAPU suggested Neruda or another Socialist besides Allende, and the Communists put forward the name of the MAPU senator, Rafael Gumucio, but without success.

The first break in the deadlock took place the following week, when the sole parliamentary representative of the Social Democratic Party, Luis Fernando Luengo, came out for Allende. On January 9, Baltra's offer to withdraw was rejected by the Radicals, but a week later they decided that his candidacy had no real possibility of success. On January 19, MAPU said it would only support a candidate linked to the working class, that is, a Socialist or Communist. Finally, on January 20, the withdrawals of Alberto Baltra and Pablo Neruda as candidates of the Radical and Communist parties paved the way for the selection of Allende. The Radicals agreed to vote for Tarud on the first ballot, continuing the tie with Allende. On the next round, Allende was nominated and, as a compromise, Tarud was named chairman of Allende's campaign committee.[17]

The Communist Party had been so certain of Allende's victory that it had already announced a mass rally for the following day. Indeed, throughout the negotiations, the Communists had taken the lead, and without their pressure and political skill, as well as what appears to have been an early decision on their part in favor of Allende, the heterogeneous coalition that now backed his candidacy would never have materialized. The candidacy of Alessandri, announced in November, also added psychological pressure to the effort to find as strong and well known a candidate as possible. Whatever Allende's weaknesses, he was well known all over Chile and had received 39 percent of the votes in 1964. This augured well for the possibilities of the left in the three-way contest which had emerged for September 1970.

CHAPTER SIX

The 1970 Presidential Election

On January 8, 1970, the presidential campaign began with a major speech by Jorge Alessandri attacking the nationalizations proposed in the Unidad Popular program. Social reform, he asserted, must be carried out "in accordance with the possibilities of the economy." Using figures on national income and population, he argued that if socialism were carried to its logical conclusion, and the entire national income except for taxes and payments to the public sector were distributed equally to each working Chilean, "each one would receive the modest sum of 775 escudos a month" (about $65 at then current exchange rates). The problem, as Alessandri saw it, was not distribution, but economic growth. "Private enterprise has not failed. The crisis in which we live and the misery of so many sectors is the reflection of an economy based on demagoguery and the politicization which has asphyxiated us."[1]

The speech indicated the emphasis Alessandri was to give in his campaign—opposition to politics and politicians, and a stress on economic growth stimulated by a vigorous private sector. Alessandri never formally published a platform, since he was running as an independent, although with very close links to the National Party. However, in his January speech and subsequently, he and his advisers filled in details. In the area of political reform, he proposed a further increase in the powers of the president, including the power to dissolve congress and to call plebiscites in the event of conflict with the legislature. Influenced programmatically as well as ideologically by Charles De Gaulle, he proposed a further limitation of the powers of Congress to initiate economic and financial legislation and a restructuring of the Senate to depoliticize it and make it an advisory body to the president. As in France, he called for the creation of an economic and social council with representation from economic groups and (different from the French example) the armed forces.[2]

In the social area, Alessandri made a special appeal to women voters, who he (correctly) thought provided the bulk of his support. His program called for the distribution of protein-rich foods such as fishmeal, whose effects on physical and intellectual growth made them especially suitable for preschool children. Alessandri also proposed a system of compulsory social service for young unmarried women at the age of eighteen which would be analogous to obligatory military service for men.

Alessandri took credit for the fact that the first agrarian reform law had been passed under his administration, but he criticized the excessive politicization of the program under the Christian Democrats and promised that individual titles of ownership would be distributed to members of the *asentamientos* who wanted them. In industry, he called for the establishment of "factory committees" to provide greater communication between labor and management, and he promised to depoliticize the trade unions while making them more representative of the workers.

Alessandri was not really running on the basis of a formally elaborated program, and his speeches and campaign were more designed to communicate a mood—the promise of a return to strong government above parties, a decrease in "politicking" (*politiquería*), and a return to authority in government. This kind of appeal evoked a response from a hyperpoliticized country, and Alessandri's emphasis on law and order took on more appeal as the Revolutionary Left (MIR) organized a series of bank robberies, assaults, and airplane hijackings in the months following Alessandri's announcement. Bank robberies and armed attacks took place in Santiago on November 13 and December 26, 1969, and January 21, January 29, February 23, June 1, and June 10, 1970. Hijackings were attempted with or without success on November 12 and December 19, 1969, and February 6, 1970—in the last case resulting in a gunfight that left one dead and four wounded. In February, the MIR announced that it was donating the money obtained from one of the bank robberies to the 26th of July Camp, which had been organized by homeless slum dwellers under the leadership of the MIR. Like other *campamentos* organized subsequently, it forbade outsiders, including the police force, to enter, maintaining order with its own "popular militia."

Meanwhile a wave of strikes began in January and reached a peak in March, when the coal miners, the nitrate miners, the port workers, and a large number of agricultural workers were on strike. The rural strikes were accompanied by the occupation of farms, which the government resolved by negotiation and occasionally by force.

The atmosphere of disorder aided Alessandri, but it also provoked movements further to the right. On February 7, General Viaux spoke at a banquet in his honor which was attended by over five hundred present and former officers and supported by letters and cables from elsewhere in the country. After referring to the Tacnazo, Viaux recalled that in 1924 and 1925 the armed forces had been responsible for the reordering of Chilean institutions "necessitated by the state of political and moral chaos in which the country found itself" and ending a long period of "misgovernment and parliamentary anarchy." Returning to the present, he called for a new constitution for Chile, written by a "genuinely national" constitutional convention, which would reform the political, economic, and social organization of the country. While it was being written, the country should be governed by "the directing authority of a strong government" which would not be dominated "by one party or coalition of parties, nor one ideological tendency, but by all, that is, by the nation."[3] The meeting led to the establishment of a "Viaux Movement." Whether it was organized to promote Viaux's presidential candidacy or to organize a military coup was not clear. Viaux's political position was somewhat compromised in the following month, when a court martial sentenced him to a suspended sentence of a year in jail for subversion.

The political panorama for the September elections thus took final form early in 1970. On the extreme left was the MIR, which rejected elections and was carrying out a series of actions which made violence a central issue in the campaign. A sector of the Socialist Party was sympathetic to the MIR, but the party as a whole was committed to the candidacy of Salvador Allende, who was supported by the Unidad Popular coalition. In the center, but leaning to the left, was the Christian Democratic candidate, Radomiro Tomic; while on the right, the "independent" Jorge Alessandri was supported by the National Party and by a right-wing group which had split off from the Radicals, the Radical Democrats. Further to the right were the forces grouped around General Roberto Viaux, who had come into prominence during the Tacnazo and continued to be a center for dissident right-wing military men and civilians who did not exclude a military coup from their planning.

The Programs of the Candidates

The program of Popular Unity contemplated the establishment of a unicameral legislature, the acceleration of agrarian reform, and a vast expansion of government control of the economy, principally through nationalization of basic industry, banking, and foreign trade. It was later supplemented by a list of "The First 40 Measures of the Government of the People," which added specific campaign promises including the dissolution of the police riot squad (Grupo Móvil), free distribution of a half liter of milk to all school children (an expansion of an already existing program), tax exemptions for small houses inhabited by their proprietors, a reduction of rents to 10 percent of income, and the termination of the readjustment of housing loan repayments in accordance with increases in the price index. Allende also announced "20 Basic Points" for agriculture, including an expansion of the cooperative system, the establishment of a national peasant council with representation from peasant organizations, and programs for housing, insurance, credit, and literacy for the rural population.[4]

The Alessandri program also spoke of social welfare and favored strong government, but it emphasized the need to reduce government expenditures and to release the energies of private enterprise, without abandoning the mixed economy that Chile had been developing over many years. Economic development and efficiency in public and private enterprise were seen as the means to achieve development, and too rapid redistribution of income was viewed as an impediment to economic growth, especially if such redistribution was carried out under the influence of the political parties and politicians.

The basis for the Tomic program had been adopted the preceding August, but its detailed formulation was not completed until mid-1970. By far the longest of the campaign documents, *El Programa de Tomic* took a position between those of the other two candidates but seemed to lean more closely to that of Allende. By the time it appeared, the qualifications introduced earlier by the Freiista sector of the party had disappeared. "Immediate and integral nationalization of copper with equitable conditions of payment" was described in the Tomic program as the source of "an important volume of additional resources for Chile." The program attacked the capitalist and "neocapitalist" system and proposed the creation of a "New Economy" which would be financed by a "Fund for National Independence and Development" based on copper revenues, individual and group savings, and new taxes on upper-income groups. The fund would promote, finance, and in some cases create worker enterprises, in both industry and agriculture, which would be managed and run by the workers, "both manual and administrative." The profits of the enterprise would go to the workers themselves or to the fund, when appropriate. Further anti-capitalist elements in the program included the establishment of increased controls over the banking system and the nationalization of foreign banks, as well as measures to prevent foreign firms from dominating the new Andean Common Market enterprises.

Like the other two candidates, Tomic proposed the reform of Chile's political institutions, but in this area, his program leaned more closely toward that of Alessandri. He proposed that the Congress vote a basic government plan as a whole—or, if it refused, that such a plan be adopted by plebiscite. Tomic repeated Frei's proposal to grant the president the right to dissolve the Congress once during his term, and hoped further to strengthen the executive by holding congressional and municipal elections at the same time as those for the presidency. Tomic and Allende's programs also agreed in calling for "the modernization and democratization of the legal system," including free legal services for the poor.[5]

The Second Round Proposal

In early 1970 there had been a brief flurry of interest in one of the proposals incorporated in the Tomic program—a constitutional amendment providing for a second round in the presidential elections. As things stood, it seemed highly probable that the Chilean electorate would divide almost evenly behind the three candidates. Both the Christian Democrats and the left had received about 30 percent of the vote in the 1969 elections. The National Party had received 20 percent, to which should be added the support of the right-wing Radical Democrats who had left the Radical Party after the elections, plus whatever additional support Alessandri personally could attract. Even in terms of program, it was difficult to know what issues were most salient to the voters. This was especially true of the Tomic voters. Was a vote for Tomic a rejection of Marxism, as the 1964 Frei vote had seemed to mean? Or was it a rejection of the present, still largely capitalist, economic structure of Chile, as the Tomic propaganda implied when it spoke of "the replacement of capitalism" as its prime objective? Frei's program, the "Third Declaration of Millahue" of April 1964, had spoken of "replacing the exploitation of capitalism with a social order which will overcome our present state of underdevelopments," but its specific proposals and Frei's conduct of his administration demonstrated that a drastic restructuring of industry was much less important to him than were reforms in other areas. The only way to determine how this appeared to the voter was to hold a second election between the two top candidates, as is done in France, whose multiparty and presidentialist system is similar to that of Chile.

The 1925 constitution provided that fifty days after the election, a joint session of both houses of Congress would formally ratify the election of the candidate who had received "more than half of the valid votes." However, if no candidate received an absolute majority, "the full Congress will choose between the citizens who have obtained the two highest pluralities." The formal text seemed to leave the Congress free to choose the second candidate, but Chilean tradition and, more important, the balance of political forces within the Congress had always favored the leading candidate. This time, however, it was not at all unlikely that if either Alessandri or Allende won, the Tomic forces might combine with the left or right to elect their own candidate if he ran second in the popular vote or another candidate who opposed the front-runner if Tomic ran third.

A bill for a second round could count on the support of the Christian Democrats, since they felt that if either Alessandri or Allende won and Tomic came in second, the chances were good that the opposition would vote for Tomic on the second round. The proposal was introduced, however, by the two MAPU senators, Rafael Gumucio and Julio Silva. Gumucio argued that a clear decision of a majority of the electorate was necessary to give the next president legitimacy. However, the right saw the move as an effort to block the election of Alessandri, since there were already rumors of negotiations between Tomic and Allende to support each other in the congressional run-off if Alessandri came in first. The director of the Electoral Registration Board spoke publicly in favor of the proposal, but *El Mercurio* (which in the last year had become more and more slanted in favor of Alessandri) denounced the scheme on the grounds that the present system had worked in the past and that the new proposal did not give enough time between rounds. The real reason seemed to be a suspicion of the move as a plot to deprive Alessandri of what *El Mercurio* thought was a certain victory. The Socialists probably opposed the measure because it might favor Tomic, and when the Popular Unity committee followed suit, it was clear that a proposal which would have avoided the chaos and violence of the following September and October had been rejected for trivial or partisan reasons.[6]

Campaign Issues and Controversy

In late February, Chile announced the signing of a trade agreement with Cuba, which marked the beginnings of a reversal of the decision to break relations with that country taken by the Alessandri government six years earlier. Rafael Moreno, the head of the agrarian reform agency, announced that Chile had agreed to sell three million dollars' worth of agricultural products to Cuba during the current year, and another eight million dollars' worth in 1971. The foodstuffs were to come from the agrarian reform *asentamientos* and cooperatives. The secretary general of the National Agricultural Society (SNA) complained that private producers had been excluded from the arrangement but approved the opening of trade relations as "very positive," thus indicating that Cuba was no longer an important internal issue in Chile.[7] Three years earlier, the establishment of a branch of the Latin American Solidarity Organization in Chile had created an uproar over Cuban subversion, but the clear failure of the Cuban effort to export revolution and Castro's own more recent turn to internal problems meant that Chilean-Cuban relations were likely to improve regardless of which candidate was elected in September.

In early March the Congress reassembled, and the first item before it was a move to impeach the minister of defense, Sergio Ossa, for a delay in distributing the wage readjustments to the armed forces which had been voted in late 1969. The impeachment of Ossa was the fourteenth attempted impeachment during Frei's term of office (many more were to be moved during the Allende regime), but until May 1969 there had never been any possibility that such an action would be successful, since Frei controlled the lower house, which was supposed to bring the indictment. In the Congress elected in March 1969, several impeachments had been attempted, but they had usually failed in the Senate for lack of the required absolute majority of the entire body. In late 1969, in the case of an attempted impeachment of the minister of the interior for taking control of the media during the Tacnazo, the Communists had once again supported Frei. In the Ossa case, however, all the opposition parties wished to demonstrate their support for the armed forces, and on March 19, the impeachment was easily adopted in the Chamber of Deputies. However, on April 4, the Senate failed by one vote (probably that of Senator Julio Durán) to support the indictment by an absolute majority, although the opposition parties appeared to possess exactly the number of votes (twenty-six) needed to carry the motion.[8] (Impeachment of cabinet ministers did not require a two-thirds vote as in the case of the president.) The renewed combination of left and right against the Christian Democrats reflected the increasingly intense partisanship in the country as the presidential campaign approached, and the impeachments provided precedents for those voted during the Allende regime.

The presidential campaign was not supposed to begin officially until early June, but the candidates were already making campaign speeches in various parts of the country. In the conservative rural area of Cautín, Alessandri was warmly applauded, while in the coal-mining area of Coronel and Lota (where there had been a ninety-six-day strike during his administration) strikes and violence attended his visit and he was declared *persona non grata* by the municipal councils. The sensationalist newspaper *Clarín* published an exposé of the substantial state pension which Alessandri, president of Chile's major paper company and a director of seven other enterprises, was receiving. The impact of the revelations—which were aimed at Alessandri's references to his "most modest" fortune when he announced his candidacy—was somewhat diminished by the publication of a full list of the politicians (including many leaders of the left) who received sizable pensions proportionate to their years and rank in the public service. *Clarín* continued to attack Alessandri, but mainly through references to his age and his private life as a bachelor. It called him "The Old Lady" ("La Señora"), said that the "mummies" on the right had hired a funeral cosmetician to improve the appearance of the candidate for "First Lady," and remarked that smoking was not permitted at Alessandri's public appearances since he might have a fit of coughing and that could be "very dangerous."[9]

The Assassination of Hernán Mery

At the end of April, the assassination of Hernán Mery, the head of the agrarian reform zone involving the provinces of Linares and Maule in the south, became the center of the next political controversy associated with the campaign. When the incident was debated in the Congress and that body resolved to send a letter of condolence to Mery's widow, Victor Carmine, a National Party deputy, exclaimed, "This is only the first death" and said, "If a CORA functionary came to rob me of my farm and animals, I would put a bullet in him and kill him."[10] That same afternoon, the National Party expelled Carmine from the party, but the incident considerably undercut the claim of the right to be the upholders of law and order in the face of the violence of the extreme left.

The threat from the left was underlined by the discovery at the end of May of a guerrilla training camp organized by the MIR in the southern province of Valdivia. On June 1 a branch of the National Bank of Labor was robbed for the second time, and on June 10 an armory was attacked in order to secure arms. The latter attack, however, was organized by the Vanguardia Organizada del Pueblo (VOP), a group which had split off from the MIR and a year later organized the assassination of one of Frei's former cabinet ministers. The MIR itself announced in June that it would suspend armed attacks and bank "expropriations."

The Schneider Statement

A week after the Mery incident, a statement by the army comander in chief, René Schneider, concerning the army's role in the election became a new source of dispute. Interviewed by *El Mercurio*, General Schneider responded to a question concerning the attitude of the armed forces toward a possible decision by the Congress to elect the runner-up as president in the event that none of the candidates received an absolute majority in September. Schneider replied, "Our doctrine and mission is support and respect for the constitution. . . . The Congress is sovereign in the case mentioned and our mission is to support its decision." What appeared to be a simple reassertion of the devotion of the armed forces to the constitution was taken in the highly politicized context of the election as an endorsement of a combination of the Christian Democrats and the left to deprive Alessandri of the presidency. *El Mercurio* denounced military intervention in politics, and rumors began to circulate that Schneider was plotting with Frei to cancel the September elections, turn over the presidency to Schneider, and call new elections in which Frei would be eligible to run.

Anticipation of the Congressional Run-off

For most of the rest of the campaign, political discussion centered around various combinations which were possible during the period between the popular election and the congressional run-off. In view of what happened after the election, it is interesting that only the National Party insisted that it would observe the tradition that the Congress should elect whoever received the largest plurality. Near the end of the campaign, Tomic asserted that he would also observe the tradition unless the difference between the two candidates was not substantial.[11]

Frei's possible candidacy was discussed because it was evident that despite the loss of support his party had suffered during his administration, and the noticeable lack of enthusiasm for the party's 1970 candidate, Frei retained very substantial popularity. A poll published in April 1970 showed 61 percent of those interviewed in Greater Santiago rating him as good or excellent, 29 percent as fair, and only 7 percent as bad or very bad.[12] Even allowing for bias in sampling, this was an extraordinary rating after six years, and it made Tomic's criticisms of Frei seem counterproductive in terms of electoral effect.

Frei's State-of-the-Nation Address

On May 21, Frei had his last opportunity to sum up the accomplishments of his regime. In education, Frei pointed to an expansion of 46 percent in enrollments, an increase of 14,000 primary- and secondary-school teachers, a reduction of the illiteracy rate from 16.4 percent to 11 percent, and an expansion of university enrollments by 124 percent. In housing, Frei listed the construction of 260,000 houses and 210,000 housing sites with sewage and electricity (the total of 470,000 "housing solutions" was well over the goal of 360,000 announced in 1964). Twenty-eight thousand families had received land from the agrarian reform program, and 100,000 farm workers were unionized (compared with 1,658 in 1964). Unemployment had dropped from 6.5 percent to 4.4 percent; exports had increased by 50 percent; and the balance of payments showed a large surplus.[13]

If the picture was so favorable, why was there such an acute sense of crisis in Chile? Frei attributed it to excessive partisan politics and to "a new feudalism—the struggle between interest groups to maintain and advance their economic and social position to the detriment of the others." He also blamed inflation (up to 30 percent in 1969 and rising at the same rate in 1970), which "is no longer an economic problem, but a political one," on the lack of self-restraint by interest groups and the parties, and on the incapacity of the nation's political institutions to adjust the objectives of the various groups to the country's economic capabilities. This led Frei to comment once again on the need for a stronger executive. Yet, only a few paragraphs later, he called for more organized participation by the people in politics, without observing that it was precisely because of the political and economic organization of the Chilean people that the various interest groups could exert such pressure on the economic system.

The message concluded with a defense of the "revolution in liberty" as a way to development "without coercion, political police, control of the media, rationing, or mass emigration." With clear reference to the MIR, Frei remarked, "I know that a revolution which is bloody, dramatic, and totalitarian, exerts a fascination for some . . . that there are those who cannot conceive of their country except as a copy of other models . . . but I am convinced that violence cannot rule in Chile. On the eve of an election of such importance, I am certain the Chileans will reject violence no matter from which extreme or for what reason it comes."

Frei's message elicited diverse responses. The National Agricultural Society referred to a report it had issued in March which observed that resettling 25,000 families was costing $12,000 per family—an amount which could have built 200,000 houses or irrigated 750,000 hectares of land. The SNA noted that the land had not really been redistributed, since most of the farm workers were on *asentamientos* and only a few had received actual title to the land. (The figures the SNA cited included, of course, the salaries of the administrators of the program, costs of unionization, and funds lent which were to be paid back.)[14]

Frei's speech was also used by *Punto Final,* the Castroite publication, as the basis of an extended comparison between Chile and Cuba, the aims of which were both to minimize the progress under the Christian Democrats and to undercut the adverse impact of Fidel Castro's speech at the end of the sugar harvest on July 26th, confessing to the economic failures of his regime. In a special supplement, *Punto Final* compared Cuba's progress since 1958 with Frei's claims of progress in Chile since 1964. In education, Cuba had risen from 634,881 students to 2,289,464, while Chile had gone from 1,840,000 to 2,689,000; and Cuba had increased the number of primary- and secondary-school teachers from 23,648 to 103,129, while Chile's increase had been from 36,835 to 51,015. Cuba had reduced its illiteracy from 23.6 percent to 3.9 percent, while Frei had claimed a reduction from 16.4 percent to 11 percent. In 1970, Chile had 7 percent unemployed (Frei had cited 4.4 percent for 1968), while Cuba had 2.9 percent. In the last decade, Chile had suffered a 248.6 percent inflation, while Cuba had none. Cuba had a higher minimum wage, free medical care, a far-reaching agrarian reform, and no strikes. Chile had had 1,700 strikes since 1965 and was paying out over $1 million each day to foreign enterprises in profits, interest, and amortization.[15]

The reference to strikes was, of course, an indication of the differences between the two regimes, one a dictatorship and the other a democratic system. *Punto Final* did not compare university enrollments, since the Cuban figure had actually gone down under Castro's rule. Nor was there any discussion of Cuba's foreign indebtedness, since Chile's increases in this area, principally for the expansion of copper production, did not begin to compare with the estimated $500 million a year of aid that the Soviet Union had given Cuba. Finally, it said nothing about economic growth, since the Chilean figures (5 percent average increase in GNP, or 2.5 to 3 percent per capita), low as they were in comparison with some other countries in Latin America, were still much higher than those of Cuba, which had had a negative per capita growth rate between 1960 and 1970.

The election, however, was not going to be decided on the basis of figures on education, literacy, or economic growth. A general sense of dissatisfaction with the continuing struggle to make ends meet, augmented by the continuing inflation and the atmosphere of tension produced by strikes and sporadic violence, was more important, despite the real improvement in living standards most Chileans had experienced. Most important of all was the personal factor, as Frei's continuing popularity in the face of dissatisfaction with his government demonstrated.

The Role of Television and Radio

Personal factors were even more important in 1970 than in 1964, because for the first time in a presidential election, television played a major role. The number of television sets in Chile had increased from 30,000 in 1964 to almost 500,000 in 1970, and all three TV stations ran programs geared to the impending election. The most important in terms of national impact and attention was "Decision '70," in which each of the three presidential candidates was interviewed on successive Sunday nights. Much more formal than U.S. interview programs, it consisted mainly of lengthy answers by the candidates to complicated questions put by a panel of representatives from various interest groups or parties. At the outset Alessandri refused to appear on the program, but finally, on May 24, he agreed to be interviewed. Unfortunately, he made this appearance after a tiring visit to a northern province of Atacama and a night without sleep. He thus appeared very tired, and just as he spoke of the need for strong government in Chile, the TV cameras, apparently operated by cameramen hostile to his candidacy, focused on an evident tremor in his hand. The incident gave symbolic expression to the doubts about Alessandri's age and health, and it was clear even in the pro-Alessandri polls that support for his candidacy was adversely affected. (Polls showed a 4 percent drop in Greater Santiago after the program.)

According to Chilean law, political propaganda cannot appear until ninety days before the election. In fact, radio "spot" advertisements had been playing regularly on the many Chilean radio stations earlier than that, and the campaign songs of the three candidates were already familiar to all Chileans. The Alessandri forces entitled their anthem, "Alessandri Will Return" ("Alessandri volverá") and emphasized that *tranquilidad* and *austeridad* would characterize a government headed by "Don Jorge." Tomic spots used the curiously negative theme "Not one step backward" (Ni un paso atrás). Allende's advertisements borrowed Castro's theme, "Venceremos," and referred to "Dr. Allende's" proposals for medical centers and free milk. In June, campaign posters on many houses supplemented the wall slogans which had already been painted for some time. Advertisements appeared in the newspapers sponsored by Chile Joven (Young Chile) with pictures of firing squads, the Iron Curtain, political imprisonments, and the heading: "This is Communism. Do you want this for Chile?" Thirty-second radio dramas that were sponsored by Acción Mujeres de Chile (Women's Action of Chile) called on women to elect "an independent government" and say "No! to systems that destroy liberty. No! to petty politics which leads us to disaster."

CIA Intervention

A similar propaganda campaign had been carried out against Allende in 1964. Both campaigns were financed, it was later revealed, by the U.S. Central Intelligence Agency. After months of debate as to whether to intervene, the interdepartmental Forty Committee, which supervises the CIA, had voted in March 1970 to authorize $125,000 for an anti-Allende "spoiling operation" of propaganda without giving direct assistance to any of the candidates. The funding was increased to $300,000 on June 27, at which time Henry Kissinger is supposed to have said of the decision, "I don't see why we need to stand by and watch a country go Communist due to the irresponsibility of its own people."[16] The State Department was critical of the operation and successfully opposed a request by the ambassador for approval of a $500,000 contingency plan to influence the congressional run-off which seemed likely in September.

The propaganda campaign was directed against both the Christian Democrats and the left. Hence, when it was proposed in the Chamber of Deputies that a congressional investigation be carried out of the "legality, finances, and persons or companies responsible for the activities of the organizations called Chile Joven and Acción Mujeres de Chile," both the Christian Democrats and the left voted in favor of the investigation, and a leading Christian Democrat, Bernardo Leighton, chaired it.

The work of the investigating committee (the right called it "The Dracula Committee" while the left termed the object of its investigations "The Campaign of Terror") was aided by access to the confidential documents of the advertising agency that was handling the Alessandri campaign. On July 21, 1970, five young men entered the agency in downtown Santiago and forced the manager at gunpoint to turn over all his records, including his financial accounts. Five days later, two journalists who said they had received the documents from "anonymous sources" gave them to the committee. They included the planning of the campaigns of the two organizations, records of meetings with leaders of the National Party, payments to the Catholic University Student Federation (which was controlled by the supposedly nonpolitical *gremialista* group) and to the polling organization, CESEC, as well as financial records indicating the receipt of funds from *El Mercurio,* from two U.S. banks, $5,000 from the Anaconda Copper Company, and a total of $600,000 from a mysterious "Charlie" who seems to have been a conduit for money from ITT and other U.S. businesses.[17] By the time the committee made its report in mid-August it was lost in the last-minute electoral propaganda, but it served to discredit a campaign which, effective as it might have been in 1964, was considerably less important in discouraging votes for Allende in 1970.

The situation had changed. Castro seemed a distant figure. Since 1968, by his own admission, his revolution had run into serious economic problems, and it had not been exported elsewhere in Latin America. The church, which had supported Frei in 1964, was now divided; if anything, the recent issues of the Jesuit magazine *Mensaje* seemed to favor Allende. (Allende repeatedly made a point of his being supported by "Marxists, secularists, and Catholics"—the last a reference to MAPU.) The U.S. embassy, in keeping with the "low profile" that Ambassador Edward Korry had espoused since his arrival in 1967, did not appear to be intervening and seemed to be divided between Tomic and Alessandri. It was clearly a different psychological situation from 1964, and *El Mercurio*'s efforts to use the invasion of Czechoslovakia and the brutalities of Eastern European communism as arguments against a vote for Allende seemed to be much less effective.

The anticommunism of the right was matched by equally extreme propaganda on the left. It attacked exploitation by capitalists and imperialists and drew on the abundant literature which had emerged in the last several years on Chile's *dependencia* on the United States. It also attacked the age, sexual proclivities, and authoritarianism of Alessandri and promised that if Allende were elected, low-income groups would benefit from the distribution of the fabulous profits being made by foreign companies and their domestic allies.

Between the two camps, the Tomic campaign failed to develop an equally persuasive set of issues. Until nearly the end of the campaign, Tomic attempted to project an image of himself as distinct from, and to the left of, Frei. In his public appearances he spoke in general terms about the necessity of replacing capitalism and ending foreign exploitation in a way that sounded much like Allende, but without Allende's common touch or the specificity of Allende's "Forty Measures." Television often hurt him because he sounded bombastic, and his reputation as a brilliant orator was turned against him as Chileans dismissed him as demagogic and verbose (*"bla-bla-miro"*).

The "law and order" issue continued to be important. On June 26, two students were killed and several injured in a confrontation with the Grupo Móvil, and this led to a series of student demonstrations and finally a general student strike on June 29. The government reacted by closing the schools early for winter vacation and decreeing a state of emergency for the Santiago province. The government blamed the MIR and the left wing of the Socialist Party, while the left used the issue of police repression to denounce the government. Particularly vehement was ex-PDC Senator Rafael Gumucio of MAPU, who claimed that the government was now responsible for thirty-five deaths, if one added those killed in various police confrontations with workers, students, and slum dwellers since 1966.

The sporadic violence continued up to election day, despite the MIR's announced policy of suspending its activities until that date. On August 25 and September 2, two Santiago banks were robbed (the MIR denied responsibility), and on September 2, just before the election, the main building of the Catholic University of Santiago was occupied by shanty-town dwellers demanding that the university turn over its land outside the city for the construction of homes.

The Situation Before the Election

In the final month of the campaign, after the order of the candidates' names on the ballot had been decided by lot, campaigning consisted of raising fingers corresponding to the ballot position of the favored candidate (one for Tomic, two for Alessandri, and three for Allende). An informal poll I conducted in Santiago revealed that most of those driving cars were in favor of Alessandri, while those in buses endorsed Allende. A similar division was evident in the posters outside houses. In the fashionable Barrio Alto, Alessandri's advantage was clear, while in the lower-class areas, Allende was the stronger candidate. The hills of Valparaíso were illuminated by neon signs for the various candidates, and there the contest was between Allende and Tomic (as the election results were to confirm).

The rallies for the candidates built up to final preelection "concentrations" in which each attempted to outdo the others and to match the massive outpouring for Frei in 1964. The first rally, for Alessandri, was held on the Sunday morning before the election in front of the railroad station and through the park beside the Mapocho River. It was difficult to estimate numbers, but they were substantial and by no means restricted to the upper and middle classes (as the anti-Alessandri cameramen of the state television network attempted to imply through selective filming of the participants). Alessandri spoke of the failure of socialism in Cuba, the crushing taxes and inflation, and the need for austerity, frugality, and sacrifice in government.

On Tuesday night, the Allende rally seemed to have a larger turnout, since it stretched down the length of Santiago's main street to the presidential palace and featured performances by dancers and singers on improvised stages every few blocks. Allende promised nationalization of big business, but protection for the small and medium enterprises. He asserted his belief in using legal means to bring about necessary changes, and he had special words of reassurance for the armed forces.

The Tomic rally on Wednesday night started later and seemed less well organized, but it turned out nearly the same number of people. (Comparisons were possible because it was held in the same location as the Allende rally.) Tomic spent most of his final speech attacking foreign companies and promising that the wealth of the country would stay in Chile if he were elected.[18]

After the Tomic rally, the right circulated stories that participation had been inflated by the left in an effort to prevent anti-Communist Tomic supporters from deserting their candidate in a "stop Allende" movement. The Alessandri campaign managers had been attempting to persuade independent Tomic supporters that he was likely to come in third and that they should therefore cast their votes for Alessandri if they wished to prevent a Marxist triumph ("If you want Allende to win, vote for Tomic"). Public wagers were made in newspapers that Tomic would be third, and the (mostly right-wing) polls were cited to demonstrate that a vote for Tomic would only help Allende.

All three candidates made last-minute appeals for the women's votes, whose importance is emphasized by Chile's separation of polling places by sex. Frei issued an endorsement of Tomic (he had been staying out of the campaign in accordance with Chilean tradition, but this had given rise to rumors that he really favored Alessandri), and a right-wing newspaper issued a list of 150 companies which would be nationalized by the Allende government. On September 4, Chileans went to the polls to choose between three clearly defined, ideologically distinct candidates for the presidency for the next six years.

The Allende Victory

In retrospect, it is difficult to understand why more students of Chilean politics had not predicted a victory for the left in 1970. Allende began with a reasonably solid 30 percent base in the two Marxist parties, and with his opposition split, he needed to pick up only a small proportion of the Radicals, left Christian Democrats, and independents to win. He had received 39 percent of the vote in 1964, and if he could maintain something close to that percentage six years later, he could win.

And that is what he did. After a tense evening in which tanks were called out as a precautionary measure, the official results announced shortly after midnight indicated a victory for Allende. He had received 36.2 percent of the vote to Alessandri's 34.9 percent, a margin of 39,000 out of 3 million votes. Tomic was a poor third with 27.8 percent. As expected, Alessandri had carried the middle- and upper-class areas of Santiago, Tomic had narrowly carried Valparaíso, and Allende had won in the copper-mining areas of the north, in the areas in and around Concepción, and in the extreme south. As in 1964, Allende had much more support among male voters (41.6 percent) than he had among women (30.5 percent).

There were some changes, however, in relation to 1964. In terms of percentages, Allende had a *lower* percentage of the vote in every province of Chile except Tarapacá and Atacama in the extreme north and Chiloé and Llanquihue in the extreme south. Alessandri's appeal and the progress of agrarian reform combined to account for Allende's loss in the percentage of the vote in the Central Valley provinces (such as Aconcagua, where he dropped from 47 percent to 39 percent among male voters and from 32 percent to 26 percent among women), where he had made substantial inroads in 1964. In the lower-class communes of Santiago, he received percentages very similar to those he had received in 1964, but the much higher voter turnout in these areas gave him an 86,000-vote plurality in the communes of San Miguel, La Cisterna, and La Granja in Santiago's Second District, which cut down the lead Alessandri needed in Santiago to counterbalance Allende's strength in Concepción and in the north. (Tomic's strength in Valparaíso, the only area where he won, prevented possible Alessandri pluralities there). In the working-class commune of San Miguel, Allende received almost the same percentages as he had received in 1964 (52 percent of the men and 40 percent of the women), but now nearly 113,000 voters turned out (compared with 95,000 in 1964), considerably more than the 93,000 who voted in the upper- and middle-class communes of Providencia and Las Condes. The one other area of Alessandri strength, the conservative southern province of Cautín, gave him an 11,000-vote plurality, but this was more than counterbalanced by Allende's strength in the northern copper-mining areas (except for the Anaconda mine at Chuquicamata, which Alessandri carried!).[19]

Thanks to the heavy Allende vote in working-class areas, Alessandri did not pile up the 100,000-vote plurality in Santiago which he had expected to carry him to victory; his plurality was only 41,000. Allende's margin of victory was provided by his 50,000-vote plurality in the province of Concepción, much of it from the depressed coal-mining areas of Coronel and Lota, plus his traditional support in the north. By comparison with 1964, Allende lost ground nationally, but his parties had solidified their hold on the working-class areas where he had already been strong in

1964. Still, he would never have come close to winning had it not been for the split in the opposition.

What can one say, then, about the theory that the Chilean voter moved left between 1964 and 1970—either because of "the failure of reformism," as the left put it, or because Frei was *El Kerensky chileno*, as the right would have it? The 1970 election results seem to demonstrate that a substantial part of the Chilean electorate (34.9 percent) moved right—away from the Christian Democrats to Alessandri and the classic rightist position he represented. Another part, in the lower-class working areas of Santiago, the unionized workers in the copper, coal-mining, iron ore, and meat-packing areas of the north, Concepción, and the extreme south, voted for Allende in roughly similar percentages in 1964 and 1970, with a sizable minority still voting for the other candidates.

The Radicals seem to have helped Allende only marginally, since traditionally left-wing Radical areas voted for Allende in both elections, while right-wing Radical areas supported Durán in 1964 and Alessandri in 1970. The other minor groups did not have any detectable influence, although it has been asserted that Chonchol appointees in agrarian areas assisted MAPU in getting out a rural pro-Allende vote.[20]

As the losers of election wagers paid off their bets, either in cash or in the traditional bath in the pool in front of the presidential palace on the day after the election, political analysts of various persuasions attempted to analyze the mistakes of the losing candidates. On the right, Alessandri's disastrous TV performance was the most frequently mentioned, while others cited his failure to make more specific campaign promises. This criticism was applied with more justification to the Tomic campaign. It had indeed failed to emphasize the genuine improvements in living standards under the Frei government, and it had not made specific promises of further improvements in the next six years. Tomic had devoted his speeches to attacking foreign capital and discussing worker control of industry—themes that did not loom large in the ordinary voter's consciousness.

Tomic's choice to pitch his campaign to the left also came in for criticism. It was argued that he should have appealed to Chile's large middle class and the basically anti-Marxist women's vote which had supported Frei in 1964, since the left vote was effectively controlled by the Marxist parties. However, apart from the effect such a move would have had on the left wing of his own party, it probably would only have reduced Alessandri's percentage somewhat without increasing that of Tomic by enough to defeat Allende. The only possible way that a more middle-of-the-road position might have defeated Allende would have been if Tomic had persuaded Alessandri to drop out of the race in his favor. However, given the strong support Alessandri demonstrated, especially in Santiago, it seems most unlikely that the rightist parties, by now thoroughly disillusioned with the Christian Democrats, would have taken such a step, unless it had been very clear that Allende was likely to win. Thus, it seemed almost predestined that there would be a three-way race, and the order of nominations (Tomic, Alessandri, and Allende) made this all the more certain. And once it was certain that there were three candidates, the chances of the left were greatly improved.

What would have happened had Senator Gumucio's proposal for a runoff been adopted? Almost certainly Alessandri would have won. It is true that one way of interpreting the results was to add the Tomic and Allende figures together and conclude that nearly two-thirds of the Chilean electorate wanted a change in the system. However, a breakdown of the Tomic vote, particularly its large female component, seems to indicate that a large proportion would have gone to Alessandri rather than to a Marxist candidate. (This is also demonstrated by the fact that even in the 1971 municipal elections, after an artificially stimulated economic boom and after six months of Unidad Popular had not brought the Marxist dictatorship that many feared, the Unidad Popular candidates fell short of an absolute majority.)

Were there alternative strategies that the Frei government could have pursued to avoid the debacle of 1970, in which the Christian Democratic candidate came in a poor third? Perhaps a more energetic effort by Frei to involve the Radicals in supporting his government would have made a difference, since it would have taken away what may have been Allende's margin of victory in 1970 (although it is by no means clear that this would have meant a victory for the PDC). As noted earlier, however, the Radical Party was identified with the right in the early years of the Frei administration, and an agreement with it would have infuriated the left sectors of the Christian Democrats. After 1967 the Radicals were clearly bent on an alliance with the Communists and Socialists.

Tomic, on the other hand, dreamed of an alliance with the Communists —presumably behind his candidacy since the Communists would know that a member of their party could never win. The Communists seem to have encouraged Christian Democrats to think along these lines in order to ensure that the 1964 de facto alliance with the right was not reestablished, but their links to the Socialists were so close and their opposition to the Frei government so intense that this never was even a remote possibility. The only other alternative was a Christian Democratic alliance with, or tacit support by, the right. For reasons of timing and the personalities involved, this was simply out of the question as long as Tomic and Alessandri had such powerful support among their respective backers.

What about an appeal to the unaffiliated voters beyond the parties? In Italy and Germany, despite the existence of multiparty systems, the

Christian Democrats had been able to maintain electoral success in this way for decades. The strategy would have been to attempt to counterbalance the loss of some middle- and upper-class voters, alienated by high taxes and the pace of reform, with newly organized groups among women, youth, peasants, slum dwellers, and (here there was a dispute within the party in 1966) workers. The problem was that many of the workers in key areas were already effectively captured by the Marxist parties through the trade unions, and many of the slum dwellers were organized by the left rather than by the Christian Democrats after 1964. The agrarian reform did not move quickly enough to add large numbers of voters to the Christian Democratic fold. (By the time the law was adopted in 1967, the left wing of the party, which was most active in this area, was beginning the agitation which led to the departure of the *rebelde* sector and of Jacques Chonchol in 1969). Young people were polarized by the climate of agitation and violence, and women, while more faithful to the Christian Democrats, were dissatisfied with the government's failure to control inflation.

Frei was right in perceiving that economic growth and control of inflation were central to the success of his program. It was economic success that gave the European Christian Democrats their electoral strength, and it was the continuing erosion of purchasing power that led many who had supported Frei in 1964 to look to another party in 1970 (although paradoxically, if Frei had been eligible to run, his personal popularity was so great that he is almost certain to have won). Despite the considerable improvement since 1964, the perennially dissatisfied Chilean voter was dissatisfied once again, and ready to try other solutions on the left and right.

A Revolution with Two Months' Notice

There had been a verdict—although not a very straightforward one—at the polls, but the provisions of the Chilean constitution made it clear that, as the Alessandri campaign headquarters immediately reminded the country, the election was not yet over. In fifty days, the Congress was supposed to choose between Allende and Alessandri. The combined votes of the parties in the two houses gave Allende 80 votes (out of 200) and Alessandri 45. The constitution provided that to be elected, a candidate must receive a majority of the votes in a secret ballot. The 75 Christian Democratic votes were crucial.

On the day following the election, Tomic went to Allende's residence and said to the journalists there, "I have come to greet the President-elect of Chile, my grand old friend, Salvador Allende." On meeting Allende, he was reported to have said, "You finally have won." However, the decision on how to vote in October was to be made by the Christian Democratic Party, not by Tomic. The PDC Council met on Monday and voted to reject as "illegitimate" the offer the Alessandri forces had made immediately after the election calling on "the democratic forces which are the vast majority to unite." However, they postponed a decision on how the party would vote in the Congress until a larger meeting of four hundred of the party leaders later in the month.

The reaction of financial circles and of the ordinary citizen to the likelihood of a Marxist president was an immediate rush on the banks and massive withdrawals from savings and loan associations. The black-market rate of the dollar skyrocketed, and members of the upper classes prepared to depart for other countries. (Augustin Edwards, publisher of *El Mercurio* and a special target of the left, quit the country immediately after voting.) But this was a revolution with two months' notice, so there was still time to attempt to prevent an Allende victory in the congressional run-off. The first step in this effort was another and more subtle approach by the right to the Christian Democrats.

On September 9, Jorge Alessandri issued an official statement in which he thanked those who had voted for him. Then, referring to the possibility of his being elected by the Congress in October, he said that during his campaign he had insisted that he would have to receive "an ample plurality," without which, regardless of the constitutional provisions, he did not feel he could exercise power. Then came the significant sentence, "In case of my election by the Congress, I would resign the post which would give rise to a new election. I can state categorically, of course, that I would not participate in that election under any circumstances."[21]

This was understood immediately as an offer to the Christian Democrats that if they cast their votes for Alessandri, new elections could be called in which Frei would be eligible to run. In the absence of a right-wing candidate he would be certain to be elected. This was backed up by a series of editorials in *El Mercurio* extracting suitably horrifying phrases from the Allende program, such as the provision for a single legislative "assembly of the people" elected at the same time as the president and subject to recall by the people, and the reorganization of the judicial system and the selection of the Supreme Court by this unicameral assembly.

Allende's response was given at a mass rally on Sunday, September 13. He referred to plots to subvert the country by bribing members of the armed forces and creating economic chaos. If "the people" were defrauded of their victory he said, the message would be spread through the trade unions, the Unidad Popular committees, and by radio. "Those who are insanely trying to provoke such a situation . . . should know that the whole country will stop, that there will not be a company, an industry, a workshop, a school, a hospital, or farm that functions—as a first demonstration of our strength. They should know that the workers will occupy the factories and the peasants the land, the white-collar workers [*empleados*] will be in the public offices awaiting the orders of Popular Unity."[22]

On Monday, September 14, the National Council of the Christian Democrats met. The party had three alternatives before it with respect to possible action in the Congress in late October. First, it could accept the Alessandri offer and attempt in effect to steal the election from Allende, while arguing that he had not received the support of a majority of the electorate. Second, it could abstain and thus allow Allende to be elected by the seventy-five representatives of the Popular Unity parties, with their abstentions counting for Allende in the second round as article 65 of the constitution provided. Third, it could support Allende, despite the serious reservations which many in the party had about the preservation of democracy under a Marxist president heading a coalition dominated by two Marxist parties.

A committee of PDC leaders had been meeting during the week after the election and had opted for the third alternative, with one important condition. In order to receive the support of the Christian Democratic representatives in Congress, Allende was to agree to the incorporation of a statute of democratic guarantees into the constitution as a set of amendments. This would specifically guarantee freedom of party organization, education (including the right of nonprofit private education to the continuation of the state subsidy it then received), trade unions, private associations, and the mass media, as well as the independence of the armed forces from political control. The Party Council approved the statute, and the next step was a lengthy series of negotiations with Allende and his Popular Unity coalition.

The U.S. Government, ITT, and Allende

In the meantime, outside pressures were also being exerted against the possibility of Allende's accession to power. Because of the publication in April 1972 of the confidential records of ITT concerning Chile, as well as subsequent investigations by various committees of the U.S. Congress, especially the Senate Select Committee on Intelligence Activities, a great deal is known about behind-the-scenes activity in both Santiago and Washington.

ITT and the Central Intelligence Agency had been in touch in June and July concerning efforts to prevent Allende's election. As it had done in 1964, the CIA had turned down an ITT request that it channel a "substantial" sum in ITT funds to the Alessandri campaign, but it had given the company advice on how to pass $350,000 of its own money and an equal amount from other companies to the candidate and the parties backing him.[23]

The contact between ITT and the U.S. government was renewed after the popular election in September. On Friday, September 11, an ITT representative telephoned Viron Vaky, an assistant to Henry Kissinger, then President Nixon's chief adviser on foreign affairs, and informed him that ITT was concerned about the fate of its Chilean investments. He added that Harold Geneen, chairman of ITT, wished "to come to Washington to discuss ITT's interest" in preventing an Allende victory, and that "we are prepared to assist financially in sums up to seven figures." "All along," he added, "we have feared an Allende victory and have been trying unsuccessfully to get other American companies aroused over the fate of their investments and to join us in pre-election efforts."

Vaky indicated that he would pass Geneen's message on to Henry Kissinger and would keep Geneen informed. According to the Senate testimony by Vaky, the message was never passed on to Kissinger, but a few days later, John McCone, former chief of the CIA and a director of ITT, came to Washington and personally relayed the offer to both Kissinger and CIA Director Richard Helms. Kissinger indicated that Geneen would hear from him, but no further contacts were made.

Immediately after the Allende election the CIA had produced an intelligence memorandum which concluded: "(1) the U.S. has no vital national interests within Chile. There would however be tangible economic losses. (2) The world military balance of power would not be significantly altered by an Allende government. (3) An Allende victory would, however, create considerable political and psychological costs," including a threat to "hemispheric cohesion" and "a definite psychological advance for the Marxist idea."[24]

The Forty Committee met on September 8 to discuss what actions should be taken in response to the Chilean election. According to the CIA memorandum of the meeting, Richard Helms reported that the Chilean congress was likely to vote for Allende and thereafter the opposition to him was likely to disintegrate. He added that a military coup "would have very little chance of success unless organized soon." The committee decided to ask the CIA and the ambassador for their views. Korry replied that "opportunities for significant U.S. Government action with the Chilean military are nonexistent," and the CIA answered that "military action is impossible; the military is incapable and unwilling to seize power. We have no capability to motivate or instigate a coup."

The Forty Committee met again on September 14 and decided to authorize a massive anti-Allende campaign involving propaganda and economic pressure. Reportedly over State Department objections concerning "subornation," it also approved a contingency fund of $250,000 for "covert support of projects which Frei or his trusted team deem important," including bribery of members of Congress. The committee decided to instruct

Ambassador Korry to try to persuade Frei to accept the Alessandri offer, and it authorized Korry and other "appropriate members of the Embassy Mission" to approach Chilean military officers with regard to their willingness to support Frei if he turned power over to them with a view to holding new elections. The instructions issued as a result of this meeting were presumably the basis of the ITT memos written from Santiago on September 17 which reported, in somewhat exaggerated terms, that on September 15 Ambassador Korry had received a message from the State Department "giving him the green light to move in the name of President Nixon . . . to do all possible, short of a Dominican Republic type action, to keep Allende from taking power." Following these instructions Korry reported to Washington that he had sent a message to President Frei through his defense minister that "not a nut or bolt will be allowed to reach Chile under Allende. . . . We shall do all in our power to condemn Chile and Chileans to utmost deprivation and poverty."[25]

On September 21, Korry reported that he had been told by a leading Christian Democrat that for "the Frei gambit" to work, General René Schneider, the army commander in chief, who opposed any interruption

Edward M. Korry, U.S. ambassador to Chile, 1967–71. (U.S. Department of State)

of the election procedure prescribed in the Chilean constitution, "would have to be neutralized, by displacement, if necessary." On September 25 he sent a cable to the State Department and Henry Kissinger in which he wrote, "I am convinced we cannot provoke a military coup and that we should not run any risks simply to have another Bay of Pigs. Hence I have instructed our military and [the CIA] not to engage in encouragement of any kind." Again on October 9 he cabled, "I think any attempt on our part actively to encourage a coup could lead us to a Bay of Pigs failure . . . an unrelieved disaster for the U.S. and for the President."[26]

Track II

Korry's messages were prompted by a suspicion that the CIA was "up to something behind my back," as indeed it was. Besides the pressure on Frei, the propaganda, and the economic program, there was an additional secret effort by the White House to use the CIA to provoke a military coup in Chile. This effort, known to the White House and the CIA as Track II, began on September 15 with a meeting of President Nixon, Henry Kissinger, Richard Helms, and Attorney General John Mitchell. Earlier in the day Kissinger and Mitchell had met Augustin Edwards, the publisher of *El Mercurio*, at the request of Don Kendall, president of Pepsi-Cola and a personal friend of President Nixon's, to discuss Edwards's view of the situation in Chile. According to Helms's handwritten notes, the participants in the White House meeting agreed that although there was only "one chance in ten" of success to "save Chile," it was considered worth the risk, and Helms was informed that $10 million was available to the agency to prevent Allende from coming to power. In July 1975 Helms testified to the Senate Select Committee, "If I ever carried a marshal's baton in my knapsack out of the Oval Office, it was that day." On September 21, the CIA chief of station in Santiago received the following instructions: "Parliamentary legerdemain has been discarded. Military solution is objective. . . . This is authority granted to CIA only, to work toward military solution to problem. . . . We were explicitly told that 40 Committee, State, Ambassador, and the Embassy were not to be told of this Track II or involved in any manner."

The CIA had already indicated its doubts about the possibilities of a coup, but it had been given an explicit presidential order and proceeded to attempt to implement it. On September 23, the CIA station in Santiago reported that the "constitutional coup" solution involving the cooperation of Frei and Schneider was by then "utterly unrealistic" since "neither will act," and that the only possibilities lay in "promoting an Army split" by "overtures to lower echelon officers." The cable specifically named General Camilo Valenzuela, chief of the Santiago garrison.[27]

Those overtures do not seem to have been made until early October. In the meantime, efforts continued on Track I, involving diplomatic, propaganda, and economic pressure. On September 16, Henry Kissinger, in a press briefing in Chicago, said that the election of Allende would create serious problems for U.S.–Latin American relations and might influence neighboring countries like Bolivia and Argentina in a leftward direction. On the basis, it seems, of Ambassador Korry's cables, he added that if Allende ("the man backed by Communists and probably a Communist himself") were elected by the Congress, he did not believe that there would ever be another free election in Chile. (In the three years following this statement, there were two general elections in April 1971 and March 1973 and four by-elections for deputies or senators.) But not all the U.S. pressure was against Allende. In his speech of September 13, Allende was able to quote a statement by the U.S. Ambassador to the Organization of American States, Sol Linowitz, urging respect for Chile's constitutional processes; and on September 23, the *Washington Post* published an article by Ralph Dungan, the former ambassador, urging that the United States remain neutral (it was described in the ITT papers as "Ralph Dungan's stupid piece").

On September 23, possibly as a result of U.S. pressure, the Chilean finance minister, Andrés Zaldívar, spoke to the nation about the serious economic crisis which had followed the election. He reported that before the election, the economy had been growing at a rate of 5 percent, with agricultural production expanding at a considerably faster rate (12 percent). The balance of payments was again favorable, with an expected surplus for 1970 of $200 million. Since the election, however, there had been withdrawals of nearly 1 billion escudos from the banking system and a reduction of 50 to 80 percent in sales of durable goods, of 60 percent in housing construction, and of 70 percent in automobile production. The government had supported the banks through the issue of currency by the Central Bank, and industry was able to secure credit to tide it over, but Zaldívar expressed the fear that this situation would release dangerous inflationary pressures as well as massive unemployment. Zaldívar's report was attacked by the left as a propaganda move directed against Allende's election by the Congress or as an indication that the Christian Democrats were preparing to turn over a bankrupt economy to Allende in November.

On September 29, an ITT memorandum from Buenos Aires reported that "President Frei wants to stop Allende . . . constitutionally, that is either through a Congressional vote upset or an internal crisis requiring military intervention." It claimed that "the armed forces are ready to move to block Allende—but only with Frei's consent, which does not appear to be forthcoming." The same memo described Frei as "double-dealing to preserve his own stature and image as the champion of Latin American democracy," telling "some of his ministers he would be quite willing to be removed by a military coup, while telling the military chiefs that he was totally against a coup." The memo also mentioned "undercover efforts . . . to bring about the bankruptcy of one or two of the major savings and loan associations" and asserted that "an economic collapse is being encouraged by some sectors in the business and political community and by President Frei himself."[28]

A memorandum written on September 29 to Harold Geneen by ITT's senior vice-president, Edward Gerrity, listed a series of steps "aimed at inducing economic collapse" in Chile to be taken by U.S. banks and companies at the suggestion of the CIA. The memo quoted Gerrity's CIA contact, William C. Broe, as saying that "of all the companies involved, ours alone had been responsive and had understood the problem." Gerrity also reported that other companies had told ITT headquarters that "they had been given advice which is directly contrary to the suggestions received." On October 7, the ITT Washington office reported that "repeated calls to firms such as GM, Ford, and banks in California and New York have drawn no offers of help."[29]

Witnesses from ITT later testified to the U.S. Senate Foreign Relations Committee that Anaconda and IBM had been contacted but that the whole plan for creating economic chaos in Chile had been rejected as "unworkable" and "self-defeating." Anaconda denied having been contacted by either the CIA or ITT, and although IBM admitted having been called by ITT on September 29, it asserted that there was no mention of a plan to put economic pressure on Chile. Representatives of four New York banks with interests in Chile also said they had not been contacted, and one even added that its lines of credit to Chile had increased from $68 million to $72 million from September to November.[30]

It appears, therefore, that very little, if anything, was done by ITT to follow up on the CIA suggestions, since they rightly assumed that such a program would have little chance of success. Furthermore, as Senate witnesses from banks and corporate institutions observed, in the event of an economic collapse in Chile U.S. investors would be likely to lose their investments or loans. Moreover, by the time the program was suggested, it was too late to influence the Christian Democrats, who had already begun negotiating with Allende to give him their support in the congressional run-off in exchange for the insertion of the statute of democratic guarantees in the constitution.

No more success was experienced by those in Chile who were attempting to promote violence so that the military might feel obliged to step in. On September 24, a mass rally was held by the Movimiento Patria y Libertad, organized by a young lawyer, Pablo Rodriguez, and committed to opposing Allende's accession to power. Rodriguez called on the Congress not to give power to "a third of the electorate" but to "give the people of Chile the opportunity to make an historic choice between freedom and slavery, between democracy and totalitarianism." Referring to a possible coup, he said, "Freedom will not be defended by a coup d'état [*golpe de estado*] but by a blow [*golpe*] for patriotism. Freedom will be defended with a blow in which youth, men, women, and workers—all go out into the streets to offer our lives if necessary because freedom must exist in Chile."[31] (In 1975 the Senate Select Committee revealed that as part of the Track II effort Patria y Libertad received $38,500 from the CIA during this period.)

A few days after the rally, a series of right-wing bombings and acts of terrorism broke out in various parts of Santiago. As the ITT observers reported at the time, they failed to arouse anything except rapid police action to arrest the bombers. The hope apparently was to provoke the MIR to return to its earlier ways, but the MIR had agreed with Allende not to engage in violence, and it was devoting its activities to infiltrating right extremist groups. As Arturo Matte had told the ITT representative in mid-September, "The Marxists will not be provoked. You can spit in their faces in the street and they'll say, thank you."[32]

The Statute of Democratic Guarantees

The real action which would determine the political future of the country was being taken in negotiations between the Christian Democrats and Allende on the subject of the proposed statute of democratic guarantees. In a long debate on September 30, the other members of the Allende coalition overrode the opposition of his own Socialist Party and voted to support the appointment of a joint committee to work out a text to be adopted by the Congress.

When the Christian Democratic Assembly met two days later, it debated two resolutions on the future conduct of the party. No one argued for the acceptance of the Alessandri proposal, since as the party president, Senator Benjamin Prado, put it, "This would amount to telling 35 percent of the electorate that you may participate in elections, but you cannot win. You can come in second or third, but not first." Prado referred to the Spanish Civil War, *la violencia* in Colombia, and Chile's own brief civil war in 1891 in arguing that such a course would lead to bloodshed and civil conflict in Chile. He reported that the PDC Council had rejected a proposal from the former minister of the interior, Edmundo Pérez Zujovic, that the PDC should seek to enter the Allende government as a way of assuring its adherence to democracy, and proposed that the party agree to support Allende on the condition that the agreed guarantees be voted as constitutional amendments by the Congress.

The more conservative members of the assembly, headed by Juan de Dios Carmona, the former minister of defense, made a counterproposal that contacts with the Allende coalition be broken off and that the PDC introduce its constitutional amendments on its own in the Congress. If the left supported them, the PDC Assembly should meet again to vote on support for Allende.

President Frei took no part in the deliberations, although it was assumed that he favored the second proposal. After thirty-two hours of discussions and debate, the assembly finally voted 271 to 191 to support the proposal put forward by the party leadership. But to satisfy the supporters of the second proposal, it agreed to follow the procedures described in the alternative resolution if negotiations with the Popular Unity representatives could not produce a common text.[33]

Following the meeting, three PDC representatives (Senator Renán Fuentealba and Deputies Bernardo Leighton and Luis Maira) met with three representatives from the Allende coalition (Senator Anselmo Sule from the Radicals, Orlando Millas, a Communist deputy, and Luis Herrera from the Socialist Party). In a surprisingly short ten-hour session, the joint committee was able to reach agreement on the text which was presented to the Chamber of Deputies on October 8, after being approved by both the Christian Democratic Council and the Popular Unity High Command (Comando). Within a week it had been adopted by the lower house and sent to the Senate. On October 22, two days before the Congress was supposed to vote on the presidency, the Senate gave its approval after a debate in which Salvador Allende gave his last speech as a member of the Chilean Senate, a body of which he had been a member (and several times an officer) for twenty-five years. Allende described the guarantees as "not only constitutional principles, but a moral commitment to our conscience and to history."[34] Following the provisions of the Chilean constitution, the amendments were approved once again by a joint session of the Congress on December 21, 1970, and after immediate approval by President Allende they became part of the constitution on January 9, 1971.

The principal change from the original Christian Democratic proposals related to the armed forces. The final text included the following sentence from the original draft: "The forces of public order [*la fuerza pública*] consist solely and exclusively of the armed forces and the corps of carabineros —institutions which are essentially professional, hierarchically organized, disciplined, obedient, and nonpolitical [*no deliberantes*]." However, a provision to which Allende had objected, that all promotions were to be made by the respective commanders, was replaced by the requirement that the assignments to posts in the military and the carabineros be restricted to graduates of the respective professional schools. Particularly important in view of later controversies were provisions that the mass media could be expropriated only by a law approved by an absolute majority of the full membership of each house of Congress (originally the PDC wished them to be constitutionally exempt from expropriation) and a prohibition against discrimination in the "sale or supply" to press, radio, and television of "paper, ink, machinery, or elements for their operation, or with respect to the authorization or permission necessary for their acquisition within, or outside of, the country."

The Statute of Democratic Guarantees was an attempt to bind Allende publicly and explicitly to what he had always supported verbally, the maintenance of the norms of pluralist constitutional democracy. It seemed to guarantee to the opposition that Chile could not become another Cuba by means of a similar process of takeover of the trade unions, universities, political parties, and the media. Of particular importance in the maintenance of these guarantees was the independence and commitment to the constitution of the armed forces, since both sides understood that if constitutional norms were respected, the military would remain out of politics, however much they might disagree with Allende's policies. If, on the other hand, the more extreme elements among Allende's supporters such as the MIR and the left wing of his own Socialist Party, were to bring about a situation in which Allende might be tempted to violate the guarantees, the military could appeal to the constitution in preventing or dissuading him from such a move.

In a lengthy interview by the *New York Times* published as the negotiations on the constitutional statute were taking place (and translated and republished immediately by the Chilean press), Allende rejected the accusation that his government would be totalitarian. Promising to form "a multiparty government, a nationalist, popular, democratic, and revolutionary government that will move towards socialism," he added, "For you to be a Communist or a Socialist is to be a totalitarian; for me, no. . . . I am a founder of the Socialist Party and I must tell you then that I am not a totalitarian. On the contrary, I think Socialism frees man." Allende claimed to have "no political agreement or understanding with the MIR" and attributed recent terrorism to the political right, which he said was ready to use "violence, economic chaos, or an assassination attempt. We will answer reactionary violence with revolutionary violence . . . [but] we reject terrorism in principle, by our very ideology, by conviction, and also out of a humanitarian spirit."[35]

The Viaux Plot

Allende was correct about the source of violence at the time he was speaking. As early as May 30, a right-wing conspiratorial group had formed around retired General Roberto Viaux. The plotters soon discovered that General René Schneider's constitutionalism was a major obstacle to a possible military coup. An ITT memo had already reported on September 17 that "one retired general, Viaux, is all gung-ho about moving immediately, reason or not, but General Schneider has threatened to have Viaux shot if he moves unilaterally." At the later judicial investigation, the plotters claimed that members of the Frei government knew of their preparations; and two prominent right-wing senators, Francisco Bulnes of the National Party, and Raúl Morales, recently expelled from the Radical Party, were also mentioned as having met with the conspirators.[36]

The CIA was probably already in touch, directly or indirectly, with General Viaux, despite a prohibition by Ambassador Korry against any contact with him or members of his family issued after Viaux led the abortive Tacna Regiment revolt in October 1969. However, the CIA lacked contacts with military officers on active duty and was compelled to make use of the military attaché at the embassy, who now began to work directly with the CIA. (It is not clear whether this was authorized by his military superiors, since the Senate Select Committee investigators were told that the relevant documents for September and October 1970 were missing from the Department of Defense files.) The agency preferred that a coup be carried out by officers on active duty, and the attaché was told not to contact Viaux directly. When the CIA Santiago station reported on October 6 that Viaux was ready to move on October 9 or 10, CIA headquarters requested that they try to stop "ill-considered action at this time," since an aborted coup would "vitiate any further more serious action."[37]

On October 5, the first of a total of twenty-one contacts was made by the CIA with Chilean officers on active duty. Officers from the army, air force, and carabineros were informed by the attaché that the U.S. government favored a military coup to stop Allende. They replied that General Schneider remained a principal obstacle to such action. An officer from the War Academy indicated, however, that he and his colleagues were studying plans to kidnap Schneider and asked whether the attaché could provide weapons which could not be traced to the Chilean military forces.[38]

By October 8, the CIA could inform the White House that it was in touch with two groups of plotters—presumably the Viaux group and another one, associated with General Camilo Valenzuela. The CIA had sent agents posing as third-country nationals to Chile in order to contact Viaux, and he had asked for an air drop of several hundred paralyzing gas grenades. A person who was probably one of the CIA emissaries was described at the later Chilean judicial investigation as having initially offered the group $1 million to purchase arms, and then withdrawing his offer in a way which led those involved to believe that "both the national forces and the countries already mentioned [the United States] did not really want a military coup." As an indication of its continuing support, on October 13 CIA headquarters authorized giving $20,000 in cash and a promise of $250,000 in life insurance to Viaux.[39]

The CIA continued to prefer a coup led by active duty officers such as

General Valenzuela, whom it quoted as describing Viaux as a "general without an army." Viaux himself had postponed his coup plans from the original date, and on October 14 the CIA Chile task force noted increasing coup activity on the part of an army general, a navy admiral, and the forces in Concepción and Valdivia. The names are deleted from the Senate Select Committee report, but the subsequent Chilean judicial investigation revealed that initial plans called for the kidnaping of the four top army generals so that General Valenzuela could succeed as army chief. Then a military junta headed by Admiral Hugo Tirado, head of the navy, was to take over, and Frei would go into exile. Six months thereafter, Frei would be permitted to run again in new elections as the candidate of all the "democratic" forces.[40]

On October 15, the CIA headquarters representative in charge, Thomas Karamessines, met with Henry Kissinger at the White House and summarized the new Chilean developments. It was then decided "to de-fuse the Viaux coup plot, at least temporarily." Viaux was to be told, "Preserve your assets. . . . The time will come when you with all your other friends can do something. You will continue to have our support." Henry Kissinger testified to the Select Committee that it was his recollection that Track II ended at this time, but the record shows something very different. On October 16, CIA headquarters cabled Santiago: "It is firm and continuing policy that Allende be overthrown by a coup." Viaux was to be encouraged "to join forces with other planners. . . . There is great and continuing interest in the activities of Valenzuela *et al.*"[41]

On October 17, two officers from the Chilean army and navy met with the U.S. military attaché and requested eight to ten tear gas grenades, three 45-caliber machine guns, and five hundred rounds of ammunition. On October 18, six gas grenades originally intended for Viaux were delivered to the officers, and a day later the machine guns and ammunition were sent by diplomatic pouch from Washington. That same day General Valenzuela informed the attaché that he and three other high-ranking military officers (the Chilean investigation mentioned Admiral Tirado, General Vicente Huerta of the carabineros, and General Joaquín García of the air force) were prepared to sponsor a coup. On October 19 and 20, two attempts were made at Valenzuela's behest to kidnap General Schneider, but both attempts failed —in the first case because Schneider left a reception in a private car with a police guard rather than in his limousine, and in the second because his abductors lost track of his car in Santiago traffic. The attaché had been authorized to pay $50,000 to Valenzuela which was to go to Schneider's abductors, but he had insisted that the kidnaping be completed before he paid the money. At 2 A.M. on October 22, the attaché delivered the three submachine guns and ammunition to a Chilean army officer associated with the Valenzuela group, but the guns were never used because the Viaux conspirators had finally moved into action.

The Death of General Schneider

The kidnaping attempts of the Valenzuela group had failed, but retired General Viaux had continued to press for a coup despite U.S. discouragement. On October 21 he sent a message to the other plotters in his group calling for a final attempt to abduct Schneider on October 22. The conspirators seem to have discussed the use of paralyzing gas for the kidnaping, but (possibly because the CIA had not delivered it to them) decided instead to capture the general at gunpoint on his way from his home to the Ministry of Defense. On the morning of October 22, as Schneider was being driven to his office in his official Mercedes, his way was blocked by four cars in front and one behind. Eight men leaped out and the windows of the Schneider car were smashed. Schneider pulled a revolver out of his briefcase, and one or more of the attackers fired several shots, four of which hit the general in the neck, arm, and stomach.[42] The attackers left the scene immediately after the assassination, and five of the group who were young right-wing ideologues from prominent families immediately fled the country. Schneider was taken to a hospital in critical condition and died three days later.

President Frei decreed a state of emergency and a strict curfew and placed the carabineros and armed forces on maximum alert. The authors of the plot were quickly identified and those still in the country apprehended. Whatever effect the plotters thought the kidnaping or assassination would have on the congressional vote, the result was to intensify the determination of the Congress, the armed forces, and the country to follow through with the constitutional processes. Two days before the assassination, Alessandri had asked his supporters not to vote for him so that "Salvador Allende may take office in a climate of tranquillity." The Radical Democrats decided to abstain, but the National Party maintained its determination to vote for Alessandri. On Saturday, October 24, Allende was elected by the Congress as president of Chile. There were 153 votes in favor, 35 votes against, and 7 abstaining.

Following the election, Allende received visits of congratulation from President Frei, from Cardinal Raúl Silva Henriquez, and from the chiefs of the three armed forces and the director of the carabineros. When General Schneider died the day after the congressional election, three days of national mourning were declared. Among the honorary pallbearers at the official requiem mass were the outgoing and incoming presidents of Chile.

The Frei Government: An Evaluation

As Eduardo Frei's term drew to a close, the uncertainty about the consequences of the election of a Marxist president overshadowed any effort to assess the "revolution in liberty" of the preceding six years. It was evident, however, that Chile was a very different country in 1970 from what it had been six years earlier. Copper had been Chileanized, with majority owner-ship in most cases in the hands of the state and with full nationalization of important mines planned for the near future. The role of the state in the promotion of development had been increased, both because of the expan-sion in state ownership (especially in copper, steel, and electricity), and be-cause of a large increase in the amounts collected in taxes, which had in-creased by 50 percent in real terms over the last six years. A strong agrarian reform law had been adopted from which 30,000 families had already bene-fited. Of greater importance to the well-being of the peasant population, peasant unionization had been legalized, nearly 150,000 farm workers had joined unions, and the minimum wage had been extended to the country-side. One hundred thousand small landholders had joined cooperatives, and 600,000 shantytown dwellers had their own organizations. The number of new houses had exceeded the 300,000 promised in 1964. Primary education had been expanded, and the Chilean universities had been restructured and their curricula modernized. If Frei were not turning the presidency over to his ideological opponents, it would seem that one could describe his regime as a considerable success.

That he was not able to pass the reins of office to a successor from his own party, however, was an indication of the problems of the democratic reformer in a free society who, as he carries out his reforms, finds increas-ing opposition from both left and right. Elected with a considerable popular mandate which was confirmed in a succeeding congressional election, Frei still had been limited both by the built-in restrictions of the Chilean consti-tutional system and by the incapacity of the country's fragile economy to respond to the demands placed upon it by its well-organized and increas-ingly numerous interest groups—aided and abetted by the opposition parties.

The left had attacked the Chileanization agreements for terms which were excessively generous to the U.S. companies and pointed out that Chilean *dependencia* had become intensified over the preceding six years because of the considerable increase in foreign investment in important sectors of the economy. It criticized the agrarian reform as aimed mainly at the *inquilinos*, the permanent workers on the Chilean *fundos*, but not assisting the *afuerinos*, the temporary farm workers who constituted the overwhelming majority of the Chilean peasantry. It accused the Frei regime of repression because of the "massacre" of eight copper workers at El Salvador in 1966 and nine land invaders at Puerto Montt in 1969, and maintained that no real changes had been made in the dependent capitalist economic system of Chile. Using these arguments, the left had been able to maintain its traditional hold on a majority of Chile's organized workers and to expand its support among the urban lower classes whom Frei had hoped to win over with his Promoción Popular program—for which he was never able to get congressional ap-proval.

The right, in turn, had made a surprising comeback from its electoral debacles in 1964 and 1965 by combining an appeal to the middle classes, burdened by the increased taxation necessary to finance the Frei government's reforms, with the projected presidential candidacy of a popular former president who was careful to appear to be above party and economic interest. It had reformed its political organization by creating a new and dynamic right-wing party and by criticizing the demagoguery of the Christian Democratic politicians for promising more than the Chilean economy could deliver. In the face of rising popular participation and an increasing number of illegal seizures of rural and urban land, universities, and occasionally factories, it called for the reassertion of governmental authority. It described Frei as a "Chilean Kerensky" who was preparing the way for a Marxist takeover. Right-wing politicians also criticized the agrarian reform as an expensive and inefficient program which did not get at the root problem—an inefficient agricultural system which had not been given sufficient price incentives to produce enough food for a largely urban society, necessitating the expenditure of scarce foreign exchange for food imports.

To the outside observer, it seemed that the criticisms of neither the left nor the right were really to the point. Frei's problems were twofold, arising from a combination of political and economic factors. From a political point of view he might have done more, particularly in the first half of his term, to give a sense of urgency to his reforms and, through dramatic speeches and charismatic appeals, to persuade Chileans to make the sacrifices they would entail, rather than expending all his energies on negotiations with the Congress on his legislative proposals. Even in the latter area, he might have given greater attention early in his term to reaching a general agreement with the Radicals. He seems also to have devoted too little time to mending fences in his own party in the 1966–67 period, before its internal divisions over the pace of reform became the basis of public disagreement. But within the limits of the Chilean constitutional system, Frei achieved everything he had set out to do in 1964—with the important exception of controlling Chile's perennial inflation.

Frei's political problems had important economic effects, since without an effective majority—both because of opposition control of important interest groups such as labor, and the lame-duck character of the Senate—Frei could not get support for inflation control programs such as the important bill for partial payment of wage readjustments in bonds. And once inflation got out of control in 1967–68, accompanied, as it happened, by a serious and prolonged drought, it was impossible to continue with reform at the same pace. The agrarian reform was slowed down, resulting in a break with the left of the party. Christian Democratic proposals for worker-controlled enterprises and banking reform were postponed indefinitely, and the dynamic image of the revolution in liberty was dissipated.

In retrospect, economics was central to Frei's success and to his failure. As long as he could keep the economy growing through a combination of public, private, and foreign investment, he could carry out his ambitious program of reform and redistribution. Once inflation outstripped growth, there was no margin left for reform, and the criticisms of left and right were able to elicit a greater response.

The special characteristics of the Christian Democratic ideology both broadened and narrowed the appeal of the Frei program. In 1964 it attracted the young, the professionals, women, reformist businessmen, and *técnicos* into a broad coalition. The Christian Democrats hoped to be able to expand their base among workers and peasants as well, and they were partly successful, as events in the Allende period would demonstrate. But the ideological character of Chilean politics and labor organization made it impossible for the PDC to make major inroads in the Marxist domination of organized labor and led to a proliferation of peasant groups, once peasant unionization was legalized. In addition, the PDC's Christian inspiration, however diluted, alienated Chileans of a more secular orientation, and there were suspicions that the party had not altogether lost the corporatist and paternalist elements exhibited by its parent organization, the Falange, in the thirties. (As the pluralist character of its labor, agricultural, and neighborhood committee programs indicated, even if party leaders had wished to pursue such a policy, it would have been impossible in the competitive party politics of Chile in the 1960s.)

Although different in their ideological inspiration, Frei's policies were similar to those of most governments in recent Chilean history in their populist orientation, based as they were on an appeal to an alliance of the middle and lower classes to secure national independence, popular participation, and social justice.[43] Like those before it and, as will be described, the Allende government that followed, the Frei government faced the problem of choice among competing goals of stability, growth, and redistribution, and had difficulty maintaining a balance among them. Like them, too, it was compelled to make difficult decisions as to which group would bear the costs of reform. Unlike the left, it did not single out the upper classes and the foreigners for condemnation but used primarily economic criteria to concentrate on selected areas for reform—the destruction of the latifundia in the countryside and the assertion of national control over the copper industry —where a national near-consensus could be achieved. The problem was whether to go further, into areas where the country was more deeply divided and where reforms would be much more costly, both politically and economically. Frei decided not to do so, since he believed that a reformist policy must proceed in a cautious, incremental fashion within the limits set by the political system of constitutional democracy, and by the need to maintain economic growth and avoid runaway inflation.

His successor, Salvador Allende, came into office with the same economic and political constraints upon his actions, but he was much less willing to take them into account. Initially he refused to recognize the economic limits on the implementation of his program, blaming Chile's inflation, inefficient agriculture and industry, and continuing social injustice on the capitalist system and promising a *vía chilena* to socialism which would solve Chile's economic problems through state ownership and central planning. When it became evident that the economic transition was not to be so easy, the maintenance of political legitimacy became central. In subscribing to the Statute of Democratic Guarantees, Allende had recognized the importance of Chile's political institutions. He seemed to have committed himself to a program which differed in degree but not in kind from that of Frei before him: securing legislative support in Congress for the deepening (*profundización*) of the agrarian reform, further state influence in basic industries, nationalization of copper, and increased welfare programs for the "marginal" groups. However, a part of his coalition—and Allende's own Marxist ideology—rejected reformism as "bankrupt" and refused to believe that "social democratic" solutions or the institutions of "bourgeois" democracy could produce the revolutionary transformations they desired. It appeared that at some point Allende would be forced to choose between a policy of populist nationalist legalism which attempted to secure broad national support for incremental but important social and economic changes, or a Marxist-inspired policy of class polarization which would sooner or later lead to a violent confrontation. As it turned out, he tried to pursue both policies at once—with tragic consequences for himself and for Chile.

CHAPTER SEVEN

Allende's First Year:
The Illusion of Success

The tense atmosphere in which it took power did not augur well for the future of the Allende regime, yet it performed surprisingly well during its first year. The climate of violence diminished although it did not disappear; the inflation subsided and the economy rebounded, producing a generalized sense of prosperity; most of the promised changes in industry (nationalization or state control of key sectors) and agriculture (elimination of large landholdings) were carried out—and all this despite external pressure from the United States and the open or tacit opposition of half the Chilean population. Beneath the surface, however, were the same economic and political constraints which had limited Frei, now accelerated in their effects and accentuated in their intensity by the polarizing policies of the government and the deepening opposition of the non-Marxist sectors. It was only after nearly a year in office, however, that serious economic problems (inflation and shortages) and political difficulties (solidification of the opposition, particularly on the part of the middle class, and a decline in legitimacy) began to emerge.

Allende was formally sworn in as president of Chile before a vast crowd which included representatives of the diplomatic community and of countries such as North Korea, North Vietnam, East Germany, China, and Cuba with which Chile did not yet have diplomatic relations. Although a Marxist, a Freemason, and a nonbeliever, he then attended a solemn ecumenical *Te Deum* ceremony of thanksgiving in the Santiago cathedral. President Nixon's failure to send a congratulatory telegram was duly noted by the press, but Charles Meyer, assistant secretary of state for Latin America, represented the United States and subsequently had a lengthy private interview with Allende, who emphasized his continuing desire to maintain good relations with the United States.[1]

Despite earlier rumors to the contrary, Fidel Castro did not attend the ceremony. Castro was reported to have sent a letter to Allende, advising him to continue to sell copper in the dollar area and to discourage skilled technicians from leaving Chile. He also warned Allende that good rela-

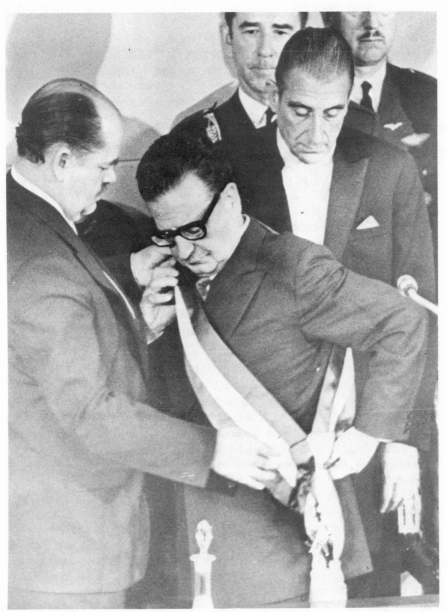

Salvador Allende receives the presidential sash from Senate President Tomas Pablo on November 3, 1970, as outgoing president Eduardo Frei looks on. (Wide World Photos)

tions with the military were essential, at least until he had consolidated popular support, and indicated that he would not visit Chile until Allende felt the time was ripe.[2]

The new cabinet, formed a few days before Allende took power, was careful to maintain a balance among the parties in his coalition. Socialists were appointed as ministers of housing, interior, and foreign affairs, the latter two of great importance. The Communists received the ministries of finance, labor, and public works. The key economy ministry went to an independent, the head of the Institute of Economics of the University of Chile and a long-time functionary in the U.N. Economic Commission for Latin America, Pedro Vuskovic; while the Radicals received mining, education, and defense (the last, so as not to put a Marxist in charge of the armed forces). The minor parties received other appointments, the most important of which was that of Jacques Chonchol of MAPU as minister of agriculture. In accordance with the agreement between the Popular Unity parties at the end of 1969, each minister was assisted by a deputy who represented a different party in the coalition, a move aimed at preventing the establishment of party fiefdoms in the ministries. Allende pointed with pride to the presence of four workers in his cabinet, the ministers of finance, public works, housing, and labor—a first in Chilean history.

The Vía Chilena

At a formal ceremony for the new president and foreign dignitaries in the National Stadium on November 5, Allende delivered an address which was his first opportunity to announce the policy of his government. He opened the speech with a tribute to the memory of heroes of the past, among whom he included President José Manuel Balmaceda, who had committed suicide in 1891 during the civil war between the forces backing the president and those behind the congress. Allende described Balmaceda as a "combatant in the patriotic effort to recover our national wealth from foreign capital."[3] He referred to the victims of police action in the José Maria Caro settlement during the Alessandri administration and to "the dead of El Salvador and Puerto Montt, whose tragic death testifies why we have come to power." Then, quoting from a reference in the writings of Friedrich Engels to a possible "peaceful evolution from the old society to the new in countries where the representatives of the people have all the power and in accordance with the constitution can do what they desire when they have the majority of the nation behind them," Allende announced, "This is our Chile. Here, at least, the anticipation of Engels is fulfilled." Promising the destruction of large landholdings (*latifundios*) and of monopolies, a reform of the tax system, and the nationalization of banking and credit, as well as of foreign-owned industries and mines, he declared that his reforms would be carried out in "our own Chilean way [*vía chilena*]," "the way to socialism in democracy, pluralism, and liberty," since "Chile is unusual in possessing the social and political institutions necessary to carry out the transition from backwardness and dependency to development and autonomy by way of *la vía socialista*." Allende called on foreign observers to bring back to their countries a vision of a Chile in spring and in celebration (*en fiesta*) determined to take the "democratic way to socialism." In a later press conference he promised that "ours will be a revolution, Chilean-style [*a la Chilena*] with red wine and *empanadas* [meat pies]."

Relations with the United States

Allende had referred in his speech to Chile's determination to recognize the governments with which it did not have diplomatic relations. One of his first acts in office was to reestablish relations with Cuba on November 12; two months later, the opening of an embassy in Peking was announced. Yet Allende did not withdraw Chile from the Organization of American States as he had threatened to do during his campaign, and his foreign minister, Clodomiro Almeyda, gave an interview on November 22 which emphasized Chile's wish to maintain friendly relations with the United States "despite the existence of present or potential areas of conflict." Almeyda expressed Chile's determination to end the "dependent relationship of Chile's economy with respect to interests which are not ours," but he distinguished Chile's opposition to imperialism, which he defined as "economic dependence and the reflection of that dependence on the political and cultural levels," from anti-Americanism, and declared that Chile was determined to act "in accordance with Chile's interest, coordinating this interest with that of the other people of Latin America and the Third World."[4]

The distinction between anti-imperialism and anti-Americanism was valid if U.S. policy also made a distinction between the interests of U.S. business and the strategic and foreign policy interests of the U.S. government. However, the two had been closely identified in the past, and this identification had been given legislative sanction in a number of ways. One was the Hickenlooper Amendment to the Foreign Assistance Act, which provides that the U.S. president "shall suspend" all foreign aid to any country which "has nationalized or expropriated or seized ownership or control of property owned by any United States citizen or by any corporation, partnership, or association not less than 50 percent beneficially owned by United States citizens" and has not within six months taken "appropriate steps, which may include arbitration, to discharge its obligations under international law toward such citizen or entity, including speedy compensation for such property in convertible foreign exchange." The Hickenlooper Amendment had not been invoked when Peru nationalized an Esso subsidiary in 1968, but Peru had a military and not a Marxist government, and the United States was able to cite the fiction of continued appeals to Peruvian courts as "appropriate steps." What would it do if Allende expropriated over a billion dollars' worth of U.S. investment property in Chile which included the remaining partial ownership of three copper companies; a minority interest in a nitrate company; three iron mines owned by Bethlehem Steel; ITT's majority interest in the Chilean telephone company and its ownership of a cable company, a telephone equipment plant, and the two leading hotels in Santiago; subsidiaries of Coca Cola, General Motors, Ford, Esso, Mobil, General Cable, Dupont, and Pfizer Chemicals; branches of First National City Bank and the Bank of America; and Dow Chemical's part interest in a petrochemical plant?[5]

U.S. investments were protected by the U.S. government in another way. The Alliance for Progress had considered private investment a major source of development capital, but in view of the instability of Latin America it was considered necessary to develop a government-financed program to insure investors against the hazards of expropriation and revolution. Such insurance was only available after an agreement between the United States and the host government, but such an agreement had been concluded with Chile and many companies had taken out policies. As of January 1971, this insurance program was to be handled by a new Overseas Private Investment Corporation (OPIC) created by the Foreign Assistance Act of 1969, with initial capital of $40 million plus income from its insurance fees, and OPIC officials feared that it might be necessary to go to Congress for considerable additional funding if Allende nationalized the U.S. investments, particularly the copper mines, without compensation.

A third way in which business and the U.S. government were interrelated was through the general commitment of the U.S. diplomatic establishment to protect the interests of U.S. citizens overseas, and included under that rubric were U.S. companies and investors. On the other hand, the Roosevelt administration had exerted only limited pressure on the Cárdenas administration in Mexico when it nationalized the oil companies in 1938, and the recent Peruvian oil case was even more striking since, in effect, it involved disregarding a mandate by the U.S. Congress to take action.

It was important, then, what methods the Allende government would take to end "dependency," and especially what the nature of the compensation arrangements would be. Allende came into office with a large reserve of foreign exchange some of which could be used for compensation; but if the ideologues in his own party (and some in the Christian Democratic Party as well) had their way, not one centavo was to be paid for what was viewed as decades of exploitation and robbery.

Legal Loopholes

Allende's policy on nationalization of both foreign and domestic firms was cautious but determined. Making a careful calculation of the political and legal situation, he decided to distinguish between copper nationalization, where he knew he could get support outside his own coalition, and the other takeovers, where it was doubtful that he could get a legislative majority. (In late 1970, his Popular Unity coalition had 20 senators out of 50 in the upper house and 60 deputies out of 150 in the Chamber of Deputies.) He resolved, therefore, not only to nationalize copper by law, but to do so by constitutional amendment, so that there would be no doubt about either the legality of the move (which in effect nullified the contractual agreements so laboriously worked out with the companies under the Frei regime) or the national and legislative consensus in favor of it.[6] In the other areas mentioned in his program—basic resources, domestic and foreign monopolies, banking, and foreign trade—he would have to use other means.

Those means were not lacking to a determined president. Under a decree law adopted during the hundred-day government of Carlos Dávila (decree law 520 of August 30, 1932) and succeeding legislation in 1952 and 1966, the president had the power to "requisition" temporarily industries and businesses which produced or distributed articles "of basic necessity" if they ceased production, failed to produce articles "of primary necessity" contracted by the government, or "unjustifiedly" produced deficiencies in supply to the population. Under the same decree law the government could permanently expropriate the firms for similar reasons, but outright expropriation required full payment in cash and approval by a government board of legal advisers, and it was used in only seven cases during the Allende period. Article 5 of the law, which had created the Directorship of Industry and Commerce (DIRINCO), also authorized "intervention" (temporary takeover of management) of industries which were not functioning because of labor disputes. Government control of prices and wages could also be manipulated to keep prices down and raise wages, thus bringing industries to bankruptcy or to such deep indebtedness to the state banking organs that a takeover was simple. In addition, the State Development Corporation (CORFO), which had been created by the Popular Front government in 1939, could simply persuade owners and shareholders to sell out to it if the terms were favorable.

The use of these "legal loopholes" (*resquicios legales*; the term he initially used was *recursos legales*—"legal resorts") to carry out the Popular Unity program in the absence of a congressional majority was recommended by Allende's legal adviser, Eduardo Novoa. From the outset, these legal provisions—originally intended in most cases to authorize only temporary government takeovers of private firms—were employed by the Allende administration to establish permanent state control of many sectors of the economy.

Purchase of shares from private stockholders was the tactic decided upon for the takeover of the twenty-six private banks (two of them U.S.-owned), which were a priority target of the government's nationalization program. The Central Bank was to extend a special credit line to CORFO in the amount of 400 million escudos which would then be used to offer bank shareholders especially attractive terms for selling to the state. The Banco Continental was sold to the government soon after Allende came to power, and three others were taken over in the same period. However, the largest private bank, the prestigious Banco de Chile, resisted the effort and even collected funds to outbid the state in the purchase of shares from private holders who wished to sell. The Allende government used a different method in taking over another large bank, the Banco de Edwards which, because of its connection with the wealthy Edwards family, the proprietors of *El Mercurio*, was a leading target of left-wing criticism. There was no likelihood that the Edwards bank would sell out to the government, but the new directors of the Central Bank discovered shortly after Allende's accession to office that the bank had violated banking regulations in guaranteeing a $7,350,000 loan from U.S. banks to a Chilean automobile company. The guarantee had not been approved by the supervisor of banks as required by Chilean law and was in excess of the limits on foreign loans to domestic industries. Citing the need to have full access to the bank records for possible prosecution, the bank was "intervened" in 1971, and in July 1972 it was formally dissolved.

The government's explanation for its effort to take over the banks was that they represented a "concentration of economic power" which the Popular Unity parties were determined to break. Because so much control of credit was in the hands of a few private banks, loans could be given to large firms on terms which, owing to Chilean inflation, amounted to a negative interest rate. Smaller firms and individuals could not get credit or were forced to pay usurious rates. In addition, credit was centralized in Santiago, so that in 1965, Santiago received 62.5 percent of all credit. The Allende government argued that access to credit should be based on national priorities and made available to individuals and smaller firms.[7]

Divided Christian Democrats

Banking reform had been an issue within the Christian Democratic Party during the Frei administration. In 1967, when the *rebelde* sector controlled the party, they had supported a bill providing for stricter government control of private banks and giving the president a majority of the membership of the directors of the board of the Central Bank. However, lacking Frei's support (he felt other reforms were more important and that this one would have adverse effects on an increasingly weak economic situation), and with stronger rival proposals made by the left, the bills were never adopted. After the *rebeldes* left the party in 1969 to form MAPU, the *tercerista* sector which formed the main Tomic support in the party also continued to press for banking reform. The Tomic program had called for the board of directors of the Central Bank to be composed entirely of representatives of the state, and it had demanded that voting of shares in the private banks be democratized, that credit be assigned on a more "democratic and decentralized" basis; and that foreign banks be nationalized.

The Christian Democratic attitude toward the banking policy of the new government illustrated a more general policy problem for the PDC. Should it support the Allende government on major issues where the two groups agreed and deemphasize the differences between the two programs? Or should it follow a policy of "constructive opposition" which would point out where it felt Allende was making errors while being prepared to vote for him when his policy coincided with that of the party? The difference was one of emphasis, but it also reflected personal and ideological differences between Frei and Tomic.

The December 12 meeting of the party's National Assembly was rapidly shaping up as the arena in which these differences would be brought out into the open. The pro-Tomic sector, most of them former *terceristas*, had begun calling themselves the Christian Left (Izquierda Cristiana), a term Tomic had used to describe his position during the campaign. Their candidate for the post of party chairman was the perennial party chief, Senator Renán Fuentealba, while the group closer to Frei appeared to favor his former finance minister, Andrés Zaldívar. Yet, the split between the two groups was not so wide as it appeared to be in the progovernment press, which was already furiously attacking Frei in the hope of dividing the party. Even before the assembly met, the outgoing president of the party, Benjamin Prado, announced that the Christian Democrats would not support the Allende banking policy, since they felt that an extension of the power of the Central Bank and the nationalization of foreign banks was sufficient to achieve the government's announced purposes without requiring a takeover of all private banks. (Probably also in the background was a fear of what government control of all banks would do to PDC financing.)

The expected confrontation of views did not take place. Frei spoke only briefly on the need for party unity and left the meeting. Tomic defended his program and denied reports that he and Allende had agreed before the election to support whoever came in first in the election against a bid for congressional support by Alessandri, if he came in second. Most of the assembly was spent attempting to work out a unity list of candidates for party office. The two lists headed by Fuentealba and Zaldívar remained in competition until 3 A.M. on December 13, but finally at 5 A.M. a common set of officers was arrived at, headed by Senator Narciso Irureta, who was not a clear partisan of either group. The newly elected president announced that the Christian Democrats would support the Allende proposals which were "positive" but would be "inflexible in our opposition" to proposals which jeopardized fundamental values.[8]

The new officers announced that they would support the proposed nationalization of copper and favored the same step for foreign banks, but they proposed that the private banks be transformed into cooperatives. They also endorsed the extension of agrarian reform, but denounced the illegal land seizures (*tomas*) then spreading through the southern part of the country. In the parliamentary debates in succeeding weeks, the Christian Democrats also expressed their concern for what they called the political persecution of PDC members in the public administration, and they added an amendment to the budget bill to forbid the removal of career civil servants from their posts.

The position of the Christian Democratic Party was thus not finally resolved at the December assembly. The differences between the two wings were papered over, and the entire question of party policy toward the Allende government was postponed. It was clear, however, that time would be on the side of those who wished to take a harder line with the government.

The Christian Democrats were under increasing pressure from their membership in the large public administration sector to protect them from ouster. The Tomic policy had been discredited by his poor showing in the election, and it was obvious that Frei, the proponent of the harder line, was likely to be a very strong contender in the 1976 presidential elections. The attacks on Frei forced the party together rather than splitting it apart. Last but not least, as yet another election approached (the municipal elections scheduled for April 1971) the party members knew that a split at this time would be electorally disastrous. (The same concern for party unity in the face of impending elections had postponed the departure of the *rebeldes* for at least a year in 1968 and 1969.)

Economic Policy

The impending election was also a very important consideration in the minds of government economic policy makers. When the budget of the new government was presented to the Congress at the end of November, it was apparent that the Allende government had embarked on a program of income redistribution which was aimed at securing increased electoral support in April. The lower limit for exemption from the wealth tax was raised by a third, thus exempting 35 percent of those who had paid the tax earlier; the income tax exemption was raised to two times the minimum wage, exempting 20 percent; the property tax exemption was also raised, benefiting 330,000 small property owners; and widows with small taxes still owing were forgiven. The extra readjustment payments to the armed forces which had been promised by the Frei government over a period of two years were to be paid in full, and the number of inspectors for the tax returns of the wealthy was expanded. The wage readjustment to compensate for the 1970 inflation, expected to reach 35 percent, was skewed in favor of the poorest wage earners. Those making the minimum wage were to receive a 40 percent wage increase, those earning between one and two times that wage were to receive a 38 percent increase, and those above that level were to receive 35 percent. Minimum pensions and social security payments were increased by two to three times the inflation rate. One hundred thousand houses were to be constructed in 1971, public works were to be expanded to provide increased employment, and the government proposed to enter into production contracts with private industry in order to promote economic expansion.[9]

The budget presented by the finance minister to cover these expenditures contained a planned deficit of 4 billion escudos which he defended, in terms that sounded more Keynesian than Marxist, as necessary to stimulate the economy and to employ unused capacity. When the actual deficit for 1971 later turned out to be three times that amount, the government blamed the Congress for rejecting a new excess profits tax and for reducing proposed wine, cigarette, and property taxes. However, the government had also counted on considerably increased receipts from a crackdown on tax collections and from the profits of "monopolist" enterprises which it had taken over. In fact, evasion of income and sales taxes continued; and the nationalized industries, if they had made profits before their takeover, ceased to do so thereafter as a result of the pricing policy pursued by the Allende government, a decline in labor discipline, and a lack of expertise by the new government managers appointed after the takeovers. (In accordance with an agreement signed between the government and the CUT on December 7, 1970, those managers were responsible to an administrative council composed of five representatives elected by the workers, administrators, and technicians, and five members appointed by the government, with the government-appointed manager casting the deciding vote.)

Deficit financing of the budget and the Area of Social Property (APS) could be carried out for a time without producing the inflationary effects feared by critics of the government. The government simply printed more money, while at the same time it strictly enforced price controls and attempted to persuade industrialists that they could make up for their reduced profit margins in the increased sales which would result from lower prices. Government economists assumed that inflationary pressures which such expansion might produce could be avoided because Chilean industry was operating at an estimated 32 percent below capacity.

For the first year of the Allende regime, this policy worked. Inflation was kept down to 3.4 percent in the first three months of 1971, compared with 16 percent the year before. This seemed to be an astounding performance, but the opposition continued to predict impending financial disaster from the government's policy of increasing the money supply (25 percent between January and March 1971) and promoting a consumption mini-boom without any concern for investment or long-run economic growth.

The opposition was also able to attack the effect of the new government's policy on Chilean international reserves. At the time of Allende's accession to office, Chile had foreign reserves of $343 million. The new government's economic policy led to a rapid decline in that figure. The price of copper, a principal source of foreign exchange, had dropped back part of the way from the unusually high levels it had reached in the last years of the Frei administration, and copper production did not expand as expected, owing both to strikes and inefficiency and to uncertainty about the future. In keeping with the Popular Unity program, the Allende government declared that it was abandoning the Frei policy of frequent and gradual devaluations which had kept the official rate roughly constant in real terms. This meant that the escudo rapidly became overvalued; thus, there was little incentive to export, while it was to the Chilean importers' advantage to buy foreign goods—although it was necessary to get an import license to do so. Chilean tourists soon found that while the amount they were permitted to change into dollars for foreign travel was somewhat reduced, vacations in Europe or the United States were cheap because of the exchange rate (at least until the first devaluation of the tourist rate in late July 1971). A further drain on the balance of payments came from initial down payments in hard currency for certain of the nationalized companies, such as Bethlehem Steel's iron ore plants, which CORFO purchased in early 1971.

Despite the government's assurances that foreign investment which brought new technology and aided Chilean development would be welcomed, the dollar drain was not balanced by new investment. Clearly, no foreign investor would risk his capital in what he took to be a hostile environment.

One of the most important drains on the Chilean balance of payments was the importation of food. Certain types of agricultural produce, mainly tropical fruits and coffee, had to be imported in any case, but Chile was not even self-sufficient in what it did produce. Despite the previous government's efforts to limit consumption of beef through meatless days and campaigns to persuade Chileans to eat fish and other types of meat, it had always been necessary to import considerable quantities of beef from Argentina. The effort to maintain and increase agricultural production had been both a goal of, and a limit on, the agrarian reform program of the Frei government. Now, with a government strongly committed to extending agrarian reform, and with the expansion of demand for food which resulted from the redistribution of income to the poor, problems in the agricultural sector appeared inevitable.

Land Seizures

An additional adverse factor was the climate of violence in many rural areas, especially in the southern provinces of Cautín and Malleco. Shortly after Allende came to power, a wave of strikes and land seizures swept through the south. According to police figures submitted to the Chilean senate, 1,458 farms were occupied illegally between November 1970 and December 1971. While it would be an oversimplification to attribute these exclusively to "outside agitators," there is no doubt that the seizures were encouraged by the rural branch of the MIR, the Revolutionary Peasant Movement (Movimiento Campesino Revolucionario, MCR). In some cases, the government "intervened" the seized land and appointed an administrator to run it, hiring those who had occupied the land along with their friends and relatives, and paying them the minimum wage with government bank credits. In other cases, it simply let the peasants remain without disturbing them or persuaded them to leave peacefully. In only very rare cases were troops sent in to remove the occupying peasants (and students); its own propaganda against preceding governments had taught the Allende government what political capital could be made of casualties linked to the government. The agrarian reform agency continued to expropriate landholdings above the legal limit of eighty "basic" hectares or its equivalent and, in the case of some of the seizures, used the provisions of the 1967 law for the expropriation of "abandoned" farmland to take over smaller landholdings after they had been occupied.

The situation in the southern provinces was made more complicated by demands of some of the 300,000 Mapuche Indians living in the south for recognition of their rights to land taken by settlers in the past. The Allende government was sympathetic to the Mapuche demands, and the president had appointed a Mapuche as head of the government Office of Indian Affairs.

In January, Jacques Chonchol announced that he was moving the Ministry of Agriculture to the south in order to supervise and control "the accelerated agrarian reform." Chonchol announced the expropriation of 32 large estates in January, but at least 260 farms had already been seized by the time he spoke, 50 of them by Mapuche Indians. After a meeting with the president of the National Agricultural Society (SNA), Allende issued a statement that "medium and small farmers" had nothing to fear, but the seizures were not limited to farms in excess of the legal limit. Indications that the peasants had received paramilitary training from the MCR further contributed to the tension—and to production problems.[10]

Given all these factors, it may have appeared puzzling that final agricultural production figures for 1971 did not decline, but showed a 5 percent increase. The puzzle is resolved, however, if the difference in the seasons in the Southern Hemisphere is kept in mind. The spring planting had already been finished before Allende took power, and the 1971 harvest took place early in the year, before the revolutionary ferment had reached many areas. The 1972 harvest dropped by 3.6 percent, and in 1973 the decline was a catastrophic 16 percent—influenced by a nationwide strike at the time of the planting in October 1972. Meanwhile, food imports rose from $168 million in 1970 to $260 million in 1971, $383 million in 1972, and $619 million in 1973.[11]

Violence or Bourgeois Legalism?

The question of whether the revolution was to proceed by violence or through legal processes had not been completely resolved by Allende's election. In December the president had pardoned the MIR members who had been imprisoned for terrorism and bank robberies, but they continued to announce their belief that the transformation of Chilean economic and social relations would have to be carried out by force.

In January, the Socialist Party Congress called for a new political structure based on worker control and elected Senator Carlos Altamirano as its secretary general. Altamirano had made no secret of his belief that at some point the Allende government would have to violate "bourgeois" legalism and constitutionality. Because of his dislike for the outgoing secretary general, Aniceto Rodriguez, Allende supported Altamirano, although by conviction and political circumstances he himself favored the use of the legal process. This was the main emphasis of his published conversations in January 1971 with Regis Debray, although Allende's opponents could point to his statement in the Debray interviews that his differences with apostles of violence like Guevara were only "tactical," his admission that he was observing legality "for the time being," and his assertion that he had agreed to the statute of democratic guarantees as a "tactical necessity."[12] Allende's position in favor of legality was endorsed by the Communist Party, which repeatedly attacked the position of the MIR and its allied MCR. As early as December 1970, the ideological differences between the two groups led to physical conflict in Concepción, where a street brawl between adherents of the MIR and members of the Communist Ramona Parra Brigade led to the death of an MIR student. The Concepción clash was an exception; in general there was little urban violence at the outset of the Allende regime. In the many instances of occupations of housing and apartment buildings, the government did not send in troops or police to dislodge the occupants, but sought to persuade them to leave by finding housing for them elsewhere. The Grupo Móvil, or government riot squad, had not been dissolved as Allende had promised in his campaign, but only integrated into the Prefecture of Special Services. However, until late in 1971, it was not called into action to deal with street disturbances. Beginning in 1972, it was often in evidence.

Copper Nationalization

In the Congress, the opposition complained about the rural violence and the government's toleration of extremist groups, but most of the legislators' attention during the opening months of 1971 was devoted to the government's proposed constitutional amendment to nationalize the copper mines. The original government draft of the amendment provided that compensation would be paid on the basis of the original cost of the investments less amortization and depreciation as well as deductions for installations in bad conditions and for "excess profits" since the "Nuevo Trato" agreements of 1955, when the government first began to keep accurate records of company profits. The amount was to be set by the controller general with a provision for appeals to a special Copper Tribunal. Compensation was to be paid over thirty years at an interest rate of 3 percent.

In the Congress, the government bill was only slightly modified. The major changes were the explicit assumption of the Chilean copper companies' past debts, including those connected with the 1967 and 1969 Chileanization, and the addition of a provision that compensation would be based on book value (rather than original cost) minus deductions. While the amendment specifically disallowed a revaluation made by Kennecott in connection with the 1967 Chileanization, the book value provision eliminated possible controversies about the original cost of investments made since 1908 by Kennecott and since 1922 by Anaconda. In addition the final text left it up to the president, not the controller-general, to determine the amounts of excess profits, and provided that the president's decision was not subject to review by the tribunal. The president was authorized to deduct "all or part" of the excess profits "considering" the average profitability of the foreign enterprises' worldwide operations, the agreements on maximum profits that Chile had made (for example, Decision 24 of the Andean Pact which set 14 percent as the maximum profit for foreign firms), and the 1969 tax regime on profits derived from unusually high world market prices.[13]

For reasons noted earlier, the copper nationalization was important for its effects on relations with the United States. However, the use of the complicated and lengthy procedure of a constitutional amendment meant that a possible confrontation on the issue between Chile and the United States was avoided for the time being and that a national consensus was developed in Chile behind the takeover. After the changes just described, all the opposition parties supported the nationalization, and the constitutional amendment was unanimously adopted on July 11, 1971.

After the 1973 coup, it was revealed that in 1971, with State Department approval, the U.S. ambassador had offered Allende a compromise arrangement on compensation according to which the U.S. companies would be paid in twenty- to twenty-five-year bonds guaranteed by the U.S. Treasury. This would have given the bonds an immediate market value and, assuming that Chile kept up payments, would have saved the Overseas Private Investment Corporation the insurance claims it would have had to pay the companies. According to Ambassador Korry, after an initial expression of interest the offer was rejected by the Allende government because of the opposition of Senator Altamirano and the Socialist Party.[14]

The 1971 Municipal Elections

The cancellation of a visit to Chile by a U.S. aircraft carrier in February 1971 may have been prompted by a desire not to assist Allende just before the April municipal elections in Chile, which were being billed as a referendum on his government. In the election campaign the opposition parties attacked the proposals in the Allende program to replace the Congress with a unicameral legislature and to establish neighborhood tribunals to try petty offenses. Modeled on similar institutions in East Germany, the neighborhood tribunals were to be composed of two locally elected officials and one government appointee who were to try petty crimes such as drunkenness and child neglect. The elected members were to be nominated by "labor or social institutions," and the tribunals could impose punishments up to a year of "rehabilitation" labor—two provisions which the opposition parties saw as susceptible of being used for partisan purposes. They also criticized the recent government takeover of the largest publishing conglomerate in the country, Zig-Zag, now renamed Quimantú, after government-approved wage increases had brought the firm to bankruptcy. (Zig-Zag published the respected news magazine *Ercilla,* and when the government acquired the company, it promised to respect *Ercilla*'s editorial independence. Despite the fact that it was printed on a government-owned press, *Ercilla* continued to follow an independent line; in the last part of the Allende regime, it took a strongly antigovernment position.)

The opposition found it difficult to attack the government's economic policies in the midst of a mini-boom stimulated by government spending, because at least as long as the inflation rate was held down, it meant a real increase in purchasing power for lower-class groups. Ex-president Frei could attack the groups in the Allende regime that were trying to install "a regime that will make democracy impossible," but the ordinary Chilean citizen saw no evidence of restriction on civil liberties or political freedom of the sort that had been predicted in the *El Mercurio* advertisements before the 1970 presidential election. The government concentrated all its efforts on securing as large a popular endorsement as possible in the April elections, counting on a combination of economic prosperity and the absence of the totalitarian repression predicted by the opposition to bring it a massive mandate similar to that which Frei received in the congressional elections of 1965.

The mandate Allende received in the April municipal elections was considerable, but not as large as some of his supporters had hoped. According to the usual system of computing percentages, the Popular Unity candidates received 49.7 percent of the vote (including 1 percent for Raúl Ampuero's Popular Socialist Union, which supported the government although not formally a member of the Popular Unity coalition) and the opposition 48 percent, with the rest going to independent candidates or invalid or blank ballots. By omitting the invalid and blank ballots, the government newspapers were able to claim an absolute majority of 50.86 percent, and it was an indication of the continuing press freedom in Chile that about half the papers published in Santiago used the first figure and the other half the second.

Even if he had not received an absolute majority, the election was a considerable victory for Allende. His electoral coalition had received nearly 14 percent more of the vote than he had received in the presidential elections seven months earlier. The "presidentialism" of the Chilean voter which had given Frei's Christian Democratic Party 42 percent of the popular vote and a majority in the lower house in 1965 enabled Allende's Socialist Party to increase its electoral percentage by 10 percent over 1969, so that it received 22.3 percent of the vote. The Communists increased their percentage by 1 percent to 16.9 percent, and the Radicals dropped sharply from 13 percent to 8.1 percent (although if the 3.9 percent registered by the right-wing Radical Democrats who had left the party after the 1969 elections is added to the latter figure, the drop is not so precipitous).

The opposition, on the other hand, also found some encouraging signs in the municipal election figures. Although the Christian Democrats had dropped an additional 2 percent since the 1970 election to 25.7 percent, they were still the largest party in Chile; and Carmen Frei, the former president's daughter, received 60,000 votes to achieve the largest electoral majority in the country. The chairman of the National Party polled the second largest number of votes, almost as many as Carmen Frei. The Nacionales received a larger percentage of the votes (18.5 percent) than did the Communists, and combined with their Radical Democrat allies nearly equaled the total polled by the Socialists. Owing to the differential effects of the electoral system, the opposition won 914 seats in the municipal councils to 766 won by the government coalition.[15]

In the breakdown of the election by commune, it seems clear that major progress was made by the Marxist left among lower-class urban women. In the working-class commune of La Granja, for example, the women's vote for the Socialist and Communist candidates increased from 45 percent in the 1967 municipal elections and 46 percent in the 1969 congressional elections to 58 percent in 1971. In Barrancas, it jumped from 32 percent in 1967 and 42 percent in 1969 to 54 percent in 1971; while in Cisterna, the increase was from 29 percent in 1967 and 31 percent in 1969 to 45 percent in 1971.

Young people between the ages of eighteen and twenty-one were voting for the first time in this election, but it was not easy to determine their electoral behavior or its significance. Only an estimated fifty thousand voted, because many had neglected to register.

The Popular Unity coalition was also victorious in a by-election to fill the senatorial seat in the extreme south left vacant as the result of Allende's election. In a three-way race which pitted a Socialist against a Christian Democrat and a right-wing Radical Democrat, the Socialist won an absolute majority of the votes (51 percent), a result which had generally been expected since the depressed areas of the far south had consistently supported the Marxist parties in recent years.

Christians for Socialism

In the period immediately following the election, an intense debate ensued within the Chilean Catholic church on the moral and religious implications of socialism in general, and of the socialist policy followed by the Allende government in particular. As noted earlier, Allende had been careful during his campaign to note the presence of committed Christians in his coalition. Cardinal Raúl Silva Henriquez, the Chilean primate, had strictly observed the constitutional procedures in 1970 and waited until the congressional election of October 24 before paying a formal visit of congratulation to the president-elect. Full religious ceremonies (which in keeping with post–Vatican II ecumenism included representatives of the other religious communities in Chile) in the Santiago cathedral and elsewhere in the country had accompanied the installation of Allende in the presidency, and the Pope had sent a message of congratulation. In turn, Allende made it clear that his government would continue to provide the financial support given by previous governments to nonprofit private schools, including those operated under religious auspices, and to the Catholic universities. Thus, there was no occasion for church-state conflict of the sort that had broken out in the early days of the Cuban Revolution when Castro took over the Catholic school system. On the contrary, some Catholics began to ask if it was not their duty as Christians to support the efforts of the Allende government to alleviate poverty and improve the lot of the workers and peasants.

This was the conclusion of a meeting of eighty priests in April 1971 on "The Participation of Christians in the Construction of Socialism." In the press conference which concluded their meeting the priests quoted Cardinal Silva's statement at the time that Allende had become president, "There are more of the Gospel's values in socialism than in capitalism," and called for collaboration between Marxists and Christians in building a new society because "socialism opens up the hope for the fulfillment of man." In what appeared to be an appeal to Christian Democratic workers, the priests observed that "significant groups of workers who favor change and even look forward to benefiting from it are not actively joining the process. The unity of all workers, however, whatever be their party option, is necessary at this unique opportunity offered our country to rid itself of the dependent capitalist system."

The letter was supported by twelve members of the Department of Theology of the Catholic University, but it elicited criticisms from other theologians in the university. One, for example, while agreeing that "the capitalist system is inhuman and execrable," accused the eighty priests of confusing "socialism and Marxism, social ownership of the means of production with state ownership, and cooperation with Marxists in specific projects with collaboration with them in building a Marxist state."[16] The controversy culminated in the issuance of a carefully worded document by the Chilean bishops entitled "The Gospel, Politics, and Socialisms." The use of the plural in referring to socialism was designed to emphasize that there were many ways in which the goals of socialism could be achieved, and the Marxist-inspired approach of the Allende government was not the only or morally obligatory way to reach the worthy objectives of social justice and equality. The bishops stated that while "a fully humanist socialism" was one of several possible political conclusions that Christians might draw from the message of the gospel, certain aspects of Marxism—its materialism, atheism, and fostering of class hatred—were opposed to Christian teaching. They concluded that the decision on whether to support a specific application of socialism in Chile should depend on a judgment as to its advantages and disadvantages, its appropriateness at this point in the nation's history, and the "real guarantees that a given form of socialism offers as to its implementation in accordance with the principles of a humanism which is in accord with the Gospels, i.e., a humanism which is open to all the dimensions and rights of man and society which the Gospels proclaim."[17]

Influenced by the theological discussion, but distinct from it, a similar debate was going on within the Christian Democratic Party. At the Party Congress in 1966, a debate had taken place on whether to describe the party's doctrine as "communitarianism" or "communitarian socialism." The former view had prevailed, but the *rebelde* sector and the leaders of the party youth organization had insisted that the party's anticapitalist position required it to define itself as socialist, since in reality there were only two options open as the basic economic forms of a modern society—either private profit or public ownership. The presidential program of Radomiro Tomic had taken a strongly anticapitalist position but had never formally described itself as socialist, maintaining the traditional "third-positionism" of the party in theory while moving it much closer to a socialist position in the specific measures it recommended. After the municipal elections, it became apparent to the Christian Democrats that it was now necessary to make the change that the left wing of the party had been urging for so long. In addition, this was seen as a concession to the Izquierda Cristiana group, which wanted a clearer definition of the left position of the party in the face of the attacks in the government press. At the full plenary of the Christian Democrats in early May, therefore, the party policy vote stated: "Christian Democracy is a revolutionary movement. Therefore, we are struggling for a socialist, communitarian, democratic, popular, and pluralist society inspired by the lasting values of Christianity. . . . We do not accept statist socialism because we believe that changes are for the benefit of the people and not of the state."[18]

Still unresolved was the continuing policy question of the extent to which the PDC would be willing to collaborate with the Allende government. The May council meeting had adopted a policy of "constructive opposition" and cited the party's support of copper nationalization and of the Allende budget and wage readjustment proposals as evidence that the party was willing to cooperate in "everything that contributes to the national interest." However, the group closest to Frei was already looking to a return to power in 1976 under his leadership. For this, the support of the right would be helpful, so the political options over the next several months were seen in terms of whether the party would move closer to the Allende government or would develop a formal or informal relationship with the rest of the opposition (the two rightist parties, the National Party and the Radical Democrats) resulting in a relatively unified opposition movement.

From a political point of view, Allende could only hope to have a workable majority in Congress by encouraging a split in the Christian Democrats that would bring the more left-oriented sectors into the coalition supporting his government. When the Tomic wing proposed that the Popular Unity coalition support a "progressive" PDC candidate in an impending by-election in Valparaíso, Allende was initially favorable, but he later turned the idea down because it was opposed by the Political Command of his Popular Unity coalition. Allende may also have been counting on a constitutional reform to create a unicameral legislature and new elections to bring him a working majority. The possible success of this approach had been somewhat dimmed, however, by the results of the municipal elections. Striking as was the increase in popular support for Popular Unity, especially for his own Socialist Party, it still did not have the absolute majority necessary to approve a constitutional amendment to reorganize the legislature. What it showed was an electoral deadlock which reinforced the opposition of president and Congress (and in the minds of many government supporters, the judiciary as well) and the equipoise of physical force (the possibility of a military coup, on the one side, and of a massive general strike called by the unions and possible civil war, on the other) to produce a "political stalemate" (*empate político*).

The Second Model of Transition to Socialism

In many other Latin American systems, this polarization of forces would have led rapidly to breakdown, but in the highly sensitized politics of Chile, it led to a careful calculation of how far each side could move. As the political actors became more and more aware of the development of this process in mid-1971, they came to different conclusions about the future evolution of Chilean politics. The economy was still feeling the prosperity resulting from the Allende government's economic policy, but it was clear to the opposition that in the near future the cushion provided by the foreign reserves inherited from the previous administration and by the unused capacity in the economic system would disappear and that massive inflationary forces would quickly destroy the euphoria built up since November 1970. On the government side, it was assumed that a policy designed to help the workers, the peasants, and the lower classes would receive their electoral support and that, therefore, the Chilean way to socialism could, in Allende's words in his 1971 message to Congress, be "built along democratic, pluralist, and libertarian lines." Chile would thus constitute "a second model of the transition to a socialist society," an alternative "anticipated by the classics of Marxism" to the dictatorship of the proletariat employed in the Soviet Union and in China. Because of Chile's "open institutional system," Allende asserted, Chile could adapt its economic and political structures to "the new reality." "At an appropriate time," Allende promised, he would propose "the replacement of the present liberal constitution and bicameral system with a constitution of a socialist orientation and a single chamber." This would be carried out with "full respect for legality" while recognizing "a premise that is artificially denied by some—the existence of classes and social sectors with antagonistic and opposing interests and the existence of unequal political power within the same class or sector."[19] Thus, while pledging to respect Chilean legal institutions, he continued to adhere to the Marxist conceptions of the class struggle which had led him three months earlier to contrast his position with that of his predecessor by asserting, "I am not president of all Chileans."[20]

Allende's promise to carry out the transition to socialism by legal means appeared in a somewhat different light three days after his address, when the Marxist-controlled trade unions of eight major textile enterprises seized the plants. A day later, the minister of economics announced that the plants would be requisitioned because of a "breakdown in supply" of articles of "prime necessity." There was no indication that the takeover was to be temporary; the management of the factories was reorganized on the basis of the December 1970 agreement with the CUT in a way that appeared to indicate that requisition meant permanent transfer to the "Area of Social Property." Indeed, any attempt to return the textile plants to their proprietors, most of them of Middle Eastern origin and often attacked as exploiting monopolists in the leftist press, would have met strong opposition from Allende's coalition and from the workers themselves.

In his May 1971 address, Allende was particularly critical of the illegal seizures of agricultural areas and housing sites, emphasizing the danger to Chilean "institutions, our legal order, political liberty, and pluralism" posed by "violence against the decision of the people." This description attempted to portray the threat of violence as coming exclusively from the right, but since the murder of General Schneider the extreme right had been in disarray and its leaders in prison or under indictment. At the other extreme, however, dissident sectors of the extreme left continued to inisist that only violence could overthrow bourgeois institutions.

Assassination and Polarization

On June 8, one such group, the Organized Vanguard of the People (VOP), carried out Chile's second political assassination since the 1970 presidential elections, when Frei's former minister of the interior, Edmundo Pérez Zujovic, was slain by gunmen. Allende and the progovernment press initially blamed the killing on the CIA, but the VOP involvement became clear when a VOP "death list" was published which included the U.S. ambassador and Cardinal Silva. The police moved in on the group quickly, and on June 13 the leaders of the group were killed in a shootout with detectives from Investigaciones. The circumstances of the shootout led to rumors in opposition circles that the VOP leadership had been killed rather than captured because of a desire to avoid the possible revelation of links between the group and the Allende-appointed director of Investigaciones, Eduardo Paredes.

The assassination of Pérez, the father of seven children and a close friend of Eduardo Frei's, impelled the Christian Democrats into an increasingly oppositionist stance. The party blamed the "climate of hatred" sown by the government media and demanded stronger measures against armed extremists on the left. It came as all the parties were engaged in preparations for yet another electoral referendum on the government's actions, a by-election to elect a deputy for Valparaíso on July 18. The government coalition nominated a Socialist labor leader, Hernán del Canto, and counted on the division in the opposition to bring it victory as it had in 1970. However, the right-wing parties, recognizing that Valparaíso was a fiefdom of the Christian Democrats, did not nominate a candidate and left their adherents with the clear understanding that they should vote for the Christian Democrat, Dr. Oscar Marín. The Christian Democrats insisted that they had made no deal with the right but indicated that they "would reject no support, no matter where it came from, provided that it accepted the progressive and democratic content of Dr. Marín's program." They called on all those who rejected "violence and hatred, sectarianism and illegal armed groups" and "the lying and defamation which continue to be expressed in various organs" to vote for the Christian Democratic candidate.[21]

The government, on the other hand, denounced the "collusion" (*contubernio*) between the Christian Democrats and the right. When Valparaíso suffered a severe earthquake in early July, Allende rushed in emergency assistance and extended housing loans (financed by the Interamerican Development Bank) with a largesse not unrelated to the impending election. The election resulted in victory for the Christian Democrats by a very narrow margin, once again demonstrating how evenly balanced political forces were in Chile. Marín received just over 50 percent of the vote, while del Canto received 48.5 percent, with the remaining votes invalid or blank. The election was taken as a great victory for the opposition; but, in fact, nothing had changed since the April municipal elections. In nearly every commune, the totals received by the two candidates in the July elections were almost exactly the same as those received by the government and opposition parties in April (if allowance is made for a slight decrease in participation in the July election). The Christian Democrats and the two right-wing parties received 49.9 percent of the vote in April and 50.14 percent of the vote in July, while the Popular Unity coalition parties received 48.2 percent in April and 48.5 percent in July.[22] Male voters also continued to support the government, while women continued to vote against the government.

Party Splits and Realignments

The opposition victory had an important psychological effect, since it was interpreted to indicate that the customary decline in the electoral fortunes of the government was beginning before the Allende government had been in office a year. The election also had an effect on the internal division of forces within the Christian Democratic Party. Its Plenary Council had met once again on July 24, and the meeting scheduled to last two days had continued until July 28. Threatening to secede from the party, the leader of the former *tercerista* faction, Bosco Parra, supported by two deputies and the president of the Christian Democratic Youth, had attempted to persuade the council to adopt a resolution prohibiting any understanding on the part of the Christian Democrats with the National Party or with the so-called nonpolitical interest groups (*gremios*), which were now beginning to emerge as a significant force in opposition to the government. Implicitly, the resolution endorsed cooperation with the left, and it stated explicitly that even if the Allende government refused co-operation, the party should continue on its course of opposition to capitalism.

After twenty-three hours of debate, the left group's resolution was de-feated 10 to 4, and the council adopted a resolution which, while expressing willingness to cooperate with the Allende government for the "replacement of capitalism . . . [and] the full participation of workers in the establish-ment, organization, and direction of the new society and for the political and economic independence of Chile" described itself as still in a position of constructive opposition and denounced the "totalitarian and exclusive spirit" of the government which "wishes to bring the country to an absolutist regime." Accusing the government of "intransigence, sectarianism, and hatred," the PDC announced that it intended to submit bills to the Congress which would give the worker real participation in the new econ-omy and the new society, would protect artisans, small farmers, and small businessmen, and would limit the power of the government to bypass the legislative process.

The adoption of the resolution led to the resignation from the party of Bosco Parra, of the president and two vice-presidents of the Christian Democratic Youth, and of six members of the Chamber of Deputies. At the time of his resignation, Bosco Parra announced that he would organize a pro-Allende group called the Christian Left, made up of "religious and lay people of all denominations who would struggle with the masses in support of the liberating values of socialism and the continued develop-ment of the critical and creative capacities of the worker and peasant base." The group that had resigned declared that they had done so because they wished to "be involved in the process of change in Chile and in the world from a point of view that is entirely Christian and entirely socialist," and they saw the Christian Democrats as moving toward a "confrontation" in which its natural allies would be "the forces of reaction."[23]

The extent to which this second division would hurt the Christian Demo-crats depended very much on how many would follow the six deputies and the youth leaders out of the party. As in the case of the earlier MAPU division, however, the mass of militants and voters remained faithful to the original party. Of particular importance was the attitude of Radomiro Tomic. While he had taken public positions in favor of a more leftist position, he never seems to have seriously considered dividing the party which he had helped to found thirty-five years earlier. In late July, he criticized the government coalition for its "explicit rejection" of PDC overtures, which he characterized as "odious sectarianism" that required the Christian Democrats "to commit hara-kiri." In an interview after the party split, Tomic expressed his disagreement with those who maintained that the party had moved to the right. He insisted that the PDC was the same party that had supported his program a year earlier, now specifically committed to a "socialist, communitarian, pluralist, and democratic" society. He blamed Allende and his coalition for the opposition between the Christian Democrats and the government, maintaining that there had been attempts at "political agreements" between the Christian Democrats and the Allende government, but that the "forces of the government" had replied in the negative. (He later cited four approaches to Allende between December 1970 and June 1971: a meeting by the new head of the PDC after the December assembly, feelers regarding cooperation in the April and July by-elections, and proposals for joint mayoral slates after the municipal elections.) What this meant, he said, was that Allende's second model of socialism, which depends on the support of a majority, could not be carried out because his government was in an "institutional minority" (apparently referring to its lack of control of Congress and the judiciary), so that its revolutionary spirit and program were being dissipated in day-to-day political battles.[24]

The importance of the Christian Left was increased a few days later when the four co-founders and the most prominent members of MAPU, who had left the Christian Democrats in 1969, announced that they were leaving the organization they had created to join the new party. The reason given by Senators Rafael Gumucio and Alberto Jerez, Deputy Julio Silva Solar, and Minister of Agriculture Jacques Chonchol was their disagreement with the Marxist position recently adopted by MAPU. Accusing the present leadership of MAPU of "excessive intransigence and zeal," they stated that their goal was to break "the political monopoly among Christians exercised by the Christian Democrats."[25]

A more important division on related grounds took place in the same period within the Radical Party. It was evident from the outset of the biennial Radical Convention beginning on July 29 that while all the delegates supported the Allende government, a number of the party's most prominent leaders were dissatisfied with its increasingly Marxist orientation. They were led by Senators Luis Bossay and Alberto Baltra. When it became apparent during the convention that the more left-oriented Radicals had a majority of the votes, five senators (out of the total Radical senatorial representation of seven) and seven deputies (out of nineteen) left the party and formed a group which later called itself the Party of the Radical Left (Partido de la Izquierda Radical, PIR). In the declaration explaining their action, the dissidents criticized the "climate of violence" in the convention and the lack of guarantees of free expression and attacked the clearly Marxist character of the policy vote adopted there. They described the vote as "completely removed from the characteristic and distinctive ideology of our party," both because it failed to stress the Radical commitment to democratic principles and because instead of reaffirming the conception of three areas of the economy (state, mixed, and private) outlined in the party program, it had committed itself to "the abolition of private property in the means of production." The dissidents announced that they would support the program of Popular Unity and would continue to consider themselves politically committed to the left, but despite subsequent efforts to persuade them to reenter the party in exchange for a modification of the Marxist tenor of the policy vote, they remained determined to constitute a separate party. (Within eight months the PIR was voting with the opposition.) The official Radical Party thus had lost or expelled its last three presidential candidates and seen its 1969 congressional delegation reduced from nine senators to two and from twenty-three deputies to twelve.[26]

As a result of the division in the Radical Party and the appearance of the Christian Left, the Radical ministers and Jacques Chonchol offered their resignations to President Allende. He refused them, although he made a minor change in one ministry, and he issued a statement in a press conference commenting on the new policy of the Radicals, describing it as neither Marxist nor "authentically what is and has been the image of the Radical Party." Apparently Allende wished to point to the Radicals as the representatives of the middle sectors in his coalition, and their recent action in identifying themselves with the class struggle and the workers made this more difficult.

The new shifts among the center parties seemed to widen Allende's base of support. He had added the eight new deputies of the Christian Left to those who would vote for his program. His problem, however, was that the new groups, especially the Left Radicals, were not as strongly committed to the Popular Unity program as those who had originally formulated it; nor, with the exception of Chonchol, were they formally involved in the government. He thus had a somewhat broader but considerably weaker congressional base of support for his program. In particular, Allende's projected constitutional amendment establishing a single legislative chamber seemed destined to encounter the strong opposition of the five senators and seven deputies of the Left Radical group.

The Copper Compensation Question

The opposition offered no disagreement on the nationalization of the large copper companies. On July 11, the constitutional amendment had been formally approved, and the government initiated a massive propaganda campaign to celebrate the fact that Chile had "put on long pants." The question of compensation, however, had still to be determined by the controller general and (for the determination of excess profits) by President Allende.

While the question of compensation was being considered, the U.S. government attempted to exert pressure on Chile by "postponing" a decision on a pending $21 million loan application to the Export-Import Bank for the purchase of three Boeing jets for LAN, the Chilean airline. One of the oldest of the U.S. institutions for international financial assistance, the Export-Import Bank was founded in 1934 to assist in the promotion of trade, especially where there are currency problems. On August 11, the president of the bank, Henry Kearns, told the Chilean ambassador that a decision on the application was being postponed, although it was "still under consideration," and informed him that the postponement was related to the pending decision on compensation for the expropriated copper mines. Ambassador Orlando Letelier immediately called a press conference to denounce the move. The Chilean press, including the opposition newspapers, condemned this exercise of financial pressure in defense of U.S. private interests, although the Christian Democrats noted that the bank might have done better to cite as a reason for the refusal the continual decline in Chilean dollar reserves, which they estimated at $35 million a month.

The bank's decision was reportedly related to the determination of Secretary of the Treasury John Connally to "get tough" with Latin American nations that expropriated U.S. companies. In an interview with *Business Week* published in July, Connally defended his policy on the grounds that "we don't have any friends there anyway." The State Department, aware of broader U.S. interests in Latin America than the defense of U.S. corporations, was reported to disagree with the Connally policy, but the Export-Import Bank was under Treasury control and followed Connally's direction. In addition, an interagency committee on economic policy toward Chile had been meeting regularly since Allende's election under Henry Kissinger's chairmanship to coordinate a credit squeeze on Chile, articulated in National Security Decision Memorandum 93 of November 1970, which had called for the termination of new bilateral and multilateral governmental assistance as well as guarantees of private investment in Chile.[27]

Chile called in outside consultant teams from France and the Soviet Union to advise the controller general on the value of the copper mines. They reported that in 1970 Anaconda had been extracting as much top-grade ore as possible—an action that was explicable from the company's viewpoint, since the 1969 Chileanization agreement with the Frei government provided that in the event of nationalization of the 49 percent still owned by the company, compensation would be based partly on 1970 profits.

The controller general was not required to report his findings on compensation until October 14, but on September 28 President Allende announced his decision on excess profits. In the presence of his cabinet, members of the Supreme Court, the clergy, workers, students, and representatives of the parties of the Popular Unity coalition, Allende signed a decree fixing the excess profits of Anaconda and Kennecott at $774 million. Allende argued that since 1955 profits for the companies' Chilean operations had been far in excess of those for all their other worldwide copper operations. Maintaining that he had not, in fact, deducted the total amount possible (the Foreign Ministry later explained that he had used the figure of 12 percent of book value rather than the Andean Pact figure of 14 percent), he set Anaconda's excess profit deduction at $300 million for its giant mine at Chuquicamata and $64 million for the mine at El Salvador. Kennecott's El Teniente mine was determined to have made an excess profit of $410 million.[28]

It was clear from this announcement that most of the U.S. companies were likely to end up owing Chile money, since most estimates as to the value of the three mines were well below the amounts set for excess profits. On October 11, the controller general announced his decision. It set the value of Chuquicamata at nearly $242 million and the deductions authorized in the constitutional amendment at over $318 million, including the $300 million decreed by Allende plus an additional amount for damage to and obsolescence of equipment and installations. The value of Anaconda's mine at El Salvador was set at over $68 million and deductions just under $70 million. The evaluation of a third Anaconda mine at La Exótica left a favorable balance after deductions of slightly over $10 million, so that Anaconda owed Chile a total for the three mines in excess of $68 million. The value of the Kennecott mine at El Teniente was set at nearly $319 million and the deductions at over $629 million ($410 million for excess profits, $198 million for "revaluation"—based on the provision of the amendment canceling an increase in book value of El Teniente carried out in connection with the 1967 Chileanization agreement—and nearly $20 million for defective and obsolete equipment), leaving the Kennecott company in debt to Chile by over $310 million. A mine in which the Cerro Corporation had invested heavily in the last part of the 1960s which had only begun to produce in 1971 was valued at over $18 million after deductions of nearly $2 million. Thus, Chile would pay compensation to Cerro, but not to either of the two giant copper corporations which had dominated Chilean copper production for many decades.

According to the constitutional amendment adopted in July, the companies could appeal the controller general's decision to a special Copper

Tribunal, although the presidential decision on excess profits was not subject to review. The appeal could be interpreted as the appropriate steps "to discharge its obligations under international law" mentioned in the Hickenlooper Amendment to the Foreign Assistance Act, so that the October decision did not lead the United States to cut off all aid to Chile, as some had expected. Arguing against the implementation of the Hickenlooper Amendment was the Peruvian precedent, where legal appeals had been used to justify nonapplication of the amendment's provisions. Another consideration, no doubt, was the fact that the principal aid to be cut off would be assistance to the Chilean military, a group with which the U.S. government was particularly interested in remaining in contact, especially in view of its role as a veto group against any attempt by the left to seize total control.

The Allende government continued to press ahead with its nationalization policy in other areas besides copper. On September 23, the Chilean Telephone Company, a subsidiary of ITT, was "intervened" on the grounds that it had not "fulfilled the obligations which the concession had imposed on it of furnishing efficient and modern service and that on the contrary, it was highly deficient."[29]

The intervention led the ITT Washington representatives to intensify their lobbying efforts to persuade the U.S. government to put more pressure on Chile. On September 28, ITT representatives met with Assistant Secretary of State Charles Meyer and, after describing ITT's problems in Chile, urged an embargo on Chilean copper and a complete cut-off of AID and Interamerican Development Bank loans. They received what they regarded as vague or negative answers, although the ITT memo on the meeting observed that "the pressure that Secretary of Treasury Connally is placing on them is being felt." On October 1, ITT wrote to Peter Peterson, presidential assistant for international economic affairs, protesting the continuation of "up to $1 million . . . each month" of pipeline AID assistance and the allocation of previously unutilized IDB funds for earthquake assistance, and attaching an eighteen-point memorandum listing ways to make sure "that Allende does not get through the next six months" (among them, closing off U.S. imports from Chile and a delay or embargo on U.S. exports, possibly including fuel deliveries to the Chilean military).[30]

On October 13, Secretary of State William Rogers issued a statement in response to the controller general's announcement on compensation of the copper companies. Rogers deplored the "unprecedented retroactive application of the excess profits concept" and warned that "the decision could jeopardize flows of private funds and erode the base of support for foreign assistance." A week later, Rogers held a meeting with U.S. companies with interests in Chile. According to the ITT memorandum on the meeting, the company representatives' response was "quite mixed" to Rogers's question as to whether there should be an informal embargo on spare parts and materials being shipped to Chile, with ITT taking the hardest line for strong measures. The memo writer noted that although Rogers had assured the group that "the Nixon administration was "in favor of business and its mission was to protect business," the meeting indicated that "the Secretary is pretty much going along with the [Assistant Secretary] Meyers and company soft-line, low profile policy for Latin America."[31]

While U.S. economic policy was not as hard as ITT would have liked, its anti-Allende program was being stepped up. In September 1971 the Forty Committee approved the expenditure of $700,000 by the CIA in support of *El Mercurio*, and an additional $965,000 was authorized in April 1972. In November 1971 it approved an additional $815,000 to support the opposition parties, and in December $160,000 was earmarked to help the opposition candidates in the January by-elections.[32] CIA money was important in enabling the opposition newspapers, radio stations, the Banco de Chile, and the Alessandri paper company to resist government efforts to bankrupt them or to buy them out. By September, nine domestic and three foreign banks had been nationalized through purchase and four others had been "intervened." The Chilean automobile industry was in a general state of disarray, since the Allende government had decided to standardize Chilean automobile production through mixed companies in which CORFO would own 51 percent of the shares. Foreign companies were to be awarded contracts to produce one basic type of small car, one type of medium-sized vehicle, and one standard chassis for trucks and buses. The U.S. companies which had been operating in Chile, Ford (taken over in May) and General Motors (which had decided to cease operations in Chile in December 1971), announced that they were not interested in competing, but nine European and one Japanese firm submitted bids. The bids of the Japanese, one Spanish, and two French companies were accepted.

The government also took over the textile and fishing industries despite objections, in the first case by the controller general (which were overridden by the constitutionally authorized "decree of insistence" signed by all the ministers) and in the second case by the workers involved. In both cases, the government argued it was legally entitled to take over the industries because of the threat of failure of supply (*desabastecimiento*) of articles essential to the process of production and distribution. The controller general did not disagree with the legal basis of the requisitions, only with the responsibility of the companies for failing to supply government orders. *El Mercurio* and many legal experts, however, raised questions about the use of decree law 520, both because it had not been formally legislated and because its use for the permanent takeover of the companies was a violation of the private property guarantee in the constitution. The legal adviser to the government, Eduardo Novoa, was able to cite ample precedents supporting the legality of the use of the 1932 decree, but the opposition found it more and more frustrating that, except for the nationalization of copper, the government continued to take over large sectors of the economy without deeming it necessary to consult the Congress.

The Paper Company Issue

The area of greatest sensitivity in the government's nationalization effort was the paper industry. Paper had been mentioned in the Popular Unity Program as slated for nationalization, but the Statute of Democratic Guarantees had specifically mentioned access to supplies and materials as a necessary prerequisite to a free press. The opposition legitimately feared that a government takeover of the only private supplier of paper, the Paper and Carton Manufacturing Company, headed by Jorge Alessandri, (the Chilean government owned one paper company, Industria Forestales), would lead to control of the national press or at least the exercise of pressure upon it. In early August, Alessandri and the government discussed proposals to reorganize the paper industry, possibly involving its direction by an independent council composed of representatives of shareholders, the government, the unions, and consumers. The government insisted that it wished to acquire majority control of Alessandri's company through the purchase of a sufficient number of shares to give it 51 percent, arguing that this was necessary in order to plan for the proper use of wood products. CORFO was therefore authorized to buy shares from private stockholders in the company. At the same time, price rises were decreed for the raw materials used by the industry, while price increases were denied to finished paper products—a patent effort to bankrupt the company. The pressures on the paper industry were resisted through the establishment by private shareholders (almost certainly with CIA financing) of a National Freedom Fund to buy shares from any stockholder who wished to sell. This was designed to prevent a takeover by the government through the method used in nationalizing the banks—driving the price of the stock down by threats of nationalization and then offering to buy it at a price well above that offered on the market.

Allende announced in mid-September his decision (later revoked) to expel the Chilean correspondent of United Press International for sending an article that he considered distorted over its Latin American wire. Suspicion of a government campaign against the opposition press was increased by a police raid on the office of *El Mercurio* on October 21 on suspicion of harboring arms for subversive groups. Nothing of an incriminating nature was found.

Along with the efforts to take over the paper company, an orchestrated campaign was carried out in the progovernment press against ex-President

Frei, and in September unsuccessful attempts were made to link him to a financial scandal involving a former contributor to the Christian Democrats. Frei had not taken an active part in Chilean politics since his retirement, except to give one speech shortly before the municipal elections; but he finally responded publicly to the escalation of attacks on him with a denunciation of the "sustained campaign of lies and offenses" which was, he said, "synchronized and directed . . . according to a prearranged plan." He said that the contributor in question was hostile to him personally and was linked to other groups not in the Christian Democratic Party (a reference to the fact that the contributor's brother was Rafael Gumucio, an Izquierda Cristiana senator) and accused the Communist Party of "applying a tactic which it has followed in all the countries which it has enslaved by blackening the reputation of any person who is an obstacle to the establishment of its baleful dictatorship."[33]

Hardening Christian Democratic Attitudes

The use of such strong language might be attributed to Frei's well-known hostility to the Communists, but a similarly strong denunciation of the government came from a Christian Democrat who had been identified with the *tercerista* faction in the past, Senator Renán Fuentealba. In a special senatorial session held in September 1971 at the request of his party to analyze the political situation, Fuentealba gave a three-hour speech in which he attacked the Allende government's efforts to take over the mass media and the universities, criticized the "implacable campaign" against former president Frei, and accused Unidad Popular of sectarianism and antipluralism. He read a documentary history of the relations between his party and the government, arguing that from the beginning of Allende's term, the Christian Democrats had resolved not to deny the government "salt and water" as it had been denied to them when they were in power. Announcing that recent events were forcing the party to take a harder line against the government, he accused President Allende of playing a two-faced game ("el doble juego, la política de dos caras"). The Fuentealba speech was an important turning point, since it indicated that groups within the Christian Democratic Party that were not identified with its right wing were now in favor of stronger opposition to the Allende government.

The effects of the hardening of the PDC position appeared in late October. For some months, the Christian Democrats had been considering using the opposition majority in Congress to end the executive's use of measures of doubtful legality to carry out its program of nationalization. Their decision to do so was accelerated by the Allende government's decision to use the constitutionally authorized "decree of insistence" to override the controller general's decision. The PDC was also concerned to give legislative expression to its ideology of communitarian socialism in a way which would distinguish it both from the conservative right and from the Marxist left.

The National Party had proposed the impeachment of the minister of the economy as a way for Congress to assert control of the nationalization process. After negotiations with President Allende, the Christian Democrats agreed not to support the impeachment effort in return for a promise by Allende to send legislation to Congress which would define and delimit the government's nationalization policy. On October 19, Allende submitted a bill defining the three areas of the economy (state ["social"], mixed, and private) and limiting expropriations to firms with over 14 million escudos in assets (about $1 million) as of the end of 1969. The Christian Democrats responded with a counterproposal in the form of a constitutional amendment embodying their ideas on the proper organization of the economy.[34]

The Christian Democratic constitutional amendment retained the "three areas" of the government bill and the reservation to state control of the fields of mining, transportation, communication, gas, petroleum, cement, steel, nitrate, iodine, and arms production; but it required all transfers of private enterprise to the "social" or mixed sectors to be carried out by specific congressional legislation. The amendment further required that when the 1932 decree was used as the basis for requisition of an industry for lack of production, the situation must have lasted for twenty days and have been the result of "the fault of the proprietor or administrator of the firm." All such requisitions were to be subject to appeal to the Supreme Court. Interventions for other reasons could only take place by a decree stating the reasons and subject to approval by the controller general; the maximum initial period of intervention was set at ninety days, with renewal possible for an additional ninety days. The amendment protected small and medium property holders against nationalization and provided that any purchase of shares by state entities after October 14, 1971, "for purposes of taking state control" (*estatificar*—the term used by the Christian Democrats for nationalization in order to emphasize that the enterprises were being taken over by the state, not by the nation) were to be null and void, thus discouraging holders of shares in Alessandri's paper company from selling their shares to CORFO, which had been authorized to buy its shares as of that date. Reflecting the Christian Democratic communitarian ideology, the amendment also specifically authorized the creation of "enterprises the administration of which will be carried out entirely by the workers who work regularly in them . . . in which case the workers will have the use and enjoyment of the respective properties and will participate in the profits which result from their management."[35]

Besides asserting legislative control of the nationalization procedure, the Christian Democrats were drawing on the proposals for worker participation in management and profits which had been an element in Christian social thought in Europe and Latin America for decades, in order to provide a "communitarian" alternative to the statist socialism of the Allende government. It was clear from the discussions in party theoretical organs and from the wording of the draft amendment that the example of the workers' councils in Yugoslavia also influenced the form of the Christian Democratic proposals. Citing large deficits in the nationalized enterprises and accusing the government policy of leading to inefficiency, bureaucracy, and waste, the Christian Democrats argued that worker participation would bring greater dynamism and greater democracy to the Chilean economy.

If supported by the right, the proposal would both limit the government's expropriation policy and restructure the Chilean economy in a way which was different from that envisioned by the Marxists who were directing economic policy. Earlier, the Christian Democrats had been reluctant to challenge government policy directly, both because of pressures from their own left wing and because they were hesitant to go to the country in a plebiscite which the constitution authorized the president to call. But the most vociferous leftists had departed when the Izquierda Cristiana group had split with the party, and a process of political polarization had been developing. This process, along with an evident decline in the popularity of the government, led the Christian Democrats to issue a legislative challenge which was to be a source of continuing conflict between Allende and the opposition-dominated Congress and the focal point of an institutional deadlock which was resolved only by the 1973 coup.

CHAPTER EIGHT

Polarization and Brinkmanship

Between the introduction of the amendment on the three areas of the economy in October 1971 and the nationwide strike initiated by the truckers in October 1972, succeeding confrontations between supporters of the government and of the opposition eroded the framework of constitutionalism and civility which had held the Chilean polity together, and Chile began to be divided into two hostile (and, increasingly, armed) camps. By this time the economic cushions inherited from the Frei regime—a balance-of-payments surplus and substantial unused capacity—had disappeared. The worst inflation in Chile's inflation-prone history began to gather increasing momentum, eliminating most of the real gains that low- and middle-income groups had made in the preceding year. However, Allende's economic policy makers did not act on the inflation problem until mid-1972, long after the danger signals were apparent. Allende himself, while not daring to resort to the constitutionally authorized but risky plebiscite procedure, continued to engage in political and legal maneuvers designed to strengthen the position of his coalition in the March 1973 congressional elections.

On November 10, 1971, he sent Congress a draft constitutional amendment for the establishment of the unicameral legislature proposed in his presidential program. It provided that the March 1973 elections would choose the entire membership of a single legislative chamber. (Allende denied that it would be called "the assembly of the people," as in his presidential program, probably because the term had been brought into disrepute by the establishment of a similarly named body of self-appointed representatives of "workers and students" in Bolivia shortly before the overthrow of the Torres government in mid-1971.) According to Allende's proposal, the members of the new unicameral legislature would serve only until the 1976 elections; thereafter, the president and parliament would be elected simultaneously for identical six-year terms. The president would have the power to dissolve the legislature once during his term of office, and the terms of members of the Supreme Court would be coterminous with that of the president. Legislators would only be eligible for reelection once, would be required to wait six years before running for a second term, and could not hold paid outside positions.[1]

The draft constitutional amendment also included guarantees of housing, social welfare, health care, and employment for all Chileans, including unmarried mothers and illegitimate children, but its basic thrust was the subordination of the legislature and the judiciary to the executive, not unlike Mexico's political system. It was clear from the outset that the proposed amendment had no chance of being adopted by the Congress. It seems that the bill was introduced only to fulfill a campaign pledge, and to familiarize the country with the specifics of government proposals to which it might appeal in the March 1973 legislative election campaign. In December Allende referred to the possibility of a plebiscite on the proposal, but when the question was raised again in February 1972, after the Congress had adopted the Christian Democratic constitutional amendment on the three areas of the economy, Allende indicated that "for the present" he would not exercise his constitutional power to call a plebiscite.[2]

Castro's Visit and the March of the Empty Pots

On the very day that the draft amendment on the unicameral legislature was sent to the Congress, Fidel Castro arrived in Chile for what the Chilean government originally described as a ten-day visit (Castro stayed for three and a half weeks). The visit was supposed to arouse enthusiasm for the Popular Unity government, but in the tense political climate it only stirred up more controversy. The opposition press accused Castro of interfering in Chile's internal politics through the speeches of support for Allende that he gave on every occasion—particularly when he described the opposition as "fascists" and attacked the Christian Democratic proposals of worker self-management as "criminal demagoguery which creates a new privileged class and corrupts the worker." Castro criticized the institutions of constitutional democracy, describing a free press, elections, and representative institutions as "condemned by history as decadent and anachronistic." Yet he also said that Allende and he were "going toward socialism in different ways, but the final objective was the same" and, in response to a question from a member of the MIR at the University of Concepción, asserted that "the Revolution in our country took place under specific conditions . . . every road was closed—a situation in which there was no alternative. It was under such conditions that a violent struggle, a bloody struggle was waged."[3]

For the first time since he had suppressed the opposition press in 1960, Castro found himself the object of published critical comments, including some unsubtle hints about his sexual proclivities suggested by a picture in which he appeared to be dancing with Jaime Suarez, secretary-general of the Allende government. Toward the end of his visit, Castro complained that his Chilean crowds were not as large or as enthusiastic as those in Cuba. In his final press conference, he referred to the "poor mass mobilization" in Chile demonstrated by the lack of attendance at his farewell on December 2 in the National Stadium. In the speech itself he had claimed that in two hours in Cuba he could get together "ten times as many people as there are here."[4]

Castro's call for mass mobilization by the Allende supporters and his assertion in his stadium speech that "we have seen fascism in action" were responses to an anti-Allende demonstration on December 1, the "March of the Empty Pots," in which five thousand women protested the lack of food and the rising cost of living. The march was accompanied by serious incidents of violence when the women were attacked by followers of the MIR and related groups, and tear gas was used by the police riot squad. The violence led to the declaration of a state of emergency and a curfew in Santiago, as well as accusations by the opposition that the Ministry of the Interior was responsible for the attacks because it had failed to act against armed left-wing extremists. In the farewell for Castro, Allende defended his minister and commented that the march was made up of women from upper-class areas "who have never known what it is like to be without food and who arrived at the demonstration in powerful cars." He commented that he found it a "suspicious coincidence" that shortly before the demonstration a Nixon assistant who had returned from Latin America was reported in a U.S. newspaper to have told the president that the Allende regime would not last much longer.[5]

The atmosphere of violence and confrontation was accentuated by a struggle over the control of the University of Chile between the pro-Christian Democratic rector and secretary general of the university and the University Council, which had a pro-Marxist majority. The council majority voted in October to reorganize the social science faculties of the university to include the law faculty. Since the social sciences were largely Marxist-controlled, while the law school was sympathetic to the opposition, the move was seen as a maneuver to expand the control of the university by the left. The result was a series of occupations of various faculties of the university by government and opposition groups, the latter seizing the law faculty and the Popular Unity forces taking control of the university's central building. Following the procedures authorized in a recent reorganization of the university, the Christian Democrats gathered sufficient signatures for a plebiscite on the council's decision, but the council argued that it had final authority on the restructuring of faculties. The crisis lasted from October until January and was resolved only by the direct intervention of President Allende and several of the Christian Democratic leaders. The compromise they reached provided that in April new elections would be held for rector, secretary general, and council, as well as a plebiscite on the projected reorganization.

First Ministerial Impeachment

As a direct result of the incidents accompanying the March of the Empty Pots, both the right and the Christian Democrats (the latter party acted separately and by a divided vote) voted to initiate impeachment proceedings against the minister of the interior. With the combination of the two opposition forces it was clear that the impeachment would be adopted. On January 6, 1972, the Chamber of Deputies approved the impeachment indictment by a vote of 80 to 59. The minister, José Tohá, was accused of "responsibility for continued, reiterated, and serious infractions of the constitutional guarantees," including the toleration of illegal armed groups, arbitrary detentions, and infringement of constitutional provisions concerning the freedom of the mass media. Tohá replied that the impeachment was based on political rather than constitutional grounds and involved the abandonment of the presidential system and a return to a discredited parliamentarism. Allende transferred Tohá, one of his closest associates, to the Defense Ministry before the Senate formally removed him from office on January 22. Borrowing a term from chess, Chileans described Allende's maneuver as an *enroque* ("castling")—a change in the position of a castle (rook) to protect the king.[6]

January By-Election—A Turning Point

The Christian Democrats and the two right-wing parties also cooperated (while denying that they were doing so) in nominations for two by-elections in January which were billed as a crucial test of popular support for the Allende government. In the election of a new senator for the provinces of O'Higgins and Colchagua to replace a Christian Democrat who had been killed in an auto accident, the Christian Democrats nominated Rafael Moreno, the head of the agrarian reform program under former president Frei. In a by-election to replace a National Party deputy for the province of Linares (who had emigrated to Australia after Allende was elected), the National Party nominated Sergio Diez, a university professor who was well known because of his appearances on a television panel show on politics. In each case the other major opposition party did not nominate a candidate for fear of dividing the antigovernment forces. The Popular Unity coalition nominated a Socialist deputy, Hector Olivares, to oppose the Christian Democratic candidate for the senate seat in O'Higgins and Colchagua, and the widow of Hernán Mery, the agrarian reform official killed in May 1970, for deputy for the province of Linares. The tactic of the government parties was to attempt to identify the Christian Democrats with the "forces of reaction," citing the support of the Christian Democratic candidate in O'Higgins and Colchagua by the National and Radical Democrat parties (there was no formal agreement on this score, and the Christian Democrats had given their supporters "freedom of action" with respect to the National Party's candidate in Linares). The opposition parties attacked the climate of violence in the countryside, the deteriorating economic situation, and the totalitarian tendencies of the government. Once again Eduardo Frei took an active part, making speeches for Moreno in Rancagua and San Fernando at the end of the campaign.

The outcome of the election was a considerable defeat for the Allende government in both by-elections. In O'Higgins and Colchagua, Moreno won 52.7 percent of the vote to Olivares's 46.4 percent; and in Linares, the National Party candidate, Sergio Diez, received 58 percent of the vote to Maria de Mery's 40.9 percent. Once again, women voted with the opposition, voting nearly two to one in favor of Diez in Linares and giving Moreno a 12,000-vote plurality in O'Higgins and Colchagua which amply counterbalanced the 3,000-vote plurality the government candidate received among male voters. Also of interest and future significance was the substantial showing of Moreno in the El Teniente copper-mining communes of Machali and Sewell, where the antigovernment vote increased by 6.5 percent. The Christian Democrats also received increased support in rural areas, where turnouts were unusually high.

When the results of the by-elections were compared with those of the municipal elections held the preceding April, it was evident that the government had consistently lost 4 to 7 percent of the vote that it had received earlier. In O'Higgins and Colchagua, where almost the same number of votes was cast in the two elections, the government vote dropped from 72,758 to 68,338, while the opposition tally rose from 72,354 to 77,614. In Linares, government support dropped from 23,112 to 21,165, while the opposition increased its vote from 26,843 to 29,990.[7]

In the postelection analyses, the drop in government support in Linares was attributed to the continued violence in the area encouraged by the MIR and related organizations. The defeat in O'Higgins and Colchagua (where the government had won in the municipal elections) was more difficult to explain, since the agrarian reform was already well advanced there and the area included a substantial sector of organized workers in the copper mines. The government candidate had himself been a union official in the El Teniente mine and was president of the Copper Workers Confederation. The beginnings of the erosion of government support, mainly for economic reasons, and the traditionally antigovernment attitudes of the copper workers were two possible explanations for the defeat of the government candidate.

The January 1972 by-election marked a turning point in the fortunes of the Allende government which was not unlike that of the 1967 municipal elections in the case of the preceding administration—except that it took place earlier in the government's tenure. As in 1967, the electoral defeat colored the future perceptions of both government and opposition as to the government's performance; and, as in 1967, it was followed by a marked deterioration in the success of the government's economic policy, in particular, its fight against inflation. Again, as in 1967, it also marked the beginning of a pattern of regularized cooperation among the antigovernment legislators.

In an effort to broaden the base of his support, President Allende reorganized his cabinet, bringing in two representatives of the Left Radicals as ministers of justice and of mining. In early February the Popular Unity parties held an extended meeting at El Arrayán, just outside Santiago, to analyze the past and future policy of the government. The Communist Party's Political Commission prepared a confidential report analyzing the elections, the full text of which was obtained and published by *El Mercurio*. The report observed that "the elections have confirmed a deterioration in the position of the government." It noted that the government candidates had lost votes in nearly every commune and that "the UP masses have been adversely affected by the result." The bulk of the report was devoted to a polemic with the extreme left in the MIR and the Socialist Party. The Communists blamed the "preponderant participation" of the MIR for the losses in Linares, and it took issue with the assertion by the left that Allende's 1970 victory was the result of a "miscalculation by the enemy." Rather, the Communists said, it was the political action of "the popular forces" that kept the Christian Democrats and the right from uniting as they had in 1964, and the Political Commission called for further work to "neutralize and win over the social base of Christian Democracy" through "dialogue with that party." Predicting that during 1972 there would be "very strong inflationary pressures which could make our situation acute," the report blamed the electoral reverses on "sectarianism, bureaucratism, and low participation by the masses."

The MIR issued a sharp attack on the Communist assertions, claiming (somewhat illogically, since the Christian Democrats did not present a candidate there) that the defeat in Linares was due to the Communist policy of first praising sectors of the Christian Democrats as progressive and then telling the workers not to vote for that party. The proper policy, said the MIR, was to "define the PDC as a party which politically represents the interests of imperialism and of the employers. If there are some progressive sectors in the PDC, they will only leave the party when it is unmasked as fascist and reactionary."[8]

The publication of the El Arrayán report made public disagreements which were already known to exist within the Popular Unity coalition. On the side of radicalization of the revolution were the MIR (not officially part of the coalition, but cooperating with it), the left wing of the Socialists headed by the secretary general of the party, Senator Carlos Altamirano, and the MAPU (minus its original leadership, which had joined the Izquierda Cristiana in August). On the other side, favoring a policy of legality and gradual extension of socialism by the takeover of the major centers of production and by income redistribution in favor of the lower classes, were the Allendista Socialists, the Communists, and the *oficialista* Radicals. In a special position, because of their support for the general goals of the government but increasing opposition to the process of polarization, were the Left Radicals who had just joined the cabinet but were not formally members of the Popular Unity coalition.

One of the results of the El Arrayán conclave was that the government parties decided to join together for the congressional elections of March 1973 in order to maximize the number of seats they would gain against a presumably divided opposition. The Communist report had proposed the formation of a Party of Popular Unity, but the Radicals and the Socialists opposed the submergence of their organizations in a single party which, because of its superior discipline and organization, would probably be dominated by the Communist Party. The result was a proposal for the presentation of joint lists by the government parties in an electoral federation or confederation. Not surprisingly, the opposition began to think in similar terms. After negotiation between government and opposition, it was agreed that both sides would be permitted to run such lists in 1973. (The Christian Democrats indicated that they would have preferred a change in the electoral laws to allow for different combinations in different areas, thus lessening the polarizing tendency of the creation of progovernment and opposition alliances on a national level).

The Constitutional Issue

The negotiations on joint electoral lists were accompanied by negotiations with the Christian Democrats under the auspices of the Left Radicals concerning the proposed constitutional amendment on the areas of the economy. On February 19, the full Congress met in joint session as provided by the constitution, and the opposition majority adopted the Christian Democratic amendment limiting nationalizations to those carried out by law, laying down specific norms for expropriation and intervention, and mandating the establishment of worker-controlled enterprises in the state and mixed sectors. The Congress then forwarded the amendment to the president for his "modifications, corrections, or the insertion of provisions validly proposed by him during the discussion of the bill," as the constitution provided. Allende had made it clear that he was opposed to the limitation of his efforts to extend government control over the economy, and government spokesmen had denounced the proposals for worker-run enterprises as intended to turn the workers into "petty bourgeois" capitalists. The next step was for Allende to veto or rewrite the amendment within the thirty days constitutionally provided. Before that, however, a serious problem of constitutional interpretation emerged.

The broadened plebiscite provisions adopted in 1970 did not specify what type of vote was required for the Congress to override a presidential veto of a constitutional amendment. The opposition, which had a majority in each house but lacked two-thirds, argued that the elimination of a previous constitutional reference to a two-thirds majority meant that the Congress needed only an absolute majority in each house to insist on its version of the amendment; if the president disagreed with this, he was to have recourse to the new, broadened plebiscite provisions. The government, for understandable reasons, insisted that the constitutional provisions regarding presidential vetoes of ordinary legislation provided the appropriate precedent and that therefore the Congress would need a two-thirds majority to override the president. Allende also indicated that in the event of disagreement with the Congress, he would submit the matter to the new Constitutional Tribunal rather than call a plebiscite. The opposition maintained that the Constitutional Tribunal was only authorized to make decisions concerning the constitutionality of laws and plebiscites, not interpretations of amendments to the constitution, and thus did not have jurisdiction in this case.[9]

It seems that the 1970 reforms had simply neglected to specify, and the earlier congressional debates neglected to discuss, the method of legislative "insistence" to override presidential vetoes and whether or not the Constitutional Tribunal had jurisdiction over the interpretation of constitutional amendments. On both issues, each side interpreted the omissions in terms which would be helpful to it. The government was confident that it had a majority in the Constitutional Tribunal, which had ruled in its favor in January by disallowing certain congressional amendments to the budget, and it had enough votes in the Congress to prevent a two-thirds vote. Conversely, the opposition, more united than in the past, had a comfortable majority in the Congress and was confident that, given the temper of the country, it could win a plebiscite.

The Left Radicals (PIR) wished to avoid a constitutional confrontation likened by many to the one in 1891 between President Balmaceda and the Congress which had led to a bloody civil war. They were also concerned that the transition to socialism be carried out through a "process of indisputable legality." In early 1972, the PIR minister of justice, Manuel Sanhueza, carried on extensive negotiations with the Christian Democrats and claimed to have achieved an acceptable agreement providing for legal regulation of government takeovers. Demonstrating the pernicious effects of the December 1969 agreement providing for consultation with all Popular Unity parties before major presidential decisions, the representatives of the parties in the Popular Unity Political Command rejected the agreement, and on April 6 President Allende sent the Congress alternative proposals which substantially departed from the Sanhueza agreement. Because of the failure of the government to support their efforts, the Left Radicals resigned from the cabinet, a move that Allende characterized as a "dirty stab in the back" (*puñalada trapera*). In the next by-election the Left Radicals, supported by all the opposition parties, ran a candidate against the pro-Allende nominee.[10]

In April the constitutional struggle between the government and the opposition moved into the streets with rival mass demonstrations in Santiago. The government, suffering a decline in popular support because of increasing inflation, was unexpectedly aided by the publication of reports in Jack Anderson's "Washington Merry-go-Round" column concerning confidential documents which demonstrated that ITT had actively sought to prevent the election of President Allende in 1970. The documents were immediately translated into Spanish and published separately by *El Mercurio* and the Chilean government, and their references to ex-President Frei were exploited by the progovernment press to launch a massive attack upon him. On April 10, Frei addressed the country in a radio reply. Denying that there were any "direct or indirect contacts" between ITT and his government, the armed forces, or the Christian Democratic Party, Frei charged that the documents simply repeated "a mass of rumors which, everyone will remember, were circulating all over Chile at that time. It was sufficient to stand on any streetcorner in downtown Santiago to know everything that those documents contained."[11]

Brinkmanship

The conflict between the Allende government and the opposition seemed to be establishing a pattern of public, sometimes violent, demonstrations and the escalation of confrontation, alternating with periods of negotiations and recourse to the ballot box rather than the streets. Thus, the negotiations of September and October 1971 were followed by increased conflict between the two sides from November until mid-January. This, in turn, was followed by a period of relative calm and renewed negotiations during February and early March. Then, from late March until early May, intense conflict ensued; at one point Allende threatened to dissolve the Congress. In January, a by-election had provided an outlet for political tempers through institutionalized channels and resulted in a diminution of conflict thereafter. The University of Chile elections in late April (in which the Christian Democrats won the rectorship and control of the council) were followed by renewed efforts on both sides to find a compromise solution which lasted until early July. As the new U.S. ambassador to Chile, Nathaniel Davis, described it in a secret dispatch published in Jack Anderson's column in March, "The Chileans have a great ability to rush to the brink, embrace each other, and back off." Davis concluded that "the prospects for military intervention are extremely small" except in the unlikely event that "discontent [becomes] so great that military intervention is overwhelmingly invited."[12]

Contrary to the ambassador's opinion, we now know that April 1972 was the first time that the military began to consider that the conflict between the president and the Congress might lead to a complete breakdown of the constitutional order. General Augusto Pinochet, chief of the military junta which took power in September 1973, told a magazine interviewer in 1974 that according to his files, on April 13, 1972, the general staff discussed the situation and concluded that the "insuperable conflict between the executive and legislature will be without a constitutional solution."[13]

In May and June, both sides tried to avoid a direct confrontation on the issue of constitutional interpretation. Allende sent his revisions of the three areas amendment to the Congress, but in his May 21 message to Congress, he appealed to the opposition not to provoke institutional conflict. In June, at Allende's initiative, lengthy negotiations were undertaken between the president of the Christian Democratic Party, Senator Renán Fuentealba (initially without consulting his party), and Jorge Tapia of the Radical Party, Allende's minister of justice, in the hope of working out a compromise. The negotiators had some success in arriving at partial agreement, and Tapia claimed that they had finally agreed on a list of industries to be expropriated by law and were not far from a final accord. But after two weeks the negotiations were broken off by the Christian Democrats when the time limit for a Senate vote on Allende's item vetoes expired. (The decision was also influenced by the imminence of a by-election in Coquimbo; it was difficult to continue negotiations in the midst of a campaign.) In contrast to the April negotiations, where the fault for the failure of the talks lay with Popular Unity, the termination of the Fuentealba-Tapia negotiations appeared to be the result of a decision by the Christian Democrats—although they blamed it on the intransigence of the left wing of the Allende coalition on such questions as the status of the paper company, the specific regulations for expropriations, and time limits on the intervention of industry.[14] In retrospect, the negotiations appear to have been the last chance to prevent the polarization which terminated in the 1973 coup.

Increasing Polarization

The breakdown of the negotiations was followed by a further series of confrontations between the government and the opposition. Allende reiterated his intention to refer the constitutional question to the Constitutional Tribunal and to make its decision respected, "whatever it might be." In reply, the opposition made veiled references to the possibility of impeaching the president if he "violated the constitution" in this fashion. The Christian Democrats also claimed that the government parties had falsified the tallies in the Central Workers Confederation (CUT) elections held in April and May, the results of which were announced only after a long delay. They claimed to have won far more votes than the 26 percent official figure (still more than twice their earlier totals, only a few votes short of the Socialist percentage, and enough to give them control of the Santiago branch of the organization).

In July, the Congress voted a second impeachment of an Allende cabinet minister when it removed Hernán del Canto as minister of interior for "nonenforcement of the law, arbitrary actions, and violation of the customs laws." The charge on customs violations referred to the demonstrable illegality of the entry in March of thirteen large wooden crates from Cuba which had been passed without examination by the customs after the direct intervention of the Interior Ministry. The Congress and the Controller General's Office investigated the incident, and various government officials, including Allende, repeatedly stated that the crates contained "works of art." After Allende's overthrow, documents were published listing the armaments, totaling over a ton, contained in the crates.[15] Their importation at this point was an indication that the Allende government was already taking steps to arm its supporters. The publicity this incident received had a predictably negative effect on the attitude of the armed forces, since it appeared to indicate an arms buildup by the left with the aid of the Allende government.

On July 12, del Canto spoke at a government rally in the square facing the Congress and the Supreme Court and denounced the legislature and the judiciary for their "collusion with the great imperialist interests" while the crowd shouted imprecations at the judges. The demonstration resulted in the first of many open letters of protest to President Allende from the Supreme Court.

On July 16, the government was encouraged by its first by-election victory since April 1971, when the Popular Unity candidate won in the Province of Coquimbo over a Left Radical, backed by the other opposition parties, 50,482 to 42,309. However, Coquimbo was an area in which the Marxist parties and the official Radical Party had always been strong, and in April

1971, the Popular Unity candidates had had a 23,368-vote plurality over the opposition parties in an election with an only slightly higher turnout. In comparison with April 1971, the government lost nearly 6,000 votes in the by-election, while the opposition gained 9,000 (there were no independent candidates). Thus, despite the victory, the pattern of declining support for the Allende government continued to be confirmed.

The Coquimbo by-election and the impeachment of the interior minister also confirmed the entrance of the Left Radicals into the ranks of the opposition. This was further indicated by the establishment of the electoral coalitions for the March 1973 elections. On the government side was the Popular Unity Federation. The opposition formation, however, was more complex. First, two federations were created: the Federación Nacional, made up of the National Party and the Radical Democrats, and the Federación de Oposición Democrática, composed of the Christian Democrats, the tiny Democratic National Party (PADENA), and the Left Radicals. These two federations then combined to form the opposition Confederación Democrática (CODE).

Inflation Takes Off

The deterioration in the government's popular support during the second year of the Allende administration had a simple explanation: the country's increasingly difficult economic position, reflected in runaway inflation and shortages of many essential commodities and replacement parts. Allende's economic policy, under the direction of Pedro Vuskovic, had appeared to be a great success during the first year. A vast government program financed by deficit spending had resulted in a reactivation of the economy, a sharp decline in unemployment (from 8 percent in early 1971 to 3.8 percent in December in the Greater Santiago area), as well as an increase of 12 percent in industrial production and of 8.5 percent in the gross national product. The spending program had been combined with income redistribution through wage readjustments and welfare increases which had increased wages and salaries in real terms by 25 percent and raised the share of the national income received by wage and salary earners from 53 percent to 59 percent of the national income.[16] With much more spendable cash, Chileans, aware that the relatively stable prices of Allende's first year could not last, went on vast spending sprees. Because of strict price controls and because of an estimated 30 percent idle capacity in Chilean industry, this "demand push" did not produce real inflationary pressures, by Chilean standards, until near the end of 1971, so the official inflation rate for that year was 22 percent—down sharply from 35 percent in 1970.

This policy of populist consumerism was accompanied by other more traditional socialist measures. The government rapidly expanded its control of industry. In his May 1972 speech, Allende reported that the government now owned 98 major enterprises and had "intervened" 83 others. The Chilean Society for Industrial Development (Sociedad de Fomento Fabril) put the total figure at 263. No one doubted that the Chilean state now had vastly increased power over the economy. While the entire banking system had not yet been nationalized, 20 of the 26 banks in the country were owned or controlled by the government, and the rest were subject to extensive controls through the superintendent of banks. In agriculture, as much land had been taken over in 1971 as had changed hands in the entire six years of the Frei administration (although it should be noted that Frei had not had a strong agrarian reform law until midway through his term). By May 1972 the government could announce that nearly all farms in excess of the eighty-hectare limit had been taken over, with the reformed sector constituting about 25 percent of the arable land in the country.[17]

This policy was seen as producing the conditions for majority support for the transition to socialism—the *vía chilena,* or second model of socialism, of which Allende had spoken in his first presidential message in May 1971. It was expected that the lower classes, who were in a clear majority (in 1970, 60 percent of Chilean families had an income of less than twice the minimum wage), would recognize the improvement in their living standards and vote in increasing numbers for the Popular Unity government. Moreover, since the opposition had lost its economic base in its control of industry and credit, the "masses" would no longer be "mystified" by the propaganda of the right, and the possibilities for the promotion of "false consciousness" among the workers and peasants would be undercut.

This view, like the earlier Christian Democratic plans for thirty years of dominance, was excessively optimistic. It did not count on the anti-Marxism of large numbers of Chileans and the continuing appeal of the Christian Democrats to many already politicized middle- and lower-class voters who refused to see the Christian Democrats or Eduardo Frei as capitalist reactionaries. It also assumed that the opposition would not be able to finance electoral propaganda, but the Statute of Democratic Guarantees and the remaining economic resources still in private hands (as well as, we now know, outside sources including the CIA) provided a continuing economic base for antigovernment publications. Even a government-owned publishing conglomerate such as Quimantú, the former Zig-Zag, printed publications critical of the government. The government's efforts to take over the paper industry had been stoutly resisted, and strong protests were raised against efforts to bankrupt opposition-controlled radio stations by granting excessive wage increases and restricting government advertising to progovernment radio stations. The government's early withdrawal of its proposals for popular tribunals and a unicameral legislature was also in response to opposition from the Chilean public.

The chief problem in maintaining support for this government, as for those in the past, was economic. The opposition could criticize as much as it wished, but if the average Chilean was prosperous and satisfied he would support the government, as about 50 percent had in the 1971 municipal elections. The difficulty was that it became apparent by the end of Allende's first year in office that serious economic constraints on the Vuskovic economic policy would make themselves felt during the next year—with an adverse effect on the government's political position. The first constraint was the need for foreign currency to pay for imports, especially of food. The Frei administration had left its successor $343 million in hard currency reserves, but the Allende government, after a year and a half in office, had only about $50 million left.[18] The decline in foreign currency was attributable to a number of factors, and often personal ideology would determine which were emphasized in explaining the phenomenon. Minister Vuskovic attributed it to the increased consumption and prosperity of Chileans, which required an expansion of imports, particularly of food. Vuskovic also observed that foreign investment had virtually ceased since Allende's accession to power. The Allende government did not view this as a calamity, since for the left foreign investment meant an increase in *dependencia*. A third factor cited by Vuskovic was a drop of about 20 percent in the price of copper from its level at the end of the Frei administration.

Invisible Blockade?

In a speech in July, Allende himself added another factor which was to be cited often by his defenders: the "economic blockade" by the United States which had reduced Chile's possibilities of receiving foreign assistance.[19] The evidence on the so-called invisible blockade is mixed. In January 1971, Chile had received two education loans for $11.6 million from the Interamerican Development Bank, and it was granted a credit of $16.1 million in July 1971 from an earlier loan for earthquake reconstruction. As a result of U.S. behind-the-scenes pressure, these were the last loans the Allende government was to receive from the IDB, although aid "in the pipeline" continued to flow. The World Bank, while continuing the flow of aid under existing programs, also made no new loans, and it terminated its consideration of one loan in October 1971 when the terms of the compensation (or lack thereof) to the copper companies were announced. The bank cited Chile's lack of "creditworthiness" but also referred to its own long-standing policies against aid to countries which expropriate foreign holdings without compensation. In December 1971, Chile received a $39.5 million credit from the International Monetary Fund to compensate for the drop in copper export prices, and a similar loan for $42.8 million was made a year later. AID "pipeline" aid, Food for Peace, and technical assistance continued without interruption. The reduction in short-term credits from private U.S. banks from $220 million in August 1970 to $32 million in 1972 was described and documented by New York bankers in testimony to the Senate ITT investigators as a gradual response to deteriorating economic conditions in Chile, although the banks must have been aware of the U.S. government position.[20]

It would be more accurate, therefore, to describe the U.S. economic pressure on Chile as a credit squeeze rather than a "blockade." Chile was not prevented from buying or selling in the United States as, for instance, has been the case with Cuba (although this had been proposed by ITT in a memorandum to the White House in late 1971). Chile's access to credit from U.S. and international banks was reduced (although by no means eliminated), but substantial credits were secured from European and Latin American countries, as well as from Eastern Europe, the Soviet Union, and China.

In November 1971, Chile had suspended payments on all its debts except those to international agencies and for military aid, thus confirming doubts expressed earlier about the creditworthiness of the Allende regime. Chile's creditors, assembled in the so-called Club of Paris, met in April 1972. The U.S. representatives made efforts to get Chile to accept the principle of "just compensation" for expropriated foreign interests, and the Chileans agreed to do so, but added "in conformity with Chilean and international law"—a formula which left a good deal of leeway for divergent interpretation in the copper dispute. After some hard bargaining, the creditors agreed to refinance Chile's debt payments so that it would only be required to pay 30 percent of the amount it owed its governmental creditors in 1972 and would receive a three-year grace period before having to pay the remaining 70 percent. In June, Chile reached a similar agreement with the U.S. private banks.

Economic Problems

Allende blamed his predecessors for running up an international debt which he variously stated as between $2 and $4 billion. (It was actually $2.6 billion.) The Christian Democrats replied to Allende's criticisms of the size of Chile's 1970 debt by observing that the debt increase under Frei had been chiefly for the expansion of the copper industry and was supposed to have been repaid with the resulting increase in production in the early 1970s and after. Copper production had not expanded as expected, however, especially at the three big mines of El Teniente, Chuquicamata, and El Salvador, and only the entrance of two new Cerro Corporation mines had kept production in the Gran Minería from actually declining. The government blamed technical difficulties, such as the water supply problems at El Teniente, and the rundown state in which the mines had been left; the opposition cited politicization, bureaucratism, mismanagement by government-appointed mine administrators, and soaring absenteeism. As usual, the explanations by both sides were partially true. Probably the most important single factor was the mass departure of the mine technicians, mainly for economic reasons. The government had ended their special pay provisions, and the mining companies offered them positions in other countries.

On the import side, the opposition cited as one cause of the balance-of-payments problem the refusal of the Allende government to devalue until December 1971 and July 1972, which made it unprofitable for a Chilean exporter to sell his goods abroad and made foreign goods very cheap. The opposition also cited the chaos in the countryside as well as price and other sorts of discrimination against private agriculture (grain prices, for instance, were kept so low that it was more profitable to feed grain to pigs and chickens than to sell it) as reasons for the sharp increase in expenditures for the importation of food. To deal with the serious shortages of imported items, the Allende government created supply and price committees (*juntas de abastecimiento y precios,* JAP) to "advise" on the distribution of scarce commodities and the enforcement of price controls, but this raised the specter of political controls through food rationing and distribution.

Under the Vuskovic policy, it was inevitable that eventually a point would be reached at which strong inflationary pressures could be controlled or disguised. That point occurred early in Allende's second year in office. Allende's first budget had produced an actual deficit of 12 billion escudos, amounting to 36 percent of the budget. The 1972 budget sharply increased the taxes on excess profits, wealth, and property, and removed many income tax exemptions, but there were still 16 billion escudos without financing. In addition, there were mounting deficits in industrial and agricultural enterprises taken over by the government which were not included in the budget but which received a subsidy from the State Bank to keep them from bankruptcy.[21] By 1972, excess industrial capacity had been absorbed, earlier stockpiles had been exhausted, demand had been sharply increased by wage hikes and income redistribution, and the hoped-for revenues from nationalized industries (the "exploitative" profits of the capitalists) had not materialized. The money supply increased by 116.5 percent in 1971, and in mid-1972 the inflation rate reached 5 percent a month. The Chilean wage earner saw his entire 22 percent wage readjustment disappear in the first five months of 1972, and shortages of food and replacement parts led to massive dissatisfaction expressed in women's marches, shopkeepers' strikes, and continued violence in the streets.

An additional problem, the effects of which were not yet evident in early 1972, was the lack of new investment in the Chilean economy. It was folly to ask the foreign or domestic investor to put new capital into an economy run by committed Marxists, so the only possible source of new investment was the government. Yet so much was going for consumption, for redistribution, and to meet the deficits of government-run enterprises that little was left for investment. Allende admitted in his May 1972 address to Congress that investment had declined 7.7 percent in 1971, and opposition economists, by including rundowns in inventories, claimed that it had dropped 24 percent. The adverse effects of this policy on economic growth were not yet felt, however, since production continued to expand until mid-1972.[22]

The effects of inflation and the lack of foreign exchange *were* felt, and the Popular Unity parties held another lengthy meeting in May 1972 to discuss what should be done. In an action aimed at straightening out the more serious distortions in the economy, Allende removed Vuskovic as economics minister in June, and in July he announced a series of austerity measures aimed at achieving "stability at another level." In fact, however, it seems that from this point forward, government policy makers lost control of the Chilean economy, since in every month from July 1972 until the September 1973 coup, prices increased and production declined. The situation might have been different if the government had been prepared to take strong measures in late 1971, but the favorable economic indicators for inflation, employment, and agricultural and industrial production concealed the basically unsound nature of the Vuskovic policy until it was too late. Moreover, the multiparty character of the Popular Unity coalition and its lack of a majority in the legislature made it difficult to pursue a policy of economic austerity. In its report for the El Arrayán conclave in February, the Communist Party had emphasized the importance of the economic problem, but Allende with his characteristic lack of concern for (and ignorance of) economics had left the inflation problem to his economy minister until it finally became evident, in mid-1972, that his policy was a failure.

The Lo Hermida Raid

The differences among the supporters of Allende were highlighted in early August, when the police carried out a night raid on an MIR-controlled shantytown area in the Lo Hermida sector of Santiago. A force of two hundred policemen supported by armored cars and two tanks carried out a search for members of an extremist group, the "16th of July Movement." An exchange of shots resulted in the death of one shantytown dweller and the wounding of six others. The MIR denounced the Communist Party and in particular the Communist undersecretary of the interior, Daniel Vergara, as responsible for the "massacre." Allende suspended the director and assistant director of Investigaciones after the incident and went personally to Lo Hermida to talk to the *pobladores* and to express his regret.

The Christian Democrats announced that they would not fall into "the simplistic position of saying that Señor Allende and his government are assassins" (an obvious reference to the left's reaction to the events in El Salvador and Puerto Montt during the Frei administration), while the MIR announced that Lo Hermida proved that the alternatives were "either to repress the people in order to engage in discussions with the Christian Democratic Party as the left reformists [that is, the Communists] propose, or the government must get the support of the people to combat the PDC as the revolutionaries within, and outside of, the Popular Unity demand."

If the raid was related to a decision to bring the extreme left under control, it failed. It seems to have marked the end of any possibility of a shift in the government's political base of support, since it demonstrated to Allende the political costs of attempting to control the MIR—if he ever considered such a step.

The Lo Hermida raid may have had a purpose which was more symbolic than real: to indicate at a time of extreme social tension the Allende government's continued commitment to the use of existing legal institutions to achieve the transition to socialism. Allende himself had made this commitment clear a week earlier in a public letter to all the Popular Unity parties denouncing a so-called popular assembly which had been held in Concepción with the support of the Socialists and the MAPU (but not the Communists). Allende's language was strong: "I reject any attempt to develop parallel 'spontaneous' tactics on the pretext that persons or groups feel that they are the depositaries of the truth. . . . I will not tolerate anything or anybody who threatens the full authority of the legitimate government of this country." Rejecting the "lyrical romanticism" of those who espoused the thesis of "dual power," he declared that his duty was to defend democratic institutions, and he called upon the Popular Unity parties to work for a government majority in the March 1973 congressional elections which would permit institutional changes such as the amendment of the constitution "in accordance with the will of the majority of the people through the appropriate democratic mechanisms."[23]

Allende's policy thus seemed to align him with the Communists and Radicals on the use of present institutions to achieve majority support for his program. Nevertheless, he allowed the Socialists a veto on steps like an agreement with the Christian Democrats (or earlier with the U.S. ambassador over copper compensation) which would permit him to reach that goal, and he was unwilling to use force to control the proponents of violence who openly opposed a peaceful transition to socialism.

The effects of the change in economic policy in June and July were felt in mid-August, when the government authorized a series of price increases of 50 percent to 100 percent or more on basic items. The inflation rate doubled in August and jumped another 50 percent in September, bringing the increase in the official consumer price index to 99.8 percent for the first nine months of the year. Food prices rose much faster than the index as a whole. The government attempted to soften the impact of the price increases by announcing that it was sending the Congress bills providing for a bonus to be given at the time of the national holidays (September 18) and for a wage readjustment to both the public and private sectors in the full amount of the inflation registered by the end of September. It also proposed the establishment of a mini–market basket (*minicanasta*) of 15 essential items (instead of the 305 in the consumer price index) whose prices would be strictly controlled in order to maintain the basic purchasing power of the poor for essential items. The latter proposal was denounced by the opposition as an attempt to disguise the runaway inflation the country was experiencing, but the bonus and wage readjustment bills were endorsed by all political groups, leaving for political controversy only the question of how to finance the vast expenditure involved. The establishment of a rationing system was also advocated by the Christian Left group, but not by the Allende government, apparently since it feared the adverse political effects of such a move on the congressional elections coming up in March 1973.

The price increases and the general hardening of the government position resulted in a new wave of confrontations between the government and opposition groups. On August 21, the shopkeepers staged a twenty-four-hour strike, their first since the government had taken office. Mini-marches of the empty pots were held in Santiago and Valparaíso. On August 29, demonstrations and marches in opposition to the government were held by the Secondary School Student Federation (FESES). The next day, three thousand construction workers met to demonstrate in support of the government. Tension was building toward a climax on September 4, the second anniversary of Allende's election.

Violence or a Political Solution?

To avoid a violent confrontation, the opposition decreed a silent protest for September 4, when those opposed to the government were to remain at home. On the other side, the government organized in support of President Allende what it later claimed was the largest demonstration in Chilean history. In his speech in the National Stadium, Allende gave particular emphasis to the need to amend the constitution. Allende recognized that this was a particularly difficult time, since "in this period of transition Chile is suffering from all the disadvantages of capitalism without enjoying the advantages of socialism." For the transition to socialism, Chile needed a new constitution, since it "cannot function indefinitely in the face of the systematic and unyielding obstruction of the work of its government on the part of the other branches." Allende proposed "changes in the courts and in the office of the Controller General of the Republic, and modernization and democratization of the judiciary," broadening the powers of the Supeme Court, and providing that its judges be retired at the age of sixty-five. (The retirement proposals, like those of the Roosevelt court-packing plan of 1937, were aimed at opening the court to new Allende appointments. As in the Roosevelt case, the transparently political purpose of the proposal made it most unlikely to be adopted by the legislature. In fact, members of Congress were quick to point out that Allende's own minister of justice was over the age limit.) Allende also reasserted his plans for reform of the legislature, calling for "a unicameral congress or a bicameral congress including a Chamber of Workers" which would be elected concurrently with the president in elections held every six years. He also proposed that the president be authorized to dissolve the legislature and call for new elections once during his six-year term.[24]

A few days after Allende's speech, *Ercilla* published the results of a poll carried out in the Greater Santiago area. It showed what appeared to be a remarkable stability in Chilean public opinion. Asked which of the 1970 presidential candidates they would now support, 36 percent replied Allende, 31 percent cited Alessandri, and 19 percent, Tomic; while 14 percent replied that they would support none of the three. Allende thus received almost exactly the same percentage as he had secured nationally in 1970, while the other candidates still retained substantial support. When the question was phrased in terms of the 1964 candidates, Allende and Frei, Allende received 39 percent—exactly his percentage in 1964—and Frei received 51 percent—slightly below his 1964 figure, but still a majority. When the figures were broken down by socioeconomic group, Frei received 77 percent of the upper-class vote, but still gained the support of 42 percent of the lower-class respondents (Allende received 48 percent support from the low-income respondents). In addition, 62 percent of the upper class and 22 percent of the lower class blamed the Allende government for the current difficulties of the country, while 61 percent of the lower-class interviewees thought the Allende government had benefited low-income groups. Significantly, 52 percent of the middle-class interviewees thought the group most adversely affected by the Allende government was the middle class.[25]

As in the polls taken before the 1970 election, the results of this poll were somewhat skewed in an antigovernment direction by the fact that they were taken in the Greater Santiago area, which was more opposed to the Allende government than some other areas. On the other hand, the poll seemed to show a considerable consistency in the attitudes of the Chilean voter; and while it indicated important differences along class lines, it showed that a substantial minority of the lower class (probably many of them women) was still opposed to the Allende government, a factor which rendered highly improbable the realization of Allende's hopes to mobilize the lower classes into a working majority for the left.

The day after the anniversary, students at the Catholic University demonstrated in support of the secondary students. The next day, the Socialist Party issued a declaration denouncing a "September Plan" to overthrow the government at the time of the national holidays in mid-September. On September 14, Allende picked up the theme of the supposed conspiracy as a justification for rerouting out of the center of the city a mass demonstration by the opposition. Allende asserted that the demonstration was to be used by fascist groups for street incidents, and that this was part of a larger conspiracy which included cutting the country into eight parts by blowing up railroad lines and blocking highways, intercepting ships which were bringing food to Chile, and bringing back a right-wing general who had fled to Bolivia the preceding March.[26]

The government's frequent references to the danger of fascism produced an impassioned speech in Congress by a Christian Democratic senator, Patricio Aylwin, on September 13. Fascism, he declared, exalts violence, is fanatically sectarian, detests parliamentary institutions, glorifies the state, is totalitarian, engages in false propaganda, and fosters hatred and polarization. Parliamentarism stands for reason, coexistence, democracy, pluralism, and the rule of law. The fascists are not in the Congress, he said, but in "sectors of the extreme left linked closely to the government, in functionaries, newspapermen, and persons who are very close to President Allende himself, in authorities and members of the bureaucracy, in high leaders and activists in the government parties."[27]

Congressional Initiatives

One might ask at this point why the Congress, with both houses controlled by the opposition, did not do more to limit the Allende government in carrying out its program. The constitutional amendments on the three areas of the economy, for example, still had not been brought up for final action on the president's vetoes. Time was running out for the Congress to take any initiatives, since after its ordinary session (May 21 to September 18) only the president could initiate legislation. The opposition lawmakers realized that any real effort to limit the executive would meet with a presidential veto, and they lacked the two-thirds necessary to override a veto of ordinary legislation. However, three initiatives were taken by the Congress before the ordinary session ended.

The most important was a constitutional amendment, thus setting the stage for another battle with the executive over whether a simple majority or a two-thirds vote was necessary to override a presidential veto, if the president did not choose to call a plebiscite. In an attempt to eliminate the abuse of the 1967 agrarian reform law, Senator Rafael Moreno, who had been head of the agrarian reform agency in the preceding administration, introduced a constitutional amendment guaranteeing landholdings under forty basic hectares against expropriation, and providing that land taken under the reform program must be assigned to the peasants in individual or cooperative ownership within a year (later lengthened to two years) of expropriation. Like the amendment on the areas of the economy, the Moreno amendment was an attempt to define and regulate by law what the Allende administration had been doing on the basis of legal loopholes. The absolute forty-hectare lower limit was necessary because since 1970 the agrarian reform agency had been using article 4 of the 1967 law, which allowed the expropriation of farms that were abandoned or mismanaged (*mal explotados*), to take over land which was well below the eighty-hectare limit set by the 1967 law. Moreno and others cited numerous cases of the abuse of this provision to seize efficient farms. Article 4 was also used for land seizures because the 1967 law provided for sharply reduced compensation in cases of abandoned lands or those which were badly farmed.[28]

The time limit for the assignment of titles of expropriated lands was included because the Allende government had refused to carry out the provisions of the 1967 law stating that after three years the land should be assigned to peasants individually or in cooperatives. It had not even exercised the presidential prerogative of decreeing an extension of the transition period for two additional years, preferring to rely on a provision in article 67 of the law which allowed for situations in which "for technical reasons . . . it may not be possible to divide the land without deterioration of the soil or injury to the possibility of its economic management." The law provided that in these cases the land should be farmed cooperatively as *asentamientos*; but in over two hundred cases the agrarian reform agency had instead set up state-owned centers of production or ambiguous structures known as centers of agrarian reform—the latter term mentioned once in article 224 of the 1967 law for a totally different purpose (administrative centers run by CORA for infrastructure support to cooperatives or individual farmers), but now employed for units comprising several expropriated *fundos* which were democratically organized but subject to state production quotas and permitted to add many new workers to the existing labor force on the expropriated farms.

The government opposed the Moreno amendment, arguing that it would establish a "new capitalist class" of proprietors of intermediate-sized holdings in the countryside, benefiting only 7 percent of the rural peasantry, while state farming could extend the benefits of the reform to the vast mass of landless peasants. Another constitutional confrontation with the executive thus seemed to be shaping up for the coming months.

A second bill was introduced in Congress as a result of the continuing difficulties of the opposition-controlled media. Sponsored by Senators Baltra and Bossay, both former presidential candidates of the Radical Party who were now Left Radicals, and by Senator Juan Hamilton of the Christian Democrats, it provided public financing and price guarantees for the press and radio. The measure was introduced because it had become apparent that recent cost increases would soon bankrupt the Alessandri paper company (the government had granted it a 19 percent price increase while its costs had doubled and tripled), and it received further urgency when the government closed two opposition radio stations for alleged distortion of the news. The bill was vetoed by President Allende at the end of September, but the concern for the independence of the media in the face of recent government actions was thus added to the economic problems of the country as a source of opposition protest. (Allende had also ordered the discontinuance of a popular TV forum, "A Tres Bandas," in which representatives of the right, the Christian Democrats, and the government parties discussed public issues each week on the government television station.)

A third law voted by the Congress at this time was the most important of all in its long-term effects. Juan de Dios Carmona, a Christian Democratic senator and former minister of defense under the Frei government, introduced a bill strictly regulating the possession of arms and giving broad powers to the armed forces to carry out arms searches and to prosecute violators in military courts. The Arms Control Law forbade anyone other than the armed forces, the carabineros, and such governmental agencies as Investigaciones to possess "machine guns, submachine guns, automatic rifles, and any other automatic weapons" and provided that all other firearms were to be registered within thirty days at the local military garrison. It also forbade the manufacture, import, export, or distribution of arms without military authorization and provided that the Ministries of Interior and Defense, attorneys of the Appeals and Supreme Courts, local government officials, and commanders of military and police units could denounce violators of the law and call for arms searches if they "presumed the clandestine existence" of illegal firearms. The Congress also amended the bill to add a prohibition on the use of "knives, daggers, and clubs" by unauthorized persons.[29]

The Arms Control Law was aimed specifically at the illegal importation of arms which had been publicized in the case of the crates from Cuba earlier in the year. Allende was expected to veto or alter its content, but it had the strong support of the armed forces. The period for action on it coincided with the massive October 1972 strike, which was only settled with the entrance of the military into the government, so that despite opposition from his own Socialist Party, Allende signed it into law in October. Initially, the military chose not to enforce it, but when they began to do so in 1973 the arms searches revealed stockpiling of arms by both sides, which undoubtedly contributed to the military decision to take power that September.

The Fiestas Patrias in mid-September were marked by praise from both sides for the armed forces. The Senate held a luncheon on September 15 for the commanders of the armed services and the carabineros at which its president recalled the devotion of the military to upholding the democratic institutions of the country and praised it as "a unifying factor and secure promise of development and change in liberty and law in the time to come."[30] Allende reviewed the troops on September 19 and was equally generous in his tributes. Thus, both sides were maintaining their links with the only mediating force in the midst of increasing polarization.

As in the ITT case earlier in the year, just as the Allende government was in deepest difficulty, a U.S. company gave it a foreign enemy on whom to cast the blame. After the special Copper Tribunal rejected Kennecott's appeals against the 1971 decision on compensation, the company began court action to assert its property rights through other means. It notified all potential buyers of copper from the El Teniente mine that it had "rights of ownership" over such copper and its proceeds and that "we will take all such action as may be considered necessary in order to protect our rights." On September 30, it petitioned a French court to secure payment for its share of the purchase price from a French company which had bought a shipment of Chilean copper.[31] The Kennecott action was condemned by all sectors of public opinion in Chile, and the government used it to rally support for its policies. On October 10, a protest rally was held which included not only President Allende and the leaders of the Central Workers Confederation, but also the heads of the armed forces and of both houses of the Congress. As now seemed to be his regular custom, Allende quoted Cardinal Silva and Radomiro Tomic in condemnation of the Kennecott maneuver.

The Truckers' Strike

The expression of national unity did not last long. Far from Santiago in the remote southern province of Aysén, a conflict was brewing which was to pose the most serious threat so far to the Allende government. The private truckers of the province were disturbed by the governor's announcement that in view of the inadequacy of private trucking, the government intended to set up a public trucking firm. Blaming the government's own inefficiency in securing replacement parts for them, the truckers announced on October 11 an indefinite strike in which they were joined by the National Truckers Confederation. The strike rapidly spread to the entire country. The tension had been building up since August, and the day before the strike began *El Mercurio* had published in its entirety a speech made by a National Party senator, Francisco Bulnes, which argued that the effort to drive the paper company out of business by refusing it price increases while its wages and costs increased was a violation of the constitution. Bulnes concluded that systematic violations of this sort had "definitely situated the government in the area of illegality" since "it is not sufficient for a government to be legitimate in its origin. Governments must also exercise the power they have in a legitimate way. A government which begins legitimately, but which systematically and deliberately violates the constitution, is converted into a government which is illegitimate."[32]

As the strike spread, it seemed evident to the government that at least some of the strike's supporters wished to use it to bring down the government. The leaders of the strike were immediately jailed, but this only aggravated the situation. On October 13, the truckers were given the support of the shopkeepers' and merchants' organizations, which also decreed a national strike of indefinite duration. Besides the problems of the truckers, the Shopkeepers Confederation and the Central Chamber of Commerce complained of the closing of a radio station and the campaign against the paper company. The National Party and the Christian Democrats supported the strikers, and the Christian Democrats blamed the government not only for punishing the strikers, but for causing the protest in the first place by creating the shortage of replacement parts which was the strikers' initial complaint.[33]

President Allende made a radio speech at midnight on October 13 in which he accused the truckers of political purposes in calling a strike and said that many truckers supported the government. As to the shopkeepers' announced intention of striking, Allende said, "We know that hundreds of shopkeepers will open their shops. The leaders of SOFOFA [Sociedad de Fomento Fabril, the Society for Industrial Development] are wrong if they think that industry will shut down. The fascists and neofascists will not paralyze the country."

On October 14, the National Council of the PDC declared that the repression of the truckers' strike constituted a violation of the Statute of Democratic Guarantees and called a meeting of its peasant, youth, women's and professional wings to decide on a common strategy. The council also listed conditions for resolving the conflict which included freeing the imprisoned strike leaders, resolving their grievances, and providing effective guarantees of liberty of expression.

On October 16, the Engineers Association joined the strike, and they were followed by bank employees, gas workers, lawyers, architects, and taxi and bus drivers; the next day, doctors and dentists joined. In eighteen (later extended to twenty) of Chile's twenty-five provinces, the government established a midnight to 6 A.M. curfew and took over all the radio stations. It opened some of the shops in the center of Santiago by force and legally requisitioned them for failing to serve the public with essential items, a tactic which was also used against factories that stopped production. The progovernment press described the strike as a "lockout," an "employers' strike" (*paro patronal*), or, somewhat more accurately, as a strike by the middle class.

The Christian Democratic–influenced industrial unions did not, for the most part, support the strike, and their workers continued to go to the factories; but the middle class (including the lower-middle class, which was often at the same income level as the workers), the professionals, and part of the peasantry supported it. Their importance to the country was demonstrated by the serious repercussions of the strike for the economy. All the taxi drivers and most bus drivers were on strike. One hundred thousand peasants, influenced by Christian Democratic peasant unions, struck. The strike leaders estimated that at its height, 100 percent of transport, 97 percent of commerce, 80 percent of the professions, and 85 percent of the peasant cooperatives had joined the strike, with the total on strike estimated at between six and seven hundred thousand Chileans.

The government list of requisitioned industries lengthened each day. To run them and to establish some coordination in the face of splits over the strike in local government agencies, parallel organizations sprang up. A National Peasant Council which had been established earlier now began to issue statements in support of the government. Self-appointed communal commands and a coordinating committee of the industrial belts (*cordones industriales*) arose and attempted to assure supplies to industry and to the shantytown areas. Yet the observer walking around downtown Santiago felt he was in a ghost town. In that area, at least, the strike was effective, and the opposition's claim of national support seemed to be verified.

The solution was obvious to all concerned: the increased involvement of the only institution trusted by elements on both sides—the armed forces. Yet in this area Allende had to tread carefully, since the left wing of his coalition was opposed to military involvement. Thus, he used the military to maintain the transportation system and to assist in distributing food and fuel, but at the outset he did not formally involve them in his government. The complaints about "economic asphyxiation" of the paper company were undercut by granting a 93 percent price increase. On October 20, Allende met with Chile's Catholic bishops to discuss the "grave situation" in the country, and the night before he met with Masonic leaders. To the latter group he quoted, prophetically, a sentence of President Pedro Aguirre Cerda, the president elected by the Popular Front in 1938: "I will only leave La Moneda [the presidential palace] in a pine box."[34]

The Association of Radio Broadcasters of Chile (ARCHI) objected to the continued government monopoly of radio broadcasting, and independent broadcasters began leaving the official network. As a result, their transmissions were suspended by the government, but their actions were upheld by the Controller General and later by the Court of Appeals on the grounds that in the absence of a law authorizing it, a compulsory network was a violation of the Statute of Democratic Guarantees. The television station run by the Catholic University continued to operate free of government interference, and on October 23 ex-president Eduardo Frei made a speech on the current situation. Describing the state of the economy as catastrophic ("formerly a Bolivian needed twenty-five pesos to buy a Chilean escudo; now a Bolivian peso buys ten escudos"), he attacked the government for its failure to concern itself with investment: "No economy, whether capitalist, socialist, or communist, can survive the disappearance of investment. Without investment, there is no growth; without growth, there is unemployment and misery." Frei asserted that the only way to reestablish social peace was by effective control of arms, true freedom of information and expression, the reestablishment of the rule of law, and free elections.

Frei's appeal to the March 1973 elections was echoed a few days later in an article by Radomiro Tomic which predicted with chilling foresight the consequences of a breakdown of Chile's institutional structure: "No constitution, no elections, no impeachments, no pluralism in the media, no marches of protest or support, no occupations or reoccupations, no gatherings in the street to denounce or support the government, no independent trade unions, no strikes, no social advances recognized by law." Blaming the government for provoking polarization into two antagonistic blocks, Tomic urged both sides to look to the March 1973 congressional elections to resolve their differences. He suggested that a minister of interior should be appointed who would have the confidence of both the president and the opposition groups, to guarantee that the congressional elections would be held in an atmosphere of complete freedom.[35]

On October 25 Allende seemed to have reached an agreement with the strikers, but differences were not resolved until the president reorganized his cabinet to take in representatives of the armed services at the end of the following week. A cabinet reorganization, made all the more necessary because the opposition now began proceedings to impeach four members of the outgoing cabinet for violations of the constitution, had already been scheduled in order to permit the departure of the cabinet members who were to be candidates in the March congressional elections. The institutional involvement of the military in the cabinet marked a fundamental change in the politics of Chile and the beginning of the end of civilian rule.

CHAPTER NINE

The Politicization of the Military

Formal military involvement in the Allende government meant that the effective veto the military already exercised in certain policy areas—military aid from the United States, border disputes with Argentina, military pay and perquisites—now extended much more broadly to issues of law and order, including the legality of the methods adopted for the extension of state control over the economy. It also meant that the military services became collectively responsible for approving and implementing government policy, thus abandoning the fiction of their "nonpolitical" character. This was particularly true in the case of General Carlos Prats, army commander in chief, who was appointed minister of interior—a much more politically sensitive post than that of either the minister of public works, held by a navy officer, or the minister of mines, occupied by a member of the air force. Now all issues of domestic policy were to be the responsibility of the head of the senior and largest military service. In the short run, this meant a lowering of the political temperature in Chile, since both sides viewed the military as impartial arbiters. Over the longer run, however, it accelerated the politicization of the military and undermined the position of those like Prats who favored the maintenance of constitutionalism and civilian rule.

Prats immediately began negotiations with the strikers, and on the basis of a pledge of no reprisals, they agreed to return to work on November 6. The strike had cost Chile an estimated $150 to $200 million. From the point of view of the opposition, the strike had resulted in the reopening of several radio stations which had been closed by the government, the cessation of efforts to take over the paper company, and the appointment of General Prats as interior minister, which was considered a guarantee of the fairness of the March 1973 election. From the government's point of view, the strike had at least not been successful in overthrowing the Allende regime, and it had also led to the extension of state control over many new enterprises. These included all of Chile's construction companies, the industries in the northern port of Arica, manufacturers of furniture, seed, and dairy products, and many other companies.

The progovernment press cited the drop in the black-market rate for dollars in October 1972 as proof that the CIA was giving financial support to the strikes—a claim that was analyzed in the 1975 report on Chile issued by the Senate Select Committee on Intelligence Activities. The report found that on September 24, 1972, the Forty Committee authorized $24,000 in emergency assistance to the Sociedad de Fomento Fabril (Society for Industrial Development), of which $2,800 was passed to the striking truckers in contravention of CIA and Forty Committee prohibitions. An additional $100,000 was authorized on October 26, 1972, for "electoral activities" by three private-sector organizations, none of it for direct aid to the truckers. This contradicted earlier newspaper reports (*New York Times*, September 24, 1974) that "a majority" of the CIA's estimated $8 million expenditure against Allende had gone to support the strikers.

Did not the government foresee that the price increases in August would lead to riots and demonstrations? Whether it did so or not, it seems to have had no choice, since cost pressures had reached the point that nearly all enterprises in the country were losing money. As it was, around 40 percent of the budget was based on deficit spending, and most of the government-controlled "social area" of industry and the "reformed" sector in agriculture was running at a loss. Probably it was assumed that a wage readjustment and additional aid from the Western European and socialist countries would enable the government to maintain relative price stability, at least until the March elections.

Once the strike had been settled, the politics of Chile was, as so often, directed toward the next elections. In the crucial Santiago area, former president Frei was nominated by the Christian Democrats and Sergio Onofre Jarpa was named by the National Party to run for the Senate. Both would run on the ticket of the Democratic Confederation (CODE), and because of Chile's proportional representation system, both seemed certain to be elected. The Popular Unity Federation also nominated two strong candidates in the Santiago area, incumbent senators Volodia Teitelboim for the Communists and Carlos Altamirano for the Socialists. The Popular Socialists who had split off from the Socialist Party in 1967 continued to run a separate ticket but were not expected to secure many votes. The March elections were shaping up as a two-way confrontation between the government and the opposition with an unpredictable element involved—the 800,000 new voters who had registered since 1970, when constitutional amendments had extended the suffrage to illiterates and to those between the ages of eighteen and twenty-one. In late 1972 the Senate was divided 33 to 17 in favor of the opposition, while in the Chamber of Deputies the division was 93 to 57. If the economy continued to deteriorate at the current rate, the opposition could hope for substantial gains.

The opposition was encouraged by the results of student and university elections in November. The Christian Democrats easily won the Federation of Secondary School Students of Santiago (FESES), and the "nonpolitical" (*gremialista*) slate, sympathetic to the National Party, won in the Catholic University. A prominent Christian Democrat, Domingo Santa Maria, was elected rector of the Santa Maria Technical University in Valparaíso, and more surprising, the opposition gained the rectorship at the University of Concepción, which for years had been controlled by the left. With Edgardo Boeninger as head of the University of Chile, this meant that the government had lost control of all the university rectorships except that of the State Technical University.

Economic Aid from Europe and Latin America

On November 15 the finance minister, Orlando Millas, presented the annual budget speech. It became the occasion for a review of the accomplishments of the Allende government and for renewed attacks upon it by the opposition. Millas noted the difficulties the government was having with foreign exchange and gave specific figures on the decline of short-term credits from U.S. banks (from $219 million at the end of the Frei term to $32 million in late 1972). Millas noted, however, that "present short-term credits from all sources total $590 million from very diverse sources." Those sources included, according to Millas, $250 million in short-term credits from Canada, Argentina, Mexico, Australia, and Western Europe. Millas also mentioned $446 million in long-term loans from the USSR, Eastern Europe, and China, and $70 million from other Latin American countries. He did not give the figure for Western Europe, but during the period between November 1971, when payment of most of Chile's foreign debt had ceased, and December 1972, the Chilean government publication *Chile Economic News* listed over $200 million in loans from Great Britain, Spain, France, Holland, Belgium, Sweden, and Finland. Millas admitted that exports had declined by 4.6 percent, with major declines in agricultural (31.2 percent) and industrial production (24.6 percent), but this was balanced by a 7.3 percent increase in the value of copper exports, the major producers of foreign exchange. On the import side, however, there was a large increase in food imports, for which, Millas reported, it would be necessary to spend $383 million in 1972.

Reviewing the accomplishments of the government to date, Millas cited the expropriation of 3,479 farms which, with the 1,408 expropriations carried out by the Frei regime, now brought the total area in the reformed sector to 35 percent of the agricultural surface of the country. The state now owned 80 percent of the shares in the country's thirteen principal banks and had taken over 119 companies, with another 41 likely to be taken over shortly. (The latter companies seem to have been the ones which had come under government control as a result of the October strike. Whether they were to be returned to their owners was the subject of intense controversy in 1973.)[1]

The Allende Trip

Millas may have included in his figures some anticipated aid from President Allende's forthcoming trip to the United Nations and to the Soviet Union. Allende scheduled his trip to make maximum use of the fifteen days that a 1970 constitutional amendment allowed for presidential travel without senatorial permission. He stopped for fuel in Lima, meeting briefly with President Juan Velasco Alvarado, and then spent several days in Mexico. After his United Nations speech, he flew to the Soviet Union and Cuba. His trip also included brief stops in Algeria and Venezuela, where he spoke to the presidents of both countries.

In addition to seeking further aid funds, the Allende trip was aimed at securing support in Chile's controversy with the copper companies. The copper shipment which had been embargoed in September had been diverted from Le Havre to Rotterdam and back to Le Havre; workers had refused to unload it because of the possibility of its being "attached" by Kennecott through proceedings in French and Dutch courts. On November 29, the French court in which Kennecott sued rejected Chile's claim that its nationalization program was not subject to French jurisdiction because of the sovereign immunity of the Chilean state. The court ruled, however, that payment could be made to the Chilean Copper Corporation for the copper, but the money was to be kept in a separate account to be made available if a court-appointed attorney determined that it should be paid out.[2] The Chileans appealed the decision and refused to cooperate with the court-appointed referee, and the case continued in litigation.

Kennecott also sued for copper delivered in other countries. In Sweden, one purchaser deposited its payment for a copper shipment with the Provincial Council of Stockholm pending the outcome of litigation on the entity to be paid. A German court declared the copper nationalization confiscatory and discriminatory but denied jurisdiction for the imposition of an injunction; in Italy, Kennecott took action in several courts to recover the purchase price of three shipments from El Teniente which had already been delivered (one court ruled that the nationalization was "not applicable in Italy" and that the physical takeover of El Teniente was "effected without rightful title and thus illegal with the further consequence that the rights of the owners of said property never terminated").[3] All shipments of copper were thus delivered to their purchasers, but the Chilean Copper Corporation (CODELCO) was involved in costly legal battles in many European countries, and presumably some potential buyers of Chilean copper were dissuaded from such purchases by the prospect of involvement in such litigation.

President Allende's United Nations speech on December 4, 1972, gave him a worldwide forum to attack the multinational corporations in general and Kennecott and ITT in particular. Allende defended Chile's nationaliza-

President Salvador Allende denounces ITT intervention in Chile at the United Nations General Assembly on December 4, 1972. (United Nations)

tion of the copper mines and cited the "exorbitant" profits made by Anaconda and Kennecott in the fifteen years which had been used as the basis for the excess profits deduction. Anaconda, he said, averaged 21.5 percent profit on the book value of its Chilean holdings, compared with 3.5 percent for the rest of its worldwide operations. Kennecott averaged 52.8 percent of book value he said, achieving a 205 percent profit on book value in 1969 compared with 10 percent in the rest of the world.[4] Over forty-two years, he said, the U.S. companies had taken $4 billion in profits out of the country which could have been used to "completely transform Chile" through programs of health, education, and nutrition. Citing the ITT papers and additional documents published in July 1972, he accused ITT of "attempting to bring about civil war in my country. . . . That is what we call imperialist intervention." Allende also attacked the U.S. government for establishing a financial blockade, "an oblique, underhanded, indirect form of aggression . . . virtually imperceptible activities usually disguised with words and statements that extol the sovereignty and dignity of my country." He cited the cutoff of loans from international agencies, the U.S. government, and private banks, noting that this led to "limitation of our ability to secure the equipment, spare parts, manufacturing inputs, foodstuffs, and medicines which we need. Each and every Chilean is suffering the consequences of these measures." Allende called for solidarity from the Third World, supported the adoption of the Charter of Economic Rights and Duties of States proposed by President Luís Echeverría of Mexico, and affirmed "the sovereign right of all developing nations to dispose freely of their natural resources."[5]

Nixon administration officials replied to Allende's charges by saying that Chilean requests for aid had been turned down because of Chile's lack of creditworthiness. They admitted, however, that Chile's credit difficulties were also related to the policy announced by President Nixon on January 19, 1972, that if U.S. holdings were expropriated without compensation the United States would "not itself extend new bilateral economic benefits" and would "withhold its support from loans under consideration in multilateral development banks." Reporting on the controversy, a *New York Times* reporter noted that nationalization problems had not prevented the administration from giving new credits to the Chilean military in May 1972.[6]

Shortly after Allende's speech the Overseas Private Investment Corporation (the U.S.-government-financed institution that had taken over AID's program of insurance to private investors in less developed areas) announced that a settlement had been reached with Kennecott on compensation for its 1967 Chileanization loan to Chile. Since OPIC would have difficulty compensating Kennecott from its own resources without seeking a new appropriation from Congress, it was offering participation certificates to U.S. institutional investors on the remaining Chilean government debt (Chile had paid interest and part of principal on its 1967 debt to Kennecott after a U.S. court had attached its U.S. assets for payment of the installment due at the end of 1971). OPIC did not compensate Kennecott for its 49 percent equity investment, which had not been covered by an insurance agreement. Nor did it compensate Anaconda for its principal losses in Chile, since Anaconda had had only "standby" insurance on its new investments in the Chuquicamata and El Salvador mines at the time of the 1969 nationalization agreements with the Frei government. (Anaconda had changed its insurance at that time, but OPIC claimed that "effective nationalization" had already taken place and denied Anaconda's claim for $154 million. The issue later went to arbitration, where Anaconda received a favorable decision.)

From New York, Allende flew by way of Algiers to Moscow, where he conducted talks on the expansion of Soviet assistance. It was reported that Moscow had promised Chile $293 million of aid in the preceding two years —$50 million in cash and the balance in short- and long-term credits. The USSR was also reported to have agreed to buy 130,000 tons of copper and $87 million of copper products over the next three years. Allende received a warm welcome, but there was some doubt about the willingness of the Soviet Union to extend further credits to Chile's troubled economy, although Chilean specialists had been working on the expansion of technical and financial aid, in particular to the copper mines. The Soviet offer of $50 million of low-interest credits (fifty years at 1 percent) for military equipment was not accepted owing to the opposition of the Chilean military. The only new aid that the Soviets granted Chile was an additional $27 million in medium-term credits for the purchase of wheat, pork, butter, and cotton and a $20 million increase in earlier short-term loans.[7] On Allende's return from the USSR he stopped in Cuba, and Fidel Castro sweetened the trip with an announcement that he was sending sugar to Chile without charge as a gift from the Cuban people. In his speech on his return, Allende paid tribute to the aid of the Soviet Union and Cuba, but he also laid particular stress on the links with Peru and Mexico which had been promoted by his trip.

During his absence the opposition parties had complained that the promises of no reprisals made by General Prats at the conclusion of the October strike had not been observed. Because he was said to have supported reprisals against employees of the Central Bank, the Christian Democratic Party voted to support the National Party's impeachment charge against Orlando Millas. When the motion to charge Millas with violation of the constitution was adopted by the Chamber of Deputies on December 28, 1972, Allende resorted to a procedure he had used before. Without waiting for the Senate to approve the impeachment, he transferred Millas to the post of economy minister and named Fernando Flores, a member of MAPU, to the Finance post. Allende again attacked the impeachment as an attempt to return to the discredited parliamentary system and stated that he viewed the vote as particularly inopportune since it took place just before the December 31 deadline for the adoption of the budget.

Food Distribution System

On January 10, 1973, the day before the impeachment of his predecessor was finally approved by the Senate, Flores made a lengthy address to the people of Chile announcing the establishment of a new distribution system for basic food necessities. Although it was described in the opposition newspapers and by the international press agencies as the creation of a rationing program, what Flores actually announced was the establishment of a government monopoly in the distribution and marketing of thirty basic food items. What gave rise to the rationing stories was Flores's statement that distribution would be planned on the basis of "family quotas" of these items in each neighborhood unit, and that these would be distributed with the help of the government-supported JAP committees. This looked to the opposition like politically controlled rationing, but the government denied that rationing cards or programs were contemplated, only a new distribution system under the direction of a National Secretariat of Distribution headed by Air Force General Alberto Bachelet. Flores described it as an attempt to prevent products from going into the black market and an alternative to the "ferocious" price rationing inherent in the capitalist system.

Flores's speech contained two significant admissions. First, he described the October strike as "a work stoppage by nonproletarian sectors" including professionals, employees, and housewives, rather than simply as an "employers' lockout," as the government had described it up to this point. Second, he noted that the government was ending the practice of payment in kind and preferential purchase of company-manufactured goods for the workers "because in many cases they are sources for the black market," thus admitting that the opposition sectors were not the only ones responsible for the flourishing black market.[8]

In the ensuing controversy, President Allende wrote an open letter to *El Mercurio* accusing it of lying when it described the system as food rationing and a move toward dictatorship. The newspaper replied that the proposed system was de facto rationing and that the powers being given to the JAP committees were indeed dictatorial. Flores's speech also led to a statement by the military ministers dissociating themselves from the "political" aspects of the speech, but supporting measures to combat food shortages. Rear Admiral Ismael Huerta resigned as minister of public works in protest over the new measures and was replaced by another navy admiral.[9]

The opposition exaggerated the extent of the rationing proposed in the

Flores speech, but it was correct in perceiving the potentialities for political control of the JAP committees. Earlier groups which had appeared to pose such a threat, such as the Popular Unity committees in the 1970 elections, and the communal commands which had arisen at the time of the October strike, had lapsed after the reason for their creation disappeared. Because of the continuing likelihood of food shortages, however, the JAP committees were likely to continue to be active, and the government distribution agency, DINAC, channeled food supplies through them. The committees were not elected bodies, but their legal existence as advisory groups to the government price control agency, DIRINCO, had been approved by the controller general in April 1972. The Communist Party had promoted their expansion, so that by 1973, 1,000 such committees were reported to be in existence, 675 of them in the capital. Beginning in November 1972, inspectors were appointed to enforce price controls, and by January 1973, there were serious problems concerning their relation to the military in charge of distribution and to the legally elected neighborhood committees that wished to supervise their activities. The JAP committees thus raised in a more permanent and broadly applicable form the question of "dual power" on the local level which had emerged during the October strike and in the MIR-controlled settlements which had refused to be integrated into the local government and police system.

Rolando Calderón, the minister of agriculture, admitted the seriousness of the food problem. Blaming "limiting factors, both natural and political," Calderón said that it would be necessary to import 450 million dollars' worth of food in 1973. (Later figures revealed that nearly that amount had actually been spent in 1972, while the outlay for food imports in 1973 was to amount to over $600 million.) Calderón also admitted that despite the provision in the 1967 Agrarian Reform Law which allowed the peasants to divide up the reformed *asentamientos* after a transitional period of three to five years, no private distribution was being permitted. In his words, "the point has already been established that individual apportionments will not result in benefit to the nation, the farmers, or production itself."[10]

The Congressional Election Campaign

The inflation rate (the official figure for 1972 was 163 percent), the food shortages, and figures which showed that state-controlled industries had operated at a deficit of 50 billion escudos for 1972 were all cited by the opposition politicians as the campaign for the March elections began to warm up. Allende did not deny that some of the state-owned industries had been operating at a loss. In January he spent two days at the Sumar Textile firm, where he lectured the workers, citing the high absenteeism, the decline in production, and the fact that the workers had given themselves a 400 percent increase in wages while the firm had lost 132 million escudos in 1972. He warned that if the workers did not restrain themselves, "I will have no choice but to leave office, comrades." But at a rally a month before the election, he warned that "fascist reaction" was menacing the revolutionary process and stated that "if the counterrevolutionaries exceed the legal limits, the people will confront them with a revolutionary violence."[11]

The president's reference to possible violence was a rhetorical exaggeration at that particular moment. The energies that could be spared by Chileans in Santiago and Valparaíso from the customary February trips to the beach were directed at the upcoming elections. The right-wing National Party was optimistic that the economic difficulties would produce a landslide against the government, and its leaders even spoke of the possibility of a two-thirds vote against the government. If such a vote were translated directly into seats, it would give the opposition enough congressional representation to impeach the president. Ex-president Frei, if only because he knew that the Chilean system of proportional representation would make it impossible for the opposition to secure the required number of seats—particularly in the Senate, where only half the seats were up for election—did not speak in such terms, but he did describe the election as a "plebiscite" on the conduct of the government. Allende stopped speaking of getting a majority which would permit him to amend the constitution, and in a speech in Valparaíso in mid-February he predicted that "despite lines, shortages, and a campaign of lies" the government candidates would secure 40 percent of the vote. As he described it, this would be a triumph for the government, since it would mark a significant increase over the 36 percent that he had received in 1970. (He conveniently forgot the 50 percent vote in the 1971 municipal elections.) Instead of combining the Allende and Tomic votes to demonstrate that 63 percent of the Chilean voters had voted against capitalism in 1970, he combined the Tomic and Alessandri 1970 percentages to arrive at a 62.7 percent figure that the opposition was supposed to match in 1973.[12]

As the campaign progressed, the differences within the two opposing camps became more evident. In late January, Orlando Millas, the Communist economics minister, had sent a bill to Congress to regularize the situation of the companies that had been intervened or requisitioned, many of them in the October strike. It provided for the takeover with compensation of those on the government's initial list of ninety monopolistic or strategic enterprises, but also set up a special commission to study the situation of others. For the Socialists and the MIR, this raised the possibility that some companies which had entered the "area of social ownership" through (supposedly temporary) intervention or requisition might be returned to their owners, a move they firmly opposed. In the opposition, persistent rumors circulated of contacts between the leaders of the Christian Democrats and the government about the possibility of their joining the cabinet after the elections. The rumors were fostered by Christian Democratic insistence that they would only decide on whether to continue with the Democratic Confederation after the election was over.[13]

These rumors were probably false, but they did have a certain credibility, since despite the presence of extremists in both groupings there was a basic coincidence of interest between Allende and the Communists on the one side, and the Christian Democrats on the other. Both groups were committed for reasons of principle and tactics to the observance of the electoral process—the Christian Democrats because they hoped to win the 1976 elections, and Allende and the Communists because they were aware that in a coup or civil war situation, they would be the losers.[14]

In the concluding weeks before the March 4 election, Chile was blanketed with propaganda from both sides. The television stations were legally neutral, but the news coverage left no doubt about where the government station and that of the University of Chile stood, while the Catholic University station appeared to give the edge to the opposition.

Radio broadcasts were interspersed with spot announcements and one foreign observer estimated that between two-thirds and three-quarters favored the opposition. The opposition had a considerable edge in media advertising because the CIA was pouring money into their campaign. A total of $1.5 million had been authorized by the Forty Committee for support of opposition parties and media. Despite the extreme improbability of securing a two-thirds majority, the National Party campaigned on the slogan "It is not a new parliament we are electing, but a new government" and spoke of a 65 percent majority or more. Their hopes, fed as in 1970 by the strong anti-Allende feelings in the middle- and upper-class areas of Santiago, proved to be false.

Election Results

General Prats had predicted on television a week before the election, "Everybody will win the election." His comment, almost a truism for Chilean politics, proved correct. On a warm Sunday in March, 3,661,898 Chileans went to the polls, 700,000 more than had voted in the municipal elections of 1971. They cast two ballots, one for the senatorial candidates and one for the deputies. In each case the candidates were listed by name under one of three headings, the order determined by lot. The headings read Confederation of Democracy, Popular Unity Federation, and Popular Socialist Union (the small party which had split off from the Socialists in 1967) in that order; but following each candidate's name was an abbreviation indicating to which of the traditional parties he belonged. Voters selected individual candidates, but the votes for each grouping were totaled and then allocated by the electoral quotient system to the parties and candidates in the order of the pluralities received by each candidate; unused votes were transferred to the next ranking candidate in each party coalition. Thus, the voter could express his or her preference both for a given candidate and (ignoring the negligible USP) for or against the government.

Because there were separate elections for deputies and senators, and because of blank and invalid ballots, the results could be computed in a variety of ways. However, there were no independent candidates, the USP received only .28 percent of the vote, and blank and void ballots were few (1.6 percent), so the easiest way of measuring the results in percentages would seem to be to add both deputy and senatorial votes and exclude the blank and void ballots. If this procedure is used, the final results gave the opposition (CODE) 55.74 percent of the vote and the progovernment Popular Unity Federation 43.98 percent. Translated into seats, it meant only a slight shift, with a government gain of two seats in the Senate and six seats in the Chamber. This reduced the opposition majority to 30 (out of 50) in the senate and 87 (out of 150) in the Chamber.

As usual, the interpretation of these results depended on one's political position, and which previous election was chosen as the base for comparison. The opposition compared the 1973 results with the 1971 municipal elections and observed that the government had lost 6 percent of its support while the opposition had received a percentage equal to that of Eduardo Frei in 1964, generally acknowledged to be a landslide victory. The government, in turn, used the 1970 presidential elections as a base point and boasted of an increase in its support from 36 to 44 percent. It also pointed out that its results were better than any preelection estimate, including its own most optimistic predictions, and asserted that this was the first time in Chilean history that a president had been able to increase his electoral support in a midterm congressional election. (President Pedro Aguirre Cerda had also done so in 1941, but his Popular Front coalition had split before the election.) Neither side used the proper basis of comparison, which was the last congressional election, in March 1969. In that election, the combined vote of the two Socialist parties, the Communists, and the Radicals totaled 43 percent—almost exactly the 1974 result. Since then, the Radicals and the Christian Democrats had suffered party splits in contrary directions, but a Chilean government publication, while emphasizing the increase in the vote for the left since 1970, produced figures which indicated that the opposition had gained 3 percent since 1969 in the Chamber of Deputies while the progovernment parties had lost about .5 percent.[15] (The difference was accounted for by the sharp reduction in the number of abstentions and spoiled ballots.)

The losses in seats by the opposition were attributable to the vagaries of the Chilean electoral system, which overrepresents rural areas and underrepresents urban areas such as Valparaíso and Santiago, where the strongest opposition to the government was registered. (In 1973, this had almost reached a point of absurdity, since the electoral quotient used to elect senators in the tenth *agrupación* in the extreme south of Chile was 16,470 votes, while the same figure for Santiago was 269,563!)[16]

The results for individual candidates could also give encouragement to both sides. As a senatorial candidate in Santiago, Eduardo Frei received the largest vote of any senatorial candidate in Chilean history (389,637), followed by two long-time Communist and Socialist senators, Volodia Teitelboim and Carlos Altamirano, with 238,535 and 229,281 votes respectively. A strong fourth-place contender (Santiago gets five senators) was the head of the National Party, Sergio Onofre Jarpa, with 191,611 votes. Among the deputies the lead was taken, as usual, by the Socialist political boss of the San Miguel section of Santiago, Mario Palestro, with 112,534.

The election strengthened the positions of four of the major parties, the Socialists and Communists on the government side, and the Christian Democrats and the National Party in the opposition, while the small parties almost disappeared. The Christian Left, which had split off from the Christian Democrats in August 1971, dropped from nine seats in the lower house to one. The two groups which had left the Radical Party in 1969 and 1971 received 2 percent and 1.8 percent of the vote, respectively, and were left with only three deputies between them—a loss of nineteen seats. The Radical Party, which had received 13.9 percent of the vote in 1969 before its two splits, continued its decline, receiving only 3.7 percent of the vote and dropping from twelve to five seats in the Chamber. Conversely, the Socialists increased their percentage by 6 percent over 1969 and nearly doubled their representation in the lower house (from fourteen to twenty-seven seats); and the Communists, Christian Democrats, and National Party all made gains.[17] Thus, the Chilean party system seemed to be moving toward four large parties, divided into two groups, each composed of two major parties and a number of small satellites. Together, the Christian Democrats (with 29 percent of the vote), the National Party (with over 21 percent), the Socialists (with 18 percent), and the Communists (with 16 percent) managed to secure nearly 85 percent of the popular vote.

The Communist paper, *El Siglo*, emphasized the increase in female support for the government candidates, noting that the women's vote for Popular Unity had risen from 30.5 percent in 1970 to 39 percent in 1973. It did not add, however, that the 39 percent figure marked a drop of 5 percent from the 44 percent which the progovernment candidates had received from women in 1971. Women in Santiago also voted for Frei and Onofre Jarpa in much larger numbers than did men, with Frei receiving 60 percent of his votes from women and Jarpa, 58 percent. The opposition received majority support from women voters in all but two of Santiago's twenty-seven communes (Barrancas and La Granja), while the progovernment candidates were victorious among male voters in fourteen Santiago communes. The difference between the division by sex in lower-class communes and the solidarity of middle- and upper-class opposition is demonstrated by looking at the returns for Providencia and Las Condes. In Providencia, 84 percent of the women and 80 percent of the men voted against the government; in Las Condes the figures were 79 percent and 72 percent, respectively.

On a national basis, the decline in female support for the government was as great as or greater than that of male voters, and women contined to oppose the government much more strongly than men. If void and blank ballots are excluded, about 61 percent of the women voted for the opposition, while only a little more than half the men did so.[18]

The reformed sectors of the peasantry seemed to have swung behind the government. A postelection analysis of rural communes which divided them into those which had been composed of large landholdings now expropriated, those which were made up principally of intermediate-sized plots (above twenty basic hectares, but below the eighty basic hectares of the agrarian reform), and those which were characterized by small farms or *minifundios*, argued convincingly that the left vote had increased in each of the last four elections (including the 1972 by-elections) in the "reformed" areas and had declined (in the case of the intermediate-sized areas very sharply) since 1971 in the other areas.[19]

The increased turnout in rural areas was partly accounted for by the larger numbers of illiterates who were voting for the first time. It was more difficult to determine the electoral effects of the enfranchisement of those eighteen to twenty-one years of age, who voted in large numbers for the first time in 1973. Impressionistic reports spoke of 70 to 80 percent supporting the government—which might help to explain the fact that it received a higher vote than anyone, including Allende, had expected—but without survey data, it was difficult to demonstrate this in any conclusive fashion. What was clear from the figures was that new voters were an important element in the 1973 election, since 700,000 more Chileans voted in 1973 than had done so in 1970, an increase of 24 percent. The unusually large number of new voters was the basis of a study published in July 1973 by the Catholic University law faculty which claimed to be able to prove a progovernment vote fraud involving 200,000 to 300,000 votes. The study turned up a few individual cases of vote fraud, but its statistical analysis was unconvincing and its partisan purpose and sponsorship made its conclusions doubtful.

CHAPTER TEN

Prelude to the Coup

The unexpectedly high progovernment vote in the March 1973 election gave a psychological boost to the government forces, despite the fact that, technically, it had been a defeat. It also strengthened the arguments of the left wing of Popular Unity against accepting the fourteen conditions the military presented as their price for remaining in the cabinet.[1] On March 27, Allende organized a civilian cabinet, appointing Socialists to the key Interior and Agriculture posts and keeping the Communists in charge of Economics, Labor, and Justice. At the swearing-in of the new cabinet members, Allende warned of "the dark hours" which lay ahead because of the worsening economic situation.

Aside from minor shifts in the Congress in favor of the four largest parties, the election had not really altered the political stalemate in Chile. In some ways it made the situation worse, since at the same time that it closed off the electoral outlet to the opposition for three years, it also encouraged the Popular Unity coalition to push ahead with its program and not attempt to seek any compromise.

The ENU School Reform

Certainly the announcement immediately after the election of a plan to implement by decree an elaborate program to reorganize and reorient public and private primary and secondary education in a National Unified School curriculum (Escuela Nacional Unificada, ENU) contributed to an immediate escalation of political tension. The plan was described by the Ministry of Education in terms guaranteed to provoke opposition. It described as its goal "the construction of a new socialist society based on the development of productive forces, the overcoming of economic, technological, and cultural dependence, the establishment of new property relations, and authentic democracy and social justice guaranteed by the effective exercise of the power of the people" (1.1). While it called for an educational system that was humanistic and pluralist, it mandated the

202

establishment of a single educational system—including the then-private schools, which would "be obliged to adopt the content and curriculum of the ENU" (6.14); proposed that all secondary-school students engage in work in state-owned enterprises of the social area as part of their regular program (2.9); and proclaimed as its objective the "harmonious development of the personality of the young people in the values of socialist humanism" (4.2.8). The program was to be initiated on an experimental basis on June 1 with ninth-grade students. In addition, national, provincial, and local educational councils were created by decree with representatives of the government, workers, peasants, parents, and educational organizations to advise on the operation of the program.[2]

The ENU program was the result of work on educational reform which had begun under the Frei government, and its proposal that all students should develop a technical specialization by the end of secondary school had been discussed for years. Yet the vocabulary in which the reform was described had heavily Marxist overtones, and the timing of its release could not have been more unfortunate.

Predictably, it aroused strong protests from the opposition. The Christian Democrats, while agreeing with the need for education more relevant to national needs, denounced the scheme as a violation of the Statute of Democratic Guarantees and called it a "sectarian" document. They protested that despite its declaration of respect for democracy and pluralism, it had been adopted without consultation with those affected and contained "affirmations of a character clearly identified ideologically with the goals and methods of the minority Popular Unity government."[3]

The proposal also ran into strong opposition from the Catholic church. The archbishop of Valparaíso warned that the proposal could "lead to the control of education by a partisan ideology." A few days later, Cardinal Silva issued a statement which, while praising the positive aspects of the proposal such as the integration of work and study, objected that "we do not see emphasized anywhere the human and Christian values which form part of the patrimony of Chile . . . respect for man, especially for the child, cultural freedom, the search for truth and a critical spirit and the genuine conditions for its exercise, a balance between the material values involved in production and the spiritual values which contribute to the full realization of man, among them the real possibility of faith." The cardinal also observed that the report assumed that a majority in the country accepted a "socialist, humanist, pluralist, and revolutionary" orientation for its education when a considerable part of the country was in disagreement either with that goal or with the way in which it was being implemented. He therefore requested that the implementation of the plan be delayed to allow for full discussion and possible modification to take into account the views of teachers, students, and parents in both public and private schools.

In early April, the bishops of the entire country issued a joint statement expressing their opposition to the proposal and warning that "a desire for social justice could result in another model of an unjust and tyrannical society which would resolve nothing and only result in power passing from one minority to another."[4]

The Christian Democratic–controlled Federation of Secondary School Students of Santiago (FESES) denounced the proposal, and on April 9 its leaders had an interview with the minister of education in which they insisted that such a reform should be carried out by law and not by decree. After the interview they pronounced the minister's response unsatisfactory and gave the government ten days to modify its position. On April 11, the minister discussed the proposal for two hours with 150 representatives of the armed forces. The next day, a special meeting of the Christian Democratic Council issued a statement calling for mobilization of its bases against implementation of the decree and threatening to "make a pronouncement on the democratic legitimacy of the government" if it violated the freedom of education guaranteed in the constitution. In the face of such strong opposition, the Allende government decided to give in. On April 12, the minister of education wrote a public letter to the cardinal accepting his proposal that the implementation of the plan be postponed to permit "an open, democratic, and constructive debate." He expressed concern that the bishops believed that the plan did not respect fundamental humanistic and Christian values and insisted that the government reform fully respected freedom of conscience and ideological pluralism. He offered to make substantial modifications if subsequent debate revealed that they were necessary.[5] Despite the government's surrender on the issue, the secondary-school students went ahead with planned demonstrations on April 26.

The issuance of the ENU decree appears to have been a very serious political error. The net result of the controversy was to increase substantially the level of political polarization in the country and for the first time to involve the Catholic church and the military in public opposition to government policy. It also made it even more difficult to negotiate any kind of political truce with the Christian Democrats following the elections.

Relations with the PDC were also adversely affected by the murder in mid-March of two PDC activists who were sleeping in tents on a vacant lot threatened with seizure by MIR militants. This led to the impeachment of the governor of Santiago in mid-April on the grounds that he had failed in his constitutional duty of maintaining order. The MIR stepped up its seizures in a campaign which evoked a furious television denunciation from President Allende of "the demagogic attitudes" and "erroneous methods" of some worker sectors at a time when what was necessary was "working more, producing more, and studying more."[6]

Again, just when the Allende government was in most difficulty, new reve-

A photograph published in early April 1973 of a Chilean policeman being clubbed by a member of the Popular Revolutionary Brigade, which symbolized to the opposition and the Chilean military the breakdown of law and order. (Embassy of Chile)

lations of U.S. interference in Chilean politics made it possible for President Allende to rally support. On March 20, 1973, the Multinational Corporations Subcommittee of the Senate Foreign Relations Committee chaired by Senator Frank Church began to hold hearings on ITT's role in attempting to influence the outcome of the 1970 Chilean presidential elections. The Church subcommittee heard testimony from many of the figures mentioned in the ITT papers released by Jack Anderson in April 1972. A memorandum from the staff director of the investigation, Jerome Levinson, publicized by Anderson in March revealed that in May 1972 several of the Cuban Watergate defendants had also broken into the Chilean embassy, the residences of the chief Chilean UN delegate and its economic counselors, and the New York apartment of the head of the Chilean Development Corporation (CORFO). James McCord later testified to the Senate Watergate Committee that the U.S. government had also tapped the telephones of the Chilean embassy.[7] Not too surprisingly, the Overseas Private Investment Corporation announced on April 10 that it was turning down ITT's request for $92.5 million in compensation for its interest in the Chilean telephone company which had been nationalized in 1971. (The Allende government had begun negotiations for compensation at that time, but they were broken off in 1972 after the revelations about ITT's activities.) The grounds that OPIC gave were that ITT had not disclosed "material information" and had failed "to preserve administrative remedies by which proper payment might have been achieved" by OPIC, which was required by law to attempt to secure compensation after it had compensated the nationalized firm. (The OPIC contract specifically rules out compensation for expropriations which occur as a result of "provocation or instigation by the investor or foreign enterprise.")[8]

Heightened Political Tension

The tense political situation was not relieved by the Christian Democrats' decision to bring up the question of the presidential vetoes of the constitutional amendment on the three areas of the economy which had lain dormant for nine months. The move was provoked by the Allende government's decision to use the collective "decree of insistence" to override the controller general's refusal to approve the requisitioning of forty-three plants. The controller had argued that breakdowns in supply (*desabastecimiento*) were not in themselves sufficient legal cause for government requisition; the government also had to demonstrate that the owners were responsible for the breakdown. He had also noted that such requisitions were legally temporary and that it was false to speak, as the government did, of the "incorporation" of the firms into the social area. The Christian Democrats also threatened to impeach the entire Allende cabinet for its signing of the decree.

On April 26, the Congress rejected the presidential vetoes of the constitutional amendment by a majority vote, but not by two-thirds. Congressional spokesmen maintained that the president's only recourse now was to a plebiscite. Instead, Allende announced that he intended to promulgate the sections of the amendment which had been adopted and to refer the disputed sections to the Constitutional Tribunal. The opposition majority in the Congress continued to maintain that the tribunal was not authorized to decide on such matters. It was an indication either of the strength of the Chilean commitment to legalism or of the reluctance of the tribunal to become involved in a direct conflict between the other two branches that on May 31 the tribunal decided that it did not have jurisdiction in the conflict, thus accepting the congressional interpretation. Only one of the five members of the court accepted Allende's claim that a constitutional amendment was included in the term "law" in the constitutional provisions authorizing the tribunal. The head of the court referred to the necessity of express constitutional authorization and observed that while the government had cited two cases in which the term "law" was used in a general sense to include constitutional amendments, there were a hundred others in the constitution which restricted its meaning to ordinary legislation.[9]

Meanwhile, the government had moved one step further on the expansion and consolidation of the area of social property. Having overruled the controller general on the industries requisitioned in October, it sent the Congress a revised list of ninety-three industries that were to be definitively nationalized. Now included on the list (it had been excluded in the bill introduced earlier in the year) was the Alessandri paper company—sure to be a red flag to the opposition. The bill also contained a general authorization for the permanent takeover of all firms intervened or requisitioned before April 30, 1973.[10]

The move came at a time of greatly heightened political tension following a particularly violent set of street demonstrations at the end of April. After a rally of secondary-school students at the Ministry of Education on April 26, there were serious clashes between the opposition and progovernment students. The students broke thirty-six windows in the presidential palace, and the police were compelled to use water cannons and tear gas to break up the rioting demonstrators. The next day, a counterdemonstration called by the Central Workers Confederation (CUT) attacked the Christian Democratic newspaper and headquarters. One demonstrator was killed by a gunshot which, the government claimed, was fired from within the party headquarters.

The Christian Democratic vice-president of CUT, Ernesto Vogel, announced that all Christian Democratic unions would boycott the traditional First of May ceremonies in protest against the CUT demonstration. Cardinal Silva also indicated that he would not appear, explaining that he was departing from his usual custom because of "the division which has been created in the heart of the labor movement, which has produced injury and hatred and turned worker against worker."[11]

There was evidence of division among the military as well. *Ercilla* reported on a meeting of eight hundred military men on April 13 at the Military Academy at which General Prats, the army commander and former interior minister, defended the Allende government and gave specific support to its educational proposals and to its program of nationalization. Prats was said to have criticized Rear Admiral Huerta for submitting a memorandum to the minister of education critical of the ENU proposal and to have stated that if he had been minister of defense at the recent meeting of the military with the education minister, "I would have ordered the immediate arrest of those officers who spoke in such an unprofessional and partisan manner." Prats later denied the report, but subsequent events indicated that it reflected accurately the geunine divisions in the armed forces on the education and nationalization questions.[12]

The polarization between the government and the opposition was further hardened when the five-hundred-man National Assembly of the Christian Democrats met on May 12. Two policy motions were moved which, while agreeing in opposing the Allende government, disagreed in their tone and emphasis. The motion presented by the outgoing party president, Renán Fuentealba, emphasized the party's commitment to humanist socialism and recommended a policy of "revolutionary" opposition. The alternative which was adopted was presented by Senator Patricio Aylwin, who was later elected to succeed Fuentealba as party president. It accused the government of seeking to establish a "Communist tyranny" and instructed the Party Council to use "all legitimate means to assure respect for the constitution and the laws."[13] Aylwin was elected with the slogan "Don't let the government get away with one more thing" ("No dejarle pasar ni una al Gobierno"), and after his election he announced that the party would initiate a campaign to defend the legally elected neighborhood committees against the expanding powers of the government-appointed JAP committees. He threatened that unless the economy minister, Orlando Millas, took steps to assure that the neighborhood committees could exercise control over the JAP, the Christian Democrats would support an impeachment procedure against him which had already been initiated by the National Party.

A further indication of the increasing polarization came in the election of officers for the newly elected Congress which was to meet on May 21. Eduardo Frei was elected president of the Senate, and a strongly partisan Christian Democrat was also chosen to preside over the Chamber. Thus, Frei and Allende reversed the roles they had had six years before when Allende was president of the Senate and Frei was chief executive.

In 1967, Allende had refused to preside when Frei delivered his annual message to the Congress, and Frei reciprocated in 1973. On May 21, at a joint session presided over by a Left Radical senator, Allende delivered a message which was markedly more sober than those he had delivered in 1971 and 1972. He observed that the daily confrontation between the opposition and the government "has accumulated a heavy charge of social violence which so far has been contained within reasonable limits or put down when it began to exceed those limits." However, he warned of "a genuine and serious threat to our democracy" and foresaw "very difficult times for the country and for the security of all Chileans." While attributing major responsibility for the present difficulties to the "national and foreign interests affected," he also admitted that his government had not created "the necessary instruments to capture the excess profits of the bourgeoisie and that the redistribution policy has exceeded the real possibilities of the economy." Allende no longer spoke of "the battle of production" which a year earlier he had said was being won. Now he lamented that the "burden of the past" had created a situation in which Chile suffered from "limitations of productive capacity," and he admitted that "since the second half of 1972, the situation has become critical" in agriculture.

Defending the "revolutionary changes" under his government, Allende stated that during the past year, 2,192 farms had been expropriated by the agrarian reform program, bringing the total number of estates taken over to 3,570 or 35 percent of the total agricultural area of Chile. In industry, more than two hundred enterprises involving 30 percent of national production were now "incorporated in the area of social property." Ninety percent of the bank credit was under state control, as well as 33 percent of wholesale distribution. These economic changes, said Allende, had been accompanied by the establishment of peasant councils, miners' councils, JAP committees, industrial *cordones*, and communal commands, which together composed a "nascent social organization in conflict with the structure of the old dormant class."[14]

Allende criticized workers "who forget that now they are the government" and demand excessive wage increases. Using Lenin's label of "economism" for their demands, he referred specifically to the "populist" supporters of the lengthy strike at the El Teniente copper mine, which the government had not been able to settle for nearly a month. The El Teniente workers had been striking since mid-April to receive a 41 percent wage increase which the government had refused to give them as part of the 99.8 percent wage readjustment in October 1972, arguing that they had been given this amount before October in partial wage increases tied by their union contract to monthly increases in the cost of living. The striking miners received expressions of support from other sectors, including at one point a threatened sympathy strike in the large Chuquicamata copper mine. The medical professional organization sent the strikers medical supplies, independent farmers sent food in a "Caravan of Hunger," and the small business and commerce employees' organization voted to give them "unrestricted support."[15]

One of the more ironic aspects of the government's problems with El Teniente was that Frei had had similar difficulties there in 1966. Remembering his own criticism of the Frei government for sending troops to the El Salvador mine in 1966 when it struck in sympathy with El Teniente, Allende was cautious in handling the strikers. There was continual violence in Rancagua, the town nearest to El Teniente, and at one point a worker was killed.

The strike was not settled until early July, and the national economy lost an estimated $1 million a day in reduced production of Chile's principal export. The length of the strike demonstrated both Allende's determination to hold down soaring wages and the loss of confidence in his government, at least by the best-paid workers.

In June the Christian Democrats initiated their threatened impeachment action against Orlando Millas, the minister of economics, for undermining the authority of the elected neighborhood committees by vesting power in the appointive JAP committees. The Congress also gave final approval to the Moreno constitutional amendment guaranteeing landholdings under forty hectares against expropriation and requiring the vesting of individual titles within two years of expropriation. This created a second source of constitutional controversy between the legislature and the president.

The Allende government was also involved in disputes with the judiciary over court orders returning seized property, or, more often, prohibiting interventors from taking actions which might increase the indebtedness of intervened or requisitioned companies without the authorization of a representative of the owners (*medidas precautorias*). Thirty such court orders were mentioned by the president of the Supreme Court in June, and in July Allende alluded to sixty cases. In June, the opposition in the Chamber of Deputies also published a confidential circular from the Ministry of the Interior ordering the carabineros not to carry out court orders to return industries or other establishments which had been taken over, but to report the court order to the governor, who was instructed to respond that it was "indispensable" to suspend the court order.[16]

The initiation of judicial action against the government for attempting to compel radio stations to join a compulsory radio chain for a government program led to a strong campaign by the progovernment press against the *viejos de mierda* in the judiciary. In May and June the Supreme Court wrote open letters to President Allende protesting the press campaign and asserting that nonfulfillment of court orders and the abuse of legal loopholes were leading to "the imminent breakdown of the judicial order." However, the campaign against the judiciary continued, and now it was broadened to include the controller general as well.[17]

A sense of the imminent breakdown of Chilean institutions is also evident in a photostat of a document published after the coup in the handwriting of presidential adviser Joan Garcés. Dating from early June, it speaks of the need for "organization of the people to resist a confrontation beginning in three to four months" and calls for "shifts in the armed forces and carabineros in order to strengthen the constitutionalist sector." After his escape from Chile in September, Garcés wrote that on June 6 Allende told the leaders of the UP coalition that an insurrection would take place within three months unless he called a plebiscite—a move they vetoed. A post-coup interview with a retired air force general also indicates that the air force began in June to plan for a coup scheduled to take place before the middle of September.[18]

Allende's speech to the Popular Unity Federation congress in mid-June was devoted to a denunciation of the rapid expansion of the black market. Earlier in the month, *Ercilla* had estimated that sixty thousand people were now working full-time in the black market and that 35 percent of the national income was being spent or earned there.[19] Until 1973, workers in refrigerator or textile plants whose contracts permitted them each year to buy specified items of their plant's products could make a small fortune reselling them on the black market. Peasants in the "reformed" areas of agriculture received a guaranteed minimum wage but now devoted most of their energies to production for the black market. A new profession appeared, that of the *colero*, made up of those who spent all their time in lines (*colas*) waiting to purchase a scarce item for resale. (Many domestic servants found this new occupation attractive, and a maid shortage ensued in middle- and upper-class areas.) The size of the black market affected government income adversely since sales taxes of 18 percent, a major tax resource, were not collected on these transactions. It also had an effect on the government's program of income redistribution, since it enriched the black marketeers and increased consumption by upper- and middle-income groups, but undermined the effort to raise the living standards of the poor. Since January the government had concentrated its price control and distribution efforts on a limited number of basic items in order to maintain the living standards and purchasing power of the lowest income groups, which had already been seriously harmed in 1972 by the fact that food prices had increased far in excess of the government price index figure. From a political point of view the government's price policy was calculated to maintain and solidify the support of the lowest income groups while at the same time attempting to put a brake upon inflationary wage increases. The government's firmness in the face of the El Teniente demands was part of this policy, but it had led instead to a considerable increase in social and political tensions.

In Santiago, those tensions were increased by the presence of several thousand workers from El Teniente who had accompanied their leaders for the discussions with President Allende and were housed in the central building of the Catholic University. On June 21, the Central Workers Confederation (CUT) called a mass demonstration of worker support for the government. In reply, the opposition-controlled peasant, student, professional, and worker groups called their own twenty-four-hour strike and urged their sympathizers to stay indoors to avoid violence. A crowd estimated by the progovernment press at between 500,000 and 1 million (The *New York Times* estimated it at 100,000) gathered to hear President Allende speak —while bombs exploded outside the Socialist Party headquarters, the Cuban embassy, and the government television station. Two days earlier, Allende had told the nation that "subversion is under way and the order of the state is in danger." Now he announced that a new plan had been developed to fight inflation, and he referred to the concern of the government to provide adequately for the needs of the armed forces. The latter reference was an allusion to a bill which the government was preparing granting raises to the armed forces at the very time that it was urging other sectors to restrain their wage demands. The raise was felt to be necessary since there were indications of military discontent, and it was becoming increasingly clear that both the economic situation and the threat of military action against the government would soon make it necessary to attempt again to involve the military in the cabinet. Negotiations were begun, and the progovernment press, as well as speakers at the Popular Unity Congress, spoke of the desirability of military involvement. Allende seems to have seen this as the only way to strengthen his political position in view of the perceptible hardening of the position of the Christian Democrats.[20]

The government also took steps against the right. In his speech at the June 21 rally, Allende announced that he was initiating the necessary legal steps to outlaw the right-wing organization Patria y Libertad, and the Ministry of the Interior attempted to compel *El Mercurio* to cease publication for six days because it had accepted an advertisement from the National Party which asserted that Allende had "nullified his presidential mandate because of the illegitimate exercise of his power. . . . No one is obliged in law or morality to obey a government which is no longer legitimate." The Court of Appeals revoked the minister's action, arguing that the party, not *El Mercurio*, should be sanctioned, but the newspaper was not published on June 22.

First Military Revolt

During the last week of June, the Allende government put down the first attempt at a military coup since it had taken power. Never a serious threat to the existence of the government, it nevertheless gravely aggravated an already tense political situation. On the evening of June 26, Military Intelligence reported a plot against the government centered in the Second Armored Regiment, whose barracks were located to the south of the center of Santiago. A captain in the regiment who was an alleged organizer of the plot was arrested on June 27 and detained in a cell in the basement of the Ministry of Defense, opposite La Moneda.

On June 27, after a meeting of the Council of Generals had voted 18 to 6 against his recommendation that the military rejoin the government, the commander-in-chief of the army, General Carlos Prats, was involved in a strange incident while driving into the center of the city. Alejandrina Cox, a middle-aged woman, stuck her tongue out at him as she passed his car, whereupon the general drew his revolver and fired two shots at her, one of which struck her car door. The opposition, which was not fond of Prats because of his support for the Allende government, denounced his violent response to such a trivial incident, while the government argued that Prats was only trying to defend himself from a possible repetition of the Schneider assassination of 1970. The weakness of this explanation (Prats himself never asserted it) produced a skeptical reaction on the following day, when General Mario Sepúlveda held a press conference to announce that the military forces had knowledge of a plot to overthrow the government involving both civilians and lower-level military men. A similar reaction greeted the Minister of Defense on the evening of June 28, when he spoke to the Senate on the same topic. The following morning, the coup attempt took place.[21]

According to the official version issued subsequently by the Chilean army, two officers of the Second Armored Regiment had been in contact earlier with the leaders of the extreme right-wing movement, Patria y Libertad, and had planned an uprising on June 27 involving the seizure of President Allende at his residence in the Barrio Alto as well as the occupation of the presidential palace in the center of town.[22] The rightists claimed the support of three army divisions in other parts of the country, as well as of the adherents of their movement throughout the country. However, on June 26 Patria y Libertad called one of the officers to tell him that the scheduled coup had been discovered. When a captain of the regiment was arrested and imprisoned in the Defense Ministry the next day and Colonel Roberto Souper, the regimental commander, was told that he was to be relieved of his command, the remaining officers decided to carry out a rescue operation and to seize the palace as in the original plan. At 8:45 A.M. on June 29, three combat groups of tanks and armored cars left the barracks. A few minutes later they arrived at the Defense Ministry and surrounded the presidential palace, firing in all directions. The insurgents freed the arrested officer from the Defense Ministry but were not able to seize the presidential palace, which was defended by the palace guard.

General Prats was informed immediately of the uprising, and he ordered the other army units stationed in Santiago to put down the revolt and to seize the Second Armored Regiment barracks. (In suppressing the coup, Prats personally commanded the Tacna Regiment, which had supported the 1969 coup attempt led by General Roberto Viaux. Since the 1969 coup attempt was referred to as the "Tacnazo," the 1973 tank uprising was subsequently dubbed the "Tancazo.") By 11 A.M. Prats had arrived at the center of town, and after about a half-hour of negotiations he secured the surrender of most of the insurgents. Four tanks and armored cars escaped and returned to the barracks headquarters, where negotiations were going on for its surrender to the Tacna Regiment. (One tank had to stop at a service station for gasoline on the way!) According to the official account, the accidental discharge of an artillery piece by one of the defenders in the barracks led to generalized firing in which three soldiers were killed. (After the September coup the number was put at "a little more than ten.") Rumors circulated subsequently that as many as eighty had died in the occupation of the barracks, but military censorship prevented further investigation of those figures. The official figures listed twenty-two killed and fifty wounded, most of them civilians hit by flying bullets. By early afternoon the total surrender of the regiment had been achieved.

The part of the plot which involved the capture of President Allende had never been implemented, and as soon as the firing began around the presidential palace Allende was informed by telephone by Under-Secretary of the Interior Daniel Vergara. Vergara indicated that the carabineros who formed the palace guard were determined to resist. Allende then went on the air from his residence to inform the country of the uprising and to call on the workers to assemble at four or five central locations to defend the government. Allende was then informed that the military commanders and the carabineros had remained loyal to him, and two battalions and six armored cars were sent to defend him. Allende then spoke to the country a second time in a statement which was recorded and continually rebroadcast during the day. He described the uprising as organized by a "small group of rebellious military men" in the Second Armored Regiment and assured the Chileans of the continued loyalty to him of the armed forces, describing the efforts of General Prats to suppress the revolt. Allende declared that he was going to the scene of the uprising, but meanwhile, he said, "I call on the people to take over all the industries and enterprises, and to be prepared to go to the center of the city, but not as victims—to go to the streets—but not to be machine-gunned—to act with prudence with whatever material they have at hand. . . . If the coup comes, the people will have arms—but I am confident that the armed forces are loyal to the government." He then listed the units that were loyal to the government and reemphasized the fact that only one regiment had rebelled. One hour later, after the revolt had been put down, the president left his residence for the presidential palace, escorted by three armored cars and his personal bodyguard. When he arrived at 11:45 A.M., occasional sniper firing was still being heard.

A military court took jurisdiction over the prosecution of the rebels, and seven officers and two civilians were held incommunicado. Military censorship was imposed on the newspapers for several days, and a film taken by a Swedish cameraman of his own death—as he was shot by a soldier—was prohibited from appearing in Santiago theaters and newspapers. When asked why there had been so many casualties compared with earlier cases which had been handled by the carabineros, General Augusto Pinochet, then army chief of staff, replied prophetically, "When the army comes out, it is to kill."

Popular Power

The president of the Central Workers Confederation (CUT) also went on the air to call for worker occupations of factories and agricultural centers, "for as long as the CUT so directs." In a single day, the number of companies taken over by the government nearly doubled, rising from 282 to 526. The CUT support for worker takeovers seemed to indicate an attempt by the union organization—and the Communist Party which dominated it—to control and direct a movement that had been inspired by its enemy on the far left, the MIR. The industrial belts (*cordones*) and communal commands which had sprung up more or less spontaneously at the time of the October strike as coordinating groups in various industrial centers around Santiago achieved new importance, as many more factories were taken over. New *cordones* were established in areas where they had not existed, and the power of the older ones was increased as more factories were occupied. This was useful to the government to demonstrate the kind of resistance that a more serious coup attempt would provoke. However, it also created new problems, since production declined sharply after the takeovers, new force was given to the opposition's insistence that the expansion of state control of industry should be carried out through legal and constitutional channels, and the quasi-spontaneous worker occupations seemed to be creating a center of power which was a possible rival to the government. Allende's own ambiguous attitude to the occupations, which he had encouraged when the limited extent and easy defeat of the insurrectionists were not clear, was expressed in his speech to the rally of support for the government on the evening of June 29. He called upon the "comrade workers of Santiago" to "organize and create *el poder popular* [popular power], but not against the government or independent from it, for the government is the basic instrument which the workers have to advance in the revolutionary process."

In the same speech Allende denounced the cowardice of the leaders of the right-wing Patria y Libertad, five of whom (including Pablo Rodriguez, its chief) had received asylum in the Ecuadorian embassy late in the afternoon. They admitted that they had attempted to overthrow the government, "together with a heroic unit of our army," but aside from lamenting the lack of support from other units "who had previously manifested their support" they did not explain why the coup had been so easily suppressed and had not involved any attempt to capture the president. (Lacking more evidence, the explanation in the official army statement that the coup had been scheduled for June 27 and then called off seems persuasive.) More Patria y Libertad leaders sought asylum in the next few days, but the organization did not cease to function. A week later the second in command of the organization, Roberto Thieme, who had appeared in Argentina in May after earlier arranging a faked death in an airplane crash in the Pacific, made a clandestine return to Chile. Appearing on the Catholic University television station, he announced that the organization was going underground and was now committed to the forcible overthrow of the Allende government.

It does not seem to have been a direct result of the coup attempt, but the following day it was announced that the El Teniente strike had been settled and the copper workers would return to work on Monday, July 2. It was agreed that they would receive a "productivity bonus" in lieu of the wage increases they had been demanding. Since the bonuses were given to all workers regardless of productivity, they amounted to a wage increase, but since they were ostensibly related to productivity, a principle that was important to the government (that of tying wages to output) had been established—although at great cost in copper output.

On the day following the uprising, Allende requested that the Congress grant him state-of-siege powers for thirty days. These powers, which included limits on press freedom and freedom of assembly and the authority to place people under house arrest, were viewed by the oppositon-dominated Congress as an attempt to use the coup as an excuse to secure a blank check to move against the opponents of the government without any evidence that they were violating the law. It was immediately clear that the Congress would not grant Allende's request, and it was rejected in the Chamber of Deputies by a vote of 82 to 51.

On July 8 the presidents of the two houses of the legislature also issued a joint statement denouncing the establishment of "popular power," which they said amounted to the de facto creation of a "parallel army in which numerous foreigners are involved."[23]

Cabinet Restructuring

Allende now resumed conversations with the military leadership concerning their possible entry into a new cabinet. After several days in which it was expected that a cabinet with military participation would be announced, the president stated that for reasons similar to those which had motivated their departure from the cabinet on March 27—their desire "to avoid being involved in political contingencies . . . and to preserve their unity"—the military would not enter the cabinet. The declaration naturally gave rise to speculation about divisions among the military and the conditions they had set for possible entry.[24] The military commanders issued a joint declaration reaffirming their respect for "the constitution which governs us" and for their own character as "nonpolitical [*no deliberantes*] institutions." Nothing was more apparent in the evolution of Chilean politics since mid-1972 than that the armed forces had by then become a very important "deliberating" force.

In a further attempt to broaden the base of political support for his government, Allende made efforts to include in the new cabinet well-known Chilean political personalities who were not directly affiliated with the Popular Unity coalition. He was reported to have approached Felipe Herrera, former head of the Interamerican Development Bank, and Raúl Rettig, a former Radical leader then ambassador to Brazil, who both declined. Allende's most important overture, however, was to the rector of the Catholic University, Fernando Castillo Velasco. The brother of the leading ideologist of the Christian Democrats, but related to Allende through his daughter's marriage to the president's nephew, Castillo seemed an ideal person to reopen links to the Christian Democrats and was personally disposed to do so. However, as a PDC member, Castillo consulted with the Christian Democratic leadership and was told that he could not participate, since a Christian Democratic presence in the cabinet, however indirect, would require that the government fulfill a number of conditions. As outlined by the party in succeeding weeks, those conditions included enforcement of the Arms Control Law adopted in November 1972, adoption of the disputed constitutional amendment defining the three areas of property, and return of the enterprises which had been seized by the workers unless they were within the areas defined by that amendment.

After a week of negotiation, a new cabinet was announced made up entirely of members of the Popular Unity coalition. The principal changes in its composition involved the replacement of those members who were being impeached by the Congress. It was an indication of Allende's desire not to antagonize the opposition that he removed the impeached ministers entirely rather than shifting them to other posts as he had on several previous occasions. The same moderation was shown in his appointment of Carlos Briones to the Interior Ministry since, although a Socialist, Briones was known as a moderate and a legalist who had good relations with the opposition.

The Christian Democrats reacted to the new cabinet by lamenting the absence of military participation. Patricio Aylwin, the party president, issued a statement that "in present circumstances, the best guarantee for the reestablishment of democracy would have been the institutional incorporation of the armed forces in the government with effective power to carry out the corrections that are indispensable to assure the rule of law and of the constitution." The party itself issued a statement accusing the government of attempting to set up an armed militia by distributing arms in the seized factories and the *cordones industriales.* "The establishment of this de facto 'people's power' with the evident participation of state authorities is incompatible with the survival of the 'institutional power' of law established by the constitution."

As usual, there were two possible interpretations of the Christian Democrats' position. Recalling that the 1971 military coup in Bolivia by Hugo Banzer was precipitated by the establishment of a popular assembly and militia by the leftist government of Juan José Torres, the Popular Unity forces saw the Christian Democratic campaign as an attempt to persuade the military of the need for a coup before a parallel army was created and consolidated by the left. The opposition, on the other hand, argued that unless the military continued to have a monopoly on the use of force, both sides would accelerate their preparations for an inevitable armed confrontation. (Visiting Chile at this time, I was astounded at the widespread acquisition of arms by both pro- and antigovernment Chileans.)

Here as elsewhere, the Christian Democratic position seemed to be echoed in the position of the Communist Party. While the Communists supported the right of the workers to adopt "security measures in the face of the recent attempt at a coup and to maintain those measures as a precaution," it declared, "We support and will continue to support the absolutely professional character of our armed forces." The party intensified the campaign against the threat of civil war that it had already initiated and called for a dialogue between the government and the opposition.

Political Rapprochement: Attempts and Obstacles

The Communists were able to quote a declaration of the Catholic bishops of Chile issued on the feast of Our Lady of Mount Carmel, the patroness of Chile, which called for a "political truce" and a dialogue on how to attain peace with justice in Chile, to be initiated in conditions of "spiritual and physical disarmament." A similar statement was issued by another group which also conceived of itself as a bridge between the two sides— the rectors of the four private universities of Chile. The Allende government affirmed its desire for dialogue. The new interior minister declared that most of the occupied industries would be returned after agreements between the owners and the workers that an important part of their production would be supplied to the state, and Allende stated that in Chile "neither the military nor the armed people will take power, for either situation woul‹ lead to civil war."

The delicate negotiations for a meeting between the Christian Democratic leaders and the Allende government were set back when Aylwin declared that he would not negotiate with "a pistol leveled at my chest," a statement that Allende labeled as "insolent." The dialogue finally was initiated at the end of July, but by then a number of changes had taken place in the political picture. These included a report that the Allende forces had "stolen" more than 200,000 votes in the March congressional elections, the fusion of three opposition parties, the beginning of another nationwide strike by private truckers and other *gremios*, and Chile's third important political assassination in three years.

Electoral Fraud?

On July 18, *El Mercurio* published a report on research being carried out in the Faculty of Law of the Catholic University which purported to demonstrate a massive electoral fraud involving more than 200,000 votes in the March elections. The report, described as preliminary, was published by the dean of the Law School over the objections of the rector, Fernando Castillo. It argued, first, that the conduct of the Chilean electorate in the March elections seemed strangely out of line with all its previous known behavior. Opinion polls, the rising inflation, and the pattern of by-elections since mid-1971 had shown a steady decline in support for the government. This decline seemed to indicate the likelihood of only about a 35 percent vote in favor of Popular Unity rather than the 43 percent it received. Further investigation of the electoral data indicated a surprising number of new registrants for the 1973 elections—820,000 new voters since November 1970. If, the report said, the likely number of new registrants among citizens eighteen to twenty-one years of age (420,000) and illiterates (75,000) enfranchised in 1970 was added to the likely number of late registrants over twenty-one (75,000), minus the registered voters who had died during the same period and were eliminated from the electoral registration lists (70,000) the result was a figure of 500,000 new voters—far below the 820,000 new registrants since 1970 or the 750,000 since the 1971 municipal elections. The report then compared the new registration figures in the various senatorial districts (*agrupaciones*) in Chile and found that in the Tenth District, where no senator was up for election in March, registration had only increased 18 percent, while in the Sixth and Eighth Districts, where there were senatorial contests, there were increases of 33 percent and 37 percent. The report listed the various ways in which it was possible to register more than once and cited specific cases of fraud in Santiago and Coquimbo which it proved by demonstrating that the numbers of the identity cards cited did not belong to the voters in question. It also gave examples of two communes near Coquimbo with large increases in electoral registration where the new registrants voted for the government in proportions far exceeding the older voters. (It is possible to determine how new registrants vote in Chile because additional voting places are established when earlier voter lists are filled.) The report concluded: "In the March parliamentary elections, an electoral fraud of major proportions took place. Up to this point, it appears to have involved between 200,000 and 300,000 illegal votes. . . . Our electoral system has permitted a gigantic fraud to be carried out, and there is no guarantee that it will not be repeated in future elections."[25]

It was typical of the state of opinion in Chile that the report was immediately accepted as conclusive by all sectors of the opposition and rejected by progovernment spokesmen as yet another maneuver to promote a military coup. The Congress appointed a special committee composed of five Christian Democrats, three Socialists, two Communists, and three members of the National Party, but no one raised some obvious questions about the report. Why, for instance, was not the Institute of Political Science of the Catholic University consulted in the preparation of the report? (The answer seemed to be that the institute was made up of professional political scientists who might raise questions about the methodology and the appropriateness of the preliminary release of the study.) Why had the study not listed among the possible new voters those twenty-one to twenty-four years of age, who had been too young to register in 1970? Assuming that they were roughly equivalent in numbers to the estimate of new voters in the group aged eighteen to twenty-one, the missing 200,000 to 300,000 voters could be found right there. And would not the false registration of 300,000 voters by one side in a highly polarized political situation have come to light earlier, even if, as the opposition assumed, the Communist Party had carried out the operation in utmost secrecy?

Creation of the Social Democratic Federation

Two days after the release of the report, the Left Radical Party (PIR) held a convention in Santiago. Representatives of the Radical Democrats and of the minuscule National Democratic Party (PADENA) were invited, with a view to uniting the three small parties into a single Social Democratic Party which would fill the vacuum left by the increasingly Marxist orientation of the Radical Party and recoup its loss in popular support since its participation in the Popular Unity government. In addition, the organizers of the meeting invited Senator Patricio Aylwin, the head of the Christian Democratic Party, to speak at the opening session. It was a mark of the increasing cooperation among opposition groups that his speech, which recounted past errors committed by both groups, received warm applause. On the last day of the convention, procedures were initiated for the registration of the Social Democratic Federation as a new political entity which combined the Left Radicals who had departed from the official Radical Party in 1971, the more conservative Democratic Radicals who had left or been expelled in 1969, and the tiny remnant of the National Democrats (PADENA) into what they hoped would be a center-left reformist party in roughly the same position on the ideological spectrum that the Radicals had occupied before their leftward movement in the late 1960s. Given the increasingly secular character of the Christian Democrats and the decline in importance of the religious issue in Chilean politics, it was still doubtful whether the new group could successfully compete with the Christian Democrats, but it was clear that the bitter enmity which had characterized the relations between the Christian Democrats and the Radicals in the 1960s was totally absent from the relations between the PDC and the Social Democrats.

The Role of the Gremios

Too much stress should not be placed upon the shifts in attitudes and alliances among the political parties and professional politicians. Even before the strike of October 1972, independent political power had been acquired by the organized interest-group associations, trade unions, and peasant groups. Described generically as the *gremios,* most of these associations were strongly opposed to the Allende government, although the top leadership of the Central Workers Confederation (CUT) was pro-government, and the government had encouraged the formation of a Patriotic Front of Professionals and Technicians to support its policies. The peasants were divided into pro- and antigovernment groups, and the government's 1970 attempt to establish a national peasant confederation had run out of steam when it became clear that the group was likely to be dominated by opposition forces. The other groups—doctors, dentists, lawyers, airline pilots, small businessmen and shopkeepers, and, since May 1972, the trade union organization of Santiago province—were opposed to the government and since October 1972 had been coordinating their policies with one another. Most strongly opposed of all were the small truck owners, and since October their leader, Leon Vilarín, had been an important political leader in his own right. (After the March 1973 elections the CIA proposed that the *gremios,* including the truckers, receive additional support, but Ambassador Davis and the U.S. State Department opposed the proposal on the grounds that the groups were known to favor military intervention. On August 20, the Forty Committee approved a grant of $1 million to opposition parties and interest groups contingent on ambassadorial approval. A specific proposal to provide $25,000 to the truckers was not approved, although they may have received part of the funds given earlier to other organizations and parties.[26])

As the October strike had demonstrated, the power of the truck drivers was based on Chile's dependence on truck transportation for its supplies of food and fuel. As in other countries, the drivers were fiercely independent, and it was the announcement of an attempt to establish a government-owned trucking agency that set off the October strike in the first place. Part of the settlement of that strike had involved a promise to the private truckers that they would receive spare parts, tires, and so on, the lack of which the truckers had attributed to the government's desire to force them out of business. Those parts had been slow in coming, and an increasing number of trucks were immobilized for this reason.[27] By July the truckers had become exasperated with the delays, and they began to threaten a strike. At midnight on July 25, the National Truck Owners Confederation began an indefinite walkout which, given the cooperation among the various *gremios*, threatened to escalate into a stoppage on the scale of October's strike—this time more serious in its effects because reserve supplies had not yet been built up again.

Third Assassination

The political situation was further worsened a day later, when Chile experienced its third major political assassination since Allende's election. On the night of July 26, on his return from a reception at the Cuban embassy, the president's naval aide-de-camp, Commander Arturo Araya Peters, was assassinated on the second-floor balcony of his home. Allende deplored the act and appointed a special investigating committee headed by an air force general. In the investigation which followed, two suspects were detained. One of them gave himself up the day after the assassination and claimed to have been involved with a leftist group which planned to kidnap Araya; the other, arrested subsequently, was an active member of a far-right group. Roberto Thieme, the leader of the underground Patria y Libertad organization, immediately disclaimed all responsibility for the act. However, the assassination was followed by terrorist acts all over Chile which appeared to be organized by the extreme right, and the progovernment press argued that the right extremists were responsible for the assassination as well. The opposition replied that the MIR and similar leftist groups might equally well have carried out the act in order to sabotage the impending conversations between the Christian Democrats and President Allende, and they cited taped radio conversations to prove that Cuban agents were in the street outside Araya's house when he was killed. Both left and right groups appear to have been near Araya's house, and a military investigating commission appointed by President Allende rejected attempts by the government to place all the blame on the right, although it subsequently charged a member of Patria y Libertad with being the "material author" of the assassination. (Many accounts of the shooting noted that the naval aide emerged on his balcony with an automatic rifle and began shooting after an explosion had taken place in the street. Silhouetted against the light of the house, he thus presented a perfect target for a gunman in the darkness.)

The assassination has never been satisfactorily explained. The left maintained that Araya was killed by right-wing conspirators who wished to remove a pro-Allende officer scheduled to return to the navy general staff in September. The right said that he was assassinated because as Allende's aide "he knew too much" and was about to denounce government efforts to subvert the military. Both explanations seem possible; neither is fully convincing, although the theory of the left seems somewhat more plausible.

Allende-Aylwin Dialogue

On Monday, July 30, the long-awaited conversations between Allende and the president and vice-president of the Christian Democrats finally took place. Carried out in an atmosphere of cordiality and civility, they covered the four principal points that the Christian Democrats had cited as the bases for agreement: disarmament of paramilitary groups, promulgation of the Hamilton-Fuentealba amendment on the three areas (to which the Moreno amendment on small and medium-sized agriculture was added since the Congress had voted down by a majority, but not two-thirds, the president's vetoes of that document), return of the industries occupied on June 29, and strengthening of the institutional and legal order through military participation in the cabinet.

On the issue of disarmament, there was no disagreement. Allende agreed that the military forces should have a monopoly on arms and that the Arms Control Law should be enforced. More generally, he agreed that constitutionalism, legal procedures, and personal freedom were to be maintained. Allende indicated that he was willing to promulgate the constitutional amendments proposed by the Christian Democratic senators on the condition that the Congress first add another which provided that presidential vetoes of constitutional amendments could henceforth be overridden only by a two-thirds vote of the Congress. This would rectify in the executive's favor the ambiguity of the 1970 constitutional reform which had provoked so much controversy. Senator Aylwin replied that he could not accept promulgation on such conditions or expect that the congressional majority would give up what it regarded as its rightful prerogatives.

On the issue of the occupied industries, Allende noted that a few were already being returned to their owners, but allegedly answered, "We cannot expel the workers from the industries they have seized for they are the support of the government—the sole support, along with the armed forces. . . . I have 100,000 workers who are ready to defend the government and I cannot give up the only thing that supports me."[28] On the participation of the armed forces in the cabinet, Allende did not rule out military participation, but he added that he believed in bringing in the military as institutional representatives rather than on an individual basis and had made attempts along these lines earlier in the month. On these questions—as well as others, such as the control of the mass media, the black market, and problems of production and distribution—Allende proposed the creation of special committees to work out a set of joint agreements.

Following the conversations, the president of the Christian Democrats, Senator Patricio Aylwin, consulted with his party and sent a lengthy letter to Allende which reviewed the positions of both sides and reasserted to Allende his party's belief that "you would reinforce your constitutional authority and preserve the institutional stability of the Republic if you would establish a cabinet with the institutional participation of the armed forces with sufficient power at the upper and middle levels to assure effective implementation of your decisions within the framework of the constitution and laws."[29] The letter said that the establishment of study commissions on the problems listed by Allende would make it impossible to arrive at an agreement, and in exchange for the promulgation of the constitutional amendments it offered to vote another amendment guaranteeing that the amendment process could not be used to reduce the powers of the president. It concluded that the conversations had arrived at an impasse and that it seemed useless to continue them.

After the 1973 coup the military revealed that if an agreement had emerged from the conversations, the subsequent history of Chile would have been different. Even Fidel Castro recognized the importance of the dialogue in a letter to Allende sent on July 29 with two prominent Cubans, Vice-Premier Carlos Rafael Rodriguez and Manuel Pineiro, head of the Cuban secret police. (The exact nature of the Cubans' mission to Chile is still unclear. After the coup the junta claimed it was to assist in preparations for a violent takeover.) Castro's letter referred to the assassination of the naval aide, the initiation of the truckers' strike, and the impending dialogue with the Christian Democrats. He sympathized with Allende in "your desire to gain time, improve the relation of forces in case the struggle breaks out, and if possible, find a way to allow the revolutionary process to move forward without civil conflict and demonstrate to history that you are not responsible for what may occur." He reminded Allende that if the PDC demanded a "price which is impossible for Popular Unity and the Revolution to pay" he should not forget the "formidable force of the Chilean working class," which at his call would "decide the destiny of Chile once and for all." In a prophetic sentence, Castro encouraged Allende to resist the pressures of the opposition. "Your decision to defend the process with firmness and honor even at the cost of your own life . . . will draw all forces capable of fighting to your side."[30]

Whose fault was it that the dialogue did not succeed? Aylwin insisted that real progress was made in the initial conversations on July 31, but that after a break in the discussions to consult with the other members of the Popular Unity coalition, Allende returned with his unacceptable study commission proposal. Something similar also happened in the case of the Christian Democrats, since when Aylwin consulted with his party after one day of discussions, it simply announced that the dialogue was over and initiated the exchange of letters. On August 17, Allende made a final effort to revive the dialogue when he invited Aylwin to secret conversations at the residence of Cardinal Silva, but no progress was made in reaching an agreement, although informal negotiations on the matters in dispute with Aylwin and other Christian Democrats were continued by Carlos Briones in Allende's name.[31]

The "National Security" Cabinet

The Christian Democratic suspicion of Allende's delaying tactics was increased by a series of moves involving the commanders of the armed forces. Allende had already used the absence of the commander of the national police during the June 29 uprising as an excuse to remove him, but thus far he had made no attempt to interfere with promotion on the basis of seniority and the recommendations of the top leadership of each of the services.

On August 6, instead of waiting for the annual meeting of the top commanders in September which would decide on promotions and retirements, Allende used his presidential powers to retire the air force generals who were second and fourth in seniority (Generals German Stuardo and Augustin Rodriguez). He apparently did so in order to clear the way for the general who was fifth in seniority (General Carlos von Schowen) who, he believed, was more sympathetic to his government. Allende then once more made efforts to secure institutional participation by the military in the cabinet. This time, with the aid of General Carlos Prats, he succeeded.

On August 9, what Allende called the "national security" cabinet was sworn in. General Prats was appointed defense minister, a departure from the Chilean tradition of civilian control of the military, but an important basis for any operation to advance military men who were favorable to Allende and to retire those opposed. Air Force General César Ruiz took over the Ministry of Public Works and Transport, which was charged with settling the truckers' strike. The national police (carabineros) were involved institutionally for the first time with the appointment of General

Sepúlveda to the largely symbolic post of minister of lands and coloniza-
tion. The navy was represented by Admiral Raúl Montero in the key Finance Ministry. In this position, he would be responsible for the recommendation of the wage readjustment promised for the national holidays
in September, and for the preparation of a new budget at a time when the
government deficit combined with the losses in the nationalized industries
was likely to reach half a trillion escudos for 1973.[32]

The entrance of the military men into the cabinet—without control of the
vital Interior Ministry (because of Socialist Party opposition, Carlos Briones,
known for his interest in arriving at an agreement with the Christian Democrats, was removed from that ministry) and without the influence over
lower levels in the ministries that they had earlier demanded—is puzzling,
except as a final effort by the top commanders, especially General Prats,
to save Chilean "institutionality."

Almost coincident with its entrance into the cabinet, the navy became
involved in a conflict with the left wing of the Allende coalition. On August 7 naval intelligence announced the discovery of a plot to carry out an
enlisted men's revolt on August 11 in Valparaíso and Talcahuano near
Concepción. Forty-three sailors were arrested in connection with the plot.
The navy accused Socialist Senator Carlos Altamirano and MAPU Deputy
Oscar Garretón, along with Miguel Enriquez of the MIR, of being "intellectual authors" of the revolt and demanded that the immunity of the two
members of Congress be lifted. In early September, Altamirano admitted
that he had encouraged navy men to resist their insurrectionary officers.
Similar efforts by the left to infiltrate the air force were the subject of an
extensive public trial in mid-1974.

After the coup, the junta claimed that the Socialists had also been preparing files on the political orientations of military officers and units and were
developing elaborate plans to neutralize the military units around Santiago.
The Unidad Popular parties were also said to have initiated a program of
military training for their followers at this time. In judgments about responsibility for the breakdown of constitutionalism in Chile, chronology is
an important factor—who began arming when and why. The opposition
can point to the importation of arms from Cuba in March 1972 and to
Allende's mendacity about the contents of the crates containing them as an
indication that the Allende government had already begun to prepare for
an armed confrontation. Supporters of Allende cite a *New York Times* interview (September 27, 1973) with Chilean army colonels who said they decided on a coup in October 1972, or to General Pinochet's later admission
that the general staff decided in April 1972 that a peaceful solution to the
political impasse was impossible. On the other side, the White Book contains detailed descriptions of military preparations by the Popular Unity

parties. It indicates that MAPU began arms training at the end of December 1972, and that the leaders of the Radical Party approved a "war plan" on July 5, 1973.[33] The MIR, of course, had been organized on a paramilitary basis from the beginning, and the 1970 establishment by the Socialist and Communist parties of the Elmo Catalán and Ramona Parra brigades was what had first produced the demand in Congress for the Arms Control Law adopted in October 1972.

The arming was not restricted to the left. The right-wing Patria y Libertad had admitted playing a part in the June 29 tank regiment revolt and in July had announced that it was going underground in order to engage in acts of violence against the Allende government. Indeed, by mid-1973, everyone in Chile seemed to be arming himself. Peaceful middle-class neighborhoods had been organized through *juntas de vecinos* (neighborhood committees) which now took on a new vitality and began to develop plans for self-defense and for concealment of opposition political leaders. On the other side, the JAP committees became the basis for the establishment of a progovernment network in the lower-class areas, and since October the MIR had been organizing the industrial areas and some of the settlements into paragovernmental industrial belts to control highway access to the cities. The MIR also began to use some left-controlled factories to manufacture and distribute arms.[34]

By August 1973, Chile had become an armed camp—and the armed forces were well aware of the extent of the distribution of weapons because of the arms searches they had been carrying out all over Chile since the beginning of July. The searches, authorized under the Arms Control Law of October 1972, involved suspected arms caches of both left and right, but most frequently those of the left. The specific results of the arms searches were never published, but they reinforced the widely repeated comment heard on both sides: "Things cannot continue this way." Indeed, the threat to the military's monopoly of the instruments of coercion, now combined with attempts to subvert the hierarchy of command from below (the infiltration of the navy) and above (the replacement of the top military commanders) provided the classic scenario for a coup d'état.

Nevertheless, General Prats had been successful in persuading the other top commanders of the necessity of entering the cabinet once more in order to attempt again what had been accomplished in late 1972: a lessening of polarization and tension through the introduction of the armed forces as impartial arbiters. In August 1973, however, the armed forces were very much more politicized and polarized than in the preceding October, and the country had changed dramatically. Attitudes on both sides had hardened, and even the casual visitor could sense the tension and the feeling of impending crisis. The truckers now seemed determined to persist in their strike until they brought the government down. Professional people who earlier had been willing to give Allende the benefit of the doubt were now fiercely opposed to the government and frightened about their own future livelihood. Their fear was intensified as the managers of the numerous firms that had been taken over on June 29 were summarily fired. As government control of distribution expanded and was used to favor those known to be sympathetic to the government, shopkeepers feared they would be driven out of business. And underlying it all were the escalation in violence, the widely publicized (and, as it turned out, exaggerated) reports of the organization and arming of the *poder popular* groups, the class hatred encouraged by the government press and radio, and the fears of the middle and lower-middle classes played upon by the opposition.[35]

Effects of the Truckers' Strike

The first problem facing the new cabinet was the truckers' strike, now entering its third week. In Santiago, cars were limited to 10 liters (2.5 gallons) of gas, and long lines appeared at the gas pumps. Heating fuel for the Chilean winter was running out. The shortages of such staples as bread, sugar, and detergent, already a problem before the strike, now became acute. On the day on which the new cabinet was sworn in, there were one-day strikes of protest against, and support for, the government called by the shopkeepers and professionals on the one side, and the CUT on the other.

The government had the legal power to seize the idle trucks which were parked outside the major cities and guarded by the truckers, but it had been slow to do so for fear of violence. One such "requisition" did lead to violence in which opposition parliamentarians were tear-gassed by carabineros, leading the opposition to initiate proceedings for the impeachment of the minister of the interior.

Allende warned that this might be the last chance to avoid civil war. He noted that four people had been killed since the strike had begun and that more than 215 terrorist attacks had been initiated by the extreme right, including the explosion of an important oil pipeline and attempts to sabotage the rail system. (One terrorist attack blacked out Santiago for thirty-five minutes during an Allende television speech.) He assured the military that he would not tolerate the existence of paramilitary groups and would support the principle of hierarchical command in the armed forces.[36]

Allende expressed particular concern that the truckers' strike be ended since, as he noted, if it continued 50 percent of the nation's industry would be forced to cease production. However, hopes that Air Force General Ruiz could arrive at a quick settlement were ended when a new requisitioning party took over more trucks two days after the cabinet took office. Ruiz disclaimed responsibility for the act, saying it had been decided by a cabinet committee. The incident led to new protests by the *gremios*, in which the wives of the truckers were particularly active. These groups occupied the Congress grounds and took over several radio stations to broadcast their grievances. By the end of the week following the naming of the new cabinet, Ruiz had resigned as minister of public works and transport (citing insufficient powers to end the strike), the truckers had defied two government ultimatums to return, most buses and taxis in Santiago were on strike, and the professional associations and shopkeepers had announced another sympathy strike for the following week. Housing construction had ceased, distribution of milk to school children was discontinued, and 500,000 industrial workers were threatened with layoffs because industries would be compelled to shut down.[37]

When Ruiz informed Allende of his intention to resign as minister, Allende insisted that he must also resign as head of the air force. Ruiz resisted, but he finally agreed to add that his resignation carried with it "implicitly" his retirement from the air force. Allende offered the post to General Gustavo Leigh, who initially refused it, then to General von Schowen (now next in seniority and supposedly more sympathetic to the government), who also refused. The next day, Allende worked out a compromise whereby an air force brigadier general entered the cabinet and Leigh became commander in chief. The compromise, of course, infuriated Ruiz, since he had been removed on the pretext that only the air force commander in chief could be in the cabinet, and he expressed his irritation on a popular television interview program on Sunday evening.

Allende himself spent Sunday, August 19, at his vacation house just outside Santiago with Regis Debray, the French writer, as his guest. After the coup and Allende's death, Debray wrote his recollections of their conversations in "jovial, warm, relaxed" atmosphere of a winter afternoon. They discussed Allende's maneuvers with the military, and Debray had the impression that Allende enjoyed the chess game he was playing with them. Yet, Debray noted, "everyone knew that it was only to secure time or organize, to arm, to coordinate the military apparatus of the Popular Unity parties—a race against the clock which had to go on week after week." Allende was guided in this game, writes Debray, by two principles. On the one hand, he felt a

visceral rejection of civil war which, given the balance of forces, would be lost. He was not taken in by the phrase "people's power." When those on the left declared that "only the direct action of the masses will stop the coup d'état," he would reply, "How many of the masses are needed to stop a tank?" On the other hand, he was determined not to tarnish the image which he wanted to leave to history by giving in to the military on the essentials of his program. But between these two conflicting principles, Allende refused to choose, since he thought or pretended that his two fundamental aims were not contradictory.[38]

His refusal to recognize that these two principles were mutually exclusive contributed to his overthrow three weeks later.

CHAPTER ELEVEN

The Overthrow of Allende

The most important week in Chilean politics prior to the September 11 coup began on Monday, August 20, 1973, when a meeting of 120 air force officers with Generals Ruiz and Leigh ended at noon with a decision by Ruiz to resist his removal and remain as air force commander. Air force Hawker Hunter jets had already taken off from Santiago for bases in Concepción, where the navy, like the air force, was on alert status. In the afternoon, while air force wives demonstrated in opposition to Ruiz's resignation, Ruiz consulted with the other generals and appears finally to have yielded to a threat by General Prats to take control of the air force as minister of defense. Finally, at 7 P.M. (seven hours after the time originally scheduled for the ceremony), General Leigh was sworn in as commander of the air force.[1]

On Tuesday afternoon, a large number of army officers' wives, including those of several generals, gathered at the residence of General Prats to present a letter requesting his resignation. When the police broke up the gathering with tear gas, it provoked such dissension within the armed forces that after a meeting with the council of generals on the following day at which he was outvoted, 12 to 6, General Prats decided to resign both as defense minister and as army commander. (The right-wing magazine *Qué Pasa* reported that General Pinochet had supported Prats but added that as the new army chief, Pinochet would "reflect the predominant tendency in the high command which is clearly opposed to giving political support to the Unidad Popular.") In his letter of "irrevocable" resignation, Prats stated that he did not wish his continuation in office to disrupt "institutional discipline" or "provide a pretext for those who seek to overthrow constitutional government"—presumably an allusion to his belief that he could only continue in office by purging two-thirds of the council of generals. Two other generals who were close friends of his, the head of the Santiago garrison and the director of the military institutes, also went into retirement, and Admiral Montero gave up his cabinet post, but not his position as commander in chief of the navy. It was significant that the three army generals who had retired were those who had led the military forces that quelled the revolt of the Second Armored Regiment at the end of June.[2]

Allende's effort to involve the military more closely with his government had thus exacerbated previously existing divisions in the armed forces and led both to the resignation from the cabinet of all three military commanders within two weeks of their appointment and to the retirement from the army of his three strongest supporters. He did secure the continued participation of senior military men in a restructured cabinet, but they were not the service chiefs; and the army representative took the relatively minor post of minister of mines rather than the Defense Ministry, which went to Allende's close friend and former ambassador to Washington, Orlando Letelier.

Congressional Legitimation of a Coup?

At the same time, the opposition majority in the Congress began to take a much harder line against the Allende government. The right-wing National Party had been disappointed in its hopes that the opposition would secure a two-thirds majority in the March congressional elections, which would have permitted the impeachment of the president. However, it was now pressing for the use of article 43, section 4, of the constitution which gives the Congress the power to remove the president from office by a majority vote if an "impediment which prevents the President of the Republic from exercising his office is such that a new election is necessary."

The Christian Democrats rightly viewed this as a maneuver of very dubious constitutionality which could only lead to institutional chaos and the collapse of democracy. The anti-Allende forces, led by Senator Luis Bossay (now head of the newly formed Social Democratic Federation), produced another constitutional provision—article 39, section 2, which provides that by virtue of its power to review (*fiscalizar*) acts of the executive, the Chamber of Deputies may adopt "sense-of-the-house" resolutions (*acuerdos*) to be transmitted in writing to the president for a reply by him or his ministers.

After substantially modifying the original resolution, Bossay was able to secure Christian Democratic support for an *acuerdo* accusing the government of attempting to impose a totalitarian system on Chile, habitually violating the constitution and the law, and encouraging the establishment of "parallel powers" which threatened democratic institutions. While not specifically declaring the Allende government illegitimate, as the original version had done, the resolution criticized the government for by-passing the legislature through the use of legal loopholes and decrees of insistence and for refusing to promulgate the constitutional reforms adopted by the Congress. It asserted that the executive had ignored judicial orders and decrees of the controller general, limited freedom of expression, encouraged illegal takeovers of agricultural and industrial property, persecuted opposition labor organizations, and supported illegal paramilitary groups. It urged the ministers who represented the armed forces in the cabinet "to put an immediate end to all the de facto situations listed above which violate the constitution and the law" or be guilty of compromising "the national and professional character of the armed forces and the carabineros" and of violating article 22 of the constitution, which declares the military forces nonpolitical.

The Chamber adopted the resolution, 81 to 47. In the past, the Popular Unity representatives had walked out before this sort of vote, but they remained because there was some doubt until the last minute whether some of the Christian Democrats would vote for the resolution. After its adoption, the Popular Unity Executive Committee declared a state of emergency and urged all its provincial and local units to remain in continual session. Allende replied to the motion by accusing the Congress of promoting a coup d'état by asking the military forces to make governmental judgments independently of "the authority and direction of the president." He pointed out that the constitution provided the Congress with only one way of voting on the legality of presidential conduct—impeachment—and he noted that motions arising under article 39 of the constitution were to be directed to the president, not to individual ministers.[3]

The resolution was carefully worded so that it did not actually call for a coup, and the president of the Christian Democratic Party told the *New York Times*, "Neither we nor the armed forces favor anything but a democratic solution to Chile's political crisis." However, he emphasized that the only way to avoid a constitutional breakdown was to form a cabinet with at least six military men in it and to appoint military men "with real power" to key undersecretarial positions and as heads of governmental agencies, in order to provide "an effective guarantee of the constitution and the laws of the country."[4] Described as a "white coup" by the Allende supporters, such a solution would have transferred most effective decision-making power to the military, leaving Allende as what many Chileans described as a "Chilean Queen Elizabeth." Given the political composition and outlook of the Popular Unity coalition, this seemed to the left to be a complete betrayal of the "revolution."

The congressional vote was echoed by several professional associations. The Medical Association called on their "colleague" to resign, a request that was echoed by the Federation of Professionals (CUPROCH). The lawyers also issued a declaration which argued that "without attributing a malevolent intention" to the president, but simply "in the face of the incompatibility between the institutional framework within which he is supposed to exercise his office and the actions which he feels obliged to carry out in his program," Allende "would appear to be impeded in the exercise of his office," thus justifying congressional action under article 43, section 4, of the constitution.

Third New Cabinet

It was a desperate and weary Allende who went about restructuring his cabinet for the third time in two months. The military entered the new cabinet, the composition of which was announced on August 28, on the condition that Allende intensify his efforts to settle the truckers' strike and to come to an accommodation with the Christian Democrats. Carlos Briones was again appointed minister of the interior, as part of a renewed effort for an accord with the Christian Democrats. When Briones's appointment was made known, the Socialist Party, to which Briones had belonged for twenty-five years, announced that it did not approve of his participation. Allende replied that Briones was participating as an independent. Given the changes in the military, and the pressures on him from the opposition Congress and from his own supporters, no one was surprised when it was announced that Allende was canceling his planned trip to Algiers for the Conference of Non-Aligned Nations on September 5–8.

Economic Crisis

As they entered their fifth week, the strikes by the truckers and others were estimated to have caused losses of $100 million to the Chilean economy. But even without the strikes, the economic situation of the country in mid-1973 could only be described as desperate. A report published by the Society for Industrial Development at the end of July gave the figures. The inflation rate for the preceding twelve months had reached 323 percent and was fueled by gigantic government deficits both for the budget and by way of credits from the Central Bank for the nationalized industries and reformed agriculture. According to the report, the budget deficit for 1972 had been 24 billion escudos, or 40 percent of the government's expenditures.[5]

It predicted that the deficit for 1973 would run well over 100 billion escudos (it actually reached 149 billion escudos, or 53 percent of the government budget), and it estimated the deficit of the nationalized industries and agriculture at between 140 and 180 billion escudos (it actually reached 175 billion escudos). These figures made the government's attacks on the Congress for leaving a 10 billion escudo deficit in the financing of the April wage readjustment pale into insignificance. The report also predicted an expansion of the money supply in 1973 of 2,300 to 2,700 percent over the amount in circulation when the Allende government took power. (Central Bank figures indicate that the money supply rose by 3,400 percent by the end of 1973.)[6]

Combined with the huge government deficits and runaway inflation were sharp drops in production. According to the report, production of iron had dropped by 23.7 percent in 1972 and that of coal by 12 percent. Copper was up by 1.2 percent in 1972, but a drop of 5 percent was predicted for 1973. In addition to worker absenteeism and mismanagement by inexperienced interventors picked for political rather than technical reasons, the decline in production was also related to the lack of new investment. In his 1973 presidential message, Allende claimed that investment had continued at a rate of 14 percent of the gross national product in 1971 and 1972, but the Department of Economics of the University of Chile put the figures at 13.3 percent and 12.4 percent (compared with an average of 17.4 percent in the 1960s). Whatever the actual figures, there was no question that industrial production had dropped precipitously in the first part of 1973, by an amount variously estimated at between 6 and 8 percent.[7]

In agriculture, the situation was even worse. The harvest figures for 1972–73 were reported as indicating a 22 percent drop in agricultural production with particularly sharp decreases in wheat production. (Final harvest figures for 1973 indicated a 25.3 percent decline in agricultural production and a 35 percent drop in wheat.) Government spokesmen no longer blamed the reductions on sabotage and imperialism, and they admitted that a considerable proportion of the "reformed" sector was not producing crops and that much of the rest was being sold on the black market.

The figures on the balance of payments were particularly depressing. The SFF report estimated Chile's increased indebtedness since the end of 1970 at $1 billion (later figures put it at $800 million) and combined this with the $343 million in 1970 reserves which had been largely dissipated in 1971 to argue that Allende had run a foreign deficit of nearly $1.25 million a day for three years—more than Cuba had received in assistance from the Soviet Union.

The situations were somewhat different, since the Chilean indebtedness was to an astounding number of countries around the world and in some cases (for example, Holland and China) involved long-term interest-free credits. Many of those credits had been extended, however, on the basis of a favorable report from the International Monetary Fund in 1972 which attributed Chile's difficulties chiefly to the drop in copper prices. Now copper prices were up and a new report which had been prepared for a meeting of Chile's creditors in Paris in July was very pessimistic. It was still possible for Chile to receive "standby" credits from the IMF, but the Allende government had made it clear that it was not prepared to embark on the stabilization program which was a precondition of such credits. At the Paris meeting, the Chilean representative asked for a postponement of 95 percent of the 1973–74 payments due Chile's foreign creditors (estimated for 1973 at $496 million), arguing that to pay the full amount would take 40 percent of Chile's export earnings. The meeting adjourned until October, without taking any action, thus giving the Chileans a further breathing spell (pending the Paris negotiations, no payments had been made). The net result of the negotiations, however, was to discourage further lending to a country which had not paid anything to the United States since 1971, nor to other creditor countries since late 1972.[8]

Yet these negative economic indicators, widely publicized by the opposition, did not spell catastrophe for the Allende government—at least not yet. Their impact on the ordinary Chilean, at least until the truckers' strike, was not so negative as to discredit the government totally. The unemployment rate in the Greater Santiago area continued to hover around 3 percent, the lowest in Chilean history, and even if much of this was in deficit-financed make-work, it still brought in a wage. Housing starts were down sharply from 1971, but there was still a time lag in construction and many of the 80,000 houses promised in 1971 were still being built.

Even with what amounted to semiannual wage readjustments, wages had not been keeping up with prices since mid-1972. In 1971 they had gone up by over 50 percent compared to a 22 percent increase in prices, but the much vaunted 1971 increase of wages and salaries to 59 percent of the national income had dropped back in 1972, according to economists at the University of Chile, to below their share in the last year of the Frei regime. In the case of the very poor, wage increases in 1972 and 1973 were well below the increase in food prices. Yet the government kept the prices down in the market basket of basic commodities that it was distributing to the poorer areas, and some of it could be resold in middle- and upper-class areas at black-market prices. There were a near total absence of beef, long lines for bread, and shortages of staples such as toothpaste, detergent, and powdered milk, but no one was starving. With so much money in circulation, many of the poor felt that their situation had improved. The question for the future was whether the Allende government could maintain existing living standards in the face of declining industrial and agricultural production, a lack of foreign exchange, and now a breakdown in the vital road transport system.[9]

The Coup Decision

It should probably have been evident to the government that the perilous state of the Chilean economy combined with the resignation of General Prats made a coup almost inevitable. September was an obvious time for such an action, since that is when troops are moved to Santiago for the military parade on September 19. However, although it was now clear that the air force was almost solidly against the government, the situation in the other services was still uncertain. The traditionally conservative navy had never been favorable to Allende, and now the attempted infiltration of ships in Valparaíso and Talcahuano had led Admiral José Merino to demand the lifting of parliamentary immunity of Carlos Altamirano of the Socialists and Oscar Garretón of MAPU. Yet despite strong pressure from his colleagues, Admiral Montero, the navy commander, continued to maintain a constitutionalist line. The carabineros were less important, but the government assumed that being drawn from a more "popular" (that is, lower-class) background, they would be loyal. The army was crucial in the government's calculations, but given the support that Pinochet and two other generals were known to have given General Prats in the discussions after the demonstrations by the officers' wives and in the reconstruction of a cabinet with military participation, it was assumed that a divided army was not about to stage a coup.

Among the political parties, Allende's principal attention was focused on the Christian Democrats, since the reopening of the dialogue with the PDC and a possible plebiscite had been conditions for the military representatives to remain in the cabinet. Carlos Briones, once again minister of the interior, began informal conversations with the PDC on the topics in disagreement, including the reinstatement of the workers fired during the El Teniente strike, the return of the University of Chile's television station (which had been occupied by the extreme left), and, as always, the constitutional amendments in dispute between President Allende and the Congress. Radomiro Tomic had written a public letter praising General Prats, and Senator Renán Fuentealba had pronounced himself satisfied with the new military cabinet, so that at least a segment of the Christian Democrats still seemed willing to cooperate. It seemed that Allende's famed *"muñeca"* (wrist action) might still resolve the crisis by some kind of arrangement with the PDC.

Yet the truckers' strike continued, now joined by more and more of the *gremios*. Ex-president Frei was said to be convinced that the only remaining choice was between a military dictatorship and the dictatorship of the proletariat. On August 28, an army second lieutenant was killed by five "extremists" headed by a Mexican leftist who, like many others, had remained in Chile after his ninety-day tourist visa had expired. The left had its martyrs, too, as *Chile Hoy* published reports of the torture of sailors suspected of being implicated in the left's plan to seize navy ships. The magazine also gave a detailed account of pressures for a coup within the air force and the navy—but not in the army—citing the MIR intelligence unit as its source.[10]

Now that Prats had resigned, the pressure focused on Admiral Montero. On August 29, Admiral Merino, the second in command of the navy, and Admiral Sergio Huidobro, chief of the Chilean marines, went to Santiago to tell Montero that the navy wished him to resign. Allende was reported to have told them at a late-night meeting that what they had discovered in Valparaíso was only one-tenth of what the left was doing, concluding, "I know I am at war with the navy." The meeting seems to have had an important influence on the navy's decision to stage a coup.[11] On Friday, August 31, after meeting the other admirals in Valparaíso, Admiral Montero agreed to resign. Allende rejected his resignation and wrote him an open letter declaring that "the highest interest of the country" required that he continue in his post. He concluded, "Although I cannot ask that you remain indefinitely as commander in chief, I insist that Chile must have your valuable support in these hours."[12]

On the following Monday, the top naval officers met for an all-day session in Santiago. By the end of the day, Allende had agreed to accept Montero's resignation and name Merino as his successor "in a few more days." He had also accepted the admirals' demands for legal action against Senator Altamirano in return for a promise by the navy to investigate the charges of torture of the enlisted men. By the time of his next meeting with Admiral Merino on the Friday deadline set by the navy, however, Allende was still asking for more time. Newspaper accounts of Merino's meetings on that day indicate that despite the fact that Montero was still nominal head of the navy, Merino for all practical purposes was acting as spokesman for the navy as a corporate institution in negotiation with the minister of defense and President Allende.

Not only was the navy upset by Allende's inaction, it also felt that the country was lapsing into virtual anarchy—as recent events in Valparaíso, the navy stronghold, indicated. At the end of August, the Catholic University of Valparaíso was the scene of a series of armed occupations and reoccupations by the extreme right and left. The rector finally was compelled to call in the navy to restore order, but when the troops left, the violence began again. The navy officers took matters into their own hands by breaking up a televised meeting in Valparaíso protesting the treatment of the imprisoned sailors.

In the political arena, the negotiations with the Christian Democrats seemed to have reached an impasse as Interior Minister Briones and Christian Democratic President Patricio Aylwin exchanged bitter public letters, each accusing the other of systematically ignoring violations of law by their supporters. The opposition parties now concentrated on gathering signatures for a petition asking for Allende's resignation, and Santiago braced itself for demonstrations and counterdemonstrations on the third anniversary of Allende's electoral victory. Supporters and opponents of the Allende regime have engaged in a futile numbers game in estimating the turnouts for the pro- and antigovernment demonstrations.[13] Estimates on the numbers at the anniversary parade on September 4 ran from 20,000 to 1 million, while the antigovernment demonstration by women and the *gremios* on the following day was estimated to have numbered between 15,000 and 300,000.

The crisis was intensified by worsening shortages and continuing strikes. Health care was almost paralyzed; shops struck for forty-eight to seventy-two hours every week; lawyers, pharmacists, engineers, teachers, even the pilots of LAN Chile were on strike. The country faced an acute shortage of bread; on Thursday, September 6, President Allende announced to the country that there was only enough flour for three or four more days. The problem, as he explained it, was not only a shortage of imported wheat, but also right-wing terrorist attacks on the highways and railroads which prevented the wheat that was available from being brought to Santiago from Chilean ports.

Allende's relations with the military were not made any easier when the executive committee of the Popular Unity Federation issued a statement on September 4 supporting the sailors on trial for subversion. On September 6, he dissociated himself from the statement's implied support for subversive acts and reiterated his support for the rule of law, indicating that while the case was being investigated, the government "could not and should not" make any statement.

On Friday night and Saturday, September 7 and 8, the Popular Unity leaders met to discuss Allende's recurrent proposal to hold a plebiscite on his continuation in office. One advantage of the plebiscite was that it would give the country an electoral outlet for the mounting tension and confrontation. Since it would take several months of preparation, it might also give the government time to attempt to resolve the country's serious economic problems. The disadvantages—which were evident to all—were first that the Congress would probably oppose it, if only because the Catholic University Law School report on the March elections had cast doubt on the validity of the present electoral rolls, and, more persuasive, the government was almost certain to lose. Predictably, Carlos Altamirano and the left wing of the UP coalition were adamantly opposed and recommended preparation for armed confrontation, while the Communists were more favorable to the proposal. After receiving Communist support, Allende is supposed to have decided that he would propose the plebiscite in a speech on the following Monday, later postponed to Tuesday, the day of the coup.[14]

The Christian Democrats were working on their own solution to the political impasse. On September 8, at a national meeting of their provincial leaders, they adopted a proposal originally suggested by the rector of the University of Chile, Edgardo Boeninger, that both the president and the Congress resign and new elections be held in order to resolve the deadlock between them. (This was the way that the deadlock between the rector and the University Council at the University of Chile had been resolved in early 1972.) But it was already too late for a political solution.

Later accounts of the immediate antecedents of the coup indicate that the decision to stage the coup on Tuesday, September 11, was made on Friday, September 7, the day after the participation of two carabinero generals who were fourth and seventh in seniority had been secured. The joint declaration published on September 11 was signed by the three armed services on Sunday, September 9, and by the new head of the carabineros, General Cesar Mendoza, the night before the coup. Only a few military men knew of the decision, and it may have been made after Allende met Admiral Merino on Friday to ask for more time before naming him navy commander. Allende is also said to have had a stormy meeting with the army and air force commanders at which General Leigh was supported by General Pinochet when he asserted that Allende was "surrounded by thieves and liars."[15]

If the military decision was made on Friday, it was probably reinforced by the armed resistance offered by workers at the state-run Sumar plant to an arms search on Friday evening. After the coup, numerous interviews indicate that the military chiefs did not have any knowledge of the so-called Plan Zeta to assassinate the military leaders on September 19, which they used to justify their actions after the fact. General Pinochet said in a later interview that because of fear of action on the part of the industrial *cordones*, he had ordered army troops from outside Santiago not to come into the city to prepare for the military parade scheduled for September 19. Pinochet claimed that the army's plans called for an uprising on September 14, at the time of the rehearsal for the military parade, but that they were so well organized that all he had to do was "push a button" to move the date back. The navy preferred September 10, the day the fleet was scheduled to go out for the annual "Unitas" maneuvers with the U.S. Navy, but Pinochet requested a one-day postponement to allow those away for the weekend to return to their bases. Thus, the date finally agreed upon was September 11.[16]

The actual signing of the declaration by the army, navy, and air force took place on Sunday, September 9, at a birthday party for General Pinochet's daughter. Generals Pinochet and Leigh met in another part of the house with two admirals who had brought Admiral Merino's written agreement from Valparaíso. (Merino claimed later that he had not previously discussed the coup with Leigh and Pinochet, but the other two admirals must already have been in contact with them. Admiral Montero had been completely left out of the decision.) The declaration had been drafted in Pinochet's house the preceding day.[17]

The Altamirano Speech

Defenders of the coup have claimed that a violent speech by Senator Altamirano on September 9 precipitated the coup, but it is now clear that his speech was given after the decision had been made. (Pinochet also said later that the speech gave a convenient excuse to keep the troops in their quarters on Monday night.) At a midday rally to publicize the conclusions of a meeting of the Central Committee of the Socialist Party, Altamirano admitted that he had attended a "meeting to which I was invited in order to hear denunciations by a junior officer and several sailors of subversive acts which were supposed to have been carried out by naval officers." Altamirano also denounced the "brutal provocation" in the Sumar plant and the return of the University of Chile television station, "the people's channel," and said that Chile was now "a silent Vietnam." Stating his opposition to any dialogue with the opposition, Altamirano declared that "the reactionary coup should be combated by striking back, not by conciliation with sedition. You do not fight through dialogues, but with the force of the people, their industrial commands, their peasant councils, their organization. Civil war should be combated by the creation of a genuine people's power. . . . In these three years, we have aroused a combative force which nothing and nobody can contain."[18]

An account of Allende's reaction to the speech, probably based on an interview with Senator Alberto Jerez, reports that Allende heard the speech at his home in the company of Jerez and Anselmo Sule, the head of the Radical Party. Allende is reported to have said, "That madman is sabotaging me." Jerez then advised him to disavow Altamirano even if it meant splitting the Socialist Party. The politicians discussed the possibility of Allende's resignation, but he held out for the plebiscite he was planning to announce the next day along with his disavowal of Altamirano's speech.[19]

The top three officers of the national police were not informed of the coup, and Allende found the carabineros' adherence to the coup a complete surprise. Later interviews refer to that adherence as taking place "late" on September 10, and in Valparaíso it was said that the carabineros did not agree to participate until 3 A.M. on the day of the coup. The director of the carabineros was in the presidential palace with Allende when the coup began, and three hundred Special Services carabineros surrounded the palace to defend it on the morning of the coup, although they left when they learned of the carabineros' adherence to the coup.

Reports published later of the shooting of thousands of pro-Allende members of the armed forces and national police on the night of September 10 are not confirmed by any evidence in Chile.[20] Others that refer to the arrest or retirement of fifty officers, including Admiral Montero and General Bachelet (who died in prison in March 1974) seem more believable.

In Valparaíso, the navy set out to join the "Unitas" international maneuvers held each year at this time. (This was one of several factors later cited in support of accusations of U.S. involvement.) The ships waited beyond the horizon and returned in the evening. Between 8 and 9 P.M., all navy commanders received a message directing that at 6 A.M. on September 11 they were to follow the orders of the "Anti-Insurgency Plan" drawn up two months before—but omitting the "Anti" from the plan's title. Meanwhile, Allende spent the day in meetings, and his speech announcing a plebiscite was postponed until Tuesday. In his residence that evening, he discussed the situation with Carlos Briones, his minister of the interior (who later described the atmosphere in the last days of the Allende government as "something out of the theater of the absurd"), and they worked on the speech he planned to give at noon the next day.[21]

The Communist Party learned late Monday night that the navy units which had left Valparaíso that afternoon had unexpectedly returned. The Political Committee of the party met, and after midnight *El Siglo*, the party newspaper, changed its headline from "The Plebiscite will Take Place" to "Everyone to His Combat Post." At 1:30 A.M., Allende received reports of suspicious troop movements north of Santiago. Foreign Minister Letelier called General Herman Brady and received reassurances that the troops were coming to reinforce the Santiago garrison, which Brady headed, against possible disturbances after the navy court martial decision was announced on Tuesday.

The Coup

Army units had orders to report for action at 4 A.M., and three hours later they began to move. By 8:15 Concepción, Chile's third largest city and long a stronghold of leftist sentiment, had been taken over without a hitch. Government leaders were arrested at dawn; as one of them ruefully remarked, "Before we were fully awake, we were on Quiriquina Island." The army later said that it had disconnected the telephones of 1,800 progovernment leaders in Concepción just before taking over the city. Valparaíso was occupied by the navy before 7 A.M. (An indication of the independence of action of the services was the fact that navy men said privately after the coup that when Valparaíso had been taken over, the navy was still not certain that the army would join them.)

The main center, as always, was Santiago. At 6:20 A.M. Allende was informed that the navy had seized Valparaíso. He may have thought this was only a naval rebellion which he could handle by negotiation (the military later claimed the navy moved first to distract Allende's attention from the activities of the other services). Perhaps he was thinking of the symbolic importance of a last stand at La Moneda, the stately presidential palace in the center of Santiago. In any case, Allende decided to go to the presidential palace although elaborate plans had been made to defend his residence in the event of a military revolt.[22]

According to one account, at 8:20 A.M. Allende's air force aide-de-camp transmitted Air Force General von Schowen's offer of a plane to take him into exile. He replied, "Tell General von Schowen that the president of Chile does not flee in a plane. As he knows how a soldier should act, I will know how to fulfill my duty as president of the Republic." Another account describes the offer as coming first from Vice Admiral Patricio Carvajal in a phone conversation with Allende at 9:25 A.M. (In September

1974 a tape recording of the offer was broadcast in Santiago to allay doubts as to whether it had been made.)

At 8:30 A.M. Radio Agricultura, a center of opposition to Allende, interrupted its programming to announce the initiation of the coup and to demand that Allende resign.

In a direct radio message to the nation Allende replied, "I am ready to resist by whatever means, even at the cost of my life, so that this may serve as a lesson in the ignominious history of those who use force not reason." (This was a reference to the Chilean motto, "By reason or by force.") He was particularly bitter about the army and carabineros turning against him, referring to the incredible action of "soldiers who go back on their word and commitments" and describing Carabinero General Cesar Mendoza as "underhanded" (*rastrero*).

One by one, the progovernment radio stations left the air, and the military radio began to broadcast its justification for the coup. Proclamation no. 5 of the military listed fourteen points, beginning: "The government of Allende has incurred serious illegitimacy as is demonstrated by its violation of fundamental rights of freedom of expression, freedom of education, the right of assembly, to strike, to petition the government, the right to property, and the general right to dignified and secure subsistence." It accused the government of "artificially fomenting class struggle," of violating the constitution by the use of "intentionally distorted interpretations," and of failing to execute the decisions of the Congress, the courts, and the controller general. It observed that the "agricultural, commercial, and industrial economy of the country is in stagnation and decline, and inflation is increasing at an accelerated rate." All of this, said the proclamation, indicated that "the internal and external security of the country" is in danger. "In the light of classical historical doctrine" of Chile, this danger is sufficient "to justify our intervention to depose a government which is illegitimate, immoral, and unrepresentative of the overwhelming sentiment of the nation."[23]

Around 9 A.M., Allende appeared briefly on the balcony of the presidential palace. Those who had been going to work or were already there now took buses or walked back to their homes. Tubs were filled with water in anticipation of a lengthy siege (water, electricity, and gas were never cut off during the coup), and radios were turned on. At 9:30, Allende delivered his dramatic last message to the Chilean people. By mid-morning the carabineros had left, followed by the military aides and part of the Investigaciones detachment, and tanks were lined up in front of the palace.

Negotiations were carried on by telephone between Allende and the military men directing the siege from the Defense Ministry opposite, amid scattered sniper fire from surrounding buildings. (In a later interview Miria Contreras claimed to have overheard two military commanders on an open telephone line assert that Allende should be "crushed like a cockroach.")

At 11:55 A.M., the bombing of the presidential palace began. The air force sent in British-made Hawker Hunters with rockets, eighteen of which hit the palace with deadly accuracy. (It is an indication of the simplistic character of outside views that the story was circulated that the planes were flown by U.S. pilots—presumably because Chileans were incapable of such precision.[24])

Why was the palace bombed, when a tank could easily have entered it? Apart from the desire to involve the air force directly in the coup and possibly to save lives among the attackers, it seems to have been calculated as a dramatic demonstration of the power of the armed forces. The bombing was to discourage the resistance which, it was feared, might come from factories where arms had been stored. In fact, there seems to have been significant resistance only at the Sumar nylon factory, which was bombed (reportedly after it had shot down a helicopter), and in the military occupation of the neighboring La Legua sector. (The left-dominated Technical University was also the scene of shooting when it was occupied by the military on September 12.)

Shortly after 1:30 P.M., the politicians and medical personnel emerged from the side entrance to the palace behind a white flag of surrender. Patricio Guijón, one of the doctors in the palace, claims to have looked into the Independence Salon as he was leaving and to have seen Allende shoot himself. "At that precise instant, I saw that the president, seated on a sofa, fired the submachine gun that he held between his legs. I saw it, but I did not hear it. I saw his body shudder and the roof of his skull fly off." Guijón said he stayed with the body for eight or ten minutes, since the rest of the group had already left. He reported that he then saw three or four soldiers enter, led by General Palacios, whom he could identify because he had been shot in the arm. Photographers arrived, and then Guijón was taken to the Ministry of Defense and subsequently to the Military Academy, where the others were being held.[25]

Suicide or Murder?

The suicide was announced to the world by a photographer for *El Mercurio*, who said he had been summoned to take a picture of the body. Military photographers took the pictures, but they have never been published. After examination by medical and ballistics experts, Allende's body was flown to Viña del Mar to be buried in the family plot. All references to the Allende family were removed from the gravestone, which refers only to the Grove family members who are buried there. A carabinero guard was placed at the cemetery.

Soldiers enter the side entrance of the presidential palace after the politicians and medical personnel had exited behind a white flag. (Hernan Morales)

Hortensia Allende (who had remained at the presidential residence and escaped just before it too was bombed) initially accepted the suicide story, but after she arrived in Mexico on September 15, she insisted that her husband had been killed, asserting that those who saw the body had told her that there were bullet wounds in the chest and stomach.[26] Those who believe that Allende did not commit suicide also cite what is supposed to be a taped interview with Luis Renato Gonzalez Cordova, a member of the president's bodyguard, who later took asylum in the Mexican embassy. It gives an account which is contradicted by other sources in numerous details, including the time of departure of Allende's daughters, details of the design of the building, and the names of government leaders who were said to have been killed, nearly all of whom are still alive. The account says that in "the halls near the Red Room" there was a fire fight between the defenders of the palace and "a group of fascists under the command of Captain Mayor" who, after calling on Allende to surrender, wounded him mortally with "about six bullets; four in the neck and two in the thorax." According to the account, somehow the attackers were beaten back, and the president's bodyguards picked up Allende's body and took it to his office (which is located a considerable distance from where the fighting is supposed to have taken place), put him in his presidential chair with his sash of office around him, and wrapped the body with the Chilean flag (all this presumably under heavy fire). A more convincing set of arguments appears in *The Murder of Allende* by Robinson Rojas, which claims that a suicide with such a powerful weapon could not have left the body sitting rigidly in the position described by the military and Dr. Guijón. Rojas also claims that Allende's clothes were changed after he died fighting in order to eliminate obvious evidence of additional bullet wounds.[27]

How does one decide among these conflicting accounts? The junta has published a detailed medical report which describes the exact course of the bullet or bullets.[28] (The doctors admit that there may have been two in rapid succession, and other witnesses speak of seeing two empty shells by the body.) The *El Mercurio* photographer claims that he was not permitted to take a picture, but he saw the body and reported on it to Agence France Presse. Others who were in the building subsequently said they saw bullet marks high on the wall behind the sofa where Allende was said to have died, as well as pieces of Allende's skull on the floor and wall. Carlos Briones has said that Dr. Guijón told him, on the same day, the story that was later published—which would not leave much time for the military to concoct a fictitious account to which Guijón was supposed to subscribe. Allende himself had often cited the example of Chilean President José Manuel Balmaceda, who had commited suicide when he lost the civil war between his supporters and those of Congress in 1891. The tone of his last speech seems to suggest that Allende was considering suicide;

he mentioned it in his September 7 meeting with the Popular Unity parties; and he is supposed to have told one of his military aides before the aides left the palace in mid-morning that he would not surrender, indicating with his finger and thumb that he intended to shoot himself in the mouth. The weight of the evidence seems to point toward suicide, but the possibility of the staging of a suicide after his death cannot be excluded, particularly given the lengthy delay between the end of the fighting and the admission of the photographers.

The fighting continued for a time at the Sumar plant, but for all practical purposes the military controlled the country by mid-afternoon of September 11. An MIR leader later wrote that at a meeting with the Socialists and Communists at 2 P.M. to coordinate possible resistance, the Communists opposed armed resistance and the Socialist leaders were reported as taking refuge in various embassies. Estimates vary widely on the number of dead, but all agree that many more were killed after the coup than during it. Thousands were rounded up and held in the two stadiums in Santiago, as well as on islands and in detention camps elsewhere in the country. The top politicians were held in the Military Academy, but some important figures of the extreme left went underground and escaped the country. (Miria Contreras de Ropert, "La Payita," was able to reach asylum in the Swedish embassy by feigning illness and securing the help of medical personnel.) The most important figure to escape was the head of the Socialist Party, Senator Carlos Altamirano, who eventually surfaced in Cuba. Most of the leadership of the extreme left MIR also eluded capture. An exception was the much publicized guerrilla leader, Comandante Pepe, who was ordered shot by a military court in the south. (Miguel Enriquez, head of the MIR, was killed in Santiago more than a year after the coup.) Aside from Allende's close friend, Augusto Olivares, and Eduardo Paredes, one-time head of Investigaciones, no member of the leadership of the Allende regime died in the coup.

CHAPTER TWELVE

Chile's New Order

There had been speculation prior to the coup that if the military took power they would call new elections in six to twelve months in which the left would be forbidden to participate. Ex-president Eduardo Frei's intransigence in recent months had been attributed to a calculation along these lines, and there were reports at the time of the coup that, as president of the Senate, he expected to be asked to take over the government even sooner. After the coup, however, *Le Monde* published an interview with Frei dated September 7, four days before the coup, in which he said, "I do not believe in a military coup d'état. . . . If the military take action, they will certainly not do it in order to benefit a civilian. . . . As for me, I do not envisage returning to power except in a legal and democratic fashion."[1]

At 10 P.M. on September 11, the four members of the junta that had taken control appeared on television to describe their policy. To Chileans, who are highly sensitized to political nuance, their presentations appeared markedly different, giving rise to some confusion on the likely character of the new regime.

General Pinochet spoke first and announced that the junta would maintain the judiciary and the Controller-General's Office intact, but would name new military ministers and governors. He also announced the the Congress would remain "in recess" until further notice and declared that diplomatic relations would be maintained with all countries except Cuba. (The USSR and most Eastern European countries broke relations with the new government, but China and Rumania did not.)

General Gustavo Leigh, the air force commander, took a very different tone. He declared that the armed forces had been compelled to depart from their traditional apolitical position because "three years of the Marxist cancer . . . have brought us to a situation of economic, moral, and social disaster. We are certain that the great majority of the Chilean people are determined to struggle against Marxism and to extirpate it completely [*hasta las últimas consecuencias*]."

Admiral Merino took a constitutionalist position. He accused the executive of violating the constitutional requirement of balance among the three powers (legislature, executive, and judiciary) and described the breakdown of democracy in Chile as "the sad result of the loss of its characteristics as a state which the armed forces were sworn to maintain."

Carabinero General Mendoza took an even stronger constitutionalist position. In direct contradiction to what had just been said by General Leigh, he declared, "It is not a question of destroying ideological tendencies or currents nor of personal vengeance, but of reestablishing public order and restoring the country to the path of fidelity to the constitution and laws of the Republic."[2]

The same ambiguity about the intentions of the regime was evident in the declarations of the principal opposition parties after the coup. The Christian Democrats viewed the coup as a necessary consequence of the "economic disaster, institutional chaos, armed violence, and moral crisis" produced by the Allende government. They expressed confidence that once the military had completed "the tasks which they have assumed of avoiding the grave dangers of destruction and totalitarianism which threatened the Chilean nation, they will return power to the sovereign people so that they can decide freely and democratically on the future of the nation. The intention to return to institutional normality and peace and unity among Chileans expressed by the Military Government Junta reflects the general sentiment and merits the patriotic cooperation of all." In accordance with this resolution, the PDC indicated that its members would be permitted to cooperate with the government and even participate in it as technicians, professionals, or administrators.

The National Party's position indicated that it did not expect a return to the 1925 constitution. "The Military Junta," declared the Nacionales, "is opening a new step in history. We Chileans, besides freeing ourselves from Communist oppression by our own efforts, will demonstrate that . . . with imagination and efficiency, we can create a new set of institutions in a climate of national unity. . . . The Nacionales, who during these disastrous years have been in the first ranks of the struggle, return today to our work with the satisfaction of a duty completed."[3]

Not all the Christian Democrats agreed with their party's statement. Eight members of Congress and five party leaders issued another statement which did not appear until over a year later in the Chilean press. (It was finally reproduced in *La Segunda* on November 29, 1974.) The statement "categorically condemned the overthrow of the constitutional president of Chile." It blamed the extremes on both sides who had created the "false impression" that there was "no other recourse, but armed confrontation or a coup d'état," singling out "the irresponsibility of the ultra-left" for "special condemnation." It was signed by Senator Renán Fuentealba and Bernardo Leighton, a deputy, former minister, and cofounder of the party, among others.

Leighton also sued in the courts for a writ of habeas corpus (*amparo*) for several ministers, including Carlos Briones, former minister of interior, and Clodomiro Almeyda, former foreign affairs minister. The Appeals Court rejected the suit on the grounds that a state of siege had been decreed by the junta on the day of the coup under article 72 of the constitution, which authorized the "arrest and transfer of persons to places other than prisons" when a state of siege was in effect. The court did not mention that article 72 provided that such a declaration may only be made by the president in cases of external attack or by the Congress in cases of internal disturbance (the president may declare it until Congress meets) and that the constitutional rights of deputies and senators must be maintained.

The Attitude of the Judiciary

The position of the Appeals Court reflected the general attitude of the judiciary toward the new government. On September 12, the president of the Supreme Court expressed "his deepest pleasure" at the declaration of the new government that it would respect judicial decisions, and a day later the full court ratified the declaration and called on all courts to "continue carrying out their labors in the certainty that the administration will guarantee their normal functioning."[4]

The formal basis of the new government had been established by a series of decree-laws published by the junta. The first constituted the junta under the presidency of General Pinochet as "the Supreme Command of the Nation with the patriotic duty to restore *chilenidad*, justice, and the institutions which have broken down" and promised to respect the constitution and laws. The second established that the junta would legislate through a series of numbered decree-laws. A decree published on September 22 declared Chile under a "state of siege in time of war"—thus effectively destroying the judiciary's power by authorizing military tribunals to impose the death penalty for violations of the Arms Control Law, allowing summary executions for security reasons, and forbidding appeals from the decisions of the military courts.[5]

The courts had been most active in defense of those whose rights had been infringed by the Allende government, but now they gave the junta complete support. They continued to do so even after it was clear that fundamental human rights were being violated by the military, not only incidentally to the roundup of political prisoners but systematically in the places of detention where they were being held. As more and more evidence of torture and repression became available, there was no hint of protest from the judiciary. General Pinochet was greeted warmly when he made a formal visit to the Supreme Court on September 25, and the head of the court referred to the distortion of law under the Allende government and its failure to carry out legal orders, concluding, "When those in the government twist the meaning of the law and refuse to carry out the resolutions of their courts, they lose their reason for existence and their legitimacy." In his visit to the court and in a speech a month after the coup, Pinochet expressed his determination to restore the legality and constitutionalism which had been violated by the Allende government. He justified the continuation of a state of siege in time of war on the grounds that there were still Chileans within and outside the country who were bent on carrying out "their totalitarian purposes and from other countries to incite foreigners to fight against their own brothers."[6]

The Church and the Junta

The church took a much more nuanced position toward the junta than did either the opposition parties or the judiciary. Two days after the coup, Cardinal Silva issued a statement deploring "the blood which has reddened our streets, our settlements, and our factories—the blood of civilians and of soldiers, the tears of so many women and children." He called for respect for those who had fallen in the struggle and, courageously, "first

The president of the Chilean Supreme Court jokes with the members of the new military junta after a formal visit. (Rex Features)

of all, for the one who until Tuesday, September 11th, was President of the Republic."[7] Instead of the traditional *Te Deum* Mass of Thanksgiving at the cathedral on September 18, the national holiday, the cardinal authorized a mass for the reconciliation of all Chileans at the Church of National Thanksgiving built in celebration of national independence. The service was attended by the three living ex-presidents, Frei, Alessandri, and González Videla, and was considered abroad as the church's endorsement of the new regime. Those who knew the internal situation in Chile, however, realized that Cardinal Silva was continuing the policy he had followed since his election in 1958 of cooperating with whatever government was in power. As the church statement put it after the coup, "The church is not called upon to form governments or to overthrow them, to recognize them or not to recognize them."[8]

The cardinal supported the creation of the Committee on Cooperation for Peace in Chile, an interdenominational group headed by Catholic and Lutheran bishops and the grand rabbi of Chile, which was formed "to give material and spiritual aid to all persons and families affected by the current situation." This included legal assistance to imprisoned Chileans, finding jobs for those who had been dismissed for political reasons, and collecting "in a responsible and documented way" and reporting to the authorities information on "irregularities which take place." The committee kept a monthly confidential record of instances of torture and maltreatment which was publicized in May 1974 when a Mexican newspaper, *Excelsior*, secured copies. The record was one of the bases of later statements by the Chilean bishops criticizing the use of torture and arbitrary detention and calling for a return to the rule of law.

The churches also established a National Committee for Aid for Foreign Refugees to work with the United Nations High Commission for Refugees on the problems created by the coup for leftist foreigners who had come to Chile during the Allende regime. The committee and the United Nations established thirteen information centers for foreigners and set up United Nations camps to house and process those wishing to leave the country. The junta referred repeatedly to a supposed threat from the many foreigners in Chile. Before the coup, the Chilean Congress had received a report on the numbers of foreigners present in the country which indicated that many had entered on three-month tourist visas and had remained after they had expired. Allende's Cuban son-in-law, an official of the Cuban secret police, had lived in the presidential residence, and Cuban advisers were known to have been located in strategic positions in the Central Bank and to be assisting in the planning of a rationing system (long overdue in Chile's desperate economic situation). Moreover, the junta's emphasis on nationalism and Chilean unity could be made more credible if the substantial support Allende showed at the polls could be attributed to the evil machinations of foreigners. In the days after the coup, the military arrested and interned in the National Stadium large numbers of foreign "extremists" and conducted house-to-house searches for arms and subversive (that is, Marxist) literature and foreign "extremists." (A single instance of book-burning, widely reported in the foreign press, took place during the searches of the San Borja apartments, where many foreigners with government connections lived.)·

Post-Coup Repression

The Cubans were deported at the end of the week, and other foreign sympathizers of the Allende regime fled to embassies and to the refugee camps. But many, including a number of Americans, were compelled to undergo the horrifying experience of detention, maltreatment, and in some cases—including those of two Americans—death at the hands of their military inquisitors.

The *New York Times* estimated the number killed during and after the coup at 2,500. Figures as high as 80,000 have been cited by opponents of the regime. More reliable estimates put the number killed between 3,000 and 10,000. When asked about the continuing reports of bodies floating in the Mapocho River in Santiago, General Pinochet replied that they must have been killed in fighting among guerrilla groups. His reply was typical of the response of the military to foreign criticisms of torture and repression—a denial that they even took place. Claiming that the regime had nothing to hide, the military admitted newsmen and representatives of such groups as Amnesty International, the Red Cross, the OAS Human Rights Commission, the International Commission of Jurists, and the International Labor Organization, as well as many individuals and groups from the United States and Europe. When they returned with detailed reports on repression and torture, they were denounced as· agents of Moscow and part of the "orchestrated campaign" against Chile.

The day of the coup, the headquarters of the Marxist parties had been attacked and their records burned. The parties that had supported Allende were outlawed on September 22, and on October 14 they were legally prohibited on the grounds that "Marxist doctrine on the state and the class struggle is incompatible with national unity." (Once again the junta spoke of its mission "to extirpate Marxism from Chile.") The JAP committees were formally dissolved, and it was announced that no further work would be done on the ENU school reform. Congress, which had been declared in recess at the time of the coup, was formally dissolved on September 21, and three weeks later all other political parties were declared in recess. The CUT, the national trade union confederation, was prohibited because it "had transformed itself into an organism of a political character under the influence of foreign tendencies, alien to national sentiment."[9] With the takeover of local government by military decree on September 19, military control was complete.

Takeover of the Universities

The professional and interest-group associations (*gremios*) immediately announced their support for the coup and formally ended the strikes which had begun at the end of July. There remained only one group of institutions which might provide a center of resistance to military rule, the universities. As the result of university elections, the Christian Democrats controlled all the universities except the State Technical University. (They also would probably have won the 1973 elections in the Chilean Student Federation, but these had never been held.) A move against the universities, therefore, could not be justified as anti-Marxist. It simply involved the consolidation of military control of all aspects of national life.

The rector of the University of Chile, working with the other rectors, attempted to work out a program for a "reorganization" of the universities, but despite his record of consistent opposition to the Allende government, the military felt that it could not trust the academic authorities to do the job. On September 28, it was announced that all universities, including private institutions such as the two Catholic universities, would henceforth be headed by military delegate-rectors appointed with full powers by the junta. In his speech explaining the action, the minister of education said that "many university centers and schools have been converted into centers for Marxist propaganda and indoctrination, in some cases, even encouraging violence and the illegal use of arms, promoted by foreign undesirables. National Reconstruction cannot afford the luxury of permitting university life to be frustrated by petty politics, bureaucratism, and disorder. . . . It is not a question of destroying the autonomy of the university, but of reinforcing it by extirpating those who exploit that autonomy to subvert the essence and function of the university."[10]

The replacement of Edgardo Boeninger, the rector of the University of Chile who had led the fight for university autonomy against the Allende regime, and the removal of the other Christian Democratic rectors demonstrated that the sympathy with the Christian Democrats that many had detected among the Chilean military before the coup was an illusion. The junta appeared to blame the PDC for allowing Allende to come to power in the first place, and more fundamentally for politicizing a Chilean society since the early 1960s in a way which, in the view of the military, made them partially responsible for the debacle of the 1970s. When this was combined with repeated Christian Democratic insistence that any new constitution must be approved by popular vote, and their private (and later public) expressions of concern about the status of human rights, it meant that by the end of September, the PDC had become critical of the junta, although it continued to permit its *técnicos* to work for the new government.

By the time the party's National Council met on September 29, the president of the party, Patricio Aylwin, was describing the government as a dictatorship and expressing deep concern over repression. The council adopted a statement which observed that in slightly more than two weeks the military had revealed that they did not intend to move toward institutional, economic, and social "normalization," but rather had imprisoned thousands of people in the National Stadium and refused them access to the courts; had dissolved the Congress, local government, and the trade unions; and had taken over the universities, burned books, suppressed radio and television stations and newspapers, and instituted strict censorship. The junta, said the council, did not respect the constitution or the laws, and the majority of the persons with whom it worked in industry and agriculture were known to be rightists. The statement denounced the persecution of Chileans solely for their ideas and described as "typically totalitarian the effort to eliminate all political activity as contrary to the national interest." Calling for respect for the rights of the human person and of organizations of workers, peasants, and mothers, it reaffirmed the principles of "nationalization of basic resources, extinction of the latifundio, and termination of monopoly," and insisted on the ultimate right of the people to decide on the political forms by which they would be governed.[11]

The PDC newspaper, *La Prensa*, carried thinly veiled criticisms of the regime under the guise of discussions of themes such as "Stalinism" or dictatorships in other countries. In February 1974, *La Prensa* ceased publication, citing economic reasons (probably the ending of CIA aid). During 1975 the government systematically removed Christian Democratic leaders from positions of influence in labor and education, especially the universities. In November 1975 it closed its principal publication, *Política y Espíritu*, and in March 1977 formally dissolved the party.

The Arms Issue

How is one to explain the intensity and duration of the repression in Chile? Part of the explanation lies in the area of psychiatry rather than politics. Not only in Chile but everywhere in the world it seems that when men equipped with guns have others in their power, they are prone to act in cruel and inhuman ways unless restrained by strong legal and moral inhibitions. In addition, the psychology of those who are attracted to police work is often such that lacking any control they will give vent to their sadistic impulses. Some Chileans give a more subtle psychological explanation, asserting that the political neutrality of the military while the country seemed to be destroyed by the economic and political excesses of the politicians led to deep hostilities and resentments to which they gave vent in brutal ways when they came to power. The left emphasizes the deep-seated ideological hatred of Marxism among the senior military leadership who had been politically socialized during the period of the cold war—many of them conservative Catholics untouched by the changes in the post–Vatican II church. More fundamentally, there was their fear of the power of an ideology which not only could secure the support of 30 to 40 percent of the Chilean electorate, but also was beginning to threaten the military's monopoly of force. Thus, the fanatical search for arms deposits all over Chile, the curfew, censorship, and harsh reliance on force were all products of a mentality that saw Chile at war with a dangerous and well-equipped unofficial army with both external and internal support.

The paramilitary preparations and the widespread distribution of arms (not only on the left, of course) during the last months of the Allende regime, combined with the fact that the far left of the Popular Unity coalition had talked incessantly about the inevitability and necessity of a violent confrontation, only reinforced the military paranoia. The evidence that military intelligence was able to secure of large-scale spying on the military leadership and Allende's plans to remove many of the military commanders also accelerated the preparations for the coup.

After the coup, evidence was not lacking to confirm what had been suspected or partially known beforehand. The regime asserted that the coup had forestalled a civil war which would have involved the loss of a million lives. It made much of the arms training that had taken place at the presidential residence, publishing photographs of Allende himself at target practice, and claimed to have discovered eight other paramilitary training facilities at various points around the country. It also produced evidence that "intervened" factories had been manufacturing arms and (rather primitive) armored cars, and that a Soviet prefabricated housing plant near Valparaíso had been used for arms training. Documents were discovered in the Central Bank concerning Socialist and MIR infiltration of the air force which became the basis of a public trial in 1974. Those plans included proposals for seizing air bases by a combination of internal and external attacks. Files were said to have been found in the safe of the head of Investigaciones with detailed information on the families, personal habits, and political orientation of the military leaders. In the apartment of Eduardo Paredes a complete inventory was discovered of the Cuban arms that had created such an uproar in Congress in 1972 when they were passed through customs without inspection. A total of over 2,000 pounds of arms in thirteen crates was listed in the inventory which was later published in the junta's White Book justifying its takeover. Another document found in the presidential palace demonstrated that Allende had received a report on December 27, 1971, on government distribution of arms to the MIR, despite his public disavowals of their tactics.[12]

Most attention was focused on plans for an anticipated coup by the supporters of Allende, especially a so-called Plan Zeta, part of which was published in the White Book in October. Five days after the coup, the junta announced that a document discovered in the safe of the undersecretary of the interior proved that the Allende government had planned to murder the top military commanders and opposition leaders on September 17. A week later, a similar list of six hundred people marked for assassination was said to have been found in the notebook of the regional secretary of the Socialist Party in its headquarters in Concepción. When an alleged excerpt from Plan Zeta was published in the White Book, however, it described the "tentative" date for the implementation of the plan as September 19. Only the central section of the plan was published "in order not to compromise the security of those singled out as victims" and because the assassins were still being hunted. It was dated August 25, 1973, and its most sensational proposals called for the elimination of the commanders participating in the military parade scheduled for September 19 and the assassination of "the generals, admirals, and other high officers at the official luncheon that the government will give for Army Day." It also called for "the immediate detention of listed officers and leaders of the opposition and their transfer to places of detention and elimination," and for the "immobilization and annihilation of centers of sedition." The regional commands of the plan were to apply it when they received specific notification of a coup d'état, "tentatively, September 19, 1973."[13]

There was nothing in the plan to indicate that it had been approved by Popular Unity parties or by Allende himself. It is either a forgery or a document produced by the left wing of the Socialist Party or the MIR, who were known to be thinking along these lines. One cannot help but wonder, though, how they believed that a paramilitary force that was ill equipped and untrained, and could not have numbered more than 3,500 to 5,000 men, could destroy armed forces totaling 87,000.

Another document published in the White Book is supposed to be a set of instructions from the Communist Party Santiago Regional Committee to its Santiago cells, dated June 30, 1973, one day after the abortive tank regiment revolt. It instructed the party militants to equip themselves with arms and provisions for a possible confrontation in July, and informed the members in the Barrio Alto that they should leave that middle- and upper-class section in case of conflict, since designated blocks of that area would be bombed. "In case of confrontation," it continued, "a highly specialized CP team will physically eliminate the leaders of the opposition, which the membership should keep a strict secret."[14] It is unlikely that the document is authentic, since the Communist Party had not one but seven regional organizations in Santiago before the coup. The *Libro Blanco* also contains an elaborate program for the defense of the presidential residence, a handwritten analysis of the disposition of military forces in and around Santiago and ways to combat them, and plans for a field hospital for a "liberated zone" of 60,000 people including 4,000 combatants.

How could the Popular Unity parties have mounted such an operation with any prospect of success? The financing and materiel came from government funds and intervened factories. The personnel seem to have been on the government payroll in many places, especially in the Urban Development Corporation (CORMU), which increased sixty times in size between 1970 and 1973. It seems clear that the Popular Unity parties were making some preparations for an impending conflict, but that a "bloodbath" was scheduled for September 17 or 19 appears very doubtful. As the coup demonstrated, most of the plans were nothing more than that—and the divisions among the Popular Unity parties meant they were unlikely to have been approved by the UP Political Command. Thus, the 1948 "Prague Coup" mentioned by PDC President Patricio Aylwin would have been difficult, if not impossible, to carry out in mid-September.

However, the documents and the quantities of arms discovered in the arms searches before and after the coup help to explain the paranoia of the military, and the discoveries after the coup of MIR strongholds near the homes of the top military men did not calm their sense of danger. The church arranged no-questions-asked arms collections at local parishes and received large quantities of weaponry (from both left and right), demonstrating the extent to which Chile had been an armed camp before the coup.

The U.S. Role

When the rest of the world looked at the Chilean coup, it paid little or no attention to the explanations by the military. To foreign observers, it looked as if a democratic regime suffering from serious economic difficulties and deep political polarization had been overthrown by a right-wing, anti-Communist military, supported by the United States. The question of U.S. participation or complicity was raised in the very first news reports of the coup, which noted that the annual "Unitas" naval maneuvers meant that U.S. Navy ships were not far from the Chilean coup. It was also observed that Ambassador Davis had returned to Washington on September 6 for consultations. U.S. government explanations that this was part of a program of consultations with ten or fifteen ambassadors by the new secretary of state (Kissinger had been appointed on August 23) and that Davis had been discussing an appointment which he subsequently received as director general of the Foreign Service were ineffective in allaying suspicions that he had been planning the impending coup. A socialist news agency in Buenos Aires circulated a story that a U.S. weather plane located at Mendoza, Argentina, had coordinated communications for the coup. The fact that the Chilean military would be most unlikely to rely on an Argentine base and that the same story had been circulated about another military coup in Bolivia in 1971 did not deter those who wished to believe in active participation in the coup by the United States.

In contrast to the mild public reaction to U.S. intervention in Cuba in 1961 and in the Dominican Republic in 1965, the U.S. Congress received thousands of telegrams, letters, and phone calls from universities and church groups. Senator J. William Fulbright told the Senate that he was particularly impressed with the "unprecedented" unanimity of the opposition to the coup, concern for those imprisoned, and strong suspicion of U.S. involvement. The protests led to a series of hearings by numerous House and Senate committees aimed at determining the U.S. role in Allende's overthrow.

In April 1974, in testimony to the Intelligence Subcommittee of the House Armed Services Committee, CIA head William Colby gave extensive information on CIA activities in Chile since 1964, a garbled version of which was leaked to the *New York Times* in September 1974. The leaks indicated that $8 million had been authorized for CIA expenditures to "destabilize" the Allende regime. (At the end of 1975 a more accurate and detailed account of the CIA's role in Chile from 1963 until 1973 was published in the staff report of the U.S. Senate Select Committee on Intelligence Activities, *Covert Action in Chile, 1963–1973*.) Colby denied any direct role in the coup itself, but the revelation that the CIA had been authorized to intervene in a free election and presumably to reverse the results by bribing the Chilean Congress caused an uproar. In a press conference on September 17, 1974, President Gerald Ford defended the CIA activity as an effort "to help and assist the preservation of opposition newspapers and electronic media and to preserve opposition political parties. I think this is in the best interest of the people of Chile, and certainly in our best interest." He noted that the "Communist nations spend vastly more money than we do for the same kind of purposes" and promised to meet with congressional committees to determine whether changes were needed in the process of review of CIA activities.[15] The statement was widely criticized both for its assumption of a unilateral right by the United States to intervene in free elections, and for its lack of complete candor about where some of the CIA financial support went (for example, to the *gremios* and to Patria y Libertad). Congress was also angry at having been deceived by administration officials—including Henry Kissinger—in the numerous committee hearings in both houses which had dealt with U.S. activities in Chile. During his confirmation hearings on September 17, 1973, Kissinger had admitted CIA involvement "in a minor way" in the 1970 elections, but asserted that "since then, we have absolutely stayed away from coups. Our efforts in Chile were to strengthen the democratic political parties and give them a basis for winning the election in 1976." Earlier in 1973, at hearings on his appointment as ambassador to Iran, former CIA Director Richard Helms had replied, "No, sir," when asked whether the CIA had tried to prevent Allende's election, a statement proven false by later revelations.

U.S. Aid and Human Rights

Americans of a variety of political orientations were especially disturbed by the U.S. role in Chile because of the continuing reports of repression and torture. Senator Edward Kennedy was particularly concerned about what he saw as a contradiction between U.S. government willingness to intervene on behalf of the property of U.S. business concerns and its insistence that the issue of human rights was an internal matter. On October 2, 1973, Kennedy proposed an amendment to the Foreign Assistance Act stating that it was the sense of Congress that the president should cut off all aid to Chile, other than humanitarian assistance, "until he finds that the government of Chile is protecting the human rights of all individuals, Chilean and foreign, as provided in the Universal Declaration of Human Rights."[16] The amendment was not adopted, although a request that President Nixon call on the Chilean government to respect human rights was included in the Foreign Assistance Act as finally adopted in December 1973. Senator Kennedy made another effort to cut off military aid to Chile in 1974, when the foreign assistance legislation for 1975 was debated. In December 1974, in a striking rebuke to the Chilean regime, both houses of Congress voted to cut off all U.S. military aid to Chile "unless the president reports to Congress that Chile is making fundamental improvements in the observance of human rights." A year later, at Kennedy's initiative, a total prohibition on all Chilean military purchases in the United States was adopted by the Senate but later modified to reassert the previous ban on military aid.

When the Department of Agriculture announced after the coup that the Commodity Credit Corporation had granted Chile a credit of $24 million at commercial rates for the purchase of wheat in order to replace the shipments from Eastern Europe and the Soviet Union which had been turned around on the high seas on the day of the coup, Senator Kennedy issued a statement criticizing the arrangement as "the latest symbol of our willingness to embrace a dictatorial regime which came to power in a bloody coup and which continues to conduct summary executions, to burn books, to imprison persons for political reasons, and to deny the right to emigrate."[17]

Following the coup there were also news reports—which later turned out to be untrue—that the Interamerican Development Bank had granted Chile a $65 million loan—its first to Chile since January 1971. (The first new IDB loans to Chile were made at the time of the Bank's Santiago meeting in April 1974.) In November 1973 an additional CCC credit of $28 million for the purchase of corn was announced, and U.S. banks began extending short-term credits to Chile in substantial amounts, although still much less than in 1970. In December, the United States reached an agreement on rescheduling Chile's debt payments which had come due between November 1971 and December 1972. Chile agreed to pay the U.S. $60 million over a four-year period, and an additional $64 million at 6 percent interest over a six-year period, beginning in January 1975. Chile also agreed to reopen compensation negotiations with the copper companies. The first agreement on compensation was concluded in July 1974 with Anaconda Copper, which received $65 million in cash and $188 million in promissory notes at 10 percent interest for its 49 percent holdings expropriated in 1971, as well as the remaining payments due on the 51 percent nationalized in 1969. In October 1974, Kennecott agreed to a $68 million settlement for its 49 percent interest in El Teniente as well as unpaid interest. It received $6.5 million in cash, the remainder to be paid at 6 percent interest between 1975 and 1984. Chile also worked out agreements with the Overseas Private Investment Corporation to compensate it for payments to insured U.S. companies expropriated by Allende.

In February 1974, the Club of Paris held the meeting originally scheduled for July 1973 and worked out a rescheduling of Chile's 1973 and 1974 debt payments. Chile would only be required to pay 5 to 10 percent of the $1 billion in debts which were due in those years, postponing payments on the remainder.[18] In the same month, the World Bank approved the $5.25 million loan for preinvestment studies which had been ready for its board of directors at the time of the September coup. The World Bank loan was the first new loan to go to Chile from that institution since before Allende had come to power.

In 1974, when the Export-Import Bank reopened its credit lines, AID asked for $25 million in loans to Chile, and the International Monetary Fund made a $95 million "standby" loan, it looked as if the Allende charges of economic discrimination against his regime had been confirmed. Once again, however, it was necessary (and very difficult) to distinguish between political and economic criteria. The IMF had made several loans for export shortfalls to Chile under Allende, but was unable to give further assistance because the Allende government refused to accept the IMF "standby" loan provisions for an economic stabilization program. The new government accepted those provisions with alacrity, and it also requested new AID assistance, as the Allende regime had not. In December 1973 it made a $16 million payment on the Chilean debt to the United States, the first such payment in more than two years. It was able to make the payment because over $45 million in black-market dollars had been exchanged at Chilean banks for Chilean currency since the coup. In addition, production, exports, and copper prices had risen sharply, and Chile's balance-of-payments picture looked favorable for the immediate future. This induced the commercial banks to reopen lines of credit. Thus, what looked like the most blatant political discrimination in favor of a military regime, and against a socialist one, turned out on closer examination (at least in the case of the private banks and of the IMF) to be a response to a change in Chile's economic policy (and an increase in the world price of copper, which had been rising to unheard-of heights since early 1973). The slowness with which U.S. private investors returned to Chile, however, indicated that for private investors (as distinct from banks and international lenders), political considerations when weighed against economic factors often still led to a decision not to invest.

The Junta Ideology

The right-wing character of the new regime was evident in its program and ideology. Nationalist appeals to the unity of all Chileans replaced the "divisive" appeals of the parties, and despite the fact that since the early 1960s between one-fourth and two-fifths of the Chilean electorate had regularly voted for the Marxist parties, Marxism was described as a foreign ideology. The regime gave symbolic expression to its nationalism by changing the name of the government printing house, Quimantú, to Editorial Gabriela Mistral, by renaming the government newspaper *La Patria*, and by naming the building constructed for the 1972 United Nations Conference on Trade and Development after Diego Portales, a nationalist hero who was considered to be responsible for establishing the stability of the political system of Chile by creating a strong presidency in the early years of the republic. The regime spoke often of the "spirit of Portales," and it introduced compulsory courses in the schools stressing nationalist themes. In foreign policy, it continued to assert Chile's claim to control over two hundred miles of "patrimonial waters" off its coastline. Patriotism became a source of legitimacy to a regime which—although it probably began in office with the support of a majority of Chileans—felt insecure because of the lack of the electoral legitimation to which Chileans had been accustomed for 140 years. (The suspension of electoral activity became definitive in December, when the regime issued a decree-law forbidding elections at any level, even in athletic associations and educational institutions.)

Nationalism was combined, as it often is, with puritanism. A week after the coup, a decree-law announced the strict enforcement of laws against violation of good morals by the media in order to "restore the values of the moral and ethical patrimony of Chilean society, which have been seriously undermined."[19] The "girlie" magazines on Chilean newsstands, mild by contemporary U.S. or European standards, quickly disappeared. It was also announced that excessively long hair would not be permitted in the classroom. The government organized new secretariats for women and youth, and indicated a special concern for the family. The junta used the slogan "For Country, God, and Justice" when it took the oath of office and repeatedly thereafter.

The moralism of the new regime was reinforced by revelations of corruption under the one it had overthrown. It was already known that MAPU had made huge sums (after the coup the amount was estimated at 100 million escudos) by reselling on the black market cars which it had obtained at official prices. A search of one of the two houses owned by Luis Guastavino, a Communist deputy from Valparaíso, produced $145,000 and bundles of new escudos—including packets of 5,000 escudo notes which had not been put into circulation. A member of the Christian Left who headed the Valparaíso Development Corporation was reported to have fled with $80,000 and 7 million escudos in his bags. In 1975 Anselmo Sule of the Radical Party and Kurt Dreckmann of the Socialists were accused of receiving payments from the General Tire Company to prevent its Chilean holdings from being nationalized, and a year later ex-Ambassador Korry declared that ITT, Anglo-Lautaro Nitrate, and the Cerro Corporation had also bribed top Allende officials. The military regime made much of the large supplies of food and drink in the presidential residences, frequently mentioning the number of gallon bottles of Chivas Regal and contrasting this with Allende's statements to the Chuquicamata copper workers in March 1972: "Occasionally I have a drink of whiskey, but not always, because it is very expensive." The safe in the presidential residence was reported to have contained $8,666 and over 5 million escudos, while $40,000 was found at the president's weekend retreat.

A complete inventory was taken of the presidential residence and the vacation retreat (and training school for his bodyguards) which had been purchased in the name of Miria Contreras, at El Cañaveral in the foothills of the Andes. References were made to pornographic books and magazines and Scandinavian sex films found there, but no details were given, and unsubtle references to Allende's relationships with "La Payita," his personal secretary, and other women filled the Chilean press. General Leigh was the harshest in his comments. "You only have to see how the leaders of Popular Unity lived—those 'sacred cows' who said they were leading the people to their liberation. All that was found were whiskey, jewels, furs, women, and exotic objects which were really incredible. They thought that by going without a tie, they could act like workers or employees. They were hypocrites."[20] The contrast was evident between what was found in

Allende's two houses and the abstemious life that his predecessors, Frei and Alessandri, had led during and after their presidential terms.

The military government also accused the Allende government of cooperation in the smuggling of cocaine to the United States in order to finance arms purchases. The new head of Investigaciones, General Ernesto Baeza, asserted in October that the Mafia had paid the Allende police authorities $30,000 a month for protection and that cooperation with Interpol in its efforts to crack down on drug smugglers had been terminated under the Popular Unity government.[21] In 1974, however, arrests for involvement in drug traffic of foreign service officers, military men, and a police official from the Frei regime who had been removed by Allende indicated that the production and smuggling of cocaine were not restricted to leftists.

Economic Policy

After some initial uncertainty about its economic policy, the junta appointed Fernando Leniz, editor of *El Mercurio*, as minister of economics and decided to pursue an economic policy directly opposed to that of the government which had been overthrown (thus refuting the claims of Popular Unity that the changes it had undertaken were "irreversible"). First, while the "legal gains of the workers and peasants" were to be respected, the factories and farms which had been taken over by force or through the use of legal loopholes were to be returned to their owners. (Some owners were reluctant to take back their properties, since a condition of return was acceptance of debts run up by the government interventors.) In addition, many of the industries (the copper mines were a significant exception) which had been taken over legally would be returned to the private sector by offering them for private sale.

Second, the whole price control system was rapidly dismantled, prices were to be allowed to rise, and competition was to be encouraged, among Chilean companies (through the enforcement of antimonopoly laws) and with foreign industry (through a reduction in the high protective tariffs and the promotion of exports).

Third, the exchange rate, which on September 11 ranged from 25 escudos to the dollar for imported food to 3,000 escudos to the dollar on the black market, was to be simplified by gradual steps, first by having only three rates—a bank rate for foreign purchases, a rate for copper, and a rate for tourists and the purchase of currency—and then by bringing these three rates into line.

Fourth, heavy priority was to be given to the expansion of agricultural production to reduce Chile's enormous food import bill. Agricultural prices were sharply increased, and small and medium landholders received an absolute guarantee against expropriation. CORA, the agrarian reform agency, was directed to comply with the 1967 law by transforming the *asentamientos* into small independent landholdings; where the Allende government had denied the peasantry the option of dividing up the land, the junta did not permit the option of continuing as a cooperative. The government announced a goal of the distribution of land titles to 10,000 agricultural family units in 1974 and complete distribution of the 8.5 million hectares of land in the reformed sector within five years.[22]

Fifth, the massive government deficit was to be reduced by government economy and by eliminating many government jobs. To this end, the junta decreed shortly after the coup that all government positions except for the judiciary and the Controller-General's Office were interim in character, and in 1974, it announced a goal of a reduction of 100,000 in the number of civil servants. These policies were aimed at the release of market forces, which had long been distorted by the policies of previous governments, in the hope that this would result in an expansion of production and a more rational allocation of resources. To compensate for the further loss of purchasing power due to the sharp increase in prices (85 percent in October), the junta decreed on October 22 that all workers and employees should receive a bonus equivalent to two months' wages (in the case of the poorer workers, three months' wages). Pensions and family allowances were also to be readjusted, and the differences between blue-collar and white-collar allowances eliminated.[23]

The new economic policy was implemented by U.S.-trained economists, principally from the Catholic University, many of whom had done graduate work at the University of Chicago and had come under the powerful intellectual influence of Milton Friedman. The return to a free-market economy based on competition would have been impossible in a democratic system, but military rule seemed to provide the authoritarian control necessary to use classical methods to put an end to the chaos of the preceding regime, however painful it might be.

The regime's economic liberalism, influenced by the U.S. and German examples, was combined with varieties of political conservatism which were especially influenced by Catholic social thought. Thus, the economic program of austerity was supposed to be mitigated by a scheme to mandate worker participation in profits and ownership which had been proposed by Catholic social thinkers for many years. The return of seized factories and industries was made conditional on the owner's acceptance of an as yet unwritten "social statute of the enterprise," which was to give the worker a share in decision-making in industry. The draft statute, when it appeared, included provisions for elected worker representatives on corporate boards of directors and an advisory and informational worker-management enterprise committee (obligatory for all factories with over one hundred workers or farms of over twenty-five agricultural workers). It was similar to the law adopted in Germany under Christian Democratic auspices in the early 1950s providing for a *Mitbestimmungsrecht* for workers in factories over a certain minimum size. Owing to controversies within the government over some of its provisions, the text of the law was not published until May 1975, and its implementation was further delayed thereafter. Explanations of the proposals for worker participation were careful, however, to distinguish the "integrated enterprise" based on the cooperation of capitalists and workers from the "workers' enterprises" which had been endorsed by the Christian Democrats since 1970 and were now viewed as Marxist in inspiration.

Political Institutions

Most of the other proposals for the new "institutionality" which was to be established under the auspices of the military came from conservative Catholic sources. General Pinochet promised that democracy would return "although I do not know when" and the junta appointed a committee to draw up proposals for a new constitution. As an indication of the break with the 1925 constitution, the junta formally dissolved the Constitutional Tribunal which had been created by a constitutional amendment in 1970 and destroyed the "falsified" electoral register in preparation for the establishment of a new Single National Roll (RUN), a task which, it was estimated, would take several years to complete.

Reflecting recent Chilean experience, there was general agreement in the Constitutional Committee on proposals to outlaw "antidemocratic" (Marxist) parties, to raise the voting age to twenty-one, and to synchronize elections so that Chile would not live in the continuous state of election fever it had experienced in recent years. It was also agreed that, although the presidency should be strong and chosen by an electoral system which gave the president majority support, power should also be given to the courts and administrative tribunals to limit executive action.

There was disagreement on the committee, as in conservative circles in Chile generally, on the system of representation for the legislature. Early discussions seemed to indicate that the *gremios* or corporate interest groups, including the military, would be formally incorporated into the legislature. However, there was debate on one of the perennial problems of corporatist theory—which interests to recognize and how to weight them. Disagreement on this subject and the junta's evident lack of interest in surrendering power led the committee to proceed very slowly. After two and one-half years it reported that it was still working on the text of the constitution's introductory bill of rights, including the right to life, to freedom of speech, educational freedom, the inviolability of the home, broadened habeas corpus procedures, and "the foundation of all public liberties—the right to private property." The government also announced the imminent creation of an advisory Council of State with the participation of all ex-presidents (Frei pointedly refused to join) and of representatives of youth, women, labor, business, education, law, and the professional organizations. The council, which held its first meeting in July 1976, was established by Constitutional Act No. 1, described as the first step toward the creation of a new constitution. Three more constitutional acts on the bases of Chilean institutions, constitutional rights and duties, and states of emergency were promulgated on the third anniversary of the coup.

The Declaration of Principles

In March 1974 the junta published a "declaration of principles" which was strongly influenced by conservative currents of Catholic thought.[24] Reflecting conceptions developed in Pope Pius XI's encyclical, *Quadragesimo Anno*, published in 1931, it defined its goal as the promotion of the common good in the interest of the human person, which "enjoys a being and a final end which no human authority can legitimately infringe." This common good is best advanced by the employment of the principles of subsidiarity (a term also used by Pius XI) "by virtue of which no higher group can arrogate to itself the area which lower entities can satisfy, in particular, the family, nor can it invade what is properly and privately the domain of each human conscience." The state can collaborate to coordinate the activities of lower associations and to remedy their deficiencies, but not to supplant them. From the principle of subsidiarity comes as "its natural form" the right to private property, although "the state should reserve as its own, the ownership of what because of its strategic or vital importance for the country, it would not be prudent to leave in the hands of a limited group of private individuals." The declaration stated that although the government respected human rights and freedom of conscience, it could not allow that "in the name of a misunderstood pluralism, a naive democracy could permit organized groups within it to promote guerrilla violence to reach power or, pretending to accept the rules of democracy, support a doctrine and morality whose objective is the construction of a totalitarian state. Consequently, Marxist movements and parties will not be admitted again to civic life."

As to the new institutions, the junta declared that it would give power "at the opportune time" to those who have been elected by the people "through a universal, free, secret, and informed vote." It spoke of its mission as "inspiring a new, great civilian-military movement" based on decentralized and regional "vehicles of participation" which would make the corporate interest groups more than an instrument for the voicing of demands, and at the same time add technical knowledge and cooperation to government decisions. "Our democracy will thus be organic, social, and participatory." Reaffirming Chilean nationalism in an interdependent world, it described women and youth as "the bulwarks of the civic movement which culminated in the military pronouncement" and "the creative force which can transform into reality a profound national hope."

Continuing Economic Difficulties

As the junta celebrated six months and then a year in power, it continued to adhere to the main lines of the policies established shortly after the coup. In January 1974, a 500 percent cost-of-living readjustment was decreed, but this did not compensate for an inflation rate that the most reliable estimate placed at 693 percent in 1973.[25] Wages were readjusted again in July, by 20 to 40 percent, and in October, by 24 percent (by then the inflation rate had reached 307 percent; by the end of the year it had reached 375 percent), and it was announced that subsequent readjustments for inflation would take place every three months.

Taxes were increased as well, and work began on wholesale overhaul of the tax system, involving the replacement of the sales tax by a value-added turnover tax, the imposition of a corporate profits tax, and a complicated system of tax readjustments for inflation. The wealth tax used by the Frei regime was reimposed on a one-time-only basis, affecting the middle and upper classes. Economies in government administration were introduced mainly by reducing the swollen bureaucracy on the basis, first, of political criteria, and then later, of administrative efficiency. The budget was still in deficit, but by 15 percent instead of the over 50 percent rate of the last part of the Allende period. Unemployment rose to nearly 10 percent in 1974 and to 18 percent in 1975. In two vital commodities, copper and wheat, production rose sharply, since there were no strikes or absenteeism in the mines, the upheavals associated with the agrarian reform were ended, and price incentives encouraged expansion of agricultural production. (In 1973, wheat production had dropped by 37 percent; copper production had declined by 6.4 percent in the first nine months, although a spurt in production during the last three months produced an increase for 1973 of 3.9 percent.)[26] Copper prices remained at record heights in 1974 (although they dropped sharply in 1975). The cost of oil had skyrocketed, and international wheat prices had tripled since 1970. The government announced that it would still be necessary to spend $256 million on wheat imports in 1974, and nearly double that figure for food imports in general. Its balance-of-payments deficit for 1974 reached $196 million and despite an austerity program initiated in April 1975 reached $230 million in 1975, principally because of a drop in copper production and prices.[27]

Thus, while the balance-of-payments picture was improved by rising exports, Chile's international payments problem remained. It was compounded by the fact that at least some payments had to be made on the massive foreign debt. In July 1974, a Foreign Investment Statute was promulgated giving investors much better terms than those prescribed by Decision 24 of the Andean Pact, but most foreign investors were hesitant to commit themselves in a country which was still officially in a state of war. U.S. banks made substantial loans to Chile, but there was comparatively little direct private investment from the United States. Whether because they were concerned about their public image in the United States, where Chile was now associated with torture and brutality, or because of uncertainty about the compatibility of the Foreign Investment Statute with the Andean Pact, by the end of 1975 only Firestone Rubber, Minnesota Mining, two data-processing companies, a ship builder, and a lithium mining company had decided to make new investments. Conversations continued concerning possible oil explorations by foreign oil companies (thus terminating the long-standing state monopoly on such ventures) and a uranium-mining project involving the Anaconda Company. The Japanese replaced the Americans as the principal outside investors, and as the Chilean Development Corporation (CORFO) continued to sell off the concerns taken over during the Allende regime it was said that Brazilian money was financing many of the purchases by private financial groups. In late 1976 Chile formally left the Andean Pact, citing the excessive restrictions it placed on foreign investment.

Continuing Repression

Despite the government's repeated assertions that there was not a single proven case of torture and the president of the Supreme Court's public statement that human rights were "fully respected" in Chile, the evidence of repression would not go away. In March 1974 the death of José Tohá, Minister of defense and of interior under Allende, was reported as suicide by the regime, but it remained clouded by suspicion. In the same month, General Bachelet, who was in prison awaiting trial on charges of having assisted in the infiltration of the air force, also died, apparently of natural causes.[28]

International protests against the violation of human rights in Chile might exaggerate figures on those killed or imprisoned, or they might be politically inspired, but the protests from the Catholic bishops in Chile had much greater significance. This is why the episcopal statement entitled "Reconciliation in Chile" which Cardinal Silva issued on April 24, 1974, was so important. The cardinal introduced the statement by noting that its publication was proof that the right to disagree and the rule of law existed in Chile, but its text revealed something very different. While praising the regime for its explicit commitment to Christian principles in its March declaration, the bishops stated that "the basic condition" for reconciliation is "the full observance of human rights." The bishops expressed the hope that Christian principles "will be incorporated in the constitution of our country by the free acceptance of our people and after a discussion in which all citizens can participate." While claiming that "we do not doubt the honest intentions or the good will of our rulers," the bishops criticized "the climate of insecurity and fear . . . job dismissals for arbitrary or ideological reasons . . . arbitrary or excessively long detentions . . . interrogations that use physical and moral pressures . . . and limited possibilities for a legal defense." The bishops also expressed their concern that "wage earners must bear an excessive share of sacrifice" and that the educational system was being "completely restructured and reoriented without sufficient participation by parents and the academic community." The bishops declared that while "particular circumstances can justify temporary suspension of certain civil rights . . . there are rights that affect the very dignity of the human person and these are absolute and inviolable."[29]

In May the international press obtained copies of a report by the church-sponsored ecumenical Committee of Cooperation for Peace which included an analysis of the government's campaign against the left, asserting that what had been random and uncoordinated repression by five different intelligence agencies had been coordinated by the creation in January 1974 (announced officially in June) of a single National Department of Intelligence (DINA), which now directed all efforts against real or potential opposition. DINA was later reported to have 2,000 military men in its employ, an equal number of civilians, and 16,000 informers throughout the country.[30]

The junta argued that it was punishing the leaders of the deposed regime, not for their ideas, but for proven acts of sedition, including the organization of paramilitary groups, conspiracy to subvert the armed forces, and violations of the Arms Control Act. It pointed to the early release of Carlos Briones, Allende's interior minister, and subsequently of Aniceto Rodriguez, former secretary general of the Socialist Party, Anselmo Sule, who held the same post with the Radicals, and Alberto Jerez, the Left Christian Senator from Concepción. In May 1975 and January 1976, decree-laws were published providing legal guarantees for those arrested, but they are known to have been ignored by the security services. Estimates of the total number of Chileans who had been "detained" since the coup ranged from 40,000 to 95,000 (out of a total population in Chile of over 9 million).[31]

Pinochet Consolidates Power

In June 1974, when the cabinet was reorganized and General Pinochet was established as sole head of the executive and administrative organs,

General Augusto Pinochet, president of Chile since 1973, standing in front of a portrait of Diego Portales. Ironically, Portales was a strong defender of civilian supremacy over the military. (Embassy of Chile)

it was apparent that a return to constitutional democracy in Chile was far off. The junta made up of the four service chiefs pronounced itself the legislative and constituent power, so that it could legislate as well as modify, amend, or replace the constitution by simple decree. The military leaders reiterated their pledge to the judiciary of full independence in the exercise of all the powers granted by the laws and constitution, but military courts continued to handle all political cases without civilian review. On the first anniversary of the coup in September 1974, the "state of siege in time of war" was replaced by a "state of siege of internal defense." This meant that punishments were milder, civilian tribunals had broader jurisdiction, and some decisions of the military courts could be appealed to the Supreme Court. A year later the state of siege was reduced by a further degree, but the state-of-siege powers still authorized indefinite detention for security reasons without judicial order of whomever the military chose to arrest. In a few cases—three in 1974—the courts now issued writs of *amparo* to secure the release of detainees, until the junta decreed a constitutional amendment in early 1977 forbidding such writs under a state of siege.

Decree-laws continued to be adopted by unanimity among the four service chiefs, but as of June 1974, executive and administrative decisions were to be the responsibility of the chairman of the junta, now called the supreme head of the nation. Thus, it was no longer necessary for a lengthy process of collegial discussion to precede every governmental decision, and the rumored possible rotation among the services of the position of head of the junta was permanently ruled out.

The government regularly announced the discovery of new arms caches to justify the continuation of controls, and a curfew remained in effect. The exiled opposition circulated stories of worker sabotage and subtle opposition, but within Chile there was no sign of open resistance to the regime. The only expression of criticism came in the traditional Chilean political jokes, now directed at the military. One noted that ropes had replaced elevators in the building used as headquarters for the junta, "so that the gorillas can get from one floor to another." Another resurrected a ten-year-old Brazilian story that the military regime was hiring Walt Disney as a speechwriter, "because of his long experience in making animals talk." However, the knowledge that telephones were tapped, that mail was opened, and that an effective internal espionage system was in operation placed limits on the open expression of criticism of the regime. Those who voiced public attacks on the regime, such as former Senator Renán Fuentealba, Christian Democratic ideologist Jaime Castillo, and the former law faculty dean, Eugenio Velasco, were summarily deported.

By the first anniversary of the coup, it was evident that September 11, 1973, had marked a fundamental turning point in Chilean history—the end of 140 years of almost uninterrupted constitutionalism and civilian rule.

In his speech to the giant anniversary demonstration in support of his regime, General Pinochet attacked all the political parties and most of the past presidents of Chile when he declared that except for "the isolated efforts of a few enlightened public figures" Chile had been governed since 1891 by class and party governments characterized by "politicking and demagoguery." Describing his regime as the "first authentically national government" in the twentieth century, he declared that "the recess in party politics will have to be prolonged for several more years, and can only be terminated responsibly when a new generation of Chileans who are imbued with sound patriotic and civil values and inspired by an authentic national feeling can take over the direction of national life."[32] He spoke of the possibility of increasing civilian participation in the military government, but it appeared from his words and actions that Chile, formerly one of the most open and free societies in the modern world, was likely to remain under authoritarian rule for a long time.

In the second and third years of his government General Pinochet consolidated his power, eliminating potential rivals in the armed forces and destroying both the left and center as influential forces in the universities, trade unions, peasantry, and mass media. After several years of deep recession and the worst unemployment since the Great Depression, the effort to reestablish a market economy showed some results, the inflation rate began to subside, and the beginnings of economic recovery could be perceived. Nontraditional exports rose sharply in response to government incentives and to the lack of a domestic market. Industrial output remained depressed, but agricultural production increased as higher prices were offered for farm products and rural properties were returned to private hands or distributed to the peasants. The price for this economic "success" was a deep decline in living standards for the middle class and near starvation for many of the members of the lower class, the destruction of the labor and peasant movements, and a sharpening of the differences between rich and poor.

Politically, only the church (that is, the bishops) remained as an independent center of criticism of a regime which, although it lacked many of the distinguishing ("totalitarian") features of fascism—the mobilization and control of the entire population, a single mass party, and an ideology that glorifies violence and expansionism—was characterized by authoritarian nationalism, antiparliamentarism, incipient corporatism, and reliance on force and propaganda which suggested many parallels with such regimes.[33] Most of all, the continued repression that the regime felt to be necessary —less than that practiced by some contemporary governments but worse than most—combined with the publicity given to instances of murder, torture, and kidnaping in Chile and political assassinations of opponents of the regime in other countries made Chile a kind of international pariah.

The hope that Chile had seemed to embody of a civilized, humane society that sought to combine freedom, development, equality, and social justice had given way to a regime committed to order at the price of freedom, economic growth at the price of social justice, and depoliticization at the price of military dictatorship and the strengthening of the power of traditional elites. For the foreseeable future, the fate of Chile would depend more on the internal politics of the military and the economic theories of a conservative technocratic elite than on the more or less free play of competing groups within a framework of constitutional liberty which it had known throughout most of its history. Why this happened, the concluding chapter will attempt to explain.

CHAPTER THIRTEEN

The Lessons of Chile

Like the politics of Chile under Allende, the explanations of the downfall of Chilean democracy tend to be ideological and polarized. The left blames external and internal "reaction"—the alliance of imperialism (the U.S. government), the multinationals, and the domestic oligarchy who combined to overthrow Allende because he threatened their vital (that is, economic) interests. The revelations of extensive CIA intervention in the Allende period and of the economic pressures exerted by the U.S. government, as well as the violence of extreme right-wing groups such as Patria y Libertad, are cited to support this interpretation, and the rightist course pursued by the military since the coup is seen to confirm it. The right, on the other hand, sees the coup as an unfortunate necessity, in order to prevent a violent seizure of power by the left or a civil war and to put an end to the runaway inflation that was destroying Chilean industry and agriculture. The external actors involved in the rightist interpretation are the Soviet Union and Cuba, and the Marxist parties in Chile are viewed as their agents, puppets, or willing accomplices. The myth of a fascist Chilean military plotting with the capitalists from the outset to destroy the Allende experiment in democratic socialism is matched by that of Chileans in league with the worldwide Communist conspiracy planning to murder the entire civilian and military leadership of the Chilean opposition and establish a "people's democracy."

The reality is much more complex. Without either relying on a mindless empiricism because the "facts speak for themselves" or selecting only those facts which suit a predetermined thesis, I hope in this chapter to draw some conclusions from my examination of the tangled web of Chilean politics over a decade and a half, analyzing the interplay of systemic, historical, and personal elements in their contributions to the Chilean tragedy.

Allende and Frei

The first lesson that can be drawn from the narrative is that the Frei and Allende governments were both alike and different. They were alike in being subject to similar systemic constraints: a hyperpoliticized country in which ideological parties, frequent and staggered elections, and an expanding electorate combined to raise high hopes at the beginning of each president's term and subsequently to frustrate those hopes; and an economic system which appeared to give the president and the state apparatus great power only to undercut that power because of excessive state expenditures, chronic inflation, balance-of-payments deficits, and dependence on unstable world market prices for a single export. Both attempted to use the Chilean state to redistribute income for the benefit of "marginal" groups such as shantytown dwellers, the peasantry, and the poor. Both believed in democracy, although their definitions of that term differed.[1]

They were different in that Frei attempted to rely on a religiously based populist nationalism ("I am president of all Chileans"), while Allende, despite initial populist and nationalist appeals, relied increasingly on a class-oriented Marxism ("I am *not* president of all Chileans") to gain support for his program. Because his party was situated in the center and center-left of the Chilean political spectrum, Frei could disavow the tactics of the right-wing parties and extremist groups even when, as in 1964, he benefited from them. Allende, himself an admirer of Fidel Castro and a member of a party which ranged from moderate Social Democrats to Maoist would-be revolutionaries, found it more difficult to denounce extremism among his supporters. Frei's economic advisers were more concerned about inflation and productivity than were those of Allende, such as Pedro Vuskovic, who were frank to admit the political purpose of the efforts to redistribute income and to create through a rapid series of faits accomplis a large "area of social property" which would include banking, major industry, foreign trade, and most of agriculture. Both Allende and Frei were experienced politicians and parliamentarians, but (and this was both a strength and a weakness) Frei was more committed to the use of the parliamentary system to achieve reform than was Allende, who continued to discuss possible alternative forms which might achieve his goals and still maintain the democratic legitimacy necessary to avoid military intervention or civil war. Both had initial success (Frei for a longer period than Allende) followed by increasing difficulties, but Allende's problems were far more profound and shattering in their impact on Chilean political and economic life.

Chilean Political Institutions and the Coup

Implied in what has just been said is the second lesson of the Chilean experience: the difficulty of achieving "fundamental" changes within a system of constitutional democracy, especially when it contains institutional features which inhibit the formation of a majority which can legitimate such changes. Frei had trouble enough with the system of staggered elections for the president, the legislature, and municipal governments, nearly continual by-elections viewed as referenda on the conduct of the government, and a multiparty system exaggerated by proportional representation. In Allende's case the Chilean political system, having permitted him to achieve the presidency with 36 percent of the vote, gave him only three choices if he wished to govern under a system of constitutional democracy.

First, he could have attempted to establish an "institutional majority" in the Congress "through a far-reaching agreement between socialists inspired by Christianity and those inspired by Marxism," the lack of which was described in 1972 by the former PDC presidential candidate, Radomiro Tomic, as Allende's "fatal political error."[2] Yet although there was substantial agreement between the Allende coalition and a majority of the Christian Democrats on the economic aspect of his program (copper nationalization, expanding agrarian reform and "a transition to socialism"), the Christian Democrats suspected and feared the ultimate intentions of the Marxist parties and opposed Allende's political proposals (the "assembly of the people," popular courts, and the subordination to the executive of the judiciary and the controller general). The PDC was also aware that if Allende failed or resigned, Frei would be eligible to run again for the presidency and in all likelihood would win. In addition, Allende at the beginning of his term (like Frei at the beginning of his) was not willing to make a deal with the opposition. As the 1972 negotiations on the three areas amendments revealed, both sides were held hostage by their own extremes—Allende by the left wing of the Popular Unity coalition, which in accordance with the agreements of December 1969 could veto any conciliatory effort, and the PDC by its more conservative members who were fearful of losing support to the National Party. Thus, the only ones who really wanted an agreement were the Left Radicals (the Chilean equivalent of the Social Democrats), some of the Communists, and one wing of the Christian Democrats; and reasons of party and coalition solidarity prevented the latter two groups from working to secure a minimal accord which was in the interest of both. The problem for Chile thus lay neither in an intractable right-wing opposition (as the left maintains) nor with a violence-prone revolutionary Marxism-Leninism (as the right believes). It lay in a multiplicity of ideological parties followed by the polarization of Chilean politics into two groups, one of which ranged from the quasi fascists of the extreme right to those who considered themselves democratic socialists, and the other from the revolutionaries of the MIR and the left wing of the Socialist Party to moderates in the Radical Party. By 1972, if not before, the center which had dominated Chilean politics for decades had nearly disappeared.

One might speculate on the possibility of solving these problems with other political institutions—simultaneous elections on all levels as in Venezuela (which would still probably have produced a three-way split in Congress), Senator Gumucio's proposal of a second round in the popular vote for the president as in France (which would almost surely have elected Alessandri), voting procedures which discriminate against splinter parties and favor the combination of parties to secure a majority as in Germany, or single-candidate local constituency elections and a two-party system as in Britain or the United States (which would have led to a deemphasis on ideology). Such changes would at least have tempered the political rhetoric and diminished the fragmentation of the national will into warring ideological groups, each with its own constituency but none motivated to agglomerate various group interests into something resembling a nationwide majority with unquestioned democratic legitimacy. Before 1958, French politicians used to criticize proposals for reform of the decadent institutions of the Fourth Republic by observing that you cannot cure the patient's fever by breaking the thermometer. Nevertheless, you do not need to inflame and exaggerate the ills of the body politic as the Chilean political system tended to do.

Allende's second alternative was to attempt to use the recently broadened plebiscite procedure to change the constitution and establish a unicameral legislature and a subordinate judiciary. According to his adviser, Joan Garcés, Allende proposed a plebiscite to his Popular Unity coalition in mid-1971 and again in June 1973. The proposals were rejected, probably because it was felt that the result would fall short of the required absolute majority, constituting a severe blow to the claim that the transition to socialism could be carried out by democratic means.

The third possibility—the one he seems to have chosen—was to hope that time was on his side and that he could broaden his support among the low-income groups who constituted a majority of the population by appealing to the class interests of the proletariat, the peasantry, and the poor. However, election results continued to demonstrate that many members of the lower classes in Chile were not convinced that a Marxist government was in their best interests. While there was a perceptible increase in class consciousness in Chile during the Allende years, and support for the left was greater in low-income areas, it never reached the proportions necessary to give Popular Unity the effective national majority to which Allende referred when he quoted Engels on the possibility of a "peaceful transition from the old society to the new" just after his inauguration. Women, including those in low-income areas, were markedly less enthusiastic about Allende than were men. Organized workers were suspicious of him in areas like the Chuquicamata copper mines, which did not support him in 1970 or 1973, or in the El Teniente mine, where the 1973 strike contributed to his overthrow. A consistent pattern of declining support for the left after 1971 in by-elections, trade union votes, and in the congressional election of 1973 shows that Allende's strategy did not work. The theory that the coup was triggered by fear that the government was expanding its support uses as evidence a specious comparison of the 1970 three-way presidential election with the two-way congressional fight in 1973, and ignores the 1971 municipal elections. There was increasing polarization, but it did not produce a progovernment majority, and those opposing the government were more determined and effective in their opposition than those supporting it.

Lacking a majority either in the Congress or at the polls, the Allende government resorted to "legal loopholes," by-passing the legislature through measures of dubious legality such as the indefinite seizure of factories on the basis of legislation designed for temporary "interventions" to settle labor disputes or "requisitions" to assure supplies of "articles of basic necessity"—or the takeover of land, often below the legal limit, on the ground that it was being "operated unproductively" after it had been seized by the peasantry or outside groups. More important, the toleration and occasional encouragement of seizures of housing, factories, and farms and the refusal to implement court orders to evacuate seized property were part of a general pattern of the breakdown of legality and erosion of the very constitutional legitimacy which provided Allende with his only assurance of survival.

Economic Policy and the Coup

Besides his failure to recognize the inherent limits of the Chilean political system and his polarizing politics and ambivalence concerning the constitutional order, Allende also pursued a fundamentally erroneous economic policy. The policy of expansion of the money supply, wage hikes far in excess of productivity increases, redistribution of income, and limitless subsidies to state-controlled industry and agriculture, while apparently successful in Allende's first year in office, contained within it the seeds of the destructive course followed by the Chilean economy during 1972 and 1973.[3] Little or no attention was paid to investment, productivity, or economic efficiency in the government's headlong pursuit of short-range political profit and long-range economic control of banking, industry, and agriculture. The short-range goal was to stimulate the economy and make use of unused capacity in the industrial sector, while maintaining price and exchange controls and increasing the share of the lowest income groups in national income. It was hoped that this would pay off at the polls with an increase in lower-class support for the government sufficient to make feasible a plebiscite to carry out desired constitutional changes. The policy also involved a rapid takeover of the remaining latifundia in agriculture, the key industries listed in the Popular Unity program, and the nationalization of banking and credit. This in turn was seen as destroying the economic and, therefore, political power of opposition groups.

These goals were achieved, but at a very high cost in efficiency and productivity. Depending on what measures are used, estimates of the drop in investment in 1971 range from 5 to 24 percent and in 1973 from 8 to 24 percent. The money supply increased 116.5 percent in one year; and, fueled by deficit financing of the budget (53 percent in Allende's last year) and subsidies to state-controlled industry and agriculture (175 billion escudos in 1973), it rose, according to Central Bank figures, by over 1,700 percent between November 1, 1970, and August 31, 1973. After an initial increase as a result of plantings made before Allende came to power, agricultural production dropped off catastrophically—especially in the vital area of wheat production. The balance of payments turned sharply negative, principally as a result of food imports, and the $343 million surplus in foreign exchange that Frei had left to his successor rapidly disappeared. In 1971, nominal wages and salaries for all groups, not just those with low incomes, went up by over 50 percent—far in excess of the programmed 35 to 40 percent readjustment for inflation—and this had predictable effects on the inflation rate. Tax collections—which had increased by 50 percent in real terms during the Frei administration, with government revenues from income and wealth taxes increasing by 209 percent—dropped off under Allende, with taxes composing a diminishing share of the gross national product each year, from 20 percent in 1970 to only 11 percent in 1973.[4]

Yet the magnitude of the crisis was not immediately apparent, because production expanded during 1971 as a result of unused capacity and the decline in the inflation rate during the same year. When it should have been evident that drastic measures were needed to improve productivity and to straighten out the distortions in the economy, government policymakers, mesmerized by the 1971 economic figures, simply projected them into the future. Instead of taking action in September 1971, when the inflation rate began to move up and shortages began to appear, no action was taken until July 1972. By September 1972, the inflation rate had reached 100 percent, and it continued to rise thereafter, while industrial output began a decline which continued every month until the coup. The inflation blew the lid off the Chilean economy, and output began to drop *before* the difficulties created by the lengthy strikes of the truckers and other *gremios* in October and November 1972, the strike of the El Teniente copper miners from April to July 1973, and the longer and much more damaging repetition of the October 1972 strikes from July 26, 1973, until the September coup (see table 1).

There were alternatives available to Allende. He need not have ignored productivity and investment and emphasized consumption to the extent

Table 1

Fluctuations in Consumer Prices
and Industrial Output

Year	Month	Consumer Price Index	Industrial Output[a]
1970	October	35.6	− 8.0
	November	35.3	4.3
	December	34.9	− 0.3
1971	January	28.1	− 4.5
	February	22.8	− 7.3
	March	20.1	6.3
	April	20.2	1.6
	May	21.0	13.5
	June	21.1	10.7
	July	19.1	6.7
	August	17.4	10.7
	September	15.6	25.5
	October	16.5	22.6
	November	18.8	22.1
	December	22.1	19.5
1972	January	24.8	18.5
	February	32.0	11.9
	March	34.0	10.2
	April	38.1	12.6
	May	40.0	11.4
	June	40.1	2.5
	July	45.9	5.0
	August	77.2	3.6
	September	114.3	− 7.8
	October	142.9	− 7.7
	November	149.9	− 8.1
	December	163.4	−11.1
1973	January	180.3	− 6.9
	February	174.1	− 4.7
	March	183.3	− 2.8
	April	195.5	−11.3
	May	233.5	−11.0
	June	283.4	−14.8
	July	323.2	−10.7
	August	303.6	−11.9
	September	286.0	−22.9
	October	528.4	18.0
	November	528.9	5.1

Sources: Instituto Nacional de Estadísticas (National Institute of Statistics), Santiago; Sociedad de Fomento Fabril (Society for Industrial Development), Santiago.

a. Percentage of change from the same month of the previous year.

that he did. The policy he followed was dictated more by political than by economic motives. Large wage increases were supposed to win support for his government, but the salaried middle sectors, which benefited from these increases as much as the low-income groups (see table 2), were frightened by the government's hostile rhetoric, the increasing shortages of consumer goods, and a runaway inflation which appeared to be aimed at their destruction.

Table 2

Geographic Income by Type of Compensation
(millions of escudos, not adjusted for inflation)

	1970	1971	Percentage Change
Wages	12,081	18,596	+ 53.9
Salaries	21,808	33,557	+ 53.9
Employer s.s. contributions	6,206	8,921	+ 43.7
Total labor share in income	40,095	61,074	+ 52.3
Other factor payments	34,539	43,174	+ 25.0
Total geographic income	74,634	104,248	+ 39.7

Source: John Strasma, "The Economic Background to Allende's Reform," *Land Tenure Center Newsletter*, no. 43 (January–March 1974): 9.
Note: The cost of living increased by 22 percent in 1971. Much of the gain in real income made in 1971 was lost in 1972 and 1973 because wage readjustments did not keep up with the accelerating increase in the inflation rate.

Ideology also produced a distorting effect, since it was assumed that once the exploitative profits of the foreign and domestic capitalists were made available to the government, its economic problems would be resolved and that questions such as the balance of payments, the money supply, excess demand, and inflation were only concerns of "bourgeois" economists. Politics also deterred the Allende government from imposing rationing, which would have alleviated its food import problem somewhat. Whenever it was intimated that rationing would be introduced, as in January 1973, there was an outcry from the opposition which correctly understood the considerable possibilities for political control inherent in a rationing system. (Apparently plans were being drawn up at the time of the coup for the initiation of rationing in the near future.)

The economic factor is therefore central to an understanding of the breakdown of Chilean democracy, since no democratic political system, no matter how stable initially, could have withstood the pressures of runaway inflation, a very widespread black market, deepening shortages of essential commodities, and continually declining production. (Concern over the security aspects of the economic crisis also was a major factor in the military's decision to act.) Reviewing the Allende government's economic policies, it is difficult not to conclude that an important reason for its difficulties was that the economists and economic policy makers of the Chilean left had simply not given serious thought to crucial problems such as the control of inflation, the maintenance of the external balance of payments, efficiency in nationalized industries and agriculture, the development of competent administrators in the state sector, the adverse economic effects of rivalries among the parties in the Popular Unity coalition, and the financing of a vastly expanded government sector which amounted in fact, although not in name, to a huge government-financed employment program.

The Chilean economic system already possessed a large state sector before Allende came to power. This seemed to provide the tools with which to carry out considerable changes. However, just because it was so centralized, economic decision-making was politicized and subject to the action of organized pressure groups which were "economist" rather than "class-conscious" in their orientation, and because the system was so democratic it was difficult to resist those pressures.[5] Frei had seen his proposal for wage readjustment payments in bonds destroyed by the combined pressures of the left wing of his own party and the congressional opposition, and the result had been a turnaround in the inflation rate which was disastrous for his party's electoral possibilities. The drop in the vote for Allende's coalition from around 50 percent in the municipal elections of 1971 to 44 percent in 1973 was in part related to the accelerating inflation of the latter year. Even more serious were the strikes, the absenteeism, the decline in exports, and the drop in food production—all of which indicated that Chile was on the verge of national bankruptcy.

The responsibility for the economic chaos did not lie only with the government. The Chilean middle and upper classes engaged in panic buying, hoarding, and black marketeering which accentuated the inflation and shortages. The price system was so distorted by 1972–73 that peasants and workers could make huge profits by supplying the black market, which by 1973 involved a large sector of the economy providing no tax revenue to the government. The government called this "economic sabotage," but it was carried on both by those who supported Allende and by those who opposed him.

External Factors

When a nation is in economic difficulty it looks abroad for help and this leads us to the fourth lesson of Chile: the important—although secondary—influence of external factors in the collapse of Chilean democracy. Just as substantial U.S. economic assistance and political support could not make the Frei "revolution in liberty" succeed, so the now documented U.S. government economic pressures and CIA intervention could not, of themselves, assure that Allende's "transition to socialism" would fail.

The economic pressures or credit squeeze began immediately after the popular election in September 1970 and continued after Allende's inauguration in November. They involved behind-the-scenes pressures to discourage lending by international financial institutions; a cutoff of *new* loans except for humanitarian and technical assistance, such as Food for Peace (which actually increased); and an effort to persuade private banks to reduce lending to Chile. As described earlier, the cutoff was neither complete, immediate, nor effective. Pipeline assistance continued, including reactivation of an Interamerican Development Bank loan which provided politically useful earthquake assistance in July 1971; the International Monetary Fund made two loans to compensate for export shortfalls; the Interamerican Development Bank extended two small university loans in 1971; and military aid increased. The Export-Import Bank dropped Chile to its lowest credit rating after Allende's election and postponed a loan for the purchase of Boeing 707s in August 1971, but it did not terminate its loan guarantees to Chile until March 1972, five months after Chile had declared a moratorium on the payment of its foreign debts. The Commodity Credit Corporation was still granting supplier credits for the purchase of U.S. foodstuffs in late 1972 (although not in 1973). Most important, the Allende government was very successful in securing loans and credits from other countries—and not only from Eastern Europe, the Soviet Union, and China. In credits actually utilized, more loans came from Western Europe and other Latin American countries, especially Mexico and Argentina. One study estimates that the Allende government received about 80 percent as much outside assistance as did the Frei government in its last three years. The Chilean debt rose under Allende from $2.6 billion to $3.4 billion, part of it (possibly as much as 30 percent) unpaid interest on past debts, but most of it to provide foreign exchange, in particular to pay the rising bill for food imports.[6]

The drop in private supplier credits (which U.S. bankers claim was "normal" in view of the deteriorating economic conditions in Chile) made it more difficult for the Allende regime to secure spare parts and U.S. consumer goods, although many were secured elsewhere. The direct effect of the U.S.-inspired credit squeeze was a decline in long-term development loans from U.S. and U.S.-influenced financial institutions. It is difficult to see how the absence of such loans could have had a significant influence on political and economic conditions in Chile. This is not to deny the malevolence of the policy, but only to question its effectiveness and importance as an explanation of Allende's overthrow.

Nor was the Soviet Union's aid to Allende a significant factor. From the outset the USSR had made it clear that it was not willing to give the Allende government the kind of massive support that it gave to Cuba. It promised increased aid in December 1972, and wheat shipments from Eastern Europe were turned around on the day of the coup. But even if it had committed itself more strongly to Allende, it seems unlikely that massive infusions of Soviet assistance would have saved the regime. Soviet technology was backward (opposition Chileans even claimed that the Soviets were photographing and copying copper production techniques developed in Chile), shipments of food took many weeks to arrive, and it was far easier for Allende to get wheat and meat on credit from Argentina. Some of the shortages might have been alleviated a bit, but in the absence of rationing and a controlled economy, the basic economic imbalances could not have been resolved by increased Soviet assistance.

A second major external factor was the substantial financial aid (about $6 million) given by the Central Intelligence Agency to Chilean opposition parties, research organizations, newspapers (including the major private newsprint supplier), radio stations, trade unions, and professional groups (*gremios*) between 1970 and 1973. There is no question that the amount of campaign advertising and propaganda by opposition parties and groups and the number of opposition newspapers and radio stations were much increased by CIA support. In particular, the aid to *El Mercurio* (about $1.5 million, beginning in September 1971) probably prevented the bankruptcy of the most formidable and effective opposition organ. This may have made a psychological difference to the opposition, but given the politicization of the Chilean populace it is difficult to believe that the absence of some organs of communication would have led the opposition to give up the battle. Many groups in Chile, and not all of them wealthy, felt—*were*—directly threatened by Allende's policies and ideology, and they did not need CIA propaganda to inform them of that fact. Aside from outright buying of votes, which no one has claimed, it is difficult to see how the election results could have been altered in any substantial way by CIA financial aid. A possible qualification of this conclusion would be our knowledge from the Senate Intelligence Committee reports that the CIA gave what may have been crucial financial support to several splinter parties, for example, the Popular Socialists after their split from the Socialist Party in 1967, the Radical Democrats both before and after they left the Radical Party in 1969, and the Left Radicals (PIR) after their departure from the Allende coalition in 1972. However, none of these groups received significant support at the polls. The continual leaking of documents to *El Mercurio* during the Allende period may also have been the work of CIA agents, but this had a negligible impact. The CIA aid made a psychological difference, but it is doubtful that it was a necessary or sufficient cause of the Chilean opposition to Allende.

Where CIA money may have had a more important impact was in supporting the *gremios* and opposition trade unions. It is not true, as the U.S. press claimed in 1974 (*New York Times*, September 20, 1974) that a "majority" of CIA money went for the support of the antigovernment strikes of 1972 and 1973. Most went to assist opposition groups and the media. The U.S. Senate investigations have revealed that Ambassador Davis opposed strike support and that no CIA money was authorized for such purposes, although the CIA requested $25,000 to support the 1973 truckers' strike. However, $2,800 of the $24,000 authorized for the Sociedad de Fomento Fabril in September 1972 went to the striking truckers in violation of CIA instructions, and they and the El Teniente copper workers who struck from April 1 to July 1973 may have received additional amounts from other organizations assisted by the CIA, out of $100,000 approved in October 1972 for the "electoral activities" of three large private-sector organizations.

The strikes were very important in politicizing the military, polarizing the workers and the middle classes, and demonstrating the opposition to Allende of large and important sectors of Chilean society, by no means all of them members of the bourgeoisie. Without outside support it is likely that the strikes would not have escalated so quickly or lasted so long. Possibly they influenced the military to stage the coup when they did. Certainly they accelerated the breakdown of the Chilean economy and polity; but given the intense polarization of Chilean politics and the complete lack of any policy by the Allende government for dealing with the desperate state of the economy, the situation could not have continued more than a few months longer.

The third aspect of the question of external intervention is the relation of the United States to the Chilean military. Besides the general U.S. policy of cooperation with the Latin American military, which involved training programs, joint maneuvers, and subsidized arms sales, the Chilean case also involved CIA assistance ("Track II") to discontented military men in September and October 1970 and encouragement of a coup to prevent Allende's accession to power, planting "fabricated" information, publishing an anti-Allende pamphlet in late 1971, and continued contact between CIA agents and military conspirators until early 1973.[7] (Newspaper reports have claimed that contact was cut off when it became clear that a coup was imminent.) Despite extensive efforts by journalists, the left, and Senate investigators with access to CIA documents, there is no evidence of direct involvement in, or provocation of, the 1973 coup by the U.S. government. Stories of U.S. weather planes coordinating communications in Argentina, transports ready in Paraguay, or U.S. aerial acrobatic teams bombing the presidential palace are unpersuasive and only demonstrate the psychological need of the left (like that of its counterparts on the right) to blame the Chilean tragedy on outsiders. It seems clear that while the Chilean military were aware that the United States would not look with disfavor on a coup, they were perfectly capable of carrying it out without outside assistance or incitement.

It is unfortunate that with such a wealth of information about U.S. intervention we do not know more about the intervention on the other side, especially by Cuba. The Senate Intelligence Committee report states that the Cubans provided about $350,000 to Allende in the 1970 elections and that he received an additional undetermined amount from the Soviet Union. The discovery of arms shipments from Cuba in early 1972 promoted the deterioration of democratic politics which was beginning at that time. Cubans were working in the Central Bank, and Allende's daughter had married a Cuban national who was connected with Cuban intelligence. The purpose of the visit by two high-ranking Cuban officials in July 1973 has still not been explained, except to note that Castro sent a letter with them to Allende. While it does not excuse the massive CIA intervention in Chile, greater knowledge of the Cuban (and Soviet) effort at least might help us to assess the degree of the external intervention that U.S. government policymakers felt they had to counteract.

If neither the U.S.-inspired credit squeeze, CIA aid to opposition groups, nor U.S. assistance to the Chilean military accounts for the failure of the Allende experiment, this was not through any lack of desire on the part of official policy makers, especially Henry Kissinger and Richard Nixon.[8] The U.S. government clearly did not have "the kind of relationship with the Chilean government that it is prepared to have with us," as Richard Nixon claimed in February 1971. As in many other cases in recent years, the U.S. policy of permanent opposition to Allende seems to have been determined more by a visceral anticommunism combined with balance-of-power politics (the effect of the success of Unidad Popular on the politics of other Latin American countries and of Italy and France) than by its professed ideals of democracy and freedom. It exacerbated and intensified an already desperate situation. While not a central factor in the destruction of Chilean constitutionalism, it bears some share of the responsibility.

The Arms Issue

The Chilean constitutionalist tradition deterred a basically anti-Communist military from intervening until the economy was on the verge of total collapse and the Supreme Court, the controller general, and, in a tortuously worded resolution, the Congress had practically invited them to do so. While those who wish to paint as dark a picture as possible of military intentions will refer to the military conspiracy of 1970 and reports of plots in late 1972, by comparison with most other military establishments in Latin America, the Chilean military forces were remarkably slow in intervening. This was partly due to Allende's own political skill in dealing with them, in particular what looks like a conversion of General Prats from an anti-Allende position to strong support. The record seems to indicate that actual preparations for a coup did not begin until June or July 1973, by which time the arms issue had become a central concern of the military, since their intelligence services had detected escalating arms stockpiling on both sides and, as Allende government officials have admitted, arms training on the part of the Popular Unity parties and one or two cases of the manufacture of armaments in government-run factories.

It was the classic precipitant of a coup d'état—the breakdown of law and order and of the military monopoly of the instruments of coercion—that finally impelled the military to act.[9] That breakdown had begun much earlier, in the last part of the Frei regime, as the MIR began bank holdups, arms training, and seizures of housing and farms that merely increased support for the law-and-order program of right-wing candidate Jorge Alessandri. Then Allende developed a group of armed personal bodyguards whom he credited with saving his life in the crucial 1970 period, but whom the military despised (and murdered after the coup). For the first two years of his regime, the level of violence gradually increased, although the overall loss of life was remarkably low (about thirty-five killed in political violence between November 1970 and early 1973, according to a list published after the coup). The violence escalated sharply on both sides after the March 1973 election.

The initial responsibility for the rise of violence in what had been the most civilized society in South America lies with the extreme left, which both practiced and preached armed opposition to the institutions of "bourgeois democracy" and thus undermined the very institutional structure which enabled a Marxist candidate to come to power. After Allende's election, however, the extreme right, in the form of Patria y Libertad and associated organizations, responded with a campaign of rallies, sporadic bombings in September and October 1970 which it attempted to blame on the left, and at the end of the Allende period, systematic violence.[10]

The right-wing activities have been cited in order to defend the arming of the left, but this ignores the important chronological fact that the organizing of paramilitary groups began on the left, and that the illegal importation of arms from Cuba with the government's cooperation and Allende's personal knowledge took place as early as February 1971—certainly by early 1972—before the right began to arm itself. When this was combined with frequent statements by Senator Altamirano and others about the ultimate necessity of an armed confrontation, it could not fail to provoke the military. Yet the left never had the remotest possibility of victory in a conflict between a few thousand militant leftists and the 87,000 members of the Chilean armed forces. As Thomas Hobbes once said, "When no other cards are agreed upon, clubs are trumps." When it became evident that other groups besides the military were trying to acquire the new trump cards (those of constitutional democracy having been abandoned or neutralized by institutional deadlock), the Chilean armed forces ended the game.

The Allende government hoped that it could keep the armed forces divided or secure their support through conversion (the military called it *sub*version) and the use of the president's power to appoint and retire military commanders. Yet Allende's efforts to manipulate the top military leaders and the left's attempts to gain support in the air force and navy were as counterproductive as the distribution of arms and initiation of arms training—they only hastened the military decision to intervene. These efforts followed shortly after an announced government program to educate children in all Chilean schools—including the private schools to which the top military men sent their children—in the virtues of "socialist humanism." The implementation of the program was postponed, but it resulted in the intensification and unification of military opposition and the isolation of those few officers who were still favorable to the regime.

Alternative Policies

Could it have been otherwise? Were there alternatives available which would have avoided the debacle of 1973? Our review of the political, economic, external, and military factors has indicated that systemic factors sharply limited the range of maneuver of Chilean democratic governments in the 1960s and 1970s. A century of inflation, populist programs which favored urban over rural groups, increased government spending, "boom-and-bust" electoral cycles, and the internal divisions accentuated by external factors did not augur well for any government. Recent Chilean political history only made things worse—in the case of Frei, making it difficult for him to cooperate with natural allies in the center such as the Radicals, and in that of Allende, reinforcing his intention not to repeat the experience of the Chilean Popular Front, when a left-wing government was compelled to adopt an increasingly conservative course. Yet in retrospect we can identify some crucial turning points in the two administrations which, if different policies had been adopted, might have altered the history of Chile. In Frei's case they include the decision for ideological and party reasons not to seek an early alliance with the Radicals, the loss of presidential control of his own Christian Democratic Party in 1967, the related defeat by the Congress in 1968 of the proposal to give part of the wage and salary readjustment for inflation in bonds, and the absence of an effort on Frei's part to seek a candidate in 1969 more acceptable to the right than Tomic.

In Allende's case the pattern is similar, although in a shortened time frame. He too lost an opportunity at the outset of his regime to broaden the support for key aspects of his program to include a large sector of the Christian Democratic Party and the middle-class (and peasant and labor) groups for which it spoke, and for similar reasons—a desire to maintain ideological purity and not to betray his own Socialist Party. (Later in his administration Allende made efforts to get an agreement with the Christian Democrats on the crucial constitutional issue, but he was sabotaged by his own coalition in April 1972 and by the Christian Democrats in June and July 1972 and early August 1973.) Allende, too, had trouble controlling the left wing of his coalition and placating more centrist groups in the Radical Party, and he ran into economic problems as a result of a rapid increase in government spending and popular consumption combined with the headlong acceleration of takeovers of industry and agriculture. In Allende's case, the economic problems might have been avoided, or at least diminished, by an earlier attempt at holding back expenditures and by the introduction of rationing. He might also have compromised with the copper companies on the compensation issue by accepting the U.S. embassy offer and giving some token compensation. In addition, a more vigorous attempt to restrain the rising tide of violence and greater emphasis on the necessity of the rule of law might have preserved Chilean constitutional legitimacy somewhat longer, but the continuing constitutional disputes and the attacks on "bourgeois legality" by his own supporters undercut the few efforts that Allende made along these lines. As a sympathetic European observer, Emanuel de Kadt of the University of Sussex, concluded in a BBC broadcast after the coup:

> Whatever the importance of the U.S.-inspired economic blockade and of the obstructiveness of Chilean private enterprise, very few observers disagree that [the Allende government's] management of the economy was disastrous, certainly as seen in a short- or medium-term perspective. . . . Whatever the contribution of right-wing extremists, there is no doubt that the incapacity of the government to impose discipline and to maintain a sense of legality among its own supporters was a political factor of major importance. . . . The military intervened when the legality and constitutionalism which Allende continued to proclaim as the essence of the *Vía Chilena* was becoming, or had become, a figment of his imagination.[11]

Chile does not demonstrate that a democratic transition to socialism is impossible, but only that it is very difficult, particularly in a country in which inflation is endemic, groups are well organized to defend themselves against it, the middle class is relatively large, and the military are strongly anti-

Communist. The only possibility for such a transition, as Joan Garcés, Allende's adviser, and Radomiro Tomic, the Christian Democratic candidate in 1971, both wrote, lay in isolating the upper bourgeoisie from the middle and lower classes. Instead, Allende's policy and, in particular, the Marxist rhetoric of his supporters succeeded only in driving many who had been sympathetic or apathetic into fanatical opposition. It is not impossible to mobilize a majority for social change, but this cannot be done on the basis of an ideology that justifies violence, polarizes the opposition, and repels more than it attracts—radicalizing its opponents more than it does its supporters. And to speak glowingly (as some of Allende's supporters did) of the impending confrontation with "reaction" and then flee into exile or asylum as soon as that confrontation occurs is hardly likely to broaden one's support among those who are left to suffer the repression that follows.

In the absence of a major war or the total desertion of the regime by all major elites, such as occurred in pre-Castro Cuba, it is doubtful that such a confrontation is ever likely to lead to the victory of the left. The lesson of Chile, then, is not as the left would have it, that Allende went too slowly, but that knowing the constraints built into the Chilean system, he tried to move too quickly to produce "irreversible" changes in Chilean society. The result was to reverse the advances that had been made for the last thirty years and to plunge what had been one of the freest and most advanced political democracies on earth into a regime of authoritarianism and repression.

The Broader Lesson

Chile has lessons not only for less developed countries. It has been experiencing in accelerated fashion the transition from traditionalism to modernity, from hierarchy to equality, and from elite rule to democracy that began in Europe at the end of the Middle Ages and has now spread throughout the globe. It has tried the formulas of right, center, and left, which have been developed since the French Revolution as secular religions, ideological responses to the new awareness of the capacity of man to use the state to transform society and achieve justice. Yet those responses differ in their choice of values to emphasize, and they can either organize society for change or immobilize it by creating deep divisions in the body politic. In the Chilean case, ideology divided the country into three groupings, and when any one came to power the other two would combine to prevent it from governing.

In the developed world as well, political and economic centralization and rising demands for equality, participation, and social justice place strains on economic and political institutions and produce conflicting ideological solutions which in a period of economic crisis could bring heightened social conflicts, institutional breakdown, and demands for, or toleration of, authoritarian rule. The Chilean example poses the question as to whether Lord Acton's pessimistic judgment on the relation of equality and liberty quoted at the beginning of this book may also someday be the judgment on the democratic nations of the West.

The answer would seem to depend partly on economics—whether rising costs of food, energy, and social services can be absorbed without producing runaway inflation and group conflict—and partly on politics—whether the faith of the political leaders and the public in the democratic process and their willingness to propose and accept partial solutions and incremental changes can carry the constitutional democracies through the difficult readjustments required to achieve a just, productive, and free society. Chile tried and failed to achieve that goal; and if there is any lesson that its failure should convey, it is that countries wealthier than Chile must not fail to do so. If they can demonstrate that efficiency, equity, and liberty can be achieved together and even reinforce one another, there is still hope that a regime committed to genuine democracy and authentic social justice will return to Chile.

NOTES

INDEX

Notes

Chapter 1.   The Coup and Its Causes

1.   The account of the coup is drawn from the following sources: Ricardo Boizard, *El ultimo día de Allende* (Santiago: Pacífico, 1973), which reproduces the full text of Allende's last radio address; *El Mercurio,* September 23, 1973, and International Edition, September 17–23, 1973; *Qué Pasa,* no. 126 (September 22, 1973), and no. 177 (September 10, 1974); *Ercilla,* no. 1991 (September 26–October 2, 1973), and no. 2041 (September 11–17, 1974); eyewitness accounts by Carlos Briones, Allende's last interior minister, and General Sergio Arellano, in *Ercilla,* no. 1999 (November 21–27, 1973): 12, and no. 2003 (December 19–25, 1973): 16–19; Florencia Varas, *Coup* (New York: Stein and Day, 1975); and Hernan Millas and Emilio Filippi, *Anatomía de un fracaso* (Santiago: Zig-Zag, 1973), retitled in its second edition, *Chile 70–73: crónica de una experiencia.* These sources have been supplemented by numerous personal interviews. For the argument that Allende's suicide was staged by the military after his death in combat, see Robinson Rojas, *The Murder of Allende* (New York: Harper and Row, 1976), and discussion herein, pp. 244–47.

2.   For representative expressions of the interpretations of the left, see Gary MacEoin, *No Peaceful Way* (New York: Sheed and Ward, 1974), and James Petras and Morris Morley, *The United States and Chile: Imperialism and the Overthrow of the Allende Government* (New York: Monthly Review Press, 1975). For the center, see Genaro Arriagada, *De la "vía chilena" a la "vía insurreccional"* (Santiago: Pacífico, 1974), and Alberto Baltra, *Gestión económica del gobierno de la Unidad Popular* (Santiago: Orbe, 1973). The right is represented by Robert Moss, *Chile's Marxist Experiment* (New York: Halsted, 1973). The social scientists referred to, and their relevant writings, are Samuel P. Huntington, *Political Order in Changing Societies* (New Haven: Yale University Press, 1968); Guillermo O'Donnell, *Modernization and Bureaucratic-Authoritarianism* (Berkeley: University of California, 1973); and Ferdinand Hermens, *Democracy or Anarchy: A Study of Proportional Representation* (Notre Dame, Ind.: University of Notre Dame, 1941). The Chilean case is seen as a confirmation of Huntington's theory in H. A. Landsberger and T. McDaniel, "Hypermobilization in Chile, 1970–73," *World Politics,* 28, no. 4 (July 1976): 502–41.

3.   The most important books by those associated with the Allende government are Joan Garcés, *El estado y los problemas tácticos en el gobierno de Allende* (Madrid: Siglo XXI, 1974); *Allende et l'expérience Chilienne* (Paris: Fondation Nationale des Sciences Politiques, 1976); Armando Uribe, *The Black Book of American Intervention in Chile* (Boston: Beacon Press, 1975); and Pedro Vuskovic, *Acusación al imperialismo* (Mexico City: Fondo de Cultura Económica, 1975). The Chilean junta's position is best represented in the White Book (*Libro Blanco*) of documents and commentary published in English and Spanish six weeks after the coup.

4.   Dependence theory was originally developed by the left, but its goals and most of its

assumptions are now shared by all Chilean nationalists—although there is strong disagreement concerning methods. On the development and influence of the ideology of dependence in Chile, see Robert L. Ayres, "Economic Stagnation and the Emergence of the Political Ideology of Chilean Development," *World Politics,* 25, no. 1 (October 1972): 34–61.

Chapter 2. The Context of Chilean Politics

1. This is not to say that the military was apolitical. Rather, its political orientation was constitutionalist, and concerned with securing salaries, military appropriations, and perquisites by "normal" pressure-group politics instead of through the instrument of the coup d'état used elsewhere in Latin America. On the Chilean military in politics, see Alain Joxe, *Las fuerzas militares en Chile* (Santiago: Editorial Universitaria, 1970), and Frederick C. Nunn, *The Military in Chilean History* (Albuquerque: University of New Mexico Press, 1976). For an attempt to explain the constitutional stability of Chile in terms of continuity of royal authority patterns in the strong presidency, see Francisco José Moreno, *Legitimacy and Stability in Latin America* (New York: New York University Press, 1969).

2. See figures in tables 1 and 2 of Atilio Boron, "Political Mobilization and Political Crisis in Chile, 1920–1970," paper presented at the Eighth World Congress of the International Political Science Association; also published in Spanish in *Aportes* (Paris), no. 20 (April 1971): 41–69.

3. The best account of Chilean political institutions before 1973 is Federico G. Gil, *The Political System of Chile* (Boston: Houghton Mifflin, 1966). On the various Marxist groups as they existed in the early 1960s, see Ernst Halperin, *Nationalism and Communism in Chile* (Cambridge, Mass.: MIT Press, 1965). Halperin also discusses the Christian Democrats, but the best single book on that party is George Grayson, *El partido demócrata cristiano chileno* (Buenos Aires: Francisco de Aguirre, 1968). For an account of the evolution of the Socialist Party see Julio César Jobet, *El partido socialista de Chile* (Santiago: Prensa Latino Americana, 1971). The history of the Radical Party is described in Florencio Durán, *El partido radical* (Santiago: Nascimento, 1958).

4. The Klein-Saks Mission and its aftermath are discussed in Albert O. Hirschman, *Journeys Toward Progress* (New York: Twentieth Century Fund, 1963), pp. 161–223. For analyses of the economic policies of the various Chilean governments in this period and later, see Ricardo Ffrench-Davis, *Políticas económicas en Chile, 1952–1970* (Santiago: Nueva Universidad, 1973), and Enrique Sierra, *Tres ensayos de estabilización en Chile* (Santiago: Editorial Universitaria, 1969).

5. Comité Interamericano de Desarrollo Agrícola (CIDA), *Chile: tenencia de la tierra y desarrollo socio-economico del sector agrícola* (Santiago: CIDA, 1966), p. 43.

6. Atilio Baron, "Political Moblization," pp. 27, 29.

7. Ibid., p. 28.

Chapter 3. The "Revolution in Liberty"

1. Women voters register and vote separately in Chile. For the complete breakdown of the 1958 results by sex and province (in Santiago by district) see Charles H. Daugherty, ed., *Chile, Election Factbook* (Washington, D.C.: Institute for the Comparative Study of Political Systems, 1964), pp. 34–35.

2. See George Grayson, *El partido demócrata cristiano chileno* (Buenos Aires: Francisco de Aguirre, 1968), and Michael Fleet, "Ideological Tendencies Within Chilean Christian Democracy" (doctoral dissertation, UCLA, 1971).

3. Federico G. Gil, *The Political System of Chile* (Boston: Houghton Mifflin, 1966), pp. 234–36.

4. On the negotiations for the adoption of the law, see Robert R. Kaufman, *The Politics of Land Reform in Chile* (Cambridge, Mass.: Harvard University Press, 1972), chap. 2.

5. Jeannine Swift, *Agrarian Reform in Chile* (Lexington, Mass.: D. C. Heath, 1971), p. 35. Kaufman gives a figure of 1,200 (*Politics of Land Reform*, p. 67).

6. Gil, *Political System of Chile*, p. 185.

7. Daugherty, *Election Factbook*, p. 15.

8. On the complex maneuvering surrounding this decision, including an effort by the left wing of the Radical Party to ally it with Allende, and Frei's rumored offer of cabinet posts to the Radicals, see Federico G. Gil and Charles J. Parrish, *The Chilean Presidential Election of September 4, 1964* (Washington, D.C.: Institute for Comparative Study of Political Systems, 1965), pt. 1, pp. 33–39. The U.S. embassy and former president Gabriel González Videla were also said to have played a role in persuading Durán to withdraw as Democratic Front candidate and run again as a token candidate. U.S., Congress, Senate, Select Committee on Intelligence Activities, *Covert Action in Chile, 1963–1973: Staff Report*, 94th Cong., 1st sess., 1975, indicates that in 1963 the Radical Party received $50,000 from the CIA, and that money was also passed to support anti-Communist Radicals who opposed party support for Allende, although the CIA rebuffed repeated Chilean approaches concerning possible U.S. support for a coup in the event of Allende's election (pp. 15–17, 57).

9. The Chilean attitude toward violent revolution was indicated in a best-selling book published in 1963, entitled *Revolución en Chile*. Supposedly written by "Sillie Utternut," a New Zealand woman correspondent, it satirized the violent rhetoric and peaceful conduct of the Chileans.

10. Gil and Parrish, *Chilean Presidential Election*, pt. 1, p. 27.

11. On the Christian Democratic ideology see Paul E. Sigmund, "Christian Democracy in Chile," *Journal of International Affairs*, 20, no. 2 (Winter 1966): 332–42, and translated excerpts from the writings of Eduardo Frei and Jaime Castillo in Paul E. Sigmund, ed., *The Ideologies of the Developing Nations*, rev. ed. (New York: Praeger Publishers, 1967), pp. 383–404. Maritain's political theory is best summed up in his *Man and the State* (Chicago: University of Chicago Press, 1951), but his earlier *True Humanism* (New York: Scribner's, 1938), lectures he gave in Spain in 1934, influenced the Christian Democrats in Chile more directly. The term *communitarianism*, which was to be so important for the PDC, was first used by the French Catholic writer Emmanuel Mounier, but was popularized in Catholic reformist circles in Latin America in the 1950s by a French Jesuit, Joseph Lebret, S.J.

12. Eduardo Frei, "A New Policy for Chilean Copper," in Sigmund, *Ideologies*, p. 396. For other aspects of the Frei program, see the Third Declaration of Millahue in *El Mercurio*, April 21, 1964, p. 27.

13. See, for example, James Petras, *Politics and Social Forces in Chile* (Berkeley: University of California Press, 1969), chap. 6, which divides the Christian Democrats into vaguely defined "corporatists" (bad) and "populists" (good).

14. I recall a 1963 visit to a *callampa* at a time when the close proximity of two unpaved streets called respectively "Carlos Marx" and "Juan XXIII" graphically illustrated the competition taking place.

15. *Covert Action in Chile*, pp. 9, 15. The report indicates that CIA subsidies to the Christian Democrats began in 1962 with the authorization of a total of $230,000. After the Curicó by-election in April 1964, the CIA was authorized to spend $3 million to ensure Frei's election. Money was also given to PDC shantytown and peasant organizations, but an offer of $1.5 million to the CIA from private U.S. businessmen in Chile was turned down.

16. The most extreme of the anti-Communist radio spots began with the sound of a machine gun, followed by a woman's cry: "They have killed my child—the Communists." The announcer then added in impassioned tones, "Communism offers only blood and pain. For this not to happen in Chile, we must elect Eduardo Frei president" (Eduardo Labarca Goddard, *Chile invadido* [Santiago: Editorial Austral, 1969], p. 66).

17. On the importance of the Cuban issue and the change in the attitude of Chileans by 1964 see Ernst Halperin, *Nationalism and Communism in Chile* (Cambridge, Mass.: MIT Press, 1965), chaps. 6–7. On the campaign see Gil and Parrish, *Chilean Presidential Election*, pt. 1, pp. 39–44.

18. Labarca Goddard, *Chile invadido*, pp. 70–71.

19. For a breakdown of the election figures see Gil and Parrish, *Chilean Presidential Election*, pt. 2, esp. pp. 10–11, 14, 19. See also discussion in Gil, *Political System of Chile*, pp. 304–07. The CIA claimed that their support accounted for Frei's majority (*Covert Action in Chile*, p. 17), but the real reason was the lack of a rightist candidate.

20. Direccion del Registro Electoral, *Elección ordinaria del presidente de la república* (1964), and Orville G. Cope, "The 1964 Presidential Election in Chile," *Inter-American Economic Affairs*, 19, no. 4 (Spring 1966): 3–29.

21. The texts of Frei's legislative proposals are published as *Proyectos de ley enviados al congreso nacional por el gobierno del Presidente Frei*, vol. 1 (Santiago: Departamento de Publicaciones de la Presidencia de la República, 1965).

22. Kennecott's strategy is analyzed in Theodore Moran, *Multinational Corporations and the Politics of Dependence: Copper in Chile* (Princeton, N.J.: Princeton University Press, 1974), chap. 4. An important element was an AID investment guarantee against nationalization for the $80 million that Kennecott would loan back to Chile. The Export-Import Bank also loaned the new joint company $110 million for the expansion program. The arrangement is criticized in Keith Griffin, *Underdevelopment in Spanish America* (London: George Allen and Unwin, 1969), chap. 4, as more expensive to the Chileans than outright nationalization; but Moran notes that access to international finance, experience in the construction of new facilities, and the education of Chilean technicians made the arrangement advantageous to Chile. See also Markos Mamalakis and Clark Reynolds, *Essays on the Chilean Economy* (New Haven: Yale University Press, 1965), pt. 2.

23. Dirección del Registro Electoral, *Resultado, elección ordinaria de diputados* (1965). See also Orville G. Cope, "The 1965 Congressional Election in Chile: An Analysis," *Journal of Inter-American Studies*, 10, no. 2 (April 1968): 256–76, which includes a useful explanation of the effects of the electoral system in giving the Christian Democrats a larger proportion of seats than they had in votes. With a single-member district, plurality system such as those in use in England and the United States, however, the number of Christian Democratic seats would have been still higher. The CIA was authorized to spend $175,000 on selected candidates in the election (*Covert Action in Chile*, pp. 17–18).

24. To an outsider the intensity of mutual dislike between the Radicals and Christian Democrats is difficult to understand, except as a curious survival of the clerical issue of the last century. However, the predecessor of the Christian Democratic Party, the National Falange, had supported Radical candidates for the presidency in 1942 and 1952. Frei had also served in the cabinets of Radical presidents in 1945–46; and between 1950 and 1952 a Radical president, Gabriel González Videla, had initiated the policy of partial government financial support of Catholic schools. The fact that both parties appealed to a similar electoral clientele clearly had much to do with the enmity between them.

25. Arturo Olavarría Bravo, *Chile bajo la democracia cristiana* (Santiago: Editorial Nascimento, 1966), pp. 75–77, 110. This is the first of a series of annual volumes which are useful sources of political information, especially on the Radical Party, despite the bizarre views and checkered political career of their author, on whom see Halperin, *Nationalism and Communism*, pp. 46–47.

26. The details of the case, along with documentation, are contained in Irving Louis Horowitz, ed., *The Rise and Fall of Project Camelot* (Cambridge, Mass.: MIT Press, 1967). A

well-documented Latin American account is Gregorio Selser, *Espionaje en América Latina* (Buenos Aires: Ediciones Iguazu, 1966).

27. Eduardo Frei Montalva, *Primer mensaje, 21 de Mayo de 1965* (Santiago: Departamento de Publicaciones de la Presidencia de la República, 1965).

28. Ibid., pp. 5, 9. By 1969, average real worker income had increased by 55 percent, according to Frei's finance minister, Sergio Molina, in *El proceso de cambio en Chile* (Santiago: Editorial Universitaria, 1972), p. 86.

29. Frei, *Primer mensaje*, pp. 93–98. Frei's letter to the four Latin American economists and their replies appear in English as an appendix to Sydney Dell, *A Latin American Common Market?* (London: Oxford University Press, 1966).

30. On Frei's trip see the *New York Times*, July 7–8, 11, 14–21, 23, 25, 1965.

31. Olavarría Bravo, *Chile bajo la democracia cristiana*, vol. 1, pp. 208–17, gives the statements quoted.

32. Ibid., pp. 270, 315, 338–46, 361–65. See also Moran, *Multinational Corporations*, chap. 5.

33. "Allende Enjuicia a Frei," *Punto Final*, 1, no. 5 (November 1965):8, 9, 11.

34. Quotations are from the excerpts from the final version of the law as published in the *Diario oficial* (Santiago, July 28, 1967) and translated in Paul E. Sigmund, ed., *Models of Political Change* (New York: Praeger Publishers, 1970), pp. 300–08.

35. For details of the election see Boris Goldenberg, *¿Despues de Frei, quién?* (Santiago: Orbe, 1966), pp. 11–24.

36. For examples of the use of the Salvador "massacre" to prove the Frei government was pursuing a policy of repression of the workers and "accommodation of the existing investor elite," see James Petras, *Politics and Social Forces in Chilean Development* (Berkeley: University of California Press, 1969), pp. 239 ff., and Dale Johnson, ed., *The Chilean Road to Socialism* (Garden City, N.Y.: Doubleday, 1973), p. 364. It is difficult to see the Salvador incident as part of a deliberate policy, since it was the result of decisions by local military commanders.

37. Eduardo Frei Montalva, *Segundo mensaje del presidente de la republica* (Santiago: Ministerio de Relaciones Exteriores, 1966) pp. 11, 59–62, 91. Note the contrast with Allende's statement in February 1971: "I am not president of all Chileans."

38. Julio Silva Solar and Jacques Chonchol, *El desarrollo de la nueva sociedad en América Latina* (Santiago: Editorial Universitaria, 1965), translated in Sigmund, *Models,* pp. 311–12. The earlier work was Jacques Chonchol and Julio Silva S., *Hacia un mundo comunitario* (Santiago: Estudios Sociales, 1951). See also Olavarría Bravo, *Chile bajo la democracia cristiana*, vol. 2, pp. 232–33, and Grayson, *El partido,* pp. 312–36.

39. For Frei's view of the Christian Democratic "third alternative" promoting intermediate organisms between the individual and the state, see the excerpt from his 1958 book, *Pensamiento y acción*, translated as "Christian Democracy in Theory and Practice" in Sigmund, *Ideologies,* pp. 384–89. Castillo's criticism of the term *communitarian socialism* appears in a paper presented at a seminar in 1966 and translated as "Property and the Communitarian Society" in Sigmund, *Ideologies,* pp. 400–04.

40. On the three positions see *El Mercurio*'s interviews with Gumucio, Aylwin, and Parra, August 7, 1966, and articles by the three leaders in *Política y Espíritu*, 20, no. 295 (August–September 1966): 55–97. The *rebelde* text is quoted in *Ultima Hora*, August 26, 1966, p. 4; while the *oficialista* text as finally adopted by the party appears in its publication, *Acuerdos del 2: Congreso, 1966.*

41. Grayson, *El partido*, p. 404; *El Mercurio*, September 12, 1966, p. 41.

42. *New York Times*, November 7, 1966, p. 16. For a comparison of the financial terms

of the agrarian reform and the copper compensation see the July 21, 1966, speech by Senator Francisco Bulnes in Olavarría Bravo, *Chile bajo la democracia cristiana,* vol. 12, pp. 270–71.

43. Sergio Molina, *Exposición sobre el estado de la hacienda pública* (Santiago: Dirección de Presupuestos, folleto 110, November 1966), pp. 10, 29.

44. *El Mercurio,* December 22, 1966, pp. 29–30.

Chapter 4. The Frei "Revolution" Stalls

1. Secretariat, Inter-American Committee of the Alliance for Progress (CIAP), *Domestic Efforts and the Needs for External Financing for the Development of Chile* (Washington, D.C.: Pan American Union, OEA, Ser. H, XIV, CIAP 46, September 21, 1966), pp. 3, 13. Sergio Molina, *El proceso de cambio en Chile,* (Santiago: Editorial Universitaria, 1972), also attributes the inflation to a decision to promote expenditures for long-term investment in mining, education, and agriculture, the effects of which in increased production would not be felt immediately (pp. 139–40).

2. The complicated party maneuvers in the Senate are summarized in Arturo Olavarría Bravo, *Chile bajo la democracia cristiana,* vol. 3 (Santiago: Editorial Nascimento, 1967), pp. 91–107.

3. Dirección del Registro Electoral, *Elección de diputados del 7 de marzo de 1965* (mimeo, Santiago, 1965); idem., *Elección de regidores, 1967* (mimeo, Santiago, 1967).

4. Olavarría Bravo, *Chile bajo la democracia cristiana,* vol. 3, p. 166. *El Mercurio,* July 24, 1966, reported that public housing starts had dropped from 10,103 units in the first three months of 1965 to 900 units in a similar period in 1967. The private sector dropped from 4,596 to 3,465 units in the same period.

5. *Tercer mensaje del presidente de la república* (Santiago: Departamento de Publicaciones de la Presidencia, 1967), pp. 7, 19, 31, 43, 57, 66, 70.

6. Olavarría Bravo, *Chile bajo la democracia cristiana,* vol. 3, pp. 188–90. Just before the convention the CIA had been authorized to spend $30,000 to strengthen the right wing of the party. It had also been funding *PEC* (U.S., Congress, Senate, Select Committee on Intelligence Activities, *Covert Action in Chile, 1963–1973: Staff Report,* 94th Cong., 1st sess., 1975, pp. 18, 57).

7. The Chonchol plan, as it was called, was never published by the party. However, the right-wing journal *PEC* secured a copy and published it on July 28, 1967 (no. 239). Parts are translated in Arpad von Lazar and Robert R. Kaufman, eds., *Reform and Revolution* (Boston: Allyn and Bacon, 1969), pp. 59–70.

8. Salvador Allende, then president of the Chilean senate, was elected president of the Chilean branch of OLAS. After Che Guevara's death and the subsequent reorientation of Cuban policy, OLAS quietly died.

9. *El Mercurio,* July 30, 1967, p. 45. Thayer's views, which specifically attack the ideas of Jacques Chonchol and Julio Silva, were expressed in his book, *Trabajo, empresa, y revolucion* (Santiago: Zig-Zag, 1968). An excerpt in which he argues for communitarianism as "the organization of the national community and the smaller communities within it," especially the workers, rather than the abolition of private ownership, is translated in Paul E. Sigmund, *Models of Political Change* (New York: Praeger Publishers, 1970), pp. 312–15.

10. Secretariat, Inter-American Committee of the Alliance for Progress, *Domestic Efforts and the Needs for External Financing for the Development of Chile* (Washington, D.C.: Pan American Union, OEA, Ser. H, XIV, CIAP 165, September 29, 1967).

11. *New York Times,* November 25, 1967, p. 12. The details of the proposal appear in Molina's testimony to the congressional budget committee, *Exposición sobre el estado de la hacienda publica* (Santiago: Dirección de Presupuestos, 1967), folleto 112, pp. 17–19. Molina's subsequent book, *El proceso de cambio en Chile,* describes the National Capitalization Fund as an effort to create "an area of social property" (p. 145). Robert R. Kaufman, *The Politics*

of Land Reform in Chile (Cambridge, Mass.: Harvard University Press, 1972), p. 236, describes the conflict in terms of urban-rural tensions, since the defeat of Molina's proposal led to a reduction of the pace of the agrarian reform, because of lack of funds.

12. The first two occurred in the April municipal elections and a June by-election won by a Socialist. Arturo Olavarría Bravo, *Chile bajo la democracia cristiana*, vol. 4 (Santiago: Nascimento, 1968), pp. 40–41. For the Socialist attitude toward support of the Radicals, see the statement by the Socialist Executive Committee, January 3, 1968, translated in Sigmund, *Models*, p. 325–28.

13. Summary of account in Luis Hernández Parker, "Frei: Dramatico Triunfo," *Ercilla*, no. 1699 (January 10, 1968): 6–7. See also account in Olavarría Bravo, *Chile bajo la democracia cristiana*, vol. 4, pp. 67–75.

14. Olavarría Bravo, *Chile bajo la democracia cristiana*, vol. 4, pp. 89–93.

15. *El Mercurio*, May 10, 1968, p. 23.

16. *Cuarto mensaje del presidente de la república* (Santiago: Departamento de Publicaciones de la Presidencia, 1968), pp. 71–77, 65, 33, 59.

17. *La Segunda*, July 17, 1968, pp. 12–13; July 18, 1968, pp. 10–11.

18. *Punto Final*, no. 53 (April 23, 1968): 2. Frei's speech appears in *El Mercurio*, July 21, 1968, p. 45.

19. *New York Times*, August 4 and 5, 1968, p. 3.

20. David Mutchler, *The Church as a Political Factor in Latin America* (New York: Praeger Publishers, 1971), chaps. 12–16, documents the divisions among the Jesuits with original materials from the files of *Mensaje*. Mutchler is an ex-Jesuit who believes that the church in Latin America "is in effect an instrument of United States and Western European policy interests" and "an agent for the spread and legitimation of dependence" (p. xi).

21. Chonchol attributed his decision to a 30 percent cut in INDAP funds for 1969 and a lack of "understanding" of the agrarian reform program by "certain sectors of the government." See the account of the Chonchol affair in *Ercilla*, no. 1744 (November 20–26, 1968): 12–14, and the summary in George W. Grayson, "Chile's Christian Democratic Party: Power, Factions, and Ideology," *Review of Politics*, 31, no. 2 (April 1969): 158–59. The Cartegena resolution on "popular unity" appears in Olavarría Bravo, *Chile bajo la democracia cristiana*, vol. 4, p. 306.

22. Dirección del Registro Electoral, *Resultado, elección ordinaria de diputados, domingo 2 de Marzo de 1969* (Santiago, 1969). In July 1968 the CIA was authorized to spend $350,000 to support moderate candidates in the March 1969 elections. Support was also given to the Popular Socialists (USP). Between 1964 and 1970 a total of nearly $2 million was spent by the CIA on twenty covert action projects (*Covert Action in Chile*, pp. 17–20).

23. See breakdown of individual votes in *El Mercurio*, March 5, 1969.

24. Editorial of March 9, 1969, translated in Sigmund, *Models*, p. 328–30.

Chapter 5. The Emergence of the 1970 Candidates

1. *Ercilla*, no. 1760 (March 14–18, 1969): 12–13, gives the details.

2. "Dos Cartas de Radomiro Tomic," in *La D.C. primera fuerza de Chile*, special supplement to *Política y Espíritu*, May 1, 1969, pp. 24–26. The supplement also includes the policy resolutions proposed for the May 1, 1969, Party Assembly.

3. *Quinto mensaje del presidente de la república* (Santiago: Departamento de Publicaciones de la Presidencia, 1969), *passim*, partly translated in Paul E. Sigmund, *Models of Political Change* (New York: Praeger Publishers, 1970), pp. 330–38.

4. Since the late 1960s many articles and books have appeared on the theme of *dependencia*, and it has now become a major element in Latin American economic and political thought. For an influential formulation of the problem by a Chilean, see Osvaldo Sunkel, "National Development Policy and External Dependence," in Paul E. Sigmund, ed., *The Ideologies of*

the Developing Nations, 2d rev. ed. (New York: Praeger Publishers, 1972), pp. 438–46. Sunkel's more recent thinking is represented in "Big Business and Dependence," *Foreign Affairs,* 50, no. 3 (April 1972): 517–31.

5. *The Latin American Consensus of Viña del Mar* (mimeo, n.d.), paras. 15, 19, 26, 29, 33, 43. See comments and interview with Valdés in *The Economist para América Latina,* May 28, 1969, pp. 9–10, and his book *Conciencia latinoamericana y realidad internacional* (Santiago: Editorial del Pacífico, 1970), chaps. 11–12.

6. The text of Frei's statement appears in Olavarría Bravo, *Chile bajo la democracia cristiana,* vol. 5 (Santiago: Nascimento, 1970), pp. 160–63.

7. *El Mercurio,* June 27, 1969, p. 27.

8. Olavarría Bravo, *Chile bajo la democracia cristiana,* vol. 5, p. 222.

9. Ibid., pp. 240–44.

10. Julio Cesar Jobet, *El partido socialista de Chile,* 3rd ed., 2 vol. (Santiago: Prensa Latinoamericana, 1971). The original party program appears in vol. 2, pp. 193–207.

11. Olavarría Bravo, *Chile bajo la democracia cristiana,* vol. 5, p. 272. I have also used *El Mercurio* for the relevant period: Eugenio Lira Massi, *Ahora le toca el golpe* (Santiago: Editorial Te-Ele, 1969); and Florencia Varas, *Conversaciones con Viaux* (Santiago: Impresiones Eira, 1972), pp. 53–120. On the danger of ignoring the military, see Roger Hansen, "Military Culture and Organizational Decline: A Study of the Chilean Army" (doctoral dissertation, UCLA, 1967).

12. For an analysis of the changes, see Eduardo Frei, Gustavo Lagos et al., *La reforma constitucional de 1970* (Santiago: Editorial Juridica de Chile, 1970).

13. *El Mercurio,* November 3, 1969, p. 15.

14. Eduardo Labarca Goddard, *Chile al rojo* (Santiago: Universidad Tecnica del Estado, 1971), is my principal source for the negotiations that led to the formation of the Popular Unity coalition.

15. Compare the following sections of the *Programa basico de gobierno de la Unidad Popular,* 4th ed. (Santiago, 1970), and the *Programa del Partido Communista de Chile* (Santiago, 1969):

Unidad Popular Program

Controlan el comercio exterior y dictan la política económica por intermedio del Fondo Monetario Internacional y otros organismos. (p. 6)

El Gobierno Popular . . . respetará las garantías individuales y sociales de todo el pueblo; la libertad de conciencia, de palabra, y de reunión, la inviolabilidad del domicilio y los derechos de sindicalización y de organización. (p. 13)

El Gobierno Popular . . . estará integrado por todos los partidos, movimientos, y corrientes revolucionarias. (p. 14)

También se destinarán tierras para crear empresas estatales. (p. 22)

[They control foreign trade and dictate economic policy through the International Monetary Fund and other bodies.

The Government of the People . . . will respect the individual and social guarantees of all the people; freedom of conscience, of speech, of assembly, the inviolability of the home and the rights of unionization and organization.

The Government of the People . . . will be made up of all the revolutionary parties, movements, and currents.

Land will also be assigned for the establishment of state enterprises.]

Communist Party Program

Manejan el comercio exterior. Dictan por intermedio del Fondo Monetario Internacional y de otros organismos financieros internacionales normas de política económica. (p. 22)

El concepto de un Gobierno Popular es inseparable del respeto a las garantías individuales de todo el pueblo; la libertad de conciencia, de palabra, de prensa y reunión; la inviolabilidad del domicilio; el derecho de organización en sindicatos y cualquier otro tipo de asociaciones. (p. 21)

Un Gobierno Popular . . . Deberán integrarlo todos los partidos y corrientes progresistas revolucionarias. (p. 19)

Será necesario destinar una parte de la tierras expropiadas a la creación de empresas estateles. (p. 40)

[They manipulate foreign trade. They dictate the norms of economic policy through the International Monetary Fund and other international financial bodies.

The concept of a Government of the People is inseparable from respect for the individual guarantees of all the people; freedom of conscience, of speech, of press and assembly, the inviolability of the home, the right of organization into unions and any other type of associations.

A Government of the People . . . should be made up of all progressive revolutionary parties and currents.

It will be necessary to assign a part of the expropriated land for the establishment of state enterprises.]

The political proposals on pp. 15–16 and international proposals on pp. 32–33 of the Popular Unity Program also strongly resemble corresponding sections in the Communist Party Program on pp. 17–18, 30–31.

16. *Programa básico,* 4th ed., p. 20.

17. Personal interview with Alberto Baltra, July 22, 1973; Labarca Goddard, *Chile al rojo,* pp. 240–52; Olavarría Bravo, *Chile bajo la democracia cristiana,* vol. 6 (Santiago: Editorial Salesiana, 1971), pp. 83–87, 90–93.

Chapter 6.   The 1970 Presidential Campaign

1. "Hacia un gobierno de integración nacional," supplement to *El Mercurio,* January 11, 1970. See also Eduardo Labarca Goddard, *Chile al rojo* (Santiago: Universidad Técnica del Estado, 1971), p. 168; and Arturo Olavarría Bravo, *Chile bajo la democracia cristiana,* vol. 6 (Santiago: Editorial Salesiana, 1971), p. 88.

2. Besides the January 8 speech, an interview with his campaign managers ("Movimiento independiente dio a conocer program de Alessandri") appears in *El Mercurio,* July 11, 1970, pp. 31–32. These two statements are used as Alessandri's program in Waldo Fortín Cabezas, Hugo Omar Inostroza, and Mario Verdugo Marinkovic, *Esquema de los partidos y movimientos políticos chilenos y síntesis programática de las candidaturas presidenciales en 1970* (Santiago: Instituto de Ciencias Políticas y Administrativas, 1970). The interview also appears as Alessandri's program in *Política y Espíritu,* no. 317 (August 1970): 43–47. A similar statement appears as "Alessandri, su programa" in *Ercilla,* no. 1836 (August 25–September 1, 1970): 50–54. The ideas in his program are further developed in the 1970 program of the National Party, *La nueva república* (Santiago, 1970). A pamphlet of excerpts from his earlier speeches entitled *El pensamiento político de Don Jorge Alessandri* was also published during the campaign.

3. Excerpts from the speech appear in Olavarría Bravo, *Chile bajo la democracia cristiana.* vol. 6, pp. 67–70.

4. See *Programa básico de gobierno de la Unidad Popular,* 4th ed. (Santiago: Impresa Horizonte, 1970), pp. 35–48.

5. "Chile, programa de Radomiro Tomic, tarea del pueblo" appears in *Política y Espíritu,* no. 317 (August 1970): 15–42. Substantial excerpts appear in *Ercilla,* no. 1836 (August 26–September 1, 1970): 45–50, and it is used as the basis for the comparison of programs in

Fortin Cabezas et al., *Esquema de los partidos,* pp. 27–52. See also analysis and comparison of the three programs in Juan Garcés, *1970, la pugna política por la presidencia en Chile* (Santiago: Editorial Universitaria, 1971), p. 3.

6. *El Mercurio,* February 6, 1970, p. 23, for Senator Bulnes's statement; February 12, 1970, p. 19, for the Radical and Socialist positions; February 17, 1970, p. 3, for its editorial position, and p. 19 for the position of Unidad Popular.

7. *El Mercurio* (International Edition), February 16–22, 1970, p. 1.

8. Olavarría Bravo, *Chile bajo la democracia cristiana,* vol. 6, pp. 120–36, gives a list of the senators involved and summarizes the speculation as to which one broke ranks to support the Christian Democrats.

9. On the *Clarín* attacks see Labarca Goddard, *Chile al rojo,* pp. 169–72. (*Clarín* supported both Allende and Tomic for the presidency, possibly because its proprietor, Dario Sainte Marie, had received a substantial loan from a government bank. The term *momio,* coined by *Clarín,* had by 1970 become a standard slang expression for a right-winger.) On the Alessandri finances, see Olavarría Bravo, *Chile bajo la democracia cristiana,* vol. 6, pp. 116–18.

10. Labarca Goddard, *Chile al rojo,* p. 276. A slightly different version is given in Olavarría Bravo, *Chile bajo la democracia cristiana,* vol. 6, p. 161.

11. *El Mercurio,* August 8, 1970, pp. 19, 27.

12. *El Mercurio,* April 23, 1970, p. 271.

13. *Sexto mensaje del presidente de la república* (Santiago: Dirección de Informaciones de la Presidencia, 1970), pp. 19–20, 22, 25, 42, 65–67, 78–79.

14. The SNA figure appears in Olavarría Bravo, *Chile bajo la democracia cristiana,* vol. 1, p. 127. Robert R. Kaufman, *The Politics of Land Reform in Chile* (Cambridge, Mass.: Harvard University Press, 1972), places the figure at $12,500 (p. 99), while Jeannine Swift, *Agrarian Reform in Chile* (Lexington, Mass.: D. C. Heath, 1971), cites lower figures (chap. 8) and argues that a productivity tax would have been more efficient from an ecomomic point of view, but that agrarian reform is preferable from the point of view of "overall social development" (p. xiii).

15. *Punto Final,* no. 112, supp. (September 1, 1970): 2–3, 6–7.

16. *Washington Post,* September 10, 1974.

17. On the outside funding of the 1970 election, see U.S., Congress, Senate, Select Committee on Intelligence Activities, *Covert Action in Chile 1963–1973: Staff Report,* 94th Cong., 1st sess., 1975, pp. 20–21. The CIA estimated that Allende received $350,000 from Cuba and an undetermined additional amount from the Soviet Union.

18. Summaries of speeches from my notes, taken at all three rallies.

19. Dirección del Registro Electoral, *Elección ordinaria de presidente de la república, 4 de Septiembre de 1970* (mimeo, Santiago, 1970). For further analysis and evaluation of the results, see Michael Francis, *The Allende Victory* (Tucson: University of Arizona, Institute of Government Research, 1973), pp. 63–76.

20. James Petras, "La clase obrera chilena," *Los Libros* (Buenos Aires), no. 15/16 (1971): 11–13. Petras also attempts to demonstrate that the working class was faithful to Allende, but he does so by comparing Allende votes in working-class areas with Alessandri and Tomic votes separately, rather than together. If he did the latter, he would have found an Allende majority in only a few communes, and then (with the exception of the coal-mining areas) only among the male voters. A study of earlier elections by Petras with Maurice Zeitlin ("The Working-class Vote in Chile," *British Journal of Sociology,* 21, no. 1 [March 1970]: 16–29) excludes female voters in order to demonstrate a correlation between proletarian status and voting for Allende.

21. *El Mercurio,* September 10, 1970, p. 1.

22. *El Mercurio,* September 14, 1970, p. 24.

23. *Covert Action in Chile,* pp. 12–13; U.S., Congress, Senate, Committee on Foreign Relations, Subcommittee on Multinational Corporations, *Multinational Corporations and United States Foreign Policy: Hearings,* 93d Cong., 1st sess., March 20–April 2, 1973, pt. 1,

pp. 433–37. The hearings (hereafter cited as *Senate ITT Hearings*) were published in two parts, part 2 containing nearly 600 pages of documents, including the full texts of the ITT memoranda of 1970 and 1971.

24. U.S., Congress, Senate, Select Committee on Intelligence Activities, *Alleged Assassination Plots Involving Foreign Leaders: Interim Report*, 1975, p. 229.

25. Korry told the Senate Intelligence Committee on February 26, 1976, that the "nuts and bolts" cable was a deliberate overstatement made at President Frei's request (U.S., Congress, Senate, Select Committee on Intelligence Activities, *Supplementary Detailed Staff Reports*, book 4, 1976, p. 127). See also *Alleged Assasination Plots*, pp. 230–32, and *Senate ITT Hearings*, pt. 2. The report of State Department opposition to bribing Chilean congressmen appears in the *New York Times*, July 24, 1975.

26. U.S., Congress, Senate, Select Committee on Intelligence Activities, 94th Cong., 1st sess., *Hearings*, December 4–5, 1975, p. 32. The September 21 message is also quoted in *Alleged Assassination Plots*, p. 231. Korry was opposed to military intervention unless it was given a constitutional basis by the resignation of President Frei and a call for new elections.

27. *Alleged Assassination Plots*, pp. 227–29, 234.

28. *Senate ITT Hearings*, pt. 2, pp. 622–25.

29. Ibid., pp. 626–28, 643. Contrary to former Assistant Secretary of State Meyer's testimony that Broe's actions simply involved a discussion of "the feasibility of a course of action" (*Senate ITT Hearings*, pt. 1, p. 400), the approach to ITT seems to have been the direct result of a decision by the Forty Committee to step up economic pressure on Chile through such measures as "cutting off credits, pressuring firms to curtail investment in Chile and approaching other nations to cooperate." The decision was opposed by the State Department representatives present as tantamount to economic warfare and a change in existing policy toward Chile (*Covert Action in Chile*, pp. 25, 43).

30. *Senate ITT Hearings*, pt. 1, pp. 264, 347, 355, 359, 368, 379, 387.

31. *El Mercurio*, September 25, 1970, p. 24.

32. *Senate ITT Hearings*, pt. 2, p. 612.

33. The account of the meetings of Popular Unity and the PDC Assembly is taken from *Ercilla*, no. 1842 (October 7–13, 1970): 8–13.

34. The text and legislative history of the amendments are contained in Fernando Silva Sánchez, *Primeras reformas constitucionales del Presidente Allende* (Valparaíso, 1971).

35. *New York Times*, October 4, 1971, p. 24.

36. Labarca Goddard, *Chile al rojo*, p. 78. Labarca, a Communist journalist, asserts that ex-President Frei and three of his ministers were "repeatedly mentioned" during the investigation, but gives no evidence that they knew of, or were in agreement with, the plot. Labarca's principal source seems to have been a lengthy interview with one of the conspirators, Colonel Raul Igualt, published in the right-wing magazine *Sepa* on February 9, 1971. According to Igault, it was planned that Frei would resign after Finance Minister Zaldívar's speech at the end of September, but Frei had changed his mind. Igualt also claimed that in early October, Frei had sent "an indirect message" to Viaux giving him a "green light" for a coup attempt. Substantial extracts from the interview appear in Olavarría Bravo, *Chile bajo la democracia cristiana*, vol. 6, pp. 387–98. Similar claims by Viaux himself were later published in Florencia Varas, *Conversaciones con Viaux* (Santiago: Impresiones Eira, 1972), pp. 126–34. Viaux asserted there that General Carlos Prats, later a strong Allende supporter, had also indicated that he was favorably disposed. There is no evidence that Senator Bulnes did anything more than meet with Viaux in mid-September, but Senator Morales seems to have assisted in the purchase of arms. The Allende government's request that Morales's parliamentary immunity be lifted was rejected by the Supreme Court on the grounds that the government had not produced any evidence of a punishable act on the part of Morales—that is, any direct connection with the Schneider assassination. For the text of the decision, see Olavarría Bravo, vol. 6, pp. 369–71.

37. *Alleged Assassination Plots*, pp. 248–49.

38. Ibid., p. 240.
39. Ibid., p. 241; Patricio García, ed., *El caso Schneider* (Santiago: Quimantú, 1972), p. 91.
40. García, *El caso Schneider*, p. 63; *Alleged Assassination Plots*, p. 242.
41. *Alleged Assassination Plots*, pp. 242–45, which is also the source of the account in the next paragraph. See also *Senate ITT Hearings*, pt. 2, p. 659, for a surprisingly accurate account of the October 15 decisions, telephoned from San Juan on October 16 by ITT Latin American Public Relations Director Hal Hendrix. In 1976 Hendrix pleaded guilty to perjuring himself when he denied in the 1973 Senate ITT Hearings that he had been employed by the CIA. (*New York Times*, December 23, 1976).
42. As far as the Senate Select Committee investigators could determine, the CIA weapons were not used in the Schneider assassination, since only handguns were involved, although there was an unloaded machine gun at the scene (*Alleged Assassination Plots*, p. 245). The right-wing magazine *Sepa* later (December 22, 1970) claimed that Schneider had been killed by left-wing infiltrators in the group. The text of the report appears in Olavarría Bravo, *Chile bajo la democracia cristiana*, vol. 6, pp. 375–77. In Varas, *Conversaciones*, p. 192, General Viaux also cites unpersuasive evidence that the left was involved. The best account of the assassination appears in *Ercilla*, no. 1845 (October 28–November 4, 1970):12–18.
43. On Latin American populism, see Alistair Hennessy, "Latin America," in *Populism*, ed. Ghota Ionescu and Ernest Gellner (New York: Macmillan, 1969), chap. 2.

Chapter 7. Allende's First Year: The Illusion of Success

1. Minutes of the interview are published in Armando Uribe, *The Black Book of American Intervention in Chile* (Boston: Beacon Press, 1975), pp. 74–80. Allende was particularly concerned to communicate his strong determination not to allow foreign (Russian) military bases in Chile.
2. Norman Gall, "The Chileans Have Elected a Revolution," *New York Times Magazine*, November 1, 1970, p. 106, gives the content of the Castro letter.
3. *El Mercurio*, November 6, 1970, pp. 1, 23. Allende's speech was written by a young Catalan political scientist, Joan Garcés, who had recently become an adviser to Allende.
4. *New York Times*, January 25, 1971, p. 73. On Almeyda's background as a Latin American nationalist attracted to both Peronism and Maoism, see Ernst Halperin, *Nationalism and Communism in Chile* (Cambridge, Mass.: MIT Press, 1965), pp. 158–69. As foreign minister, Almeyda demonstrated a pragmatic realism which contrasted strongly with his revolutionary theory.
5. A list of the major U.S. investments in Chile appears in the *New York Times*, September 21, 1970, p. 2. There were 110 U.S. companies doing business in Chile in 1970, 50 of them wholly owned subsidiaries (*New York Times*, September 14, 1970, p. 59).
6. See discussion of the reasons for resorting to a constitutional amendment in Eduardo Novoa, *La batalla por el cobre* (Santiago: Quimantú, 1972), p. 152–59.
7. On the Allende government's banking policy, see CORFO, *Chile Economic Notes* (New York), nos. 73 and 75 (February 1 and March 5, 1971), and the advertisement by the Central Bank of Chile in the *New York Times*, January 25, 1971, p. 73. The control of credit and related enterprises by the Grupo Banco Edwards was the target of a widely read book (originally a thesis written under the direction of Professor [later Senator] Alberto Baltra) by Ricardo Lagos, *La concentración del poder económico* (Santiago: Editorial del Pacífico, 1961), esp. pp. 140–43. Before the elections, pro-Allende demonstrations would march past the main building of the Edwards Bank chanting, "Con el gobierno popular, este banco se va a expropiar" ("With the government of the people this bank will be expropriated"). Statistical methods are used to answer the charges concerning concentration of credit and to prove that large corporations receive less than their proportionate share of credit in Javier Fuenzalida

and Sergio Undurraga, *El credito y su distribución en Chile* (Santiago: Colección Estudios, 1968), esp. chap. 4.

8. See the detailed account of the assembly in *El Mercurio,* December 14, 1971, p. 3.

9. *El Siglo,* December 9, 1970, pp. 1, 4; *La Prensa,* November 28, 1970, p. 7; CORFO, *Chile Economic Notes,* no. 72, March 1971.

10. *New York Times,* January 18, 1971, p. 3; January 25, 1971, p. 3. Alistair Horne, *Small Earthquake in Chile* (New York: Viking Press, 1972), chaps. 8–9.

11. Agricultural production figures are taken from the useful summary of all economic indicators for 1966–70, 1971, 1972, and 1973 in the 1974 report on Chile of the Inter-American Committee of the Alliance for Progress, Consejo Interamericano Económico y Social, Comité Interamericano de la Alianza para el Progreso, *El esfuerzo interno y las necesidades de financiamiento externo para el desarrollo de Chile* (OEA/Ser. H/XIV; CIAP/650, January 28, 1974), pp. II-3, II-4. See p. II-14 for a breakdown by crops for each year from 1970 to 1973 and II-23 for food import figures.

12. See Regis Debray, *The Chilean Revolution: Conversations with Allende* (New York: Pantheon, 1971), pp. 77, 91, 97, 119. In his introduction, Debray stated his own position that "in the last analysis and until further notice, political power grows out of the barrel of a gun, and the popular government does not have its own armed apparatus, its own institutions of defence on a national scale" (p. 52). At its congress in January 1971, the Socialist Party also stated that "the special conditions under which Popular Unity came to power oblige it to observe the limits of a bourgeois state for now" but called on its followers to prepare for "the decisive confrontation with the bourgeoisie and imperialism."

13. The provisions of the government bill and the amendments introduced in the Senate are compared in *Ercilla,* no. 1858 (February 24–March 2, 1971): 11–12. The congressional amendments to the government text are criticized in Novoa, *La batalla por el cobre,* chaps. 11–12.

14. A detailed account of the negotiations appears in a declassified cable from Ambassador Korry, dated October 1, 1971, published in U.S., Congress, Senate, Select Committee on Intelligence Activities, *Intelligence Activities,* vol. 7, *Covert Action,* 94th Cong., 1st sess., December 4–5, 1975, pp. 128–35.

15. *El Mercurio,* April 6, 1971, p. 8. All other figures are taken from the official results, Dirección del Registro Electoral, *Resultado, elección ordinaria de regidores* (Santiago, 1971). Prior to the election, CIA funds enabled the Christian Democratic Party to purchase a newspaper and radio station, and it assisted all the opposition parties in the municipal elections and in a July by-election. Between January and July 1971, a total of nearly $1.9 million in covert assistance was authorized by the Forty Committee (U.S., Congress, Senate, Select Committee on Intelligence Activities, *Covert Action in Chile, 1963–1973: Staff Report,* 94th Cong., 1st sess., 1975, pp. 28, 59).

16. The documents involved in the controversy were published in *Pastoral Popular,* 21, no. 123 (May–June, 1971). On the emergence of an articulate segment of the Catholic church in Latin America in favor of active collaboration with Marxism, see Paul E. Sigmund, "Latin American Catholicism's Opening to the Left," *Review of Politics,* 35, no. 1 (January 1973): 61–76.

17. Conferencia Episcopal de Chile, *Evangelio, política y socialismos* (Santiago: Secretariado del CECH, 1971), pp. 35–36.

18. On the May decision and its consequences, see articles in "Trinchera Política" and "Polémica" sections of *Política y Espíritu,* 27, nos. 322 and 323 (June and July 1971).

19. Salvador Allende, *La vía chilena,* translated as "The Chilean Way to Socialism," in *The Ideologies of the Developing Nations,* ed. Paul E. Sigmund, 2d rev. ed. (New York: Praeger Publishers, 1972), pp. 447–53.

20. Allende's statement was made in a speech in Valparaíso on February 4, 1971. Three days later, he explained that he had meant that he was not president of "the speculators,

landowners, unscrupulous bankers, and international delinquents." See *El Mercurio*, February 5 and 8, 1971.

21. "Declaración del Partido Demócrata Cristiano," *Política y Espíritu*, 27, no. 323 (July 1971):69.

22. The election figures for the July by-election are broken down by commune in *La Nación*, July 20, 1971. They have been compared with the statistics for the April election published by the Dirección del Registro Electoral. Later estimates by the opposition that the government had lost 3 percent in this election seem to be in error.

23. *Ercilla*, no. 1881 (August 4–10, 1971); *Política y Espíritu*, 27, no. 323 (July 1971): 70–72; no. 324 (August 1971):77–78.

24. *El Mercurio*, July 28, August 7 and 11, 1971.

25. *El Mercurio*, August 7, 1971, p. 25. See also *Política y Espíritu*, 27, no. 324 (August 1971):79–80.

26. The text of the declaration by the dissident senators and deputies appears in *El Mercurio*, August 4, 1971, pp. 1, 10. The Radical policy vote is printed in *El Mercurio*, August 8, 1971, p. 37. Besides the phrases cited in the Bossay-Baltra declaration, the policy vote also states that the Radical Party is "an organization . . . at the service of the class interests . . . of the workers," and that "since we are socialists, we accept historical materialism and the class struggle as an interpretation of reality. . . . The class struggle is a concrete reality which is practical and observable in all class societies in the history of the world. . . . Two-thirds of humanity live under socialism and have elevated the values of democracy to real and concrete rights for the working class."

27. *Covert Action in Chile*, p. 33. The Export-Import Bank did not terminate its loan guarantee program to Chile until 1972, after Chile had defaulted on its debt payments to the bank. However, shortly after Allende took power, it dropped Chile to its lowest credit-rating category. NSDM 93 also directed that private businesses be "made aware" of U.S. government policies.

28. *El Mercurio* (International Edition), September 27–October 3, 1971, pp. 1 and 7, gives the text of the excess profits decree. The compensation decision appears in *El Mercurio* (International Edition), October 4–10, 1971, p. 1.

29. *El Mercurio* (International Edition), September 20–26, 1971, p. 7.

30. *Senate ITT Hearings*, pt. 2, pp. 943–53, 964–65. Peterson testified at the hearings that he never saw the eighteen-point memorandum (p. 431).

31. *Senate ITT Hearings*, pt. 2, pp. 975–79.

32. *Covert Action in Chile*, pp. 29, 60. The extreme rightist organization Patria y Libertad received $7,000 in 1971, but financial support was ended thereafter.

33. *El Mercurio* (International Edition), September 20–26, 1971, pp. 1–2.

34. The text of the government bill appears in *El Mercurio* (International Edition), October 18–24, 1971, pp. 1–2. The ceremony in which Allende signed the draft bill was attended by Cardinal Silva as well as by representatives of the armed forces and the head of the Supreme Court.

35. "Texto del proyecto de reforma constitucional sobre areas de la economía," *Política y Espíritu*, 27, no. 330 (February–March 1972):63–65. See also Juan Hamilton's senatorial speeches on the amendment in no. 326 (October 1971):32–39 (speech delivered October 29, 1971); and no. 330 (February–March 1972):65–71 (speech delivered February 19, 1972).

Chapter 8. Polarization and Brinkmanship

1. *El Mercurio* (International Edition), November 8–14, 1971, pp. 5, 8.

2. Ibid., December 20–26, 1971, p. 1; February 21–27, 1971, p. 1.

3. Ibid., November 8–14, 1971, p. 8; *The Speeches of Fidel in Chile* (Montreal: Editions Latin America, 1972), vol. 1, pp. 48, 79; vol. 2, p. 353.

4. *Speeches of Fidel,* vol. 2, pp. 366, 392. For an analysis of the visit, see George Grayson, "El viaje de Castro a Chile, Perú, y Ecuador," *Problemas Internacionales,* 19, no. 3 (May–June 1972):1–14.

5. *El Mercurio* (International Edition), November 29–December 5, 1971, pp. 1, 7. The original press report on the comments by Herbert Klein appeared in the *New York Times,* December 1, 1971, p. 20. U.S. Senate investigators in 1975 were unable to establish a connection between the CIA and the opposition march.

6. *El Mercurio* (International Edition), January 3–9, 1972, pp. 1, 7. For documents and details of the impeachment, see Joan Garcés, *Revolución, congreso y constitución: el caso Tohá* (Santiago: Quimantú, 1972). Before 1972 only thirty-six "constitutional accusations" had been moved against ministers in the history of Chile; four had been adopted by the Chamber, and the Senate had passed only three (p. 340).

7. *El Mercurio* (International Edition), January 17–23, 1972, p. 1. *Boletín informativo del Partido Demócrata Cristiano,* 2, no. 25, p. 8. The returns for O'Higgins, Colchagua, and Linares for the April 1971 municipal elections appear in Dirección del Registro Electoral, *Resultado, elección ordinaria de regidores, 1971* (Santiago, 1971).

8. Excerpts from the Communist and MIR statements appear in *El Mercurio* (International Edition), January 31–February 7, 1972, p. 4. The full text of the Communist report appears in *El Mercurio,* February 3, 1972. Allende also received a report from his economic advisers predicting much more serious inflation and balance-of-payments problems in 1972.

9. For the text of the joint declaration of the opposition members of Congress on the constitutional controversy, see *El Mercurio* (International Edition), February 28–March 5, 1972, pp. 1, 4. Allende's rejection of a plebiscite appears ibid., February 21–27, 1972, p. 1.

10. Full documentation on the Left Radicals' split with Allende appears in a PIR publication, *Trayectoria política del PIR* (Santiago, August 1974). The presidential veto message was the occasion for the PIR break with the government, but behind it lay a much deeper disagreement concerning the role of the middle class and of respect for legality in the transition of socialism. The incident also demonstrated, once again, Allende's unwillingness to oppose his own Socialist Party, which had bitterly denounced the proposed agreement.

11. Frei's radio address is reprinted in *Política y Espíritu,* 27, no. 331 (April 1972): 86–91. The 1973 Senate ITT hearings tended to support Frei's position.

12. *Washington Post,* March 28, 1972, p. B11. The last sentence of the Davis dispatch has been repeatedly and, it would seem, deliberately quoted out of the context to prove that the ambassador was advocating the promotion of a military coup. See, for example, James Petras and Morris Morley, *The United States and Chile* (New York: Monthly Review Press, 1972), which dates the dispatch as early 1971, before Davis had even arrived in Chile, and Joseph Collins, "Chile Suffered Invisible Blockade," *National Catholic Reporter,* 9, no. 39 (October 12, 1973):6, which quotes the ambassador as *advocating* the creation of discontent "so great that military intervention is overwhelmingly invited."

13. *Ercilla,* no. 2015 (March 12–19, 1974):14. Since September 1971 the CIA had been monitoring, and in two cases in late 1971 encouraging, coup-plotting by the military. In November, Washington CIA headquarters had warned the Santiago station that it did not have Forty Committee approval to become involved in a coup (U.S., Congress, Senate, Select Committee on Intelligence Activities, *Covert Action in Chile, 1963–1973: Staff Report,* 94th Cong., 1st sess., 1975, pp. 38–39).

14. *Ercilla,* no. 1932 (July 26–August 2, 1972):11, compares the government and PDC proposals. See also the comparison of the open letters of Tapia and Fuentealba on July 4, 1972, in Genaro Arriagada, *De la vía chilena a la vía insurreccional* (Santiago: Pacífico, 1974), pp. 184–89. A report in a progovernment newspaper that the negotiations had been broken off because of a phone call by ex-president Frei from Yugoslavia seems to have been pure invention.

15. *Libro Blanco,* pp. 103–08, publishes photocopies of the itemized list. Hernán Millas,

Anatomía de un fracaso (Santiago: Zig-Zag, 1973), pp. 101–05, quotes the various and conflicting statements by government officials on the contents of the *bultos cubanos.*

16. Salvador Allende, *La lucha por la democracia económica y las libertades sociales* (second state-of-the-nation address, May 2, 1972) (Santiago: Consejería de Difusión de la Presidencia, 1972), pp. 24, 19. By using a different accounting basis, other sources (for example, ODEPLAN, *Cuentas Nacionales, 1960–71* [Santiago, 1973], p. 41) were able to raise the 1971 wages and salaries percentage to 65.87.

17. *El Mercurio* (International Edition), June 12–18, 1972, p. 1; Allende, *La lucha,* p. 17.

18. The deficit in the balance of payments for 1971 was $368 million (*El Mercurio,* April 17–23, 1972, p. 2).

19. Ibid., December 13–19, 1971, p. 2; July 24–30, 1972, p. 8.

20. U.S., Congress, Senate, Committee on Foreign Relations, Subcommittee on Multinational Corporations, *Multinational Corporations and United States Foreign Policy: Hearings,* 93d Cong., 1st sess., March 20–April 2, 1973, pt. 1, pp. 342–98.

21. Deficit figures from government sources are given in "La economía chilena en el gobierno de Allende," *Política y Espíritu,* 27, no. 331 (April 1972): 41, 50. The new taxes are listed in *El Mercurio* (International Edition), January 3–9, 1972, p. 1.

22. The drop in investment is cited by Allende in *La lucha,* p. 21. In March 1972, Vuskovic admitted that "economic policy is subordinate in its content, shape, and form, to the political need of increasing Popular Unity's support" (J. Ann Zammit, ed., *The Chilean Road to Socialism* [Austin: University of Texas Press, 1973], p. 50).

23. *El Mercurio* (International Edition), July 31–August 6, 1972, p. 6 (Allende letter); August 7–13, 1972, pp. 1, 8 (Lo Hermida raid).

24. *Chile Economic News* (CORFO, New York), October 1, 1972, pp. 4–7.

25. *Ercilla,* no. 1939 (September 13–19, 1972):10–11.

26. *La Nación,* September 8, 1972, p. 6; *El Mercurio* (International Edition), September 11–17, 1972, pp. 1, 5.

27. Patricio Aylwin, "Dos años de destrucción" *Política y Espíritu,* 28, no. 336 (September 1972): 23–37, at pages 33–34.

28. The issues involved in the amendment are well presented in the Senate debate on the presidential vetoes published in *El Mercurio,* July 23, 1973, pp. 9–12, and July 29, 1973, pp. 26–30. On the changes in the agrarian reform under the Allende government, see Brian Loveman, *Struggle in the Countryside: Politics and Rural Labor in Chile* (Bloomington: University of Indiana Press, 1976); Solon Barraclough and José Antonio Fernández, *Diagnóstico de la reforma agraria chilena* (Mexico City: Siglo XXI, 1974); and Stefan de Vylder, *The Political Economy of the Rise and Fall of the Unidad Popular* (New York: Cambridge University Press, 1976), chap. 7.

29. Ley no. 17, 798 (*Diario official,* October 21, 1972).

30. *El Mercurio* (International Edition), September 11–17, 1972, p. 1; September 18–24, 1972, p. 1.

31. Documentation appears in Kennecott Copper Corporation, *Confiscation of El Teniente,* Supp. 3, New York, December 1972, pt. 2. Documents on the successful Kennecott action in U.S. courts in February 1972 to force Chile to make scheduled payments on the 1967 Chileanization loans by attaching Chilean assets in New York are published in supp. 2, February 1972, pt. 3, and in supp. 3, pt. 1. Payments were suspended again in 1973, and no payments were made on Kennecott's 49 percent equity nationalized in 1971.

32. *El Mercurio,* October 10, 1972, p. 19.

33. Claudio Orrego, *El paro nacional* (Santiago: Pacífico, 1972), pp. 12–19, reproduces documentation for the initial days of the strike.

34. *El Mercurio* (International Edition), October 16–22, 1972, p. 8.

35. Radomiro Tomic, "Que el pueblo decide en marzo," *Política y Espíritu,* 28, no. 337 (October 1972):70–72. The Frei speech appears on pp. 64–69.

Chapter 9. The Politicization of the Military

1. Orlando Millas, *Exposición sobre política económica* (Santiago: Dirección de Presupuestos, 1972), pp. 006, 014; *El Mercurio* (International Edition), November 13–19, 1972, p. 8; *Ercilla,* no. 1949 (November 22–28, 1972):24; and *Chile Economic News* (CORFO, New York), passim.

2. Kennecott Copper Corporation, *Confiscation of El Teniente,* supp. 3, New York, December 1972, pp. 64–66.

3. Ibid., supp. 4, May 1973, p. 31. The information in this publication concerning the various legal controversies initiated by Kennecott has been supplemented by a personal interview with Carlos Fortín, then London representative of CODELCO, July 25, 1973.

4. Kennecott claims that the excess profits deduction of $410 million was far in excess of its *total* Chilean profits between 1955 and 1970 which, it says, amounted to $253 million. See Kennecott Copper Corporation, *Confiscation of El Teniente,* supp. 2, February 1972, p. 45. Much depends on the accounting methods used, in particular, the method used to compute book value.

5. Salvador Allende, *Speech Delivered Before the General Assembly of the United Nations, December 4, 1972* (Washington, D.C.: Embassy of Chile, 1972), passim.

6. Tad Szulc, "U.S. and Chile: Is There a Way Out?", *New York Times,* December 10, 1972, sec. 4, p. 3.

7. *Newsweek,* December 11, 1972, p. 57; *New York Times,* December 7, 1972, p. 10; *Christian Science Monitor,* December 28, 1972, p. 1.

8. Flores's speech is translated in *Chile Economic News,* February 15, 1973, pp. 3–12. The English translation stops just before Flores's announcement of the "family quotas" and the use of the JAP committees to enforce them. For the original text, see *El Mercurio* (International Edition), January 8–14, 1973, p. 7.

9. *El Mercurio* (International Edition), January 15–21, 1973, p. 1; January 29–February 4, 1973, p. 4.

10. *Chile Economic News,* January 15, 1973, p. 2.

11. *Excelsior* (Mexico City), February 6, 1972, p. 1. The Sumar remarks are reported in *El Mercurio,* January 23, 1973. Allende again threatened to resign during the copper workers' strike in April.

12. *El Mercurio* (International Edition), March 12–18, 1972, p. 7.

13. The text of the Millas bill appears in *El Mercurio* (International Edition), January 22–28, 1972, p. 6, and is translated in part in *Chile Economic News,* March 1, 1973, pp. 1–3. Differences among the government parties are discussed in the *New York Times,* March 4, 1973, p. 3, and among the opposition in *Latin America* (London), 7, no. 8 (February 23, 1972):63.

14. *El Mercurio,* March 1, 1973, published a secret MAPU report problably obtained from the CIA, which described the "state capitalist" position of Allende and the Communists as not fundamentally different from that of the opposition.

15. *Chile Economic News,* March 15, 1973, pp. 4–5.

16. The figures for the *cifra repartidora* are taken from *El Mercurio,* March 7, 1973, p. 17, and *La Tercera,* March 6, 1973, p. 22. On the disproportionate number of electors required in various districts, see Federico Gil, *The Political System of Chile* (Boston: Houghton Mifflin, 1966), p. 216.

17. Embassy of Chile (Washington, D.C.), *Chile: A Summary of Recent Events,* no. 252 (March 6, 1973):1–2; *Chile Hoy,* 1, no. 39 (March 9–15, 1973):8.

18. Dirección del Registro Electoral, *Resultado, elección ordinaria de congreso nacional* (Santiago, 1973). The *El Siglo* article appeared on March 10, 1974, p. 2. The Frei and Jarpa results are reported in *El Mercurio,* March 7, 1973, p. 17.

19. *Chile Hoy,* supp. 4, Revista Agraria, April 1973, pp. 2–3.

Chapter 10. Prelude to the Coup

1. *El Mercurio,* November 22–23, 1973, published a secret Allende government document found in the Central Bank, written before the March elections, which advocated a policy of continued involvement of the military in the government. In mid-1974, General Pinochet said that he and seven other officers had signed a document on March 20, 1973, declaring that a constitutional solution was now impossible (*El Mercurio* [International Edition], August 5–11, 1974, p. 7). *Ercilla,* no. 1988 (August 27–28, 1973):7–8, lists the conditions of the military, including enforcement of arms control, adoption of the three areas constitutional reform, and mutual respect among the three branches of government.

2. Decree no. 224, Ministry of Public Education, March 6, 1973. The full plan was published with the title *Informe sobre escuela nacional unificada,* Ministry of Public Education, February 1973. Along with other documents, it is reproduced in FEUC (Catholic University Student Federation), Department of Studies, *ENU, el control de las conciencias* (Santiago, April 1973), pp. 69–88.

3. *El Mercurio* (International Edition), March 19–25, 1973, p. 6. See also PDC, *Informe técnico sobre educación,* March 1973, which discusses the relation of ENU to the educational reforms of the Frei government and proposes an alternative "communitarian" model of education.

4. *El Mercurio* (International Edition), March 19–25, 1973, p. 8; March 26–April 1, 1973, p. 1; April 9–15, 1973, p. 8; Carlos Oviedo Cavada, *Documentos del episcopado: Chile 1970–73* (Santiago: Ediciones Mundo, 1974), pp. 151–58.

5. *El Mercurio* (International Edition), April 9–15, 1973, p. 8; *Latin America* (London, 7, no. 17 (April 27, 1973):133. In response to Allende's invitation, the bishops published in June a detailed critique of the proposal, *El momento actual de la educación en Chile.*

6. *El Mercurio* (International Edition), April 2–8, 1973, p. 1.

7. *Washington Post,* March 8, 1973, p. D17; June 10, 1973, p. A6.

8. *New York Times,* April 10, 1973, p. 2. See also Gerrity and Guilfoyle testimony in U.S., Congress, Senate, Committee on Foreign Relations, Subcommittee on Multinational Corporations, *Multinational Corporations and United States Foreign Policy: Hearings,* 93d Cong., 1st sess., March 20–April 2, 1973, pt. 1, pp. 201, 239–40. OPIC had already paid out $80 million to Kennecott, Ralston Purina, Ford Motors, and Northern Indiana Brass Company. In late 1974 OPIC reversed its ITT decision at the recommendation of an outside arbitrator.

9. *El Mercurio* (International Edition), May 28–June 3, 1973, p. 1.

10. The firms are listed in *Chile Hoy,* 1, no. 48 (May 11–17, 1973):11. The text of the bill appears on pp. 16–17.

11. *El Mercurio* (International Edition), April 30–May 6, 1973, p. 8.

12. *Ercilla,* no. 1971 (April 24–May 1, 1973):9; no. 1970 (April 18–24, 1973):9. On May 23, eight air force generals protested to Allende the inconsistency of the government's firmness against the protesting students and its inaction against the MIR. See *Ercilla,* no. 2012 (February 20–26, 1974):32. General Pinochet also has cited May 28 as the first time that military planning actively began to take account of the possibility of a coup; see *Ercilla,* no. 2015 (March 13–19, 1974):14.

13. *El Mercurio* (International Edition), May 14–20, 1973, p. 8.

14. *Mensaje de Presidente Allende ante Congreso pleno,* May 21, 1973, passim. See also *Chile Hoy,* 1, no. 51 (June 1–7, 1972):13; *Ercilla,* no. 1976 (May 30–June 5, 1973):8–9; and *El Mercurio* (International Edition), May 21–27, 1972, pp. 5, 8.

15. *El Mercurio* (International Edition), May 21–27, 1973, p. 8.

16. The government did not always oppose judicial orders. For an example in which the Socialists supported a court ruling against (Christian Democratic) peasants who had tried to take over the former owner's legally guaranteed reserve property, see José Yglesias, "The Chilean Experiment: Revolution in the Countryside?", *Ramparts,* 11, (June 1973):16–20.

17. For examples, see *Chile Hoy,* 2, nos. 54, 55 (June 22–28, June 29–July 5, 1973).

18. Garcés's letter is reproduced in the *Libro Blanco,* p. 92, and he writes about Allende in *Le Monde,* December 19, 1973, p. 5, and in *El estado y los problemas tácticos en el gobierno de Allende* (Madrid: Siglo XXI, 1974), pp. 38–39. General Stuardo's interview appears in *Ercilla,* no. 2012 (February 20–26, 1974):32.

19. *Ercilla,* no. 1976 (May 30–June 5, 1973):25.

20. *El Mercurio* (International Edition), June 18–24, 1973, pp. 7, 8; *Chile Hoy,* 2, no. 55 (June 29–July 5, 1973):7, 28–32.

21. The generals' vote appears in Robert Moss, *Chile's Marxist Experiment* (London: Abbot, 1973), p. 191. The account of the June 29 coup which follows is drawn from *El tancazo de ese 29 de junio,* published by Quimantú, the Allende government publisher, in its Documentos Especiales series. It has been compared with the accounts in *El Mercurio* (International Edition), June 25–July 1, 1973, and July 6, 1973, and *Ercilla,* nos. 1981 and 1983 (July 4–11 and 18–24, 1973).

22. Government references to the location of the president's residence described it as situated in "the eastern section" of Santiago, but members of the opposition were always referred to as residents of the Barrio Alto.

23. *El Mercurio,* July 9, 1973.

24. Two of many versions of the negotiations between Allende and the military appear in *Ercilla,* no. 1982 (July 11–17, 1973): 7–10. General Pinochet later said that on July 4 active planning was initiated at his order as chief of staff for a possible urban conflict centered in Santiago. For security purposes, the plan was entitled "Internal Security War Game." See *Ercilla,* no. 2015 (March 13–19, 1974):14–15. Joan Garcés (*El Estado,* p. 42) says Pinochet and other coup-minded (*golpista*) officers argued to Allende that Prats should not become interior minister at this time because he was needed to maintain unity in the army. He also notes that part of the Popular Unity coalition was opposed to military participation.

25. The text of the report appears in *El Mercurio,* July 20, 1973, p. 23, and July 21, 1973, p. 29. Allende's former adviser, Joan Garcés, later argued that the report was devised in order to prevent any solution to the crisis through the use of a plebiscite (*Le Monde,* December 19, 1973).

26. U.S., Congress, Senate, Select Committee on Inteligence Activities, *Covert Action in Chile, 1963–1973: Staff Report,* 94th Cong., 1st sess., 1975, pp. 30–31, 61. The only expenditures from the August 20 authorization were made after the coup. In October, $25,000 was spent to purchase a radio station and $9,000 for travel by an anti-Allende trade union delegation. In June 1974, $50,000 previously committed was given to the Christian Democrats.

27. One indication of the magnitude of the spare parts problem was the fact that the number of taxis in Santiago dropped from 4,000 to about 2,000 between 1971 and 1973.

28. This account of the negotiations is drawn from the article in *Ercilla,* no. 1986 (August 8–14, 1973):9–10. Based apparently on the recollections of the Christian Democratic participants, it purports to give verbatim excerpts from the conversations.

29. The texts of Aylwin's letter of August 2, Allende's reply of August 3, and the reply of the PDC on August 4, are published in *Política y Espíritu,* 29, no. 345 (August 1973):64–69.

30. *Libro Blanco,* pp. 101–02, reproduces the letter in Castro's handwriting. In October 1973, the letter was recognized as genuine by the Cuban delegation to the United Nations.

31. Aylwin has insisted that Allende showed no interest in serious negotiation at the dinner (personal interview, January 11, 1974). Joan Garcés quotes Allende as responding to suggestions at this time that he should give in to PDC demands: "Never! That would result in the division of Popular Unity and therefore the end of the revolutionary movement" (*El Estado,* p. 36).

32. *Ercilla,* no. 1988 (August 22–28, 1973):22. The actual deficit by the time of the September 10 coup was 400 billion escudos.

33. *Libro Blanco,* pp. 197, 192, confirmed by author's interviews. See also *El Mercurio,* November 22–24, 1973.

34. After the coup, for instance, it was discovered that under the direction of a Brazilian

activist, the night shift at the state-controlled Madeco factory was adding heavy armor and machine-gun emplacements to its fork-lift trucks.

35. It should be noted that while there was an intensification of class feeling in this period, there continued to be strong opposition to Allende in lower-class areas, especially among women. Among organized workers the intensity of the opposition to the government on the part of the El Teniente copper miners had been dramatically demonstrated in the two-and-a-half-month strike which had ended in early July.

36. *El Mercurio* (International Edition), August 6–12, 1973, p. 6. That Allende was sincere in his opposition to paramilitary groups is confirmed in a document in the *Libro Blanco,* where he is quoted as insisting on "the necessity of enforcing the Arms Control Law and arresting and, if necessary, killing anyone bearing arms" (p. 194).

37. *New York Times,* August 18, 1973, p. 1.

38. Regis Debray, "Il est mort dans sa loi," *Le Nouvel Observateur,* September 2, 1973, p. 37. Patricio Aylwin claims that at the meeting at the Cardinal's residence on August 17, he had told Allende he had to choose between "the navy and the *cordones,* the Christian Democrats or the MIR."

Chapter 11. The Overthrow of Allende

1. *Qué Pasa,* no. 123 (August 23, 1974):6–7. The movement of air force jets was later described by a *New York Times* correspondent (September 27, 1973) as preparatory to a coup. The air force later said that the move had been taken because of possible MIR action at the Santiago bases.

2. *Ercilla,* no. 1988 (August 22–28, 1973):7–12; no. 1989 (August 29–September 4, 1973): 7–8; *Qué Pasa,* no. 123 (August 23, 1973):6–31. On the Council of Generals' vote, see Alain Touraine, *Vie et mort du Chili populaire* (Paris: Editions du Seuil, 1974), p. 94, quoting an article by Joan Garcés, possibly based on an Allende government recording of the meeting. General Pinochet's support for Prats led him to assure Allende of Pinochet's commitment to constitutionalism when he chose him as Prats's successor. Garcés later wrote that Allende held a midnight meeting with the Popular Unity leaders on August 22 at which he described a plan for a "joint worker-military operation" against a possible coup, which he was preparing with Pinochet and other generals. Garcés also says that Pinochet persuaded Allende to accept Prats's resignation to pacify the navy and air force and promised that if appointed army commander, he would retire six army generals who were opposed to the government (Garcés, *El Estado y los problemas tácticas en el gobierno de Allende* [Madrid: Siglo XXI, 1974], pp. 48–50).

3. The text of the congressional resolution and President Allende's reply are printed in *El Mercurio* (International Edition), August 20–26, 1973, p. 5.

4. *New York Times,* August 27, 1973, p. 12. See also similar statements by ex-president Frei in *Política y Espíritu,* 29, no. 345 (August 1973):71–74.

5. The report is summarized in *El Mercurio* (International Edition), July 30–August 5, 1973, p. 2, and in *Ercilla,* no. 1987 (August 15–21, 1973):22–23.

6. The most useful collection of figures on the actual performance of the Chilean economy in 1973 is the January 28, 1974, report of the Inter-American Committee of the Alliance for Progress *El esfuerzo interno y las necesidades de financiamiento externo para el desarrollo de Chile* (OEA/Ser. H/XIV; CIAP/650). It repeatedly uses the 53 percent figure for the 1973 deficit, although on p. LV-2, a 42 percent figure (121 billion escudos) is used.

7. Alberto Baltra, *Gestión económica del gobierno de la Unidad Popular* (Santiago: Orbe, 1973), pp. 80, 119–23.

8. *El Mercurio,* July 26, 1973, p. 2. The 1972 IMF report is summarized and strongly

criticized in *El Mercurio* (International Edition), May 7–13, 1973, p. 2.

9. For unemployment figures, see *Chile Economic News* (CORFO, New York), July 15, 1973, p. 6; and *El Mercurio,* July 21, 1973, p. 33. Figures on the decline in housing construction given in the Chilean Senate by Senator Juan Hamilton, housing minister in the Frei administration, appear in *El Mercurio* (International Edition), August 6–12, 1973, p. 8. The 1974 CIAP report contains a graph of the real purchasing power of salaries which indicates that by the end of 1971 it had risen 35 percent above the 1970 level, but in June 1972 it began a steady decline which by August 1973 had reached a point 50 percent *below* the 1970 level (p. III-12).

10. *Chile Hoy,* nos. 64 and 65 (August 31–September 6 and September 7–13, 1973).

11. Accounts of the meeting and subsequent negotiations concerning the resignation of Admiral Raúl Montero appear in the *Christian Science Monitor,* September 17, 1973, p. 2; *The Economist,* October 13, 1973, p. 47; and Robert Moss, "Chile's Coup and After," *Encounter,* 42, no. 3, (March 1974):72–80. Admiral Merino later stated that although preparations had been made earlier, it was events in the last two weeks that triggered the coup. See *Ercilla,* no. 1996 (October 31–November 6, 1973):13.

12. The text of the letter appears in *El Mercurio* (International Edition), September 3–9, 1973, p. 7.

13. See, for example, Laurence Birns, ed., *The End of Chilean Democracy* (New York: The Seabury Press, 1974), pp. 206–07.

14. Personal interview, Carlos Briones, January 14, 1974. An account of the UP meeting appears in Kyle Steenland, "The Coup in Chile," *Latin American Perspectives,* 1, no. 2 (Summer 1974): 12.

15. See interviews with Colonel Pedro Ewing in *Ercilla,* no. 1999 (November 21–27, 1973): 15, and with Admiral Merino in *Qué Pasa,* no. 152 (March 22, 1974): 7, and *La Tercera,* September 8, 1974, pp. 4–5. On the role of the carabineros, see interviews with General Mendoza in *Ercilla,* no. 2014 (March 6–12, 1974): 13, and *Qué Pasa,* no. 177 (September 11, 1974): 21.

16. *Ercilla,* no. 2015 (March 13–19, 1974): 15. Moss, "Chile's Coup," p. 76.

17. *Ercilla,* no. 1997 (November 7–13, 1973): 14 (interview with General Leigh); no. 2015 (March 13–19, 1974):16 (interview with General Pinochet); *The Economist,* October 13, 1973, p. 48.

18. From the newspaper account of the speech reproduced in Ricardo Boizard, *El ultimo día de Allende* (Santiago: Pacífico, 1973), pp. 131–36.

19. *Qué Pasa,* no. 148 (February 22, 1974):13.

20. *Latin America,* 7, no. 49 (December 7, 1973), quoting the Cuban news agency, which it admits is "not, of course, an unbiased source." See also Garcés, *El estado,* p. 24, and Steenland, "Coup in Chile," pp. 16–17.

21. Briones's account in the London *Times,* November 12, 1973, has been supplemented with a personal interview, January 13, 1974.

22. For sources used in the account of the coup, see chap. 1, n. 1.

23. *Libro Blanco,* doc. 10, pp. 248–49 (also available in English), gives the full text. Elsewhere, the proclamation admits that the Allende government was "initially legitimate" but "has fallen into serious illegitimacy." Like the reference to classical doctrine on the subject, the discussion reflects Catholic theories on the right of resistance, which had been applied to the Allende government in the right-wing Catholic journal *Tizona* and in public statements by Father Osvaldo Lira of Valparaíso. The lead articles in the July 1973 issue of *Tizona* were entitled "Rebellion and Its Goals," "Resistance to the Tyrant," and "The Right of Rebellion."

24. See, for instance, Gabriel García Márquez, "The Death of Salvador Allende," *Harper's,* 248, no. 1486 (March 1974):53. His source seems to be published interviews with Communist

Deputy Gladys Marín. See Camilo Taufic, *Chile en la hoguera* (Buenos Aires: Corregidor, 1974), pp. 81–82.

25. *Ercilla,* no. 2005 (January 2–8, 1974):10–13. Similar accounts citing Dr. Guijón appeared in *El Mercurio,* September 21, 1973, and *Ercilla,* no. 1997 (November 7–13, 1973):21.

26. See telephone interview with Hortensia Allende in Taufic, *Chile en la hoguera,* pp. 78–81.

27. Robinson Rojas, *The Murder of Allende* (New York: Harper and Row, 1976); Luis Renato González Cordoba, "The Scene from Within the Moneda," in *The End of Chilean Democracy,* ed. Laurence Birns (New York: Seabury, 1974), pp. 35–41. In *Granma* (Havana), October 7, 1973, pp. 2–3, Fidel Castro admits that it is possible that Allende was a suicide but says he was shot in the chest and "riddled with bullets" by "the fascists" and includes the account of the move from the Red Room to the presidential office and the ceremony there. See also García Márquez, "The Death of Salvador Allende," p. 53: "He resisted for six hours [and] died in an exchange of shots with that gang. Then all the other officers, in a caste-bound ritual, fired on the body. Finally, a noncommissioned officer smashed in his face with the butt of his rifle."

28. *El Mercurio* (International Edition), October 29–November 4, 1973, pp. 1, 7.

Chapter 12. Chile's New Order

1. *Le Monde* (Weekly Edition), September 20–26, 1973, p. 2.
2. *El Mercurio* (International Edition), September 9–15, 1973, p. 4.
3. *El Mercurio* (Extraordinary Edition), September 1973, p. 7.
4. For full documentation on the role of the judiciary from May until September 1973, see *Revista de Derecho y Gaceta de los Tribunales,* 70, nos. 7–8 (September–October 1973). The judiciary's reactions to the coup appear on pp. 278 ff.
5. See *100 primeros decretos leyes dictados por la Junta de Gobierno de la República de Chile* (Santiago 1973), pp. 6–19. Summary executions were forbidden after the end of October, but they are known to have occurred after that time.
6. *Revista de Derecho,* pp. 281, 291.
7. *Latin America,* 7, no. 47 (November 2, 1973):369.
8. Gary MacEoin, *No Peaceful Way: Chile's Struggle for Dignity* (New York: Sheed and Ward, 1974), p. 173. The book gives considerable, although unjustifiably critical, attention to the position of the church.
9. *100 primeros decretos leyes,* pp. 178–83, 62, 30.
10. *El Mercurio* (International Edition), October 1–7, 1973, p. 1.
11. Consejo Nacional, Partido Demócrata Cristiano, *Posición del PDC frente a la nueva situación del país* (Santiago, 1973).
12. *El Mercurio* (International Edition), February 18–24, 1974, p. 3, reproduces the document. The inventory of Cuban arms appears in *Libro Blanco,* pp. 103–08, and Allende at target practice appears on p. 8. The Central Bank documents which, from internal evidence, appear to have been written between October 1972 and March 1973, were published in *El Mercurio,* November 22–24, 1973. The Investigaciones files are discussed in *Ercilla,* no. 1991 (September 26–October 2, 1973):22, and the arms manufacture is described in no. 1992 (October 3–9, 1973):21.
13. *Libro Blanco,* pp. 49, 54–65.
14. Ibid., p. 48. At the end of October, the Italian newspaper *La Stampa* published an interview with a Chilean Communist in exile in Italy criticizing the "maximalism" of the Socialists and the MIR, but adding, "Unfortunately, there were not many who knew how to use the arms we had—the generals have only discovered a very small percentage of them—because there was not enough time to train the mass of the people." The interview is quoted

in Genaro Arriagada, *De la vía chilena a la vía insurreccional* (Santiago: Editorial del Pacífico, 1974), p. 25.

15. The transcript of the press conference is published in the *New York Times,* September 17, 1974. For follow-up investigative reporting on the CIA in Chile, see articles by Seymour Hersh in the *New York Times,* September 8–20, 1974, and October 22, 1974, and by Laurence Stern in the *Washington Post,* September 8–17, 1974. See also Marlise Simons, "The Brazilian Connection," *Washington Post,* January 6, 1974, for information about probable cooperation between Brazilian and Chilean right-wing groups. For testimony critical of the CIA role in Chile by eight university professors, including the author, see U.S., Congress, House, Foreign Affairs Committee, Subcommittee on Interamerican Affairs, *United States and Chile During the Allende Years, 1970–73,* 94th Cong., 1st sess., 1975, pp. 255–371.

In December 1974 the U.S. Congress voted to prohibit CIA clandestine operations for other than intelligence-gathering purposes "unless and until the President finds that each such operation is important to the national security of the United States and reports, in a timely fashion, a description and scope of such operations to the appropriate committees of the Congress."

16. U.S., Congress, Senate, Judiciary Committee, Refugee Subcommittee, *Refugee and Humanitarian Problems in Chile,* 93d Cong., 1st sess., September 28, 1975, pt. 1, p. 47. In 1975 the Congress adopted a general cutoff of U.S. economic assistance to any country which "engages in a consistent pattern of gross violations of human rights."

17. *Refugee and Humanitarian Problems in Chile,* pt. 1, p. 54. Later wheat agreements in 1974 and 1975 were on concessional terms of 2 to 3 percent interest with a grace period for repayment of principal (*New York Times,* August 3, 1975).

18. *New York Times,* February 20, 1974. For the agreements with Anaconda and Kennecott, see *El Mercurio* (International Edition), July 22–28, 1974, p. 7; November 21–27, 1974, p. 8; and *New York Times,* October 25, 1974.

19. *100 primeros decretos leyes,* decreto ley no. 14, pp. 34–35.

20. *Ercilla,* no. 1991 (September 26–October 2, 1973): 28. See also *El Mercurio* (International Edition), October 1–7, 1974, p. 8.

21. U.S., Congress, House, Committee on Internal Security, *The Theory and Practice of Communism: Hearings,* 93d Cong., 1st sess., November 15, 1973, March 7, 13, 1974, pt. 5, appendix C. For the (dubious) assertion that the CIA was also involved in the narcotics traffic, see *Latin American and Empire Report,* 7, no. 6 (July–August 1974):9.

22. *Ercilla,* no. 2034 (July 24–30, 1974):10. By the end of 1975, 19,200 land titles had been distributed (*Chile Economic News* [CORFO, New York], no. 62, May 1976). Another 15,000 were distributed in 1976. About 25 percent of the expropriated farms were returned to their former owners.

23. *100 primeros decretos leyes,* pp. 228–44.

24. *Declaración de principios del gobierno de Chile,* March 11, 1974, published separately and in *El Mercurio* (International Edition), March 10–17, 1974, p. 4.

25. The government later cited 508 percent as the official inflation rate for 1973. I have drawn the figure of 693 percent from the 1975 OAS report, *Situation, Principal Problems and Prospects of the Chilean Economy* (OEA, Ser. H/XIV CEPCIES 56, March 6, 1975), p. 126. Fernando Leniz, Chilean minister of economics, cited the figure of 700 percent in January, *El Mercurio* (International Edition), January 28–February 3, 1974, p. 8.

26. *CIAP Report, 1974* (OEA/Ser H/XIV; CIAP/650, January 28, 1974), pp. II-14, II-17. *El Mercurio* (International Edition), January 28–February 3, 1974, p. 8.

27. *Ercilla,* no. 2034 (July 24–30, 1974):9; no. 2049 (November 6–12, 1974):10; *New York Times,* January 24, 1976. In 1975 Chilean industrial production dropped by over 20 percent.

28. *Excelsior* (Mexico City), May 21, 1974, contains a moving account of the reaction of

Tohá's wife to his death. She was particularly bitter because of the special concern that Tohá had shown for the military as minister of defense. Sergio Poblete, a retired air force general who had been imprisoned with General Bachelet, testified in Mexico in February 1975 that Bachelet had died because of lack of adequate medical treatment in prison for his heart condition.

29. *LADOC* (Washington), no. 49 (June 1974), doc. 4, p. 41. Interamerican Commission on Human Rights, *Report on the Status of Human Rights in Chile* (OEA/Ser. L/V/II.34/ Doc. 21), published on October 25, 1974, called for the restoration of civil and political liberties in Chile and the prosecution of those responsible for "psychological and physical torture." In July 1975 President Pinochet refused to allow a previously invited delegation from the UN Human Rights Commission to enter the country, an action for which he was rebuked by the United States, which had earlier supported postponement of OAS action pending the UN report. In December 1975 the United States voted with the majority when the UN General Assembly voted 95 to 11 with 23 abstentions to condemn the "constant flagrant violations of human rights" in Chile. Having earlier criticized the U.S. ambassador to Chile for giving "political science lectures" on human rights to the Chilean government, Secretary of State Kissinger himself, speaking at the OAS meeting in Santiago in June 1976, was critical of Chile's violations of human rights.

30. The figures on the DINA appear in Robert Moss, "The Tribulation of Chile," *National Review,* 27, no. 39 (October 10, 1975):1111. In November 1975, after one of its organizers had been involved in assisting a wounded MIR leader, General Pinochet asked the churches to dissolve the committee, although the Vicariate of Solidarity, a similar group under Catholic auspices, took over its work.

31. United Nations estimates placed the number of political prisoners in March 1976 at around 4,000 and the number who had disappeared at 1,000 to 2,000. Over 1,200 political prisoners had been permitted to leave Chile, and 17,000 Chileans had fled the country after the coup. (UN Economic and Social Council, Ad Hoc Working Group on the Situation of Human Rights in Chile, *Protection of Human Rights in Chile,* October 8, 1976, pp. 43 ff.) In November 1976 the Chilean government announced that all except 20 of those detained under the state of siege had been released. It also exchanged one of the 20, Luis Corvalan, former secretary general of the Chilean Communist Party, for a prominent Soviet dissident. Those serving sentences in prison or awaiting trial for security violations were not included in the announcement. Amnesty International estimated that there were still 900 political prisoners in Chile and published the names of 86 persons who had disappeared between January and August 1976.

32. *El Mercurio* (International Edition), September 9–15, 1974, pp. 8–9. In June 1975 General Pinochet declared that "I shall die and my successor will die but there will be no elections" (*Los Angeles Times,* June 21, 1975). In August he repeated his estimate that the military might remain in power for a generation (*Ercilla,* no. 2090 [August 20–26, 1975]).

33. On authoritarian corporatism as an alternative model of political development, especially in Latin America, see Philippe C. Schmitter, "Paths to Political Development," in *Changing Latin America,* ed. Douglas C. Chalmers (New York: Academy of Political Science, 1972), pp. 83–109; Howard J. Wiarda, "Toward a Framework for the Study of Political Change in the Iberic-Latin Tradition: The Corporative Model," *World Politics,* 25, no. 2 (January 1973):206–86; Robert R. Kaufman, "Transitions to Stable Authoritarian-Corporate Regimes: The Chilean Case?", Sage Professional Papers in Political Science, no. 01-060 (Beverly Hills, Cal.: Sage Publications, 1976); Fredrick B. Pike and Thomas Stritch, eds., *The New Corporatism* (Notre Dame, Ind.: Notre Dame University Press, 1974); and James Malloy, ed., *Authoritarianism and Corporatism in Latin America* (Pittsburgh: University of Pittsburgh Press, 1977).

Chapter 13. The Lessons of Chile

1. At this point, some may object that Allende never intended to carry out his revolution within the framework of constitutional democracy, citing his toleration of illegal arms importation and his words to Regis Debray concerning the "tactical" character of his adherence to legality. However, whatever may have been Allende's belief about the ultimate inevitability of a violent confrontation (my own view is that as an incurable optimist he believed, at least for the first two years of his administration, that he would "make it" to 1976), the constraints under which he operated, especially the effective veto by the military of any departure from the constitution more serious than the employment of "legal loopholes," meant that although the increasing violence from late 1971 until the coup created serious problems, his administration remained, for the most part, a constitutional democracy until September 11, 1973, with functioning courts and Congress, and the effective exercise of civil liberties and individual suffrage.

2. J. Ann Zammit and Gabriel Palma, eds., *The Chilean Road to Socialism* (Austin: University of Texas Press, 1973), p. 38. On the relative permanence ("immobilism") of the division between left, right, and center in Chilean public opinion, see James W. Prothro and Patricio Chaparro, "Public Opinion and the Movement of Chilean Government to the Left, 1952–72," *Journal of Politics*, 36, no. 1 (February 1974):2–43. For contrasting views from Allende supporters after the coup as to whether greater efforts should have been made to secure PDC support, see Jaime Gazmuri, "Aprender las lecciones del pasado," *Chile-América*, nos. 8–9 (1975):66 ("Objective conditions made possible the goal of political unity of Popular Unity and Christian Democracy"); and Michel Raptis, *Revolution and Counter-Revolution in Chile* (New York: St. Martin's Press, 1974), p. 78 (an alliance with the PDC and the middle class was a "mirage").

3. The best-known criticism of Allende's economic policies is Paul Rosenstein-Rodan, "Why Allende Failed," *Challenge*, May-June 1974, pp. 7–13, and the *New York Times*, June 16, 1974 ("Allende was not overthrown because he was a socialist, but because he was incompetent"). For attacks on the Vuskovic policy published during the Allende administration, see José Musalem, *Crónica de un fracaso* (Santiago: Editorial del Pacífico, 1973); Alvaro Bardón et al., *Itinerario de una crisis* (Santiago: Editorial del Pacífico, 1972); Pablo Baraona et al., *Chile: A Critical Survey* (Santiago: Institute of General Studies, 1972); and Orlando Sáez, *Un país en quiebra* (Santiago: Ediciónes Portada, 1973). Sergio Ramos, *Chile, una economia de transicion?* (Santiago: CESO-PLA, 1972), defends the Vuskovic program. In a book published after the coup Vuskovic himself blames "imperialism" for Chile's economic problems and, except for a reference to the 1971 successes, makes no attempt to defend his policies (*Acusación al imperialismo* [Mexico: Fondo de Cultura Económica, 1975]). In a personal interview with the author he cited the Central Bank's lack of a monetary policy and Allende's failure to mobilize the masses as the causes of Chile's economic problems.

4. For details on tax collections under Frei, see *CIAP Report,* 1973 (OEA/Ser H/XIV; CIAP/612, June 20, 1973), pp. 167–68 (Spanish version). For Allende, see *CIAP Report,* 1974 (OEA/Ser H/XIV; CIAP/650, January 28, 1974), p. IV-2.

5. On the "economism" of the Chilean working class and the counterproductive economic and political effects of the mobilization of the proletariat by the Allende government, see H. A. Landsberger and T. McDaniel, "Hypermobilization in Chile, 1970–73," *World Politics,* 28, no. 4 (July 1976):502–41.

6. Details on the increase in Chilean indebtedness between 1970 and 1973, most of it to the West and nearly half in short-term debts, appear in the 1974 *CIAP Report*, pp. V-2, 3, 9, 17.

7. Senate investigators found no other evidence of encouragement of a coup by the CIA. The CIA paid for a trip by Chilean trade unionists to Europe to "explain" the coup, and admitted that it had prepared "arrest lists" in Chile, but denied that they had been passed to the

Chilean authorities. One wonders too, what was the direct or indirect source of the funding for the ephemeral (ostensibly leftist) magazine that appeared on Santiago newsstands in late July with the headline, "Soldiers, Disobey Your Officers" adding in tiny letters "when they violate the constitution."

8. On the record, the State Department and the two ambassadors preferred diplomacy over the Nixon-Kissinger program of economic warfare and subversion. The State Department representatives on the Forty Committee opposed covert intervention in December 1969 and June and September 1970, as well as the program of economic pressure initiated in September 1970. Ambassador Korry opposed a military coup in September–October 1970, and Ambassador Davis was against aid to the striking truckers in 1972 and 1973.

9. For discussions of the causes of military intervention in Latin America which respectively emphasize political factors (fear of the rising political power of the lower classes by a weak and divided middle class) and economic factors (populist redistribution policies which produce runaway inflation), see José Nun, "The Middle Class Military Coup," in *Latin America, Revolution or Reform?*, ed. James Petras and Maurice Zeitlin, (New York, Fawcett, 1968), pp. 145–68; and Guillermo O'Donnell, *Modernization and Bureaucratic-Authoritarianism* (Berkeley: University of California, 1973). Both factors were present in Chile, but ideological elements (fear of the establishment of a Cuban-style dictatorship) and the institutional motivation (defense of the military monopoly of force) seem to have been more important.

10. As noted earlier, Patria y Libertad received $38,500 from the CIA during the Track II efforts of 1970 and additional amounts totaling $7,000 in 1971. CIA support was supposed to have ended then, but it is possible that some of the later CIA aid to right-wing parties was passed to the organization, despite its increasing commitment to violent methods.

11. *The Listener*, December 6, 1973. See also Ian Roxborough, *Chile: The State and Revolution* (London: Macmillan, 1977) which concludes: "It would be a mistake to underestimate the role of the USA in defeating the Chilean working class, but to place the major emphasis here is to go against the available evidence. The coup would probably have occurred, even if the USA had remained strictly 'neutral' " (p. 153).

Index

232, 234; of Frei, 53, 66–67; of Pinochet, 270. *See also* Ministerial impeachments
Calderón, Rolando, 196
Canto, Hernán del, 149, 171
Carmine, Víctor, 99
Carmona, Juan de Dios, 118, 183
Carvajal, Patricio, 242–43
Castillo, Fernando, 217, 219
Castillo, Jaime, 32, 52, 63, 66, 84, 272
Castro, Fidel, 5, 34–35, 104, 128, 130, 162–63, 224
Central Intelligence Agency, 34, 87, 102, 112–17, 121–22, 156, 157, 173, 189, 198, 259–60, 285–86
Chonchol, Jacques, 52, 53, 62–63, 72, 79, 84, 89, 91, 130, 139, 151, 152
Christian Democratic Party, 17, 31–33, 47–48, 126; cleavages in, 53, 65, 72–73, 77–79, 112, 135, 149–50; and coup, 8, 249–50; *oficialistas* in, 54, 63, 79; *rebeldes* in, 47, 53, 54, 62, 63, 66, 72, 78–80; relations with Allende of, 118–19, 146, 168–69, 185, 198, 204, 206–07, 208, 217–18, 223–25, 232, 233, 237–39; *terceristas* in, 53, 54, 63, 66, 72–73, 78, 82, 135
Christian Left, 135, 146, 150. *See also* Elections
Church. *See* Roman Catholic Church
Class structure, 21–22
Communitarianism, 33, 52, 64, 145–46, 159, 160
Compensation, 132, 141–42, 153–56, 175, 197, 261. *See also* Area of social property; Copper; Overseas Private Investment Corporation
Confederación Democrática, 161, 172, 187, 197, 198–201
Congress, 7, 15, 87–88, 95, 103, 181–82, 189, 199, 207, 210, 216, 232–33, 287. *See also* Constitutional amendments; Statute of Democratic Guarantees; Unicameral legislature
Conservative Party, 27, 29, 50. *See also* Elections
Constitution: of 1833, 14; of 1925, 14–17, 27
Constitutional amendments, 16, 27, 58, 141, 152–53, 159, 161–62, 167–68, 182–83, 207, 223, 277. *See also* Congress; Statute of Democratic Guarantees
Constitutionalism, breakdown of. *See* Dual power
Constitutional reform, 87–88

Constitutional Tribunal, 17, 87–88, 168, 171, 207, 266
"Consumerism," 173
Contreras, Miria, 3, 5, 243–44, 247, 263
Controller General, 154, 180, 186, 206, 248, 265, 287
Copper, 19–20; and Chileanization, 33, 36–37, 39, 45–47, 49, 80, 82, 124; embargo of, 191–92; nationalization of, 89, 141, 152–53, 192–93; prices of, 60, 80, 234–35. *See also* Compensation
Coquimbo, 171–72
Cordones industriales, 186, 215, 218
CORFO, 133, 134, 156, 269
Corporatism, 31–32, 33–34, 266
Corvalán, Luis, 78
Council of State, 267
Coup: attempt of June 29, 1973, 212; decision for, 236–37, 239–40; of September 11, 1973, 3–7, 242–44, 288–89. *See also* Armed forces
"Creditworthiness," 174, 175, 193, 284. *See also* Aid, economic
Cuba: compared with Chile, 101; influence of, 27, 171, 224–25, 252, 256, 287; as model of change, 11; relations with, 35, 97, 131, 248. *See also* Castro, Fidel
Curicó, 29

Davis, Nathaniel, 170, 221, 258
Debray, Regis, 140, 229
Debt, Chilean, 30, 175, 225, 261
"Decree of insistence," 206
Democracia Radical, 83, 221. *See also* Elections
Democratic Front, 27, 29
Democratic National Party, 161, 172, 187, 197, 198–201, 221
Dependencia, 9, 81, 104, 124, 174
"Destabilization." *See* Intervention, U.S.
Diez, Sergio, 164, 165
Drug traffic, 264
Dual power, 178, 196, 215, 227–28, 241
Dungan, Ralph, 40, 42, 55, 58, 60, 116
Durán, Julio, 27, 29, 46, 83, 98

Economic aid. *See* Aid, economic
Economic growth, 9, 42–43, 51, 55, 64, 68, 92, 101–02 ·
Economic policy: in 1958–64, 26; in 1964–70, 59–60, 126, 275–76; in 1970–73, 133, 136–38, 159–60, 172, 174, 176–77, 226, 275–76,

Pérez Zujovic, Edmundo, 65–66, 70, 72, 77, 118, 148
Pinochet, Augusto, 50, 170, 215, 231, 237, 240, 248, 251, 271–72, 273
Plan Zeta, 257
Polarization, 167, 170, 275, 279
Plebiscite, 15, 168, 239, 241, 278
Polls, 74, 100, 102, 105, 106, 180–81
Popular Action Front, 18, 30, 39, 61. *See also* Elections
Popular power, 215, 228, 241
Popular Promotion Council, 33, 39, 43, 69
Popular Socialist Union, 71, 92, 285. *See also* Elections
Popular Unity, 88–89, 90, 94–95, 133, 165, 169, 226, 233, 239, 277
Populism, 8
Portales, Diego, 262
Prado, Benjamín, 118, 135
Prats, Carlos, 188, 194, 198, 208, 213, 214, 225, 227, 231, 237
Price control, 196. *See also* Supply and price committees
Project Camelot, 41–42
Proportional representation, 8, 16–17, 96, 109, 161–62, 189, 197, 276–78

Radical Democrats, 83, 221. *See also* Elections
Radical Party, 7, 25–26, 27; divisions in, 151–52; negotiations with Christian Democrats, 39, 46–47; negotiations with Popular Unity, 84, 85, 90–91, 108; realignment of, 60–61, 71, 72, 73, 83. *See also* Elections; Popular Unity
Rationing, 195–96, 211, 239
Repression, 50, 177–78, 253–54, 269, 270, 273–74
Requisition, 133, 148, 186, 206, 210, 228, 279
"Revolution in liberty," 9, 23, 49–50, 100–01, 123–24, 284
Rodríguez, Aniceto, 39, 71, 83, 84, 140, 270
Rodríguez, Pablo, 117–18, 216
Roman Catholic Church, 104, 144–45, 186, 204, 251–52, 269–70, 273
Ruiz, César, 225, 228–29, 231

Sáez, Raúl, 66–67
Sanhueza, Manuel, 168–69
Schneider, René, 99, 114–15, 120–21, 123
Schowen, Carlos von, 225, 229, 242

Secondary School Student Federation, 179, 189–90, 204
Silva, Julio, 52, 53, 74, 79, 96–97, 151
Silva, Raúl, 123, 144–45, 148, 184, 203, 207–08, 225, 251–52, 269
Social Democratic Federation, 220–21
Social Democratic Party, 84, 90–91
Socialist Party, 18, 68, 71, 72, 73, 84, 88, 91, 140, 184. *See also* Elections; Popular Unity
Social justice, 9, 11, 12, 20–21, 22, 41–42, 68–69
Soviet Union, 194, 284–85
State Development Corporation, 133, 134, 156, 269
Statute of Democratic Guarantees, 112, 119–20, 127, 157, 173, 187, 263
Strikes, 50, 67, 68, 93, 179, 185–86, 188–89; of copper workers, 80, 209–10, 216; of truckers, 184–85, 221–22, 225, 227–28, 234, 238–39, 280
Sule, Anselmo, 119, 241, 263, 270
Supply and price committees, 176, 195–96, 208–10, 227, 253

Tacnazo, 86–87, 93–94
Tapia, Jorge, 170
Tarud, Rafael, 79, 89, 91
Taxation, 82, 105, 125, 130, 136–37, 268, 280
Teitelboim, Volodia, 189, 200
Thayer, William, 53, 66
Thieme, Roberto, 216, 222
Tohá, José, 3, 164, 269
Tomic, Radomiro: and Christian Democratic Party, 36, 45, 72, 150–51; and the left, 26, 78; and nationalizations, 33, 80, 83, 184; in 1970 election, 68, 84, 94, 95, 104, 106
Trade Union Confederation (CUT), 7, 43, 62, 86, 148, 171, 207, 212, 215, 221, 253–54
Truckers. *See* Strikes, of truckers

Unemployment, 172, 236, 273
Unicameral legislature, 142, 161, 183
Unionization, 53–54. *See also* Communitarianism; Popular Promotion Council
United States, 10, 12, 40–41, 42, 81, 258–59, 286–87. *See also* Central Intelligence Agency; Intervention, U.S.
Universities, 61–62, 163–64, 169–70, 190, 198, 254–55
Urban guerrillas, 65. *See also* Violence

PITT LATIN AMERICAN SERIES

Cole Blasier, Editor